AMERICA'S SECRET MiG SQUADRON

OSPREY
PUBLISHING

AMERICA'S SECRET MiG SQUADRON

THE RED EAGLES OF PROJECT CONSTANT PEG

COL. (RET.) GAILLARD R. PECK, JR

First published in Great Britain in 2012 by Osprey Publishing
Midland House, West Way, Botley, Oxford, OX2 0PH
44-02 23rd Street, Suite 219, Long Island City, NY, 11101, USA

E-mail: info@ospreypublishing.com

OSPREY PUBLISHING IS PART OF THE OSPREY GROUP

A CIP catalogue record for this book is available from the British Library

ISBN: 978 1 84908 976 0
PDF e-book ISBN: 978 1 78096 867 4
E-Pub ISBN: 978 1 78096 868 1

Edited by Tony Holmes
Page layout by Myriam Bell Design, UK
Index by Zoe Ross
Typeset in AGaramond
Originated by PDQ Digital Media Solutions, Suffolk
Printed in China through Bookbuilders

12 13 14 15 16   10 9 8 7 6 5 4 3 2 1

Osprey Publishing is supporting the Woodland Trust, the UK's leading woodland
conservation charity, by funding the dedication of trees.

www.ospreypublishing.com

Contents

DEDICATION

Dedicated to the men who restored, maintained, and supported our MiG aircraft, thus permitting American fighter pilots to train realistically and achieve a formidable air combat capability.

ACKNOWLEDGMENTS

All of the Red Eagles kept their mouths shut about the MiG operations at the Tonopah Test Range in Nevada until November 2006 when Project CONSTANT PEG was declassified. After so many years, it was a struggle to recall facts and figures about the project, especially since the written records had largely been lost, either to the shredder or in the attack on the Pentagon on September 11, 2001, as has been alleged. Nevertheless, the discussions I have recently had with other Red Eagles (and Red Eagle adversaries) have enabled me to put together this story. I don't claim that it is 100 percent accurate, but it is as close as I could come given the lapse of time and the advance of age.

My fundamental encouragement came from the first Red Eagles author, Steve Davies (who wrote *Red Eagles – America's Secret MiGs* for Osprey), who has been a cheerleader for me throughout this book writing process. Steve, you will always be my friend.

I thought I knew a lot about leadership and management until I heard Simon Sinek speak at the USAF Weapons School (WS) at Nellis Air Force Base (AFB), Nevada, in 2010 and then read his book, *Start With Why!* I previously understood the basics of the "Why, How, What" and the "Golden Circle," but Simon's explanations brought the basics into focus for me and legitimized the outline I had selected – why we formed the MiG adversary program, how we built the airfield and restored the MiGs for use in combat training, and what the USA received as a combat performance dividend. Simon, I will always be your cheerleader.

And now to my friends both within the circle of Red Eagles and those on the outside cheering me on and/or critiquing this work. First, a profound word of thanks for your candor, your stories, and your help. Gen Vandenberg got this project going back in the 1970s and then applauded the results in a summer 2011 letter to me which included the lines:

All you Red Eagles can be justifiably proud of the great contribution you made in winning the Cold War. From such an inauspicious beginning to what you became and what you all accomplished is carved in stone. I am proud to be even a very small part of such an unequalled organization.

Air superiority rules!
Sandy Vandenberg

Boss Vandenberg, without you, generals Chuck Donnelly, Jim Currie, and Charlie Gabriel, and then Col (later Gen) Dick Murray, the "Gang of Three" (Glenn Frick, "DL" Smith, and I) would not have been able to make CONSTANT PEG happen.

A special word of thanks to fellow Red Eagle commanders Earl "Obi Wan" Henderson, Phil "Hound Dawg" White, and Mike "Scooter" Scott for sticking with me and providing information that helped put the pieces together with some degree of historical accuracy. Earl's son Neil Henderson has also been a champion of this project, providing insight and help. We all owe former Red Eagle commander Jack "Madjack" Manclark a word of thanks for leading the effort that led to the declassification of the project. And a tip of the hat to the guys that followed the "Gang of Three," Bill "Saki" Sakahara at the Air Staff and Joseph "CT" Wang at TAC Headquarters. These men, along with the subsequent commanders of the Red Eagles and the replacement staff at the Pentagon and Langley AFB, Virginia, kept the momentum going and ensured the success of the Red Eagle program.

I owe a special word of thanks to my 433rd TFS combat colleague and fellow FWS air-to-air instructor Ed "Fast Eddy" Cobleigh (author of *War for the Helluva It*) who gave me great advice on the "dos and don'ts" and then read and critiqued the entire manuscript, providing insight and critical comment. My F-4 FWS fellow IP and long-time friend Gen Jeff Cliver pored over the document and helped so much with the rewrites. FWS instructor Billy Gordon patiently told me combat stories that helped me lay the foundation for the story about the need for change in fighter tactics and training. My new ski buddy, and fellow fighter pilot, Gabby Hayes and his lovely wife Ava also took the time to read the manuscript and help me with the details of alternative language, organization, and flow. My Air Force Academy classmate Gen Don Shepperd and fighter pilot friends Mark Berent and Walt Boyne, all accomplished authors, provided encouragement, contacts, and pointers that are gratefully acknowledged.

A special thanks to my new friend Gholi Darehshori, a true American patriot and champion of the US military who enthusiastically offered to partner with me to be sure this work would be published. Gholi, that was a special and wonderful push from you and your lovely wife Georgia, with great help from your brother Nader.

Christine Biederer always smiled when I asked her to make another graphics art "fix" for me. And then she got it done and her product always exceeded my hopes. Thanks Red.

To Sam Moore, the Department of Energy site manager at Tonopah at the beginning, to John Pollet at Holmes and Narver (our architectural and engineering contractor), to Del Gaulker at Reynolds Engineering and Electrical Company (our construction firm), and to all the others in your organizations that lent us total support and unequalled performance, thanks and a tip of the hat.

Now to some Red Eagles that I especially treasure. Ben Galloway and Bob "Bro" Breault and Ben's lovely wife Melody – I could not have gotten this done without you guys. And at the same time you were building and refining the fidelity of our Red Eagle rosters and preparing the newsletters. Just what I would have expected from Red Eagles. Wow! Thanks for being on my team. P. Cox, the keeper of the historical personnel records and the man that can do anything. Keep charging. We love you man! Rich Samanich and Chief "Mac" McMurtrie – thanks for the stories and the pictures. Gifted artist Joe Mike Pyle and the flight doctors, especially Doc "Gerbil" Funke, fed me great information about life at Tonopah after my watch was over. Joe Mike, perhaps we can energize your talent and beg you to do a painting depicting our jets on the tarmac at Tonopah for the National Museum of the Air Force. Possible?

The enlisted team put together by Bobby Ellis was without equal anywhere. You guys could do anything, and you did it regularly. Over the years I have kept up with the initial Assistant Chief of Maintenance Don Lyon, along with master aircraft mechanics Steve Hovermale and Tommy Karnes, and jet engine mechanic Ike Crawley. Our chats, laughs, and memories have been the fuel that motivated me. I love hanging out with the pilots too, but you guys, along with the rest of the initial cadre, make me smile just to think about you. Thanks so much for everything that ALL of you Red Eagles accomplished. My heart still aches over Bobby's loss.

To the USAF, US Navy, and the US Marine Corps Red Eagle MiG pilots and controllers, and to the combat fighter pilots that scored kills and validated our project, I'll fly or drink with you anytime, anywhere. You guys are my heroes. US Navy pilots Tom "Squid" Morgenfeld and Chuck "Heater" Heatley and the sea service pilots that followed brought a tremendous dimension to the Red Eagle team.

Jim "Bluto" Keys and Bud "Chops" Horan were more than exquisite ground control intercept (GCI) controllers. Our analyst Bob "Darth" Drabant contributed so much. In addition to their regular duties, these men also did the jobs that had to be done and never whined. You guys are great.

This acknowledgment would not be complete without a word of thanks to Osprey Publishing for seeing the wisdom of adding this story to its list of publications, and for having the vision to see this work as a part of a larger picture that surely will be worthy of books to follow this one. I look forward to meeting in person the people that have supported me with this project at Osprey, namely John Tintera, Kate Moore, Tony Holmes, and the other members of staff that operate behind the scenes, thank you. And, John and Kate, thanks for answering my e-mails and making this happen.

And, finally, a special word of thanks to the 18th Chief of Staff of the Air Force, Gen "Buzz" Moseley, for his total support over the years and for preparing the foreword for this book. Gen Moseley trained against the MiGs and then taught others how to fight them when he was the "F-15 Barnyard Commander" at the FWS at Nellis AFB. Gen Moseley's words echo the frustrations that those of my generation shared over the Vietnam era training shortfalls, and his words express the passion that drove our daily effort to make CONSTANT PEG successful.

FOREWORD

You are about to get a rare glimpse into a unique United States Air Force combat training program and into a collection of dedicated and amazingly innovative airmen. Through these individuals' singular commitment to "fix" the tactical execution failings they experienced over North Vietnam and specifically to prepare for the uncertainty of future combat, these airmen were instrumental in "changing the game" in America's approach to air combat. Through their focused efforts and passion to fix the failings of Vietnam, these airmen were center stage for the "post-Vietnam" revolution in air combat training in the skies over the high desert of Nevada.

Through the eyes and experiences of Col "Evil" Peck you are about to have a front row seat into a previously "classified" program named CONSTANT PEG, and into an organization that was specifically created to address the frustrations and many failings experienced in air-to-air combat over North Vietnam. This air war was singularly characterized by a lack of focused American air combat preparation and, to a certain extent, a lack of experienced, tactically savvy leadership.

During the period after the Korean War and prior to entry into the Vietnam conflict, the very senior leadership of the USAF chose not to prioritize or even emphasize tactical leadership development, advanced air combat training or the most basic of combat preparation. The hard-earned "fighting" skills that American fighter pilots learned and honed in the World War II skies of the Pacific and Europe and over the Korean Peninsula in the early 1950s atrophied "away" to the most basic of non-combat airmanship. During this critical period, the USAF's senior leadership consisted primarily of officers with bomber and transport experience. And these senior leaders' priorities centered primarily on nuclear delivery, maintaining a comfortable status quo in Washington, D.C., and on minimizing peacetime training accidents.

Through these short-sighted priorities, the combat-focused, fighter pilot community was marginalized and ultimately ill-prepared for the challenges they were to face in the most hostile skies over North Vietnam. Their knowledge of enemy aircraft and their understanding of potential opposing tactics was limited at best, as was their ability to execute even the tactical fundamentals of air combat.

The individuals involved in this combat-focused "training renaissance" are legends in the fighter communities of the USAF and US Navy. Col "Evil" Peck has masterfully captured the contributions made by these many professionals. From the incredibly talented and visionary Col "Moody" Suter tothe senior ("fighter experienced") leadership willing to take a chance on this idea; to the CONSTANT PEG/4477th commanders; to the USAF, US Navy, and US Marine Corps pilots and maintainers; to the many support players – these creative individuals made such a big difference!

My personal contact and experience with this program began when I was a student at the USAF's Fighter Weapons School. Our F-15 Eagle syllabus at the time had at least one "adversary" sortie against the MiGs! What an experience. I'll never forget the professional level of the briefing and the detailed discussion of performance characteristics, etc. As an experienced F-15 Instructor Pilot, I had absolute faith in my Eagle, and I had read everything I could find on this "critter" called a MiG-21. The sortie was everything I had imagined. The MiG proved to be quite agile, but not of the caliber of the Eagle. The instruction and "debrief" was the most memorable, generating a whole new level of appreciation for the MiGs – but also for the talented fighter pilots of the 4477th!

I next had a chance to fly with the Red Eagles in 1982 whilst returning to the 18th Tactical Fighter Wing at Kadena from a WILLIAM TELL competition-winning deployment. En route home, we stopped off at Nellis for a week of sorties with the 4477th and to share ideas and tactics with the experts. Again, it was just outstanding.

My next opportunity to work with the 4477th was when I commanded the "Barnyard" (the F-15 division of the USAF's Fighter Weapons School) of the 57th Fighter Weapons Wing at Nellis AFB. We were tasked with taking the Combat Air Forces' most experienced, air-to-air Instructor Pilots from the F-15 Eagle community through the most rigorous and challenging academic and flying course imaginable. The "Barnyard" course syllabus content was 100 percent focused on air-to-air skills, tactics, and how to train the F-15 Eagle community to dominate any airspace from "day 1." From the "Barnyard" we were always looking to include the Red Eagles into our syllabus development discussions and in the "exposure" of our students to their world of MiGs. It was an ideal marriage. The tactical awareness, the appreciation of the MiGs' capabilities and, more importantly, the confidence generated out of those sorties and the understanding realized from those exposures later paid off in spades over Iraq and the Balkans.

The impact of these talented airmen and this unique organization was realized not only in the increased lethality and tactical awareness of USAF and US Navy/Marine Corps fighter pilots and aircrew, but also in the overall development of skilled, prepared leadership across the board. I suggest both outcomes were key in thinking through the emerging air combat challenges as they presented themselves from the 1970s to the present over the Mediterranean, over a variety of locations in the Middle East and over the Balkans. Throughout this period, I suggest CONSTANT PEG was a key, essential building block in the development of training templates, the honing of leadership skills, the gaining of confidence, and in the development of winning air-to-air tactics. I also suggest that the individuals involved in this program are owed a debt by all who fly and fight and look to win! They delivered on their vision and their promise!

We certainly don't know what the future holds relative to the next air combat location or adversary. But we do know that we, as a country, have had a "100 percent" fail rate on predicting where and when we'll deploy and fight next. I would suggest that after World War II, the military leadership and planners in the United States did not see the "next fight coming." Whether we consider the combat experienced over Korea, Vietnam, Iraq I, Somalia, Bosnia, and Kosovo, the 12 years of "Iraqi no fly zones" or the post-September 11, 2001 realities of Afghanistan and Iraq II, *we did not see these fights coming.*

As we look out into this most uncertain future, it will serve us well to consider the lessons taught and re-enforced in the sky over the high desert of Nevada. We simply must be prepared, across the board, to deal with increasingly lethal potential adversaries and/or their equipment. To best serve the country, we must not allow ourselves to "repeat" the same deadly failures witnessed during the Vietnam era as a result of taking our eye off the ball in prioritizing what is required to fly, fight, and win.

Col Gail "Evil" Peck has painted a detailed and rich picture of what it takes to "stay on top" in this business of air combat, and what it takes to focus "organizationally" on these required combat skills. He has highlighted not only a USAF flying unit but, more importantly, a set of amazingly talented individuals, commanders, maintainers, officers, enlisted, and civilians that made up this "joint" program named "CONSTANT PEG." Through his eyes and his words, we also clearly see what it takes to move a vision through a bureaucracy to create a capability that has had lasting impact. Well done "Evil!" And, from fighter pilots everywhere…

"Sierra Hotel" CONSTANT PEG … "Sierra Hotel!!!!"

General (ret.) T. Michael "Buzz" Moseley
Chief of Staff of the United States Air Force, 2005–08

PROLOGUE

The Fighter Weapons School (FWS) at Nellis Air Force Base (AFB), just outside Las Vegas, Nevada, is where the US Air Force (USAF) sends its outstanding fighter pilots to train to a doctorate level of knowledge and performance. The classroom is the laboratory of the sky and the tools of the trade are jet fighters. In this school the pilots, and in two-seat jets their weapon system operators, master their combat aircraft and, along the way, learn to think innovatively. Their reward is a FWS graduate patch to wear on their flightsuits, along with the probability of a rich future in the military.

In the beginning only fighters and attack aircraft "played" at the FWS. Now, the school has expanded to include the full spectrum of air force combat capability, including bombers, helicopters, airlift, special operations, intelligence, space, command and control, and reconnaissance. Recently, an unmanned aircraft course was initiated too. Thus, the Nellis "fighter school house" has evolved into the USAF Weapons School. The reward for the graduate is still "The Patch."

I attended the FWS and mastered the F-4 Phantom II, as did my close associates and friends Glenn Frick and David "DL" Smith. Later we were to become the "Gang of Three" within the MiG program.

FWS for me came after I had completed a Vietnam War combat tour in the F-4. Flying from Ubon Royal Thai Air Base (RTAB) with the 433rd Tactical Fighter Squadron (TFS), I completed 163 combat missions – nearly 100 of them at night. Glenn Frick was a highly experienced fighter pilot when he attended the FWS. Prior to the F-4, Glenn had been an Air Commando involved in Special Forces operations, in addition to undertaking combat ready assignments flying the F-100. "DL" Smith had two combat tours in Vietnam and attended the FWS in between those tours. During the summer of 1972, "DL" is credited with destroying the Paul Doumer Bridge just north of Hanoi, in North Vietnam, during the LINEBACKER I campaign. After his second Southeast Asia assignment, "DL" came to Nellis as a part of the initial cadre of USAF Aggressors, where he flew the T-38 as a MiG-21 surrogate. The Aggressors' mission was to train all USAF fighter pilots against a realistic adversary threat.

Along the way the three of us all had the chance to fly real Russian MiGs. And that experience stimulated our entrepreneurial juices and set the stage for action that culminated in the creation of a training program using real MiGs as adversaries.

GAIL PECK, "PATTY 02," AND THE PHANTOM IIS

Here I am, an F-4 flight instructor at the USAF's FWS! And today I am airborne in a real MiG-17. I love flying this little jet. The MiG-17 is truly a machine you "put on" instead of "get in." It smells funny and it makes weird and unfamiliar noises, at least to an American fighter pilot, but it is an honest airplane. I'm "buried" in the cockpit with my helmet just above the fuselage. My head is encased in the clear Plexiglas canopy, with a periscope over my head allowing me to glance up and see directly behind me. I'm just chugging along getting ready to give four dudes flying F-4 Phantom IIs the dogfight of their lives. This airplane reminds me of the little train engine working its way up the mountain. *I think I can, I think I can* the ditty goes.

How lucky could one American fighter pilot be to have the chance to fly this thing? And my thanks goes to the men that restored this wreck of an airplane. Their work transformed the jet from a museum display piece into a safe flying machine. These men are mechanical geniuses. God, I LOVE working with them and just hanging around with them.

The aircraft radio blasts into my headset, disturbing the reverie. "'Patty 2,' 'Dream Control.' Climb and maintain 'Angels 20,' turn right heading 090° and when established look for bandits, four F-4s, 090°, 20 miles." The crisp radio call from our radar-equipped GCI folks snaps me back to the reality of the moment. "Roger 'Dream,' 'Patty' turning to 090 and looking!" It is time to go to work. "Chase, Control. Hold west of 'Patty!'" "Chase. Roger that Control!"

Okay, that gets Norm Suits in the T-38 chase airplane out of my way.

What kind of call sign is "Patty 2" anyway? Why "Patty"? If I'm ever in charge the call sign will be "Shark" or "Killer" or "MiG" or "Bandit" or something, but not "Patty" for Christ's sake.

Whoa! Good vector from GCI. And my climb put the F-4s right against the haze layer on the eastern horizon. The smoke trails from their engines show up against the earth's haze layer like a moth fluttering on a movie theater screen when illuminated by the projector!

"Control, 'Patty 2,' I have visual on four smokers at 090°." "Roger 'Patty 2,' Control. Visual contact is your group of playmates. Vector 100° for a single side offset intercept. Have fun."

Won't those F-4 drivers ever believe what we tell them? They *have* to be in minimum afterburner power at least 20+ miles from the target or their damn engine smoke trail makes them stand out like a whore in church! Put the damn throttles into minimum afterburner and the smoke disappears. Jeez!

"Roger, 'Patty 2' steering 100°. I have a tally-ho on four F-4s. Chase, stay above the fight and to the west, out of the way." I don't know why we have to have a test pilot-flown T-38 chase aircraft mucking up the training opportunity. Oh well, rules are rules. At least he is staying out of my way.

Hmmm, I can't believe they have seen me yet, but it looks like they are trying to point at me so they must be getting good GCI. I'm turning south a little bit more to 120° so I can conserve some turning room. When they pass line abreast of me that will make my conversion turn to a position behind them easier.

Oh Boy! That's not working. I just gave *them* turning room. They are now only about five or six miles in front of me at "ten" to "eleven o'clock." The wingmen are in fighting wing. This is truly going to be a learning situation. Lead is level with me and is pointing his nose at me, while Nos 3 and 4 are in trail with Lead and No 2. So now I'm going to start a turn into them and see if either Lead or No 3 are smart enough to climb into the vertical.

Nope! We briefed this tool of using the vertical to match the turn circle. I guess he has to learn the hard way. Here he comes right across the circle, with his wingman in fighting wing. No 3 is right behind him. Unbelievable! A classic mistake.

Okay, now he sees me for sure, and he is trying to put his nose on me so I will harden my turn into him just a little bit and see if he takes the bait. He's maybe two miles back, trying to keep his nose pointing at me. Be patient Peck, wait for him to get in closer. I'll make my move when he closes to about 3,000 to 3,500ft, which is still well outside his accurate gun range. Patience, patience ... one more second!

Now! He's at my left "seven o'clock." Back stick pressure in my MiG-17 and instantly my turn causes his nose to fall behind the gun-firing position. He does not have a gun-shot and he is too close to shoot a Sidewinder heat seeking missile at me, so I guess it is about time to render *the big surprise*. Full back stick and top rudder in the MiG-17 as the F-4 harmlessly passes behind me and to the outside of my turn circle. The MiG is snap rolling to the right, and if I have timed this right he will be at my right "three o'clock" grossly overshooting my turn and setting me up for a guns kill. I'm looking over my left shoulder and now transitioning to the periscope to judge his overshoot.

There he is! Right "four o'clock," moving to "three" and out in front of me. Still level. Why doesn't he zoom into the vertical? I move my control stick forward to end the snap roll and let the ailerons handle the roll control, and now stick and ailerons to get the pipper onto his canopy. YES! "Guns tracking on the F-4. KILL" – simulated in this training event of course!

What about the wingman? Quick roll back to the left and there he is about to hammer me. But, my friend, I've got one more trick up my sleeve – the same one that your leader just experienced.

Hard back stick. He is starting to overshoot! Why can't they learn to roll out and go into the vertical? Yep, yep, that's why we are doing this. It's called training! Okay, now full back stick and top rudder and there he goes. "Guns tracking on the F-4. KILL!" Wow, that was an instant replay of the kill on his leader.

Now, where's No 3? I roll back left and check my left "seven o'clock" and there he is, maybe two miles back, with No 4 in fighting wing. Watch this! An instant replay generates two quick kills on Nos 3 and 4 the same way Lead and 2 "died." Okay, that's enough for now.

"Chase, let's go 'Button 2!'" Chase responds, "'Button 2.'" Now I switch my radio to the F-4 frequency and transmit, "Okay guys, knock-it-off." "Roger that 'Patty.' Lead knock-it-off, 2 knock-it-off, 3 knock-it-off, 4 knock-it-off." "'Patty 2' is heading 270 degrees and starting a left hand turn, accelerating to 300 knots. F-4 leader, corral your wingmen and call tally-ho on me for the join-up."

"Phantom Flight, 'Patty 2.' Do you have tally-ho?"

"Roger, Lead has tally-ho, 2 has tally-ho on Lead and 'Patty,' 3 tally-ho all, 4 tally-ho all."

"'Patty,' Phantoms have tally-ho and are joining up."

"Okay, Lead and 2 join on the left wing and 3 and 4 join on the right. I'll level out heading about 360 degrees and let you guys take a look at my jet for a couple minutes and then I will have the element [Nos 3 and 4] hold out with the chase T-38 and we can do 2-versus-1 perch attacks. Then we will swap with the element until Bingo Fuel [when we have to go home due to our fuel state].

"And I want you to think about the briefing and the vertical. Using the vertical is how you defeat me. I will turn inside you all day long unless you use the vertical. Remember the chalkboard lesson? Using the vertical is like tying a knot in a rope. It makes the rope shorter. How high into the vertical and when to do it is what you have to learn in order to kill this little guy. That's why we're here.

"Let me know when *show and tell* is over and you are ready to get back to work!"

Such was one of my early encounters as a fighter pilot training American aircrews in how to fight the MiG-17.

How sweet it is!

OVERVIEW

This book is the story of a group of military "pioneers" who were intent on using their experience, knowledge, and love of their country to develop a new air-to-air training paradigm for fighter pilots.

Chapter one will tell you why the "Gang of Three" created a super-secret squadron, built a remote and secret airfield, and equipped it with real MiG jet fighters manufactured in the Soviet Union. Those jets were completely restored from wrecks by gifted USAF mechanics. The MiGs were then used as adversaries to train American fighter pilots.

This chapter will also reveal the origin of the names CONSTANT PEG and Red Eagles.

To make this story clear and concise, "Fluid Four," "fighting wing," and a host of other fighter pilot terms will be explained as we work through the history of why.

Next, the book is going to relate how the idea was sold in Washington, D.C., how the project was financed, and how the airfield was constructed in about two years from initial concept until MiG tires were on the airfield ramp, all without competitive bidding from contractors.

We will look inside the operation, discuss the jets, and detail how the talented American aircraft mechanics assigned to the Red Eagles took these grounded wrecks and restored them into safe flying machines. Memories from and about the leadership and the men who made this project happen will be chronicled. Short anecdotal stories taken from personal memos and diaries are designed to help the reader understand who these Red Eagle people were, how they worked and played, and generally how they did business.

I wish that every man's story could be included, but many of them have died or, in pilot speak, "Flown West." Others just disappeared from our telephone, mailing, and e-mail rosters. We have searched for these missing men, and that task is still ongoing.

The story will conclude by telling you what the United States of America harvested from this project in terms of a fitting reward. That return on investment came in the form of American combat performance over the Gulf of Sidra, during DESERT STORM and, in a residual sense, during the war for Kosovo in the Balkans. Combat success was the goal, and that success is a tribute to the US military. The program was richly rewarding personally for the men who built an airfield, and restored, maintained, and operated American MiG jet fighters. These men provided the capstone on the training program that produced the American fighter pilots of our era.

CONSTANT PEG was a gift to our country from the men that made it come true. These men recognized a need for this training program and took aggressive steps to fulfill that need with a super secret concept. Then, the same men made it come true. The Air Force and Navy did not ask for the program, and no one was tasked to do it. Instead, a determined group of American patriots made it happen. Once understood, the program was embraced by the military services, causing problems and resistance to melt away. The program lasted until the end of the Cold War, when defense spending reductions took over as the nation rejoiced, new threats emerged, and spending policy shifted. Thus, the changing national priorities and the "peace dividend" mandated cuts or elimination of many programs, including CONSTANT PEG.

I loved working with every one of the members of the Red Eagle team at the time when, together, we were making things happen. Further, I treasure their ongoing friendship today and look forward to hoisting a cool brew with every Red Eagle I meet when we next get together.

Gail Peck
Colonel, USAF (retired)

INTRODUCTION

Government secrets! Everybody is curious about what the government is up to, but will not talk about.

The "mouse came out of the pocket" on one highly classified government program in November 2006 when the USAF declassified a closely guarded project with the code name CONSTANT PEG.

Knowledge that the USAF and US Navy trained American pilots using Soviet MiG jet fighters as adversaries is not new information. But, the odds are that most people know only little pieces about the program. Even those that may have participated know only their part of the story. That includes those who were trainees engaged in air combat with the MiGs and even most of the American instructor pilots who were actually flying the Soviet-built aircraft.

The program was established in the late 1970s, with operations commencing at the Tonopah Test Range in Nevada in July 1979. The project was named CONSTANT PEG and the organizational unit operating the MiGs was initially designated the 4477th Test and Evaluation Flight (TEF). This was later upgraded to the 4477th Test and Evaluation Squadron (TES). Initially it was thought that a flight organization instead of a squadron would be less visible, thus helping with security. Deception was built into its name from the beginning.

The American pilots and ground crewmen assigned to the unit elected to call themselves the Red Eagles because of the belief that the Soviet Union had a fighter weapons school. It was also believed that the Soviet pilots called themselves Red Eagles. The USAF Red Eagles patch was based on information alleging the existence of this Soviet squadron, and its symbol. LtCdr (later Capt) Charles "Heater" Heatley of the US Navy can be credited with designing the patch – in 1979 – that we wore on our flightsuits, hats, and work uniforms. "Heater" also led the way in naming the squadron Red Eagles.

Throughout its operational duration, the CONSTANT PEG program was conducted as a secret/must know project. Participants were briefed just before assignment to the program and were debriefed as soon as their association with it was complete. The debriefing admonished personnel from ever talking about their experiences outside the community of air crewmen, mechanics, and support personnel that had participated, or "played." The project was highly regarded, ensuring that the security was respected by all participants. It is indeed a tribute to the players that security was maintained throughout the project's entire active period ending in 1988, and for 18 years after flight operations terminated.

The USAF publicly declassified CONSTANT PEG during a press conference held at the National Museum of the Air Force at Wright-Patterson AFB, Ohio, in November, 2006. This public announcement provided an overview of the program, and a press conference was hosted by Maj Gen (ret) Charles D. Metcalf, the curator at the museum. Attending the event were four former Red Eagle commanders, along with the widow and family of one of the pilots killed during the program in the crash of a MiG-23. The commanders that attended the "coming out" were myself, Pentagon architect of the program and the first commander at the Tonopah operating location, Earl Henderson, the second commander at Tonopah, Jack Manclark, the sixth Tonopah commander, and Mike Scott, the seventh and final commander at the Tonopah operating location. Mike Scott's tour as a commander was his second Tonopah assignment flying MiGs. Mike was also a MiG pilot hired by me as a member of the initial cadre at Tonopah.

Two pilots and one NCO lost their lives during the project. Lt Hugh Brown (US Navy) died in a MiG-17 and Capt Mark Postai (USAF) was killed in a MiG-23. It was Postai's family that attended the declassification press conference at the National Museum of the Air Force. TSgt Rey Hernandez died in an industrial accident at Tonopah when he was overcome by jet fuel fumes while repairing a T-38 fuel tank.

CONSTANT PEG lasted nearly ten years, and during that time the program evolved and expanded. People came, served, and left to be replaced by new personnel, all of whom accumulated rich and largely untold experiences.

Chapter 1

Why the need for a MiG training program?

Setting the Scene

You might end up with an interesting list of aviation events if you assemble a group of pilots and bait them with the question, "What is the most difficult activity that you can do with an airplane?" Aviators with differing levels of experience will offer widely varying opinions on the most difficult maneuvers. Those opinions would be based on the situation that they remember providing them with the greatest challenge, and/or the most frightening aviating experience.

A novice pilot might stress take-offs and landings or stall approaches, spins, and instruments. The more experienced pilots might bring up aerobatics, and soon the list will expand to include weather flying and low visibility approaches. Some will mention formation flying, and then formation flying in bad weather or at night. Finally, formation aerobatics might be added to the list.

While all of these aerial events provide challenges of an increasing magnitude, air-to-air combat is the ultimate challenge. Anytime you are maneuvering for a life or death advantage it is easily argued that few, if any, aviation challenges will be equal to that of the air combat engagement. Surviving an air combat engagement is probably an odd combination of luck and skill. Luck reigns supreme, but it won't ensure survival over the long haul without significant skills. Air combat maneuvering skill is not innate. Instead, this skill is only developed by dedicated and intense training.

Harkening back to the beginning of aerial warfare, World War I pilots on opposite sides initially waved and later shot pistols at each other. Technology soon provided machine guns. The next iteration was a machine gun synchronized to shoot through the aircraft propeller without striking the blades. World War I air combat involved fiercely fought close encounters with pilots shooting at other aircraft from tens or hundreds of feet, preferably from an in-trail position. When head-on firing passes were made, the passes were close, and very scary! It was chaos until the German combat leaders of the day (specifically the great fighter ace Oswald Boelcke) began to develop techniques associated with formation flying that encouraged mutual support in order to obtain a tactical advantage.

Despite having no radios, they worked out a system of providing mutual support and taught it to their squadron mates. It didn't take long for the Royal Flying Corps and the French *Armée de l'Air* to catch on and develop formation tactics of their own. When the Americans entered the war in late 1917, they learned from the veterans.

In World War I aerial combat was not as personal as engaging an enemy with rifles and bayonets in trench warfare, but it was pretty damned close to it. By the start of World War II, however, providing your squadron mates with mutual support and a tactical advantage through formation flying had become doctrine.

During World War II the aircraft flew faster, had armor to protect the pilot, and were also more heavily armed. But the principal weapon in aerial warfare was still the machine gun, and the firing distances involved were still only slightly greater than in World War I.

The conflict in Korea added jets to the fray, although they were still armed with machine guns, which meant that aerial combat remained a very close range experience.

At some point early in this journey of air combat tactics development, the notion emerged that the shooter needed a wingman. This evolution probably formalized during World War II when the leader needing a wingman to cover him while he was concentrating on machine gunning the adversary. With the insurance provided by a wingman serving as a lookout and perhaps a shield, the leader was less vulnerable to coming under attack himself. And that is how it was done in Korea. Indeed, Korean War tactics ultimately developed into a combat formation known as Fluid Four, and we went to war in Vietnam using this tactical formation.

However, we quickly found out that our training with Fluid Four had not prepared us for North Vietnamese MiG-21s shooting missiles at us from a mile in trail. Our formations and tactics were not appropriate for this threat, and many of our airplanes were shot down. Some men died, some were rescued, and others became prisoners of war. We struggled to change and adjust, but the process was slow. Tactics emerged from the Vietnam combat theater wherein the FWS graduates and other talented pilots invented new ways to do business.

Fortunately, during the early stages of the Vietnam War, the United States acquired MiG-17 and MiG-21 aircraft. These were flown extensively, being thoroughly exploited during testing and evaluation by American pilots, maintainers, operations analysts, and engineers. They were also flown in air combat scenarios against all of our frontline fighter aircraft, USAF and US Navy alike, and thorough performance comparisons were made. These early programs were called HAVE DRILL and HAVE FERRY for the exploitation of the MiG-17 and HAVE DOUGHNUT for the exploitation of the MiG-21. Still and video footage was gathered and included in the exploitation reports.

Sadly, unlike these early programs, CONSTANT PEG was not carefully documented for historical purposes due to security issues and the classification of the project. That was a mistake we made. The files, photos, and records that were accumulated during the project were filed away in a vault in the Pentagon when the CONSTANT PEG project was terminated. That vault, according to credible reports, was destroyed along with all of it contents on September 11, 2001, when American Airlines Flight 77 crashed into the building.

Thus, with the exception of unclassified social events, what photo documentation that did exist on CONSTANT PEG was in the personal possession of individuals that participated in the program.

Later, a MiG-23 was acquired and exploited in a program called HAVE PAD. No photo documentation of this exploitation has appeared, although the USAF did declassify the test report. The photographs included in the photocopies of the report were black smudges, completely without photo documentation value.

My good friend Billy Gordon was a key participant in the HAVE DOUGHNUT exploitation. A war story about him illustrates the errors of warriors preparing for the last war and helps set the stage for the changes that followed.

TESTING VERSUS TRAINING

So, what are the differences between testing and training? The difference between the early US MiG programs and CONSTANT PEG is best described as a testing environment versus a training environment.

The HAVE DRILL/HAVE FERRY, HAVE DOUGHNUT, and HAVE PAD aircraft were flown during those tests by a limited group of highly skilled test pilots and a few very experienced operational fighter pilots, all of whom wrote reports about their experiences. Comparisons were made with friendly aircraft likewise flown by a select group of pilots who wrote their reports on what worked and what did not work in various maneuvering scenarios against the MiGs. The combat ready operational fighter pilots labored over these reports to extract the maximum amount of learning from the written word and the in-flight experiences of the test pilots.

The missing link was the void in the combat fighter pilots' actual experience. Book knowledge can never compete with actual experience and, until CONSTANT PEG, only a few of our pilots had actually flown against the MiGs. Fewer still had flown the MiGs.

First, let me point out that the fighter pilot community is comparatively small. And, while not involved directly in CONSTANT PEG, my good friend Billy Gordon had a major role in my training and also in the MiG-21 exploitation program HAVE DOUGHNUT.

Billy Gordon was the radar and AIM-7 air-to-air missile instructor when I went through the FWS in the fall of 1970. I clearly remember Billy standing in front of our class of future weapons officers, dressed in a flightsuit and holding a yellow legal pad of radar notes, as he explained to us in great detail the workings of the F-4 radar and the details an F-4 pilot and his weapons systems officer (WSO) needed to know in order to properly operate the radar in combat. As weapons officers, we were destined to become the chief instructors in our fighter squadrons, and it would be our job to teach these lessons to our men. Billy knew why and how because he had experienced combat like few others.

Indeed his experiences, more than any other that my research uncovered, dramatized the need for evolution, or revolution, or some kind of renaissance in fighter air-to-air tactics. Billy's experiences also support the fact that old tactics worked at the beginning of the Vietnam War but did not work once the enemy had air-to-air missiles.

Billy Gordon likes to refer to his combat opportunities in Southeast Asia as "more than one."

A veteran fighter pilot and retired colonel, he had a career any man with an adventurous spirit would envy. Even in retirement Billy is remarkable. In the summertime he flies his Pitts S-1 biplane in aerobatic displays at airshows in New England and in the winter he is a ski instructor in Colorado. I am in a ski group along with Billy that is rich in fighter experience. As in a fighter squadron, all the guys and most of the gals have nicknames. Billy Gordon is known as "Jean Claude Billy," a reference to the Olympic champion skier Jean Claude Keely. Billy is really that good!

During the early days of the Vietnam War, Billy Gordon was stationed at Yokota Air Base (AB), Japan, flying the single-seat F-102 Delta Dagger in the air defense mission. He was thus a very junior officer on his first operational fighter assignment when he and a group of pilots were sent temporarily to Tan Son Nhut AB near Saigon, Republic of South Vietnam, for air defense duties. On the way from Japan to Vietnam, the F-102 pilots made a short stop in the Philippines near Clark AB to attend the jungle survival school. The lasting piece of information Billy stored in his brain were the words of the instructor that suggested "if you get shot down in Vietnam get over the mountains or the ocean and you will probably get rescued. Don't ever get shot down over the Mekong delta because no one has ever been rescued from there."

Billy Gordon and another pilot were scheduled to conduct a local area orientation in the vicinity of the Mekong Delta and then undertake day and night intercept training as the sun set and day gave way to night. It was strictly a new guy orientation and training mission, and certainly not a planned combat mission. All went as expected until the flight split up for GCI radar vectors for a radar handoff to the ground control approach (GCA) facility at Tan Son Nhut. GCI vectors properly position the fighter for the final instrument approach and landing, which is completed by following directives from a ground radar approach controller.

As Billy was about to be handed off to GCA he noticed a considerable amount of ground fire adjacent to his flightpath and realized that he was observing his first war. He decided to take a better look and moved in closer. Mortars were being fired and small-arms fire was equally evident to the wide-eyed fighter pilot. He felt a jolt and thought that somehow he had inadvertently jettisoned his external fuel tanks. While trying to sort this out, the cockpit suddenly went black with complete electrical failure, the control column froze with complete hydraulic failure, and the jet pitched up out of control.

Billy ejected over the dreaded Mekong Delta. Coming down in his parachute, he noticed a little village with numerous huts or "hooches" as Americans called them, and he could hear people on the ground and see figures scurrying about. He landed in a briar patch with thorns an inch long and almost immediately could see people in black dress and wearing the coolie hats associated with the Viet Cong (VC). At jungle survival school he had been taught that the VC didn't keep prisoners. Upon capture by the VC American pilots could expect immediate execution, probably with one's own sidearm – a bullet to the forehead was the preferred method.

Billy Gordon abandoned his survival gear and began to evade through the briar patch in the opposite direction from the advancing people, who appeared to be searching for him. Somehow he managed to escape the patrol, and armed with only his sidearm, contemplated the challenge of getting rescued. He later learned that the guys he had initially seen were actually good guys dressed to look like bad guys as a part of a special operations effort.

Billy found a hole within sight of the village and hid. He was on the ground for several hours when he heard a helicopter that appeared to be patrolling up and down a road. It was equipped with a searchlight, and when it got to the village it illuminated each hooch as if looking for something. He hoped it was him. The helicopter seemed to progress, stop, turn around, and repeat the pattern almost in a precisely timed search pattern. Billy finally made his way to a ditch by the road, and when it approached he jumped up and waved his arms.

When the UH-1 Huey pilot saw him and visually authenticated Billy as a friendly he landed. Billy ran to the side door jumped in and embraced the gunner. The gunner was totally shocked and threw him out of the helicopter. Sensibility prevailed and Billy Gordon was invited back into the helicopter, but admonished to knock off the hugs. A new chapter had been written with the Mekong River Delta rescue. The loss of the F-102 was officially judged to have been caused by mechanical failure. Billy did not hasten to clarify the matter.

After the Delta Dagger tour, Billy Gordon checked out in the F-4D Phantom II and was assigned to the 555th TFS, nicknamed "Triple Nickel," as a part of the 8th Tactical Fighter Wing (TFW), better known as the "Wolfpack," under the command of then Col Robin Olds at Ubon RTAB.

The F-4 was a two-seat fighter that could perform either the air–to–air or air-to-ground mission. The second crewmember was initially another pilot. By 1968 the USAF had started the changeover from pilots in the back seat to WSOs with navigator aeronautical ratings. The pilot up front referred to the officer in the back seat as his "GIB" (Guy In Back). It didn't matter if the GIB was a pilot or navigator. He was still the GIB. One of the great personnel injustices of the Vietnam War was the policy that existed for a time that mandated USAF pilots volunteer for a second combat tour in order to obtain an upgrade to the front seat of the F-4.

The weather in Vietnam and Thailand is always bad one place or the other. This condition is caused by the monsoon weather flow pattern. If the monsoon is causing severe thunderstorms and heavy rain in Thailand, it is generally clear in Vietnam and vice versa. To allow the Vietnam War to continue in bad weather, USAF engineers and other behind the scenes experts re-engineered the function of the Strategic Air Command (SAC) scoring system for nuclear weapons training. SAC used a radar system to grade its simulated air drops. The radar would track the bomber, which would transmit a "pickle" or drop signal when the bomb delivery button was pushed. Using the radar-tracked bomb release point and known winds aloft, the radar bomb scoring (RBS) system would provide the crew with a hit or miss rating. It could also calculate the distance and radial from a perfect bulls eye.

The USAF reasoned that if targets were well mapped, then the RBS equipment could guide an aircraft to a drop point irrespective of the weather, and by dropping a string or stick (meaning several bombs rippled off the bombing aircraft) it could be reasonably expected that the ordnance would hit the target. The bombing system was labeled COMBAT SKYSPOT.

On October 26, 1967, Billy was flying as No 3 in a flight of four F-4s – Capt John Logeman was leading. The formation was Fluid Four and the mission was to escort two RF-4C photo-reconnaissance jets that had been tasked with validating the mapping of targets for COMBAT SKYSPOT in the heart of North Vietnam. Logeman and Gordon and their wingmen were to escort and protect the RF-4Cs from enemy fighters.

It was expected that following COMBAT SKYSPOT validation, fighter-bombers could be launched even when faced with terrible weather in North Vietnam and continue to rain bombs accurately on major targets in enemy territory.

A few days earlier the fighter-bombers had attacked the Vietnamese Peoples' Air Force (VPAF) airfield at Phuc Yen for the first time. The results and details of that raid are a subject for a different story. But, having no idea what was coming their way on October 26, eight MiG-17s were scrambled from Phuc Yen to defend the airfield as the RF-4Cs and their escorts approached on the photo run.

Initially, it was a head-on set-up, with the four escort missile-armed F-4s facing down the guns-only MiG-17s. Logeman attempted to boresight his radar on the lead MiG for a radar missile shot. He didn't get a lock-on but fired anyway. One missile didn't come off the jet but the second weapon roared away, leaving a great smoke trail. It speared the MiG in the wing root. The wing came off and the pilot ejected as the Phantom IIs roared through the initial merge.

The MiGs had set up a defensive wheel or circle wherein each jet could clear the tail of the MiG in front of him. Logeman repositioned the flight, and on the second pass through the wheel Billy boresighted his radar on a MiG and to his amazement his back-seater called "Locked!" Billy fired two missiles, and a few seconds later the Sparrow did its job. There were now two parachutes in the middle of the MiGs' defensive circle.

Through all of this the Nos 2 and 4 in the F-4 formation had been faithfully flying fighting wing to protect their element leaders from gun attack. As previously mentioned, the only weapons these MiGs had were guns – specifically two 23mm and one 30mm cannon. Billy noted that as he flew by the MiGs they sometimes seemed to be firing their guns, but at nothing he could identify as a target in front of them. Billy's wingman flying in Fluid Four welded wing called numerous breaks to his leader, but Billy assessed the nose position of the MiG attempting to gun him as he roared through their circle in pursuit of another kill. That nose position was such that the VPAF jet did not have enough lead to be a threat to him, so he pressed on.

Billy's wingman, Capt Larry D. Cobb, observed a MiG breaking out of the defensive wheel and broke away from his element leader to pursue a kill of his own, which he obtained with an AIM-4 infrared or heat-guided missile. This was a monumental breakdown of wingman discipline, especially since the wingman didn't radio Billy that he was no longer supporting his element leader. Soon there were three parachutes, all VPAF pilots in or near the defensive circle of the MiGs. The battle had raged and a trio of MiG-17s had been shot down without any Phantom II losses. Then it was over almost more suddenly than it had started.

The USAF jets headed for the tanker prior to commencing the long ride home to Ubon. At that time Billy's wingman reported an extremely low fuel state, which surprised Billy as he had conserved his own gas. Actually, as Billy tells the story, "The wingie was screaming for a tanker." That was the first time Billy realized his wingman was no longer with him in fighting wing. They made their airborne rendezvous with the tanker, got the fuel needed to make it back home and all survived. But, the famous "Wolf Pack" commander, Col Robin Olds, grounded Capt Cobb for a period due to his breach of discipline, even though he had scored an aerial victory. The grounding didn't last too long, just enough time to get everyone's attention.

The importance of grounding for a breach of discipline zeroes in on the problem we were facing in Vietnam. Fighting wing was a perfectly appropriate formation for the circumstances that were faced in this engagement. Keep the Phantom II wingmen in fighting wing formation to cover the element leaders who were the designated shooters. The threat was only armed with guns. However, when "Atoll" air-to-air missiles appeared on VPAF MiG-21s the game began to change.

By the time Billy next headed into North Vietnam on November 8, he had a snazzy red star on his helmet compliments of the NCOs in the life support section. His wingman on this occasion was an inexperienced pilot with a big itch to go to Route Package (RP) VI. Billy was the 555th's scheduling officer, and he had some control over who did what. On numerous occasions he had told this particular pilot that he just wasn't ready to go that far north.

Military planners divided North Vietnam into six geographic regions that they called Route Packages. These were numbered from I to VI and generally flowed from the south to the north. RP I was just north of the Demilitarized Zone between North and South Vietnam. The exception to this division was the area around Hanoi and nearby Haiphong, which was designated RP VI. "Pak 6," as the pilots referred to the area, was further divided into RP VIA (Hanoi) and RP VIB (Haiphong). Generally, the USAF had responsibility for operations in RP VIA and the US Navy dealt with targets in RP VIB. This split between the services placed the US Navy area of responsibility (AOR) closest to the aircraft carriers in the Gulf of Tonkin, while the USAF AOR to the west was closer to its air bases in Thailand.

Finally, Billy relented, thinking that as a highly experienced combat pilot with a MiG kill he could certainly take this man to North Vietnam safely. The mission was on. On this raid Billy and his flight were providing escort Combat Air Patrol (CAP) for F-105s. Billy was No 3, with the new guy on his wing.

A MiG-21's under ground radar vectors converted unobserved to their rear and blazed through the formation at more than 600 knots. The flight leader immediately detailed Billy to continue the escort of the F-105s while he pursued the MiG. Looking down through the haze at the jungle and attempting to pick out the Thunderchiefs in their jungle camouflage required a lot of concentration, and the first indication that Billy Gordon had that he himself was under attack was the thump of the impact of the missile fired by the second MiG-21.

Billy's new-guy wingman had seen the MiG approaching, but, as he freely admitted, was paralyzed by fear and was unable to push the radio microphone button and warn Billy of the impending attack. The MiG-21 with an air-to-air "Atoll" missile and a high quality radar vector had completed the intercept and taken its toll with a kill from about a mile in trail, in spite of Billy having a wingman supposedly covering him from the fighting wing position.

If Billy had ejected at that point he would have been over the flat land near Hanoi, and almost certainly would have been captured. Fortunately, the jet continued to fly for more than two minutes allowing him to maneuver to the west away from Hanoi and into very high mountain terrain, where he and his GIB, 1Lt Richard C. Brenneman, ejected. Landing in heavy elephant grass near the town of Lao Phou Van, Billy's back-seater was captured almost immediately. He threw away his helmet and then remembering the red star, searched and found it again. He removed the red star and continued his evasion until rescued some hours later. The worry with the red star was that if he were captured and his equipment found, as it almost certainly would have been, the bad guys would have known without interrogation that he had previously shot down a MiG.

It was after this excitement that Billy was brought back to the United States to participate in the HAVE DOUGHNUT MiG-21 exploitation program. He told me he was slated to be a MiG pilot, but doing so would have precluded his return to the combat zone due to security sensitivities. HAVE DOUGHNUT was very highly classified, and initially the USAF was not willing to take the risk that one of its MiG-21 pilots could be shot down, captured, and interrogated. Hence, travel restrictions were placed on personnel performing the MiG pilot task, and the combat theater in Southeast Asia was one of those restricted areas. Billy Gordon declined the opportunity to fly the MiG to avoid the travel restrictions. Oddly enough he still participated, but instead of flying the MiG-21, Gordon flew the F-4 against the MiG in the exploitation phase of the program.

Later, other HAVE DOUGHNUT MiG pilots, notably Fred Cutthill, did have combat tours after flying the MiG-21. Fred was in the 433rd TFS with me at Ubon, but few, if any, of us knew at the time that he had actually flown the MiG-21. Such was the classification level of the program, even though HAVE DOUGHNUT lessons were being widely briefed to aircrews across the USAF.

HAVE DOUGHNUT analyzed the MiG-21F "Fishbed C" against all US combat fighter aircraft. According to the report, the purpose of the program was to identify deficiencies and limitations that could then be exploited to defeat the MiG-21 over North Vietnam.

Air combat maneuvering engagements were simulated during the exploitation and tactical maneuvers were flown to validate effectiveness. From these evaluations the results were extracted and documented into published material that included the words "Lessons learned that could save you." This exploitation and use of captured or borrowed MiGs was a great start to the training of our pilots. However, only a handful of pilots got to fight against the MiGs, and even fewer got to fly them. Thus, while a great event, it was not satisfying from a training standpoint.

FIGHTER WEAPONS SCHOOL

The Fighter Weapons School at Nellis AFB is the graduate school for USAF fighter pilots. After mastering the basics in a frontline fighter squadron, the very best pilots are sent to this school to develop their skills further and prepare them for duty as a squadron weapons officer. The latter's principal task is to be the unit's chief tactician and instructor, training the remaining pilots in the squadron so that they are ready to go to war. Graduating from the FWS also sets the stage for a fighter pilot's career because all subsequent assignments are aimed at positioning the officer so as to allow commanders, especially in combat, ready access to his Nellis experience.

Our class at the FWS was a notable group that included Bob Lodge, who shot down three MiGs, and John Madden, who was also credited with three MiG kills. All six victories came during the LINEBACKER I campaign against North Vietnam in the summer of 1972. Another classmate was Mike Ryan, who later became the USAF Chief of Staff. Joe Hicks was the Outstanding Graduate in our class and George Branch won the flying award. Dick Swope later made "three star" rank. My squadron mate from my combat tour in the 433rd TFS, "JD" Allen, was also one of us.

An important part of the FWS curriculum is air-to-air gunnery against a towed target. In the 1970s the "Dart" was the towed target. Wood framed, it was pointed and weighted on the front end. The aft end of the 16ft long target resembled an X, with each of the four wings tapered in a straight line from the front to the rear. The wingspan at the rear of the Dart from tip to tip was about six feet. The dart was covered with a heavy aluminum foil over the basic wooden structure, the latter being strengthened with honeycomb material under the foil.

For take-off the Dart was stowed under the wing of the F-4 tow aircraft on a pylon. Upon a combination of switch commands from the cockpit, the Dart tow pilot released the Dart, which spooled out on a steel cable housed in the pylon to a position 1,500ft behind the tow aircraft. At the completion of the mission, or in the event of an emergency, the tow pilot could trigger a cable cutter and jettison the Dart. There is a peak to the northwest of Nellis AFB called "Jettison Hill," and aviators flying over it can still easily see the sun reflected sparkles from the aluminum skin of the Dart wrecks on the ground.

A complete handbook could be written about the various set-ups used for aerial gunnery training using Dart targets. Three typical set-ups that we were allowed to use over the years were the racetrack, butterfly, and combat Dart. The FWS used the butterfly set-up for their training syllabus at the time

I attended the course as a student. Shooters and the Dart tow jet launched in single ship take-offs and then joined in formation. With the area behind the tow aircraft clear, the Dart was launched into the tow position on its 1,500ft steel cable. Next, the Dart was inspected by the leader of the shooter aircraft formation, who was usually an instructor pilot at the FWS. The integrity of the Dart, and its flying qualities, were of special interest during the inspection. If the Dart was doing rolls due to damage during launch or an unforeseen aeronautical imbalance, it was deemed unsuitable as a target, the mission was aborted and the Dart jettisoned.

If there was more than one shooter involved, the second shooter aircraft would typically fly fighting wing on the first shooter. Then, they would swap positions. The pilot in any extra aircraft in the formation hoping for a turn as a shooter would hold well clear until called to shoot by the flight leader. The opportunity to shoot might or might not happen for the extra shooters depending on damage done to the Dart during the initial gunnery passes.

The butterfly set-up was initiated with both the shooter and the Dart tow aircraft in close formation. Upon the briefed radio command the fighter and the tow aircraft turned 45 degrees away from each other. When enough separation was obtained, a second turn back towards each other was commanded by the Dart tow pilot. Thus, with about two miles spacing, the tow and the fighter turned toward each other, resulting in a head-on pass. When the two passed each other the fight was ON and both turned. If the F-4 decided to turn into the target, a single circle fight resulted, and it was possible, but not probable, to shoot the towed target in about 17 seconds or so in a high deflection gun shot. Or the fighter could turn the same way as the tow aircraft, resulting in a two-circle fight. In the latter the time to reach a firing opportunity was substantially longer, but the deflection angle was greatly reduced, increasing the probability of a hit.

At the time we were only starting to understand clearly the dynamics of a single circle versus a two-circle dogfight. As it turned out, the single circle/two-circle dogfight was a fundamental of modern aerial warfare that in 1970 no one had previously explained to fighter pilots. If two fighters meet head on and, as they pass, both turn towards each other, a two-circle fight results, as both fly circles that when observed from above would resemble a figure 8. On the other hand, a single circle fight results if one pilot turns in the opposite direction. In this case the "God's Eye View" of their tracks would just be a single circle. The first pilot to turn establishes the option for the second pilot to make the fight either single circle or two circle.

There are reasons that fighter pilots will select a single circle fight versus a two circle fight. The most important of these is the ability to achieve a quick gun kill. On the other hand, the quick gun kill comes with risk attached because the firing pass will happen very quickly and at a high crossing angle.

During a single circle fight the attacking fighter cuts across that turn circle using the vertical. Since the sky is three dimensional, so is the circle. The circle then actually resembles an egg, with the tighter turns at the top. If the pilot elects to dive, his airspeed and turn radius increases. On the other hand, if he climbs his jet slows, and his slower speed results in a smaller turn radius. These aerodynamic factors define the air combat maneuvering "egg." Therefore, a pilot can attain the minimum time from the head-on pass to the gun firing position by diving across the circle defined by the Dart tow, following the bottom of the egg.

In the modern world, heat-seeking missiles like the AIM-9X, coupled with a helmet-mounted sighting device, can be fired at an opponent from inside or across the circle, hastening the kill. But during the early part of the Vietnam War the heat seekers had more primitive guidance systems that required shooting from an in-trail position straight behind the opponent.

Or in the case of a turning fight these early missiles were shot from outside the turn circle in what we called a "belly shot." Visualize a circle and draw a line tangent to the circle. That line would define the acceptable position for firing an infrared guided missile against a turning target to complete a "belly shot." Lots of technical stuff goes into describing the circumstances a fighter pilot faces in aerial combat.

My only claim to fame among my FWS group of classmates was a great air-to-air gunnery mission in which I went single-circle with the Dart and managed a kill in record time. It is probably true that a couple of years later my Dart mission caused the leadership at Nellis AFB to select me to come back to the FWS as an air-to-air instructor. In the interim after FWS I returned to MacDill AFB in Tampa, Florida, looking forward to serving as the weapons officer for the 46th TFS.

MOODY AND SOME OF THE BOYS

Maj "Moody" Suter was the air-to-air flight commander at the FWS when I returned to Nellis to be an instructor in July 1972. Richard M. Suter was a visionary who had orchestrated the evolution of the Aggressors and would soon invent Red Flag during his future assignment at the Pentagon. Red Flag is the dazzling training exercise at Nellis AFB that continues to this day, and it has grown to include similar exercises historically in the Philippine Islands and currently in Canada and Alaska.

Moody and his "fighter mafia" colleagues came up with the notion that if a fighter pilot could survive the first ten combat missions of a war, he had a highly increased probability of surviving his entire combat tour. Red Flag was established to bring the various combat air force elements (Intelligence, command and control, fighters, bombers, reconnaissance, aerial refueling tankers, etc.) together at Nellis in a large two-week exercise aimed at giving the participants ten missions that would be as close to combat as training could permit. The participants face "enemy" air and ground forces, and when a mission is complete and all have landed, both sides then participate in and contribute to an exhaustive debriefing aimed at identifying and recording every lesson that can be harvested from the sortie – both good and bad.

At the FWS Moody had assembled around him a group of stunningly capable officers, all of whom were air-to-air instructors in the F-4. It is important to mention the names of some of these men that trained us to be instructors at the FWS level.

Roger G. Wells was one of the most respected and forceful of the group. A flight briefing followed by a Basic Fighter Maneuvers training mission and a debriefing with Roger Wells was truly an event to remember. I credit Roger as the originator of the now ever popular expression "Situational Awareness" or "SA" for short. I was present in one of Roger's debriefings when I first heard the term. He was explaining to one of our students the errors of his ways after a disastrous series of events during an FWS training mission. Roger said something like, "Man, you just had no *SITUATIONAL AWARENESS*, and it was evident because if you had known what was going on around you, you would never have let that happen!" Roger barked it out, his flattop haircut glistening, his ice blue eyes almost glowing, his finger jutting right in the student's face, almost touching him. The other instructors in the room looked at each other thinking and almost uttering, "WOW! Did I just hear what I heard?" The details of the student's error are long forgotten, but the term or the meaning of "SA" will never be forgotten!

In addition to "Moody" and Roger were Ross Truesdale, Dick Berdan, Bill Sakahara, and Ed Cobleigh. Lloyd "Boots" Boothby, who later became the first Aggressor squadron commander, was an attached instructor and a gifted pilot. All were excellent aviators and incredible instructors. Gary Skarit, like Billy Gordon, had been an instructor when I was a student, but he had departed before I returned to the FWS as an instructor. These FWS instructors were especially effective, and they laid the foundation for the next step of the training evolution that Joe Hurd, Dave Smith, Don Gish, and I inherited as the air-to-air replacement team of instructors at the FWS in 1972. Others of our squadron mates were also notable. No one individual or group can take credit or be credited with the changes that were coming. It was truly a team effort.

When "Moody" left Nellis for duty in Washington, D.C., in the Air Staff's Tactical Division ("fighter shop") of the Deputy Chief of Staff (DCS) for Operations and Readiness, I was selected to replace him as the air-to-air flight commander at the F-4 FWS. About a year later I was on my way to intermediate service school at the Armed Forces Staff College in Norfolk, Virginia, with a follow-on assignment to the same "fighter shop" office in the Pentagon where "Moody" worked.

While stationed at the Pentagon "Moody" was selected for advancement to lieutenant colonel, and also received a well-deserved reward for "inventing" Red Flag. The reward was a Legion of Merit, one of the highest non-combat decorations awarded to a USAF officer. The award was followed by a mid-tour transfer to take command of an F-15 squadron at Luke AFB, near Phoenix, Arizona.

My assignment at the Pentagon's Tactical Division was initially in the weapons shop working for Lt Col B.V. Johnson. An entire book could be written about B. V. He was a true warrior and a great leader, friend, and man to know and work for.

As luck would have it when "Moody" left the Pentagon, once again I inherited the job he vacated.

At the time his job was referred to as the "Air Force tactics officer." Moody's duties involved unclassified or "white world" responsibilities that included support of Red Flag and the Threat Training Facilities. But "Moody" was also in charge of many of the highly classified, or "black world," projects that were ongoing related to testing and training. One of those had to do with US government owned MiG jet fighters.

OUR GANG

Much of the focus of this book is the United States flying enemy aircraft to train our fighter pilots. But let me stress that is was our maintenance men and other members of the support team that refurbished the MiGs and made them safe for flight.

And, there were other influential people in my life who facilitated our training improvements overall.

The man who gave me my start into the higher levels of fighter operations was my squadron commander at MacDill AFB, Lt Col Daniel O. Walsh, or "Firecan Dan." He was the operations officer of the 46th TFS when I arrived at MacDill in late 1969. A month or so earlier I had met him briefly at the MacDill Officers' Club, and later learned that he had arranged for me to be assigned to the squadron. Soon, I had built a rapport with "Firecan" to the point that I could remind him regularly that he should send me to the FWS. To make that happen I worked every job I was given as hard as I could, and in late August 1970 the FWS dream came true. I graduated in December 1970 and returned to MacDill AFB and the 27th TFS. In the summer of 1972 my tour with the unit at MacDill AFB ended when I was selected to return to Nellis and report to the 414th FWS as an F-4E FWS instructor. The stage was set.

Among the FWS F-4 instructors at the time were officers destined for very high rank and responsibility. Dick Myers made four stars and went on to become the Chairman of the Joint Chiefs of Staff. I clearly remember one Halloween when Dick's wife Mary Jo dressed him up in a yellow "Big Bird" costume for a party. Always a gentleman on the ground, despite being a fierce fighter pilot in the air, I have never heard a disparaging word said about Dick Myers.

John Jumper came through the FWS as a student on my watch and later served with the school as an instructor. Johnny did a lot of writing in the *Fighter Weapons Review*, our quarterly magazine. His subjects varied, but they were universally good. He is credited with first describing the building-block approach to training that we were developing and using.

Another student who came back as an instructor was Ron Keys. Ron became famous in USAF circles with his 1978 "Dear Boss" letter outlining why many good officers were dissatisfied enough with the Air Force to be leaving the Service.

In addition to Myers, both Jumper and Keys made four stars, with Johnny serving as the USAF Chief of Staff and Ron taking the helm at Air Combat Command.

One of my best friends in life, Joe Hurd, who had been a weapons officer colleague in another squadron at MacDill was also an instructor in the air-to-air flight at the FWS. Hurd, Gerry Huff, and I also hung out together socially and threw some memorable parties. Joe Hurd made three stars and served with distinction in the Western Pacific, Central Command, and at the Pentagon in a variety of jobs during his career.

It was great to fly again with my combat roommate Ed Cobleigh. After Ubon, Ed had flown a second combat tour and was then assigned to the FWS. Upon completion of the course he remained as an instructor. For a time he worked in the "smart bomb" business, teaching aircrews how to employ terminally guided weapons. Ed then became one of "Moody's" guys in the air-to-air flight until his tour ended. He was present with "Moody" and I as the last three standing after a great party at my house at 724 Delta in Las Vegas. It was during a semi-drunken conversation that we verbalized the thoughts that eventually "Moody" used to develop the Red Flag training exercise.

"Whiskey Bill" Wilson, our operations officer, went to the Air Staff in the Pentagon when he left Nellis. Col Wilson called Joe Hurd and me (both majors) to his office in the summer of 1975 shortly after Joe and I reported for duty in the "fighter shop" in the Operations Directorate (AF/XOO) within the "five-sided squirrel cage" (otherwise known as the Pentagon). Joe and I had three straight assignments together – MacDill, Nellis, and the Pentagon.

Wilson was a Division Chief in the DCS for Programs and Resources (AF/PR). That meant that he and his people determined how money would be spent in the USAF. It was Bill Wilson's boss, Maj Gen Jim Currie, that subsequently lent me a guiding hand as we worked money issues for CONSTANT PEG. "Whiskey Bill" reminded Joe and I that you can have the best plans in the world for the best operation in the world, but if it isn't sprinkled with money (like water), it won't grow. His counsel was well taken when the seed of CONSTANT PEG was planted a short time later.

Back at Nellis in the early 1970s our training practices were overly restrictive in some areas. It was mandated that we would not engage in dissimilar air combat training (DACT). It was judged to be too dangerous. The opposite was the truth. Engaging in exclusively similar aircraft training was actually much more dangerous because it was hard to tell a "good guy" from a "bad guy," and the risk of a mid-air collision was increased because all aircraft exhibited roughly the same performance capabilities.

Nevertheless, in the early 1970s, our air-to-air training in the USAF F-4 community was conducted almost exclusively with F-4s fighting other F-4s. As Roger G. Wells liked to say, "In a one-versus-one air combat training mission, we were forced to attack each other with identical aircraft using the same tactics, while neither pilot was much more skilled than the other. That is NOT GOOD!"

F-4 against F-4, or worse still a pair of F-4s against another pair of F-4s, was not the advanced air-to-air training we needed, especially at the FWS. Instead, we needed to visually see other types of aircraft in flight and learn to tell whether they were turning away or into us. Further, some jet engines smoke and some don't. An F-4 smoking is not in afterburner and an F-4 that isn't smoking is in afterburner. This is a dead giveaway as to the power setting. Most adversaries don't give up such an obvious clue.

We also needed to practice engaging aircraft that could turn better than the F-4, and that had other dissimilar characteristics and capabilities including small size and vertical (zoom) capability. Our prime adversary, the MiG-21, is tiny compared to an F-4 and the engine is almost smokeless. We needed to learn to look for glint and canopy shimmers instead of big smoking aircraft that gave away both their power setting and position by their smoke trails.

Eventually a regulation was written authorizing DACT. As might be expected, the regulation was initially very constraining, but it was a start. In the meantime we plowed along doing what we were told to do, all the while knowing that what we should be doing was "new world thinking." We were reliving history's previous wars tactically, but in a completely new environment brought about by the air-to-air missile.

During our pre-combat training our instructors had taught us as best they could. We tried to be professional and follow orders, while learning the hard way that the techniques and tactics our instructors had taught us did not match the situations that we had faced in combat, and that others were still facing in combat in the skies over North Vietnam.

In the fall of 1972 the F-4 FWS's third class of the year was cancelled and the weapons school instructors were redirected toward preparing three different groups of pilots for action in Vietnam. The training program for one of these groups of pilots and aircraft was code-named RIVET HASTE. The latter group was a full squadron of experienced F-4E pilots and WSOs headed for an assignment at Udorn RTAFB and destined to join the air war over North Vietnam. The F-4Es that belonged to this squadron were brand new, and they had the tech order modification known as 556 which was the beginning of HOTAS (Hands On Throttle and Stick) switchology for weapons employment. Instead of reaching all over the cockpit for different switches to select various weapons and modes of radar operation, HOTAS put all of these switches in an ergonomically proper arrangement on the aircraft control stick and throttles – hence HOTAS.

The jet was capable of launching the AGM-65 Maverick rocket-powered air-to-ground missile that was designed to destroy tanks. It also had a telescopic identification system called Target Identification System, Electro-Optical, or TISEO for short. At this time in history, the combat rules of engagement required a visual identification prior to shooting air-to-air missiles. The purpose of TISEO was to identify missile targets beyond visual range. The TISEO and the system's telescope looked wherever the aircraft radar was looking and presented a magnified image of the target in the cockpit. With positive target identification at very long distances, it was thus possible to take advantage of air-to-air missile shoot ranges without the risk of fratricide. For the first time aircrews could lock onto a distant target, visually identify the target with the TISEO and shoot from beyond visual range.

The RIVET HASTE pilots and WSOs arrived at Nellis combat ready from their previous F-4 units. The entire mission at Nellis was to learn to operate the AGM-65 Maverick, including some live firing opportunities and to polish their air-to-air skills. This included learning to use the 556 modification to the weapons delivery system and to achieve proficiency with the TISEO telescopic identification system. These officers were a dream to fly with and their training proceeded without incident.

It was during the training of this squadron that Randy O'Neil and I first flew the MiG-17 as an adversary in their training. It was a memorable experience. I will never forget the line Suits spewed out at Randy O'Neil and me the day we showed up to check out in the MiG-17. "Stormin Norman," as he was called, made it clear that we were worthless TAC scumbags that were encroaching on sacred Edwards territory without an invitation from the "King" (him). Finally, Randy, a true southern gentleman from Virginia, had had enough and the young captain (me) watched in awe while the majors went at it. Randy ate Norman's lunch. From then on all was cool, and we had a great time checking out and flying the MiG during the RIVET HASTE adversary missions.

These sorties were one MiG vs two or four F-4s, and as described in the prologue, the squadron employed Fluid Four tactics against us. They quickly learned to use the vertical and avoid trying to turn with the MiG. The F-4's wing-loading was much higher than the MiGs, and efforts to engage the latter in a turning dogfight always led to the F-4 overshooting the MiG and becoming defensive as soon as the communist fighter reversed direction. By using the vertical the F-4 pilots learned to stay behind the MiG through zoom-like maneuvers as they were approaching the overshoot point. As soon as the MiG started to drift out front again the F-4 could be positioned back down and to the inside of the MiG's turn circle, enabling another gun pass.

The idea of getting a squadron of MiGs and using them as training adversaries had been dreamt about for some time by the FWS instructors, and probably by other fighter pilots in the USAF as well. With the RIVET HASTE training opportunity, some of us had now gotten a taste of how good that would be.

With the completion of RIVET HASTE training, the men and the F-4Es deployed from Nellis AFB to Udorn RTAFB. Upon arrival they became the 555th TFS or the "Triple Nickel," or just the "Nickel" in fighter pilot speak. Airplanes and people that had been members of the "old" Nickel squadron were reassigned, being farmed out to other units to make room for the new *hot shots*. That made a lot of the former "Nickle" members unhappy, as the unit had a rich history and the old crowd was proud to be in the unit, and thus were resentful of the "new guys." The new jets and highly trained aircrew were expected to bring a new dimension to aerial warfare, and the leadership decided they should carry the sword and shield of the "Triple Nickel." However, they never got into any significant air-to-air combat before the Vietnam War in the north ended.

The second group of pilots being trained by the 414th FWS also had previous F-4 experience, but most recently had been assigned to non-flying staff tours. These officers were also headed for the combat theater. The officers in the third, and final, group were all recent F-4 trainees who had just completed gunnery school. Their next assignment was to be in combat. So, the 414th was tasked to write an air-to-air training top-off syllabus for these officers and then conduct the training. All of this training was going on simultaneously and, with some notable exceptions, for the most part went smoothly.

The staff officers and the young pilots had no opportunity to train against the MiG. All of their training was F-4 vs F-4, and on more than one occasion the results were scary. All of these groups used the same old fighter tactics, which meant flying Fluid Four and welded wing formation.

At around this time USAF leadership at some unknown level came up with a plan to make air-to-air training more effective when using similar aircraft on both sides of the mock dogfights. Our maintenance folks were directed to paint the tips of the horizontal stabilizers orange on half of our Nellis F-4 fleet. The plan was to have all orange tails on one side of a dogfight. "They" thought this would enable the pilots to keep track of who was who. This was an ironic step because from the distances that we initially engaged it was impossible to see the orange tips. Confusion raged. The orange tails also became a maintenance generation and operations scheduling nightmare, as efforts were made to have all orange tails on half of the flying schedule and no orange tails on the other half. The entire exercise would have been laughable if it were not for the energy wasted while trying to make it work.

On one such training mission I was the instructor pilot of record flying in the back seat of the No 4 F-4 aircraft on one side against four other F-4s. Students were in the front seats and at the controls of all eight jets. My guy in the front seat was hanging on for dear life in fighting wing formation when he flew though the jet wash of his element leader about 1,000ft behind him. We were supersonic at the time, and my head hit the side of the canopy so hard that a piece of my helmet about the size and shape of a silver dollar spalled off. When I recovered from my disorientation we were in a steep dive, and I looked out to the left and counted seven airplanes several miles away. I asked my student in the front seat if he still had our element leader in sight and he responded, "No I lost him!"

I braced myself and suggested he recover from the dive and save our lives. I had my hands in a V-shaped position with my thumbs locked together right behind the F-4 control stick in the rear cockpit. I did this to prevent him from over-stressing our aircraft by exceeding the maximum structural g limitation. The student responded by snatching 7gs on the aircraft in about two heartbeats of time and nearly broke my thumbs. But my hands prevented the over-g. The entire sequence really made me mad, and I took over at that point, called for a join-up and took the miserable gaggle back to Nellis. I radioed the operations desk and asked the squadron commander to meet me at the aircraft and he complied with my request. He agreed that we should never do that again, and we didn't.

Air-to-air training was about to change, and lurking in the back of all the FWS instructors' minds was the determination to follow the RIVET HASTE model and add actual MiG exposure to the training of combat fighter pilots.

Throughout this period we continued to learn how to do the air-to-air job better. We found over time that the overall skill required to be successful in air combat can be distilled into pieces of training we called building blocks. Start with simple maneuvering relative to the maneuvering of another aircraft. Increase the abruptness and magnitude of the maneuvers. Then, cast the players as offensive, defensive, or neutral advantage at the beginning of a training session, and have them practice maintaining or reversing their circumstance. Then, add additional aircraft to the fray, both friendly and adversary, and extend engagement distances to beyond visual range, with both sides depending on ground based and/or on-board radar in the attempt to generate an offensive advantage prior to transitioning to the visual dogfight. The building block scenarios go on and on until the trainee has mastered the entire package and has become skilled in air-to-air combat operations in a training environment.

One set of starter building blocks is satisfied if the offensive advantage is maintained throughout a series of aggressive maneuvers on the part of the adversary. In another building block set, the defender maneuvers effectively and becomes the offender in a two aircraft engagement, reversing the roles of the fighters in spite of the best efforts of the adversary. Or take the building blocks to the next level and start the engagement without advantage to either pilot with a head-on pass, and see if one pilot can gain the offensive advantage over the other.

Each of these dogfighting engagements consist of maneuvers the pilot must perform, and each must be precisely timed to respond to the maneuvers of the other pilot so as to either gain or maintain the advantage. If the maneuvers are performed correctly at the right time by one of the pilots, either the offensive advantage is maintained or the defender becomes the offender. If the maneuvers are not timed correctly or performed without accuracy the offender can become the defender and lose the dogfight and, in actual combat, perhaps his life.

Learning to fight together as pairs of fighters follows as the next level in assembling the air-to-air training building block sequence.

Even with the completion of all of the training building blocks, thrusting the young pilot into real combat takes the training challenge to another level that is quite different. The live combat arena, with real bullets and missiles, often brings a change in pilot behavior and a potential breakdown in the ability of the engaged pilot to maintain the needed intensity and discipline. Bad luck, fear, loss of a flight member in a shoot-down, or any combination of circumstances can result in a performance breakdown for a "green" aviator. Even if everything goes exactly right, the excitement of first observing an enemy aircraft in an aerial dogfight can turn the almost perfectly trained pilot into a target. Fighter pilots call it "buck fever" and strike a corollary with learning to hunt deer. As the deer is centered up in the rifle sight, the gun starts to shake, the hunter hesitates, and suddenly the advantage is lost. And this happens in spite of the fact that the deer isn't even equipped to shoot back.

In spite of the lessons we were suffering, change came slowly. By 1972 the instructors at the F-4 FWS were becoming increasingly frustrated while trying to make Fluid Four work. They pored over the operations reports coming in from the combat theater and specifically Udorn RTAFB during LINEBACKER I. We paid attention because Steve Ritchie, Bob Lodge, John Madden, Fred Olmstead, Dan Cherry, and others were scoring combat victories in North Vietnam and were developing new fighter tactics as they went along. The FWS instructors became the students.

A notable input from the combat theater was an improved method of turning the four-ship formation called the delayed 90. The leader gives a sharp visual signal by making a wing dip in the direction to be turned. The turn is then initiated by whichever element leader is on the outside of the turn – i.e. if the formation is turning left, the turn is initiated by the right element. In the case of the left hand turn with the lead element initially on the left, the leader hesitates to allow his element leader to turn first. When the element leader has, in his turn, drifted back to an angle of about 45 degrees (line aft) the flight leader commences an aggressive 4–5g 90-degree turn to the left.

The element leader may signal his wingman to start the turn and then hesitate, or he may maneuver a little less aggressively to permit his wingman to move to the opposite side during the 90-degree turn. After 20 seconds or so, and at the end of 90 degrees of turn, the formation is once again line abreast. This is at least three times faster than a fluid turn. The risk is that if the flight leader rolls out of the turn after only 45 degrees of turn, as could happen in an initial move in a tactical engagement, the element is trapped or "sucked" back to a line well aft of line abreast. In a worse case situation the element would be sucked to trail, losing the mutual support of the lead element.

The tacticians of the day quickly realized that with a radio call, leaders could adjust the turn by keying the rest of the formation to look for a different angle in their delayed turn. For example, a turn of 45 degrees (versus 90 degrees) can be accomplished with the formation ending up line abreast if the delay is held until the line aft of line abreast is nearly 70 degrees. Eventually communications-out techniques were developed as pilots became more accustomed to gauging the intentions of the leader.

A complete 180-degree turn can be accomplished very quickly in two ways. If the leader calls for an in-place turn left or right, all four fighters make a 4–5g turn in the same direction. This could apply if the leader needed to reverse direction and displace the formation one direction or the other for patrol purposes, or to face an enemy approaching from a direction slightly offset from an absolute trail.

The other 180-degree turn is called a cross turn. At the signal to initiate a cross turn the element leaders turn into each other while visually assuring vertical separation. At the completion of the 180-degree turn the formation has reversed course. The wingmen must maneuver to position themselves so as to be on the correct side of their element leader. The cross turn also permits each element to clear the "six o'clock" of the other element during the turn. This is sometimes called delousing, or ensuring that no "parasites" are stalking a formation at deep "six o'clock."

We worked hard at the FWS to learn the lessons from the combat theater and to include these new tools in our air-to-air training programs. But the FWS, with a colonel as the commandant, was several layers below the general officer masters at Headquarters Tactical Air Command (TAC) at Langley AFB. That generation of fighter pilot generals still hung on to the notions about air-to-air combat that were learned during the Korean War. Thus, we FWS instructors were forced to continue to use the tactics of the past – slow Fluid Four turns while on patrol, and once the four-ship formation engaged in aerial combat, the wingmen were expected to collapse into fighting wing and cover their respective element leaders from the gun attack. These continued to be the rules of the day.

WHAT MOTIVATED THE PROJECT?

So, where do great stories start and end? From the very beginning it is important to make the point that the US military air forces struggled through a renaissance in both training and tactics during the period of time that included the Vietnam War. During this conflict personnel in our air forces began to realize that the world of fighter aviation was changing largely due to the weapons available to the fighter airplanes/pilots, along with the defensive forces on the ground.

The US Navy was first to take action to fix the training and tactics problem. A study called the Ault Report was the beginning for the air-to-air training renaissance in the US Navy and Marine Corps. The Ault Report recommended establishment of an "Advanced Fighter Weapons School" to revive and disseminate community fighter expertise throughout the fleet.

The USAF FWS has existed at Nellis AFB for many years, producing hundreds of graduates. The mantra for air-to-air combat training at the FWS was based on the experience and writings of Maj Gen (ret.) Frederick "Boots" Blesse and his documentary publication *No Guts, No Glory*. It explained the tactics and techniques shown to be effective during the Korean War, and mandated that fighters employ in pairs with one shooter and one flying cover for the shooter. In the preceding explanations and stories in my book, the goal has been to show that at the beginning of the Vietnam War, the Korean War tactics were workable. Of note is the gun-armed MiG-17 kill that Billy Gordon scored on October 26, 1967. Billy had missiles, but no gun. The MiGs he attacked had guns but no missiles. Later, when the MiGs were equipped with missiles, things changed, and on November 8, 1967, Billy Gordon was shot down by a North Vietnamese MiG-21 that targeted his F-4D with an "Atoll" air-to-air missile.

A period of dither followed. USAF combat pilots, including Col Robin Olds, the commander of the 8th TFW "Wolfpack," used the Korean War tactics and scored numerous kills. But, overall, we had mixed results. The FWS attempted to follow the lead of the US Navy and the Air Defense Command Weapons School by introducing tactics and training changes that abandoned the Korean

War four-ship Fluid Four tactics in favor of a two-ship focus, with both fighters cleared to be shooters. But fierce resistance to these changes came from TAC middle and senior leadership and change came slowly. The Air Force FWS embraced the new two-ship ideas and eventually began to train pilots in accordance with the lessons emerging from the combat theater during LINEBACKER I. While the path was slow and rocky, eventually the road into the next generation of aerial combat tactics was paved based on the combat success from LINEBACKER, along with fresh ideas about training and tactics.

So, this story about the USAF renaissance in fighter thinking and application could start with lessons experienced, but not necessarily learned, at Udorn RTAFB in 1969, or in aerial combat in the skies over North Vietnam on May 10, 1972.

THE ROLE OF "MOODY" SUTER

I first met Richard "Moody" Suter at Udorn RTAFB in 1969. We were attending a tactics conference and he was a weapons officer from the 366th TFW at Da Nang AB, Republic of South Vietnam. This meeting could serve as another start point for the CONSTANT PEG story. I was a delegate to the tactics conference from the 8th TFW at Ubon RTAB. The 433rd TFS "Satan's Angels" was my first operational fighter assignment, and it was truly an honor to be selected to attend the conference. By the time of this gathering I had flown 36 daylight combat missions into North Vietnam and had also completed about 100 night combat missions, mostly in Laos. President Johnson called off the North Vietnam bombing campaign known as ROLLING THUNDER on October 31, 1968 – my 28th birthday. The RF-4C reconnaissance guys continued to fly over North Vietnam, however, and sometimes escorts also went there too if the communist forces showed a pattern of shooting at the recce Phantom IIs.

We had a great tactics conference at Udorn, the agenda of which is long since forgotten. But the gist was the need for better combined or integrated tactics among the players conducting the air war in Laos and the protective reaction escorts into North Vietnam during the bombing halt. Those players consisted of F-4 fighters from Udorn, Ubon and Korat RTABs, Da Nang AB, Vietnam, and F-105 fighter-bombers from Takhli and Korat RTABs. It is important to include the RF-4C reconnaissance assets from Udorn and the KC-135 tankers that came from Utapao RTAB too.

Another key player in operations at this time was the Search and Rescue force at Nakhon Phanom RTAB. These units flew either H-3 and H-43 helicopters or big, slow, propeller-driven A-1E aircraft. The latter carried enough fuel to stay in a rescue area for a long time, and were equipped with a variety of weapons that were very good for covering the helicopter rescue assets. The A-1Es, call sign "Sandy," along with the rescue helicopters, call sign "Jolly" (Jolly Green Giants as they were affectionately called), were vitally important to those of us fighting the so-called out-of-country war in Laos and North Vietnam.

At the conclusion of the conference, with all the problems "solved," the participants gathered socially, decked out in their specially tailored and brightly colored flying suits covered with unit patches and the occasional tasteless statement emblazoned on a custom patch. We called these flightsuits "party suits," and the party suits were the uniform of the day when we embarked on a trip to Bangkok for a weekend to remember. The transportation was a C-130, call sign "Klong," and the cargo was all of us and numerous coolers filled with beer, ice, and Bloody Marys.

There was a substantial delay in leaving Udorn that morning, and we were all avoiding the tropical summer sun sitting around under the wings of the C-130 waiting for the signal to board. Naturally, everybody was thirsty and so the booze flowed. By the time we boarded most of the passengers were hammered, and the scene aboard the airplane could best be described as a combination of a *Star Wars* bar and a zoo. Guys were swinging from the overhead tie downs, and at one point while airborne a colonel stuck his head back into the cargo area from the cockpit to attempt to quiet things down. He was pelted with ice cubes and driven back into the cockpit. Throughout this chaos I sat next to Maj "Moody" Suter, who I had just met. We chatted, drank, and set the stage for a life-long friendship.

Very quickly I transitioned into receive mode as "Moody" ranted on and on about training. He spoke about how we had to do more for the young inexperienced wingman referred to as Blue No 4 (Blue was usually the call sign adopted by friendly forces, with Red being used by the enemy, while No 4 referred to the fourth jet in the formation, flown by the junior pilot) and keep them alive and out of PoW camps, etc. It was a fascinating experience, and set the stage for my post-Vietnam life work in the USAF. All the while drunks were doing their best either to outdo each other or entertain the group with their antics. It was a wild scene, and yet "Moody" quietly explained things to the slick winged captain sitting next to him.

I next ran into "Moody" when I was a student at the FWS in the fall of 1970 and he was the air-to-air flight commander. Little did I anticipate during either of these first two meetings that I would be cast to follow in his footsteps through many bureaucratic battles both at the FWS and later at the Pentagon.

Finally, in the search for the beginning of this story, fast forward to the warriors at Udorn RTAFB in 1972. In addition to the summer of 1969 at Udorn RTAFB – when I first met "Moody" – another possible start date for this story is May 10, 1972, because that is the day Bob Lodge died.

Maj Robert A. "Bob" Lodge, an Air Force Academy graduate in the Class of 1964, was a FWS classmate of mine, and a very close friend. He and I really got to know each other while we were students attending the FWS. Bob had a little silver sports car, and during the rare breaks in our schedule he would call me and we would head for Binion's Horseshoe Casino in Las Vegas, where Bob would gamble. My job was to help him keep track of his money. He did very well as he understood the game and the bets thanks to his computer-like mind. After a couple of hours we would rake in the money and head back to Nellis to plan our next FWS mission.

One of the more memorable training hops that Bob and I flew together took us and two others in a flight of four in combat spread formation into Death Valley, California. We descended until our altimeters read below sea level as we overflew the Death Valley area known as Bad Water – the location of the lowest elevation in the US. Then we screamed past the Furnace Creek airport and resort at 500 KIAS (knots indicated airspeed) below 500ft AGL. You'd go to jail today if you pulled that stunt in a national park. Less than two years later Bob Lodge was at Udorn RTAFB, and the air war in North Vietnam was again raging. Bob had shot down two MiGs prior to the fateful May 10, 1972, mission.

Along with Bob Lodge, Steve Ritchie was among the "band of brothers" at Udorn that were developing new F-4 fighter tactics and formations to deal with the MiG threat. Steve had been an upgrading instructor at the FWS when I was a student. Before he was done in Vietnam he had shot down five MiG-21s, all with AIM-7 Sparrow radar guided air-to-air missiles, to become the only USAF pilot ace of the war.

After FWS Bob Lodge had blossomed into an awesome tactician, and he was the 432nd Tactical Reconnaissance Wing's Weapons Officer at Udorn. The combined skills of the Udorn fighter pilots including Bob Lodge, Steve Ritchie, Fred Olmsted, John Madden, and others lifted the fighter community out of the historic Korean War mindset of gun warfare. They acknowledged each challenge they met in air-to-air combat and adapted with solutions that were intellectually "outside the box" of historical fighter tactics. Fluid Four formation survived but was adapted, and wingmen were allowed to detach from their element leaders and use their weapons to kill – two totally nontraditional notions by historical measure.

Two of the back-seaters from Udorn, both Weapons System Operators or WSOs (Steve Debellevue with six kills and Jeff Feinstein with five), scored five or more kills, bringing the number of American aces during the Vietnam War to five when US Navy F-4J pilot Randy Cunningham and his back-seater Willy Driscoll are included.

During the Vietnam War, a significant number of the US aircraft shot down were lost in air-to-air combat. The kill ratios quoted vary widely because of the way they are calculated. The Red Baron reports clearly describe the various kill ratio methodologies and numbers. The point to be made was not that the USAF and US Navy pilots were not good at air-to-air combat, but instead that American forces were slow to adapt to the "slash and run" tactics used by the VPAF. No longer were guns the total threat. Missiles could be fired from many times the effective range of a gun. These facts were exacerbated by the excellent radar coverage the VPAF had over its own territory, while the attacking US forces had virtually nothing to help them see the air picture except on-board aircraft radars, eyeballs, and distracting and often incorrect radio warning calls.

On May 10, 1972, Bob Lodge was leading "Oyster" flight – four F-4Ds from Udorn – when it was engaged by four MiG-21s nearly head-on. Bob was on the right and his element leader, Steve Ritchie, was on the left. Both Bob and Steve took head-on shots, and each downed a MiG-21. John Markle, Bob's wingman, was authorized to detach and shoot also. He did so and shot down a third MiG-21. Bob was pursuing the fourth MiG, with Markle maneuvering back into fighting wing, when two blue and green MiG-19s rose from the camouflage of the jungle below and gunned him. We came to call them "snakes in the grass!" All the while Markle was commanding Bob to defensively react with a break turn.

Bob had briefed his wingman to be a shooter, and in fact the wingman was repositioning to support his leader after himself shooting down a MiG-21. In Bob Lodge's view every fighter should be a shooter and all firepower should be brought to bear. Thus, initial results were mixed as highly skilled pilots attempted to develop new tactics in fierce combat situations. When Bob Lodge was gunned down by a MiG-19 he paid the ultimate price for leading the way into the next generation of tactics. A few tactics were yet to be worked out.

There was one ejection – the back seat. Bob had elected not to eject, perishing when his jet hit the ground. He had stated to his colleagues that he would never eject because as the wing weapons officer, he had too many secrets locked in his cranium and would never want them to be compromised in an enemy interrogation. He paid the ultimate price for this inspirational execution of his sense of duty. It is a miracle that Roger Locher, Bob Lodge's WSO, avoided capture and was rescued 23 days after he and his pilot were shot down. Locher was far luckier than many of his compatriots who either died in the skies over North Vietnam as a result of bad luck and inadequate training or spent years as "guests" of the North Vietnamese in prisons cynically nicknamed "Hilton," "Zoo," and "Plantation," to name three. By May 10, 1972, several hundred American fighter pilots and other crewmembers were either missing in action or languishing in these prisons. Why?

There are a lot of answers to this question ranging from bad luck to potentially lifesaving information denied the pilots by the intelligence community. This was a so-called ploy to allegedly protect the methods of collection and sources being used by the intelligence community. All of these and other reasons led to the sad experiences of these unfortunates who were incarcerated for so long.

TRAINING

So where did the Red Eagles project begin? I freely admit it could easily be argued that this story started at some time and place other than the Udorn "Moody" Suter experience in 1969, or with Bob Lodge's loss in 1972.

I think this story started in 1969 at Udorn the day I met "Moody" Suter. That is when and where, because of Moody Suter's lesson aboard the C-130, I first became truly aware of a major training problem with my fellow fighter pilots. Up until that point I was just one of the young guys.

So, what about training? Were all the missions' elements adequately covered in training? *Inadequate* and *no* are the answers to these two questions. Were the pilots and other crewmen adequately prepared to go to war in a hostile air-to-air arena? Were their tactics validated? What of their weapons and the weapons of the enemy? What role did training play in all of these areas? There are no easy answers to these questions. But the one lingering doubt was the issue of fundamental training, especially in air-to-air combat. Were the officers adequately trained to do what was being asked of them? "Moody" Suter thought not, and those of my generation came to agree. We dedicated our careers to try and fix the problem.

Training goes far beyond the physical experience of a dogfight in the sky. It includes thinking through the air combat engagement process. People do not naturally know how to think through the planning and execution of an aerial campaign. They must be taught this skill though challenging scenarios of increasing complexity and numbers followed by a comprehensive debriefing of each element of the scenario, wherein lessons are extracted and points to ponder are identified and discussed. Then comes repetition with more complex scenarios because circumstances never recreate themselves the same way twice.

As time has passed, the building blocks and the points to ponder when the air plan doesn't work out have widened in challenge and grown in complexity as experience paves the way toward combat success. The building blocks are much like the so-called house of cards wherein if any one card is removed the final product comes tumbling down. This is not learning designed to execute scripted tactics. Instead, it is learning aimed at recognizing situations and then adapting to whatever the situation presents by way of a challenge.

In sports you could characterize American football as the execution of scripted tactics. The quarterback calls the team to the huddle and then announces the play. Everyone has a specific assignment, which, if executed perfectly, will result in positive yardage. Basketball and soccer, on the other hand, are games of continuous motion and change. Teams call plays in basketball and set up formations in soccer while the game is in motion, and then adapt to the defense presented by the actions of the opponent.

The goal of the fighter pilot is to be like the basketball or soccer player. Have a playbook, attempt to execute the plan, or variations thereof, and adapt to changing adversary responses and other unforeseen events.

Thus, this tale zeroes in on one of the more advanced building blocks of the training issue – how to ensure that we are not surprised or paralyzed into inaction when we first meet the enemy head-to-head.

CHANGE AT LAST

By the end of 1973 the two Nellis AFB Aggressor squadrons were traveling throughout the United States providing realistic adversary training opportunities as they simulated MiG-21s. The Aggressors were humiliating the F-4 community and its Fluid Four formation. The same experiences in North Vietnam were being replicated in the hometown airspace, with the Aggressors flying their T-38s as the "bad guys."

After numerous attempts to emerge from the dark ages of Fluid Four, success finally came when the FWS advocated a new formation called Fluid Two. This formation was essentially the same as Fluid Four, but using delayed 90-degree turns instead of fluid turns. The big difference was that Fluid Two was flown as a two-ship with "phantom" wingmen. Thus, both fighters were shooters. Terms like "detached mutual support," "engaged fighter" versus "free fighter," and "shooter-cover" evolved to describe the relationship between the two fighters while engaged in a swirling dogfight. Then, we assembled two more line abreast two-ship formations of fighters flying Fluid Two. The result was a four-ship formation with greater spacing, and with each fighter a shooter. We called it "the wall," and this is a basic four-ship formation that has been used for decades by the F-15 community that followed our generation of F-4 warriors.

Important and exciting things were finally happening to fighter employment in TAC. It is important to stress how hard this transition was to accomplish. Years later it was reported that one F-15 wing was being forced to fly Fluid Four, probably by a closed-minded wing commander schooled in the Fluid Four formation at a young age and then sent off to various promotion-accelerating staff jobs, where he essentially fermented and lost track of what was happening in the community.

The evolution of Fluid Two coupled with the initiation of the Aggressor program and Red Flag had finally created a stage for realistic training. By this time both the Aggressor program and Red Flag experiences had completely validated the ineffectiveness of Fluid Four and welded wing formations.

Chapter 2

How was the MiG airfield created in record time?

The Pentagon is said to have been the largest government office building in America in 1975. It may still be. Located on the Virginia side of the Potomac River, the massive structure is a commanding presence directly across the water from the center of power for the United States of America, Washington, D.C. Construction started in 1939 and the initial building was completed in 1943, where it served as the War Department in World War II. Since then, the building has been extensively modified and updated, with one of the most dramatic changes being the addition of the subway access and underground train station that became operational in the 1970s.

From its name, the shape of the Pentagon, as viewed from above, is evident. What isn't so obvious is the building's five-floor layout above ground and multiple underground floors. Above ground and looking down from above, the building has five sides. It also has a large interior plaza, whose five sides form the interior walls of this mammoth structure. From each of those five interior corners two corridors extend out and are perpendicular to the five outside walls. There are ten of these corridors. Moving from the interior to the outside, the building is organized into five rings called A Ring through E Ring. So, a hypothetical above ground office address could be 4E950. That means the 4th floor on the E Ring adjacent to the 9th Corridor, Suite 50.

There is order to the part of the building above the ground. Stairwells vertically connect the floors of the building, and on the A Ring there are ramps from one level to the next. Adjacent to the ramps are escalators that can expedite the ascent or descent of an action officer (AO) on his or her way to "coordinate" a package. AOs are generally majors or lieutenant colonels assigned tasks by their superiors. The AO first organizes the subject material, describes the task to be accomplished in what is called a staff summary sheet, and then presents a menu of options as possible solutions, along with a final recommendation. Attachments are typically added to further clarify and present the arguments fundamental to the issue. Assembled and ready for the next step, the accumulated papers are called a "package."

The AO's next task is to hammer out the details of the final solution in what is called the coordination of the package. Coordination means getting every other affected office in the Pentagon to sign off or agree with the conclusions and recommendations in the package. This process is called "top lining" because the majors sign first and then they recommend that their superior, the lieutenant colonels and colonels, sign and, finally, on the top line, the general signs – or non-concurs. Thus, completion of the coordination signals the final approval or disapproval of the action.

To gain all the coordination signatures, the AO personally visits the appropriate offices and explains the package, as necessary, at each rank level in the hope of obtaining the top line signature and completing the action item. This was true in the 1970s, but e-mail has assuredly changed and expedited the process in recent years. To complete an "action" 40 years ago the AOs moved about the Pentagon at a power walk clip. It has been calculated, but long since forgotten, the number of extra packages over a three-year tour here that a power walking AO could coordinate compared with a person walking normally. This is simply because of his or her pace as they raced through the building, aided by the "backstairs" short cuts that they learned.

In contrast to the upper floors of the Pentagon, the floors below ground level are on an entirely different layout. The underground levels are sometimes referred to as the basement and the sub-basement. I'm not sure how many levels there actually are, but I know that there are at least two. For as long as I can remember the USAF operations and readiness offices have been located in the lower level sub-basement, and that is where my office was, along with the office suite of the Director of Operations and Readiness, Maj Gen Hoyt S. "Sandy" Vandenburg Jr. The general's Air Staff office symbol was AF/XOO. Gen Vandenburg is a well-known fighter pilot, and the son of the first USAF Chief of Staff.

The sub-basement level also contains the USAF Command Post and the chamber known as the Air Force Council room, where USAF three star generals meet, usually in private, to make major policy and financial decisions. It was in this room that Lt Col "Moody" Suter received the Legion of Merit for "inventing" Red Flag.

The sub-basement is also the location of major industrial support areas that largely engage in printing Pentagon publications in huge quantities.

The underground corridors are generally wide, with high ceilings lined with multiple pipes and conduit. The hallways usually run perpendicular to each other, and it appears that the stairwells from above that depart the orderly upper floors penetrate the basement randomly. New visitors routinely get lost on their initial trips into the bowels of the Pentagon. Near the basement exit point of stairwell 94 stood a purple ceramic water fountain that was a well known landmark that most visitors to that part of the basement relied upon for orientation. From my offices, if I turned right and then left I passed the purple water fountain and found Stairwell 94. This stairwell is the quickest path to the offices of the USAF Chief of Staff and his immediate staff on the fourth floor above ground level on the E Ring, overlooking the Potomac River.

General Support Agency (GSA) personnel are the dominant neighbors to the blue suit USAF residents of the sub-basement, and one must be careful to avoid getting run over by a civilian courier riding a two or three wheeled bicycle or a GSA employee driving a forklift with a pallet loaded with either blank paper or freshly printed material.

Turning left out of my office suite, the corridor passes by two large adjacent men's restrooms. Two adjacent facilities were originally built, and they still exist today as reminders from the days of segregated restrooms. Continuing on this path, the hallway forms a tee intersection adjacent to the doors of the USAF Council Room and the Air Force Command Post.

Such was my world in the "five-sided squirrel cage" when I inherited "Moody" Suter's job taking care of Red Flag and the USAF "black world" or highly classified and compartmented programs. I settled into my new job and was soon meeting regularly with my new "black world" boss, Gen Vandenberg. This relationship skipped over at least two layers of full colonels that weren't briefed on the classified and compartmented programs. The usual subject of these meetings was to obtain approval for the next event in the ongoing arrangements that permitted very limited training using the MiGs as adversaries.

At one such meeting in the spring of 1977, Gen Vandenberg and I were engaged one-on-one in his office in the sub-basement. It was my goal to obtain his signature and complete an action that would approve the use of the MiGs for a "test." The test was in reality a disguise for a training opportunity aimed at providing MiG adversary support for Aggressor F-5E training at Nellis AFB. This training was vaguely required by the Aggressor Upgrade Syllabus so as to preserve security while directing the training. Calling training opportunities "tests" was the charade we were then playing in order to gain access to the MiGs.

To schedule the MiG assets for a training event we were required to write a test plan, including all of the details necessary to conduct an orderly flight test. The procedure required that the plan be approved by Gen Vandenberg and then countersigned by the head of the Air Staff's Research and Development (AF/RD), Deputy Chief of Staff LtGen Alton Slay. At the conclusion of the training using the MiGs as adversaries, a formal "test report" was written that required a similar approval process in respect to obtaining signatures of the AF/XOO and AF/RD to close out the action. Gen Vandenberg clearly understood and completely detested the process because he knew the essential value of training. Further, he knew the MiGs had been totally exploited, and that there was no further learning to be gained by additional testing. Nevertheless, in order for us to fly the MiGs as adversaries in training, the jets' profiles were mandated to be test sorties.

It would seem that this entire process could have been updated and the problem existing between testing and training resolved with the stroke of a pen from the right government official. With that said, as operations were conducted, there were National Security reasons that made this impossible to accomplish.

So, on this day my task was to get a test plan signed so we could fly Aggressor F-5s against the MiGs in support of the Aggressor syllabus of training for newly assigned pilots. Gen Vandenberg was extremely agitated over the emphasis testing was getting versus training with respect to the use of the MiGs. As I pressed him to sign the test plan, he essentially melted down and directed me to "either get me that program or get me out of it!"

Startled by his outburst, I reacted and verbally proposed to Gen Vandenberg that we build a remote airfield and equip it with our own MiG aircraft and use them exclusively for training. With such a facility and operation we could augment the Aggressor and FWS programs as the next building block in the training process – using actual MiGs as adversaries. Perhaps one day, I suggested, we can acquire and restore more MiGs and they can be used for wider applications in training, including Red Flag. Gen Vandenberg looked at me incredulously for a long moment, then he rolled back his chair, stood up, walked around for a moment and on the spot instructed me to meet with BrigGen Chuck Donnelly, who was the Deputy Director of Plans, and see if he could help achieve this. Gen Vandenberg arranged the meeting.

Oddly, while the test community had operational control of the MiGs, the USAF planners, instead of the research and development test community, had cognizance or ownership of the MiG assets.

Like Gen Vandenberg, Gen Donnelly was also a fighter pilot, and I knew that was a positive aspect. I hoped for a favorable decision. However, in spite of my hopes, inside I doubted anything would come of the idea.

To comply with Gen Vandenberg's instructions I did a little staff preparation and headed for the fourth floor office and my appointment with Gen Donnelly. I headed out of my office, went down the corridor, past the purple water fountain and up Stairwell 94 to the fourth floor of the Pentagon. Once there, I turned away from the direction of the Chief's office and made my way to Gen Donnelly's office. After a few minutes of waiting in the outer office, the executive officer invited me into the general's office and closed the door. During our meeting I looked over the general's shoulder and had a stunning and forever memorable view of the US capitol, the Washington monument and the Jefferson Memorial.

Gen Donnelly listened intently as I laid out the plan. He, like Gen Vandenberg, was also initially astonished at the proposal. But he listened, thought briefly about the idea and then quickly became enthusiastic – once he had finished laughing. With gusto he suggested I report back to Gen Vandenberg with a positive response and then talk to Maj Gen Currie, the Chief of Air Force programs and resources (AF/PRP), as a first step in mounting a major advocacy of the proposal.

The deal he offered me was to give us the MiGs for training IF we could restore those we already owned to flyable status, AND if we could arrange to build a very remote airfield for the conduct of the absolutely and totally secret air combat training program, using the actual MiGs as adversaries. Now, it was my turn to be astonished. I immediately reported the results of my meeting with Gen Donnelly straight back to Gen Vandenberg. I was about to get a lot more exercise racing up and down Stairwell 94.

Gen Vandenberg walked over to his desk, opened a little wooden box and picked up two steel balls. He then slumped in his chair grinding the steel balls in his hand while staring intensely at me. It was like a scene from the book *The Caine Mutiny*, reminiscent of the antics of Capt Queg. Finally, looking at me over his reading glasses, Gen Vandenberg's instructions were, "Go for it!" or words to that effect. I was stunned over this order, and could only think about coming up with an alternative name to clearly separate the training program from the exploitation and testing conducted during HAVE DRILL and HAVE DOUGHNUT.

I asked, "Sir, what's your call sign?" Gen Vandenberg growled "Constant" and I was dismissed. As I walked back to my office in the sub-basement, my heart was pounding with excitement while my brain was numb with concern. "How am I going to do this?" My thoughts drifted to my wife Peggy, and it came to me that CONSTANT PEG would be a great name for the program. It is often asked if Peggy knew about the program. She did.

At the time CONSTANT PEG was evolving Peggy was also working in the Pentagon as a secretary for the Deputy Chief of Staff for Logistics in the transportation division and had a Top Secret security clearance. One Saturday we were working on an element of the MiG project that required typing. We had no typist available in my office and those that were immediately available did not have the appropriate security clearances. Gen Vandenberg caustically asked, "doesn't anybody in this building know a secretary that has a clearance?" I answered, "Yes sir, my wife does." Gen Vandenberg said, "Well get her in here and brief her up and let's get this done." With big eyes Peggy listened attentively, did the job, and never asked further questions. I think we scared her so bad during the brief that during much later years in conversations with me, she was reluctant to even acknowledge that she knew what was going on.

But during the time I was in command of CONSTANT PEG, it was apparent she had completely gotten the message. This was evident as she skillfully dealt with the squadron wives, who at times became frustrated or suspicious about the odd schedules and frequent overnight absences of their husbands. It was immensely useful for her to know and understand what we were up to.

OUR GENERALS AND KEY LEADERS

The position and roles of generals Vandenberg and Donnelly have already been discussed. The other general officer at the Pentagon who was a key contributor to the program was Maj Gen Jim Currie, Director of Programs (PRP). In that capacity he was in a position to channel the spending of the USAF'S finances. The conduit for spending was managed by the Controller of the USAF, and the key officer was Col Dick Murray. Murray later retired as a two star general. He had an action officer that was especially key to the project, Dana Whitmore, an air force civilian employee.

When I left the Pentagon to take command of CONSTANT PEG, I handed the job of Air Force Tactics Officer and the CONSTANT PEG project over to another FWS graduate and instructor, Maj Bill "Saki" Sakahara. He admirably expanded the project's vision and depth. Saki was responsible for acquiring both the T-38s and the MiG-23s, as well as working with the F-117 community on the airfield expansion and utilization. Bill Sakahara was a very close personal friend as well. As FWS instructors we had worked side-by-side for almost three years at Nellis AFB. To his credit after I turned the program over to him, he never broke security and leaked any of the planning information to me ahead of the formal releases. I have always admired him for avoiding that indicator of crony behavior. Saki eventually retired from the USAF and worked as a defense contractor in southern California until finally totally retiring to keep an eye on his grandchildren.

At Langley AFB, the headquarters of TAC, the AO was Maj David "DL" Smith. Within the brotherhood "DL" was also known phonetically as "Dog Lima." "DL" was both a FWS graduate and an initial cadre Aggressor pilot. Like my job at the Pentagon on the Air Staff, "DL" had a visible job at TAC Headquarters and also a "black world" job. He really got the ball rolling at TAC, setting up the squadron as a training organization and smoothing the road with all the generals that were a little bit unsure about what we were up to.

"DL" had made himself famous in Vietnam as the pilot, during LINEBACKER I, that used laser guided bombs to drop the Paul Doumer bridge in Hanoi during the summer of 1972.

Right in the middle of the CONSTANT PEG evolution "DL" was selected to lead the Thunderbirds, briefly leaving the MiG team in somewhat of a vacuum. Sadly, he was later killed upon ejection on take-off when a T-38 lost power during a non-airshow mission at the Burke Lakefront airport in Cleveland, Ohio. The T-38 had suffered power debilitating bird strikes at a critically low altitude on take-off. Both crewmembers in the jet ejected. One made it safely – "DL" did not.

When "DL" left TAC to take command of the Thunderbirds he was replaced by Joseph "CT" Wang who, along with Bill Sakahara at the Air Staff, did remarkable work. Wang is also a FWS graduate and another close personal friend. He and I were in the same fighter squadron at MacDill AFB when we were captains.

At Nellis AFB Lt Col Glenn Frick was the officer charged with the responsibility for completing the Red Baron reports at the Tactical Fighter Weapons Center (TFWC). The Red Baron reports detailed all of the air-to-air engagements of the Vietnam War. This was Glenn's "white world" job. He also had "Black World" responsibilities, and with that "hat" on he became "Mr Nellis" for what was to become the CONSTANT PEG project. This ultimately led to Glenn's selection as the first 4477th TEF commander. An FWS graduate, he was widely known as one of the most enthusiastic and energetic officers in fighter aviation. He had also served earlier as an Air Commando. A man of many talents, Glenn masterfully restored an ancient Model A Ford pickup that he often drove to work at Nellis. When I arrived at the base as his relief in the spring of 1978, Glenn was building a Christen Eagle aerobatic biplane. The construction was ongoing in the living room of his family's home in Las Vegas. Wife Gracie put up with a lot of Glenn's shenanigans.

After retiring from the USAF Glenn became involved in the US National Aerobatic Championships and was captain of the Advanced Team in 1999. During and after a second career at Lockheed Martin in Fort Worth, Texas, he bought a grass airfield and continued to fly and restore light aircraft. Glenn died of leukemia in May 2001.

One of Glenn's henchmen was Chuck Holden. I knew Chuck from the RIVET HASTE program, as he was one of the pilots in the squadron of F-4Es that came through Nellis for training. At the time I was an instructor at the FWS, detailed to fly the MiG-17 as an adversary during their training. While Glenn had a team of pilots, including operations officer Ron Iverson, during the CONSTANT PEG work-up, Chuck essentially became one of Glenn's special assistants. One of his greatest contributions to CONSTANT PEG was his knowledge of general aviation and his currency in flying light aircraft. Chuck was also a key player in the development of the CONSTANT PEG project book, which was used by the architects to design the airfield facility.

Finally, at Nellis, Mary Jane Smith was at the other end of Col Dick Murray's money conduit. Murray would fill the pipe with money and his guy, Dana Whitmore, would operate the pipeline from the Pentagon with Mary Jane owning the spigot at Nellis. Mary Jane was a joy to work with. She loved her job and especially the elements from the "black world." Mary Jane later retired, married a former Air Force officer and moved to Pahrump, Nevada. She is now deceased.

BOBBY BOND AND HAVE BLUE

In the spring of 1974, while serving as the Air-to-Air Flight Commander at the F-4 FWS, I was detailed to participate in a study group that was convened in Washington, D.C., and at Wright-Patterson AFB. The task of the Tactical Fighter Modernization Study Group was to examine the lightweight fighters and other contenders, and reduce the list to viable candidates for purchase by the USAF. The study group was chartered by Gen George Brown, the USAF Chief of Staff, who personally briefed the team in his Pentagon conference room at the beginning of the study. The study group was under the direct leadership of Maj Gen Dick Cross, DCS for Research and Development (AF/RD) at the Pentagon. His two action officers were Col Bobby Bond and Lt Col Gordon Williams. The study was extensive and continued for about three months.

Other notable members of the group at the senior officer level included colonels "Firecan Dan" Walsh, Dave Young, Bob Russ, and Bob Kelley. As outlined earlier "Firecan Dan" sent me to FWS when we served together in the 46th/27th TFS at MacDill AFB. He remains one of my very best friends. Dave Young had been the wing commander at Nellis. Bob Russ was the commander of the 4th TFW at Seymour Johnson AFB, South Carolina. Russ later became the four-star general in command of TAC who gave the order to terminate CONSTANT PEG. Bob Kelley was later the commander of the TFWC at Nellis AFB, and in spite of our close friendship in the early days he was the officer who relieved me of the CONSTANT PEG command. At my level in the study group the other action officers were "DL" Smith, Bill Ricks, and other notables. Bill Ricks and I had been squadron mates during our initial F-4 training at MacDill AFB.

Col Bobby Bond and I hit it off well, and remained in touch following the completion of the study group's work. Shortly after Gen Vandenberg gave the go-ahead for CONSTANT PEG, Col Bond called me to his office in the Pentagon. He was still in RD but at a higher post than during the Fighter Modernization Study Group timeframe. Col Bond greeted me when I entered his office on the E Ring of the fourth floor of the Pentagon. His office had a window overlooking Crystal City and National Airport (now Reagan National Airport). Col Bond asked me to close his office door and he carefully opened a two drawer safe next to his desk. There was no chitchat or casual conversation at this point. He removed a manila folder and handed it to me, instructing me to take a look.

I couldn't believe my eyes. It was an airplane straight out of a science fiction movie. Col Bond went on to tell me the project was called HAVE BLUE and that the test aircraft was invisible to radar. He indicated his belief that the aircraft would enter production and that he thought it might somehow fit into the program that Gen Vandenberg had authorized. It was the first inclination I had that he knew about our efforts to build and operate a MiG airfield. He concluded the meeting by telling me he did not have the authority to brief me on the project but that I should figure out a way to get briefed on the HAVE BLUE program. He offered no ideas or suggestions for accomplishing that task. Bond, who subsequently became a three-star general, was later killed in an aircraft accident in Nevada in April 1984. It did not happen during flight operations from Tonopah, as is widely speculated, nor did it involve CONSTANT PEG aircraft.

Armed with the knowledge of the existence of HAVE BLUE, I engaged in an extensive research effort. Most of the information I gathered came from the "Filter Center" column of *Aviation Week*. I found numerous disconnected references to contracts that had been let for various aircraft subsystems including landing gear and flight controls. When the dots were connected the material seemed to point to the HAVE BLUE test article. Using this open source information I wrote a "white paper" speculating that an advanced technology project was in the works and danced as close as I felt I could to the details. When I dropped my unclassified paper on key players in the "black world" the response was close to nuclear. I was ordered to report, along with all copies and records. After reporting as instructed, I was briefed on HAVE BLUE and told that the aircraft was not invisible to radar but had the radar cross section of a sparrow.

The briefing was intense and the threats to me personally for any security breach were enormous. It was clear I was inside, and thus I was sworn to secrecy. I will always remember the little room inside a vault. It had a table with an interrogation-like single light hanging from an overhead cord. Two chairs were in the room and I was in one of them, with the light in my face. The other was pulled back from the table and was occupied by the briefer. Other people were standing in the room. When it was over and I left, while now briefed and inside "their" program, it was clear to me that I really wasn't a part of their team. Nevertheless, I was now able to build a strategy for constructing the airfield.

The main thrust of the strategy was based on the apparent fact that the USAF would need a discrete operating location for basing the operational derivative of the HAVE BLUE article, assuming ongoing testing validated the stealth capabilities. No one that was briefed on HAVE BLUE could disagree, and a ground swell of momentum quickly developed. The highly classified and compartmented mantra became, "Build the airfield and fly MiGs by day and the stealth fighter by night."

MONEY MAKES THINGS GROW

The source of funds and the methodology for making it all happen evolved largely through the leadership and knowledge of Gen Jim Currie and his associates and advisors. When I briefed him on progress he would often get up from his desk, personally shut the door to his office and don a World War II leather jacket that hung on a coat rack in his office. He would then invite me to sit with him in easy chairs around a coffee table in front of his desk.

It was through one of these discussions that I learned we could advocate funding for our project from the Secretary of Defense's emergency military construction fund. This was a $10 million bucket of money that existed within the annual DoD appropriation bill (at least for that particular year). To spend the money DoD only had to notify the chairmen of the Senate and House Appropriations and Armed Services Committees. Congressional approval was implied in the legislation and was not required.

Thus, we found money to finance the project but the big challenges were yet to come. How could we get the project designed and constructed without public scrutiny? It was important to avoid the competitive bid for both security reasons and to permit meeting our self-imposed timeline to have the MiGs flying, or in aviator's jargon "rubber-on-ramp," as soon as possible.

Usually, big government construction projects were subject to the open and competitive bidding process. The solution to this dilemma came in a two-stage revelation. First, we learned that money could be transferred from one government agency to another government agency. This authority came from a little known law that was reported to us as the Economic Recovery Act of 1932. According to the pundits in the Pentagon at the time, the law stipulated that appropriated funds could be transferred between government agencies through a process called a Multi-Interagency Procurement Request or MIPR. This Economic Recovery law was alleged to be a part of the Hoover legislation that preceded President Franklin Roosevelt's New Deal – old, but still applicable. In recent years I have searched long and hard for the "law." I never found it.

We still had to avoid the public eye for our highly classified program. So, the second stage of the solution to our design and construction dilemma came when we learned that Congress had authorized the Department of Energy (DoE), through legislation, the right to engage in sole-source contracting. This meant that DoE could hire a contractor to do whatever architect and construction work it deemed appropriate without a competitive bidding process. The DoE sole source contractors were Holmes and Narver of Orange, California, for the architecture and engineering and Reynolds Electrical and Engineering Company (REECo) of Las Vegas for construction.

Now, all I had to do was coordinate a package through all the generals on the Air Staff to obtain authority to go to DoD to request that we empty the SECDEF's Emergency Military Construction fund. I knew the Pentagon fourth floor where the USAF generals worked, but was terrified over the prospects of winding my way though OSD on the third floor in search of someone short of the SECDEF that had the authority to say okay to my scheme. Assuming the funding was possible, I then had to somehow convince the DoE that it should accept our money and use its design and construction resources to build an airfield somewhere!

What had I gotten myself into? It was time to quit whining and get to work.

Where to Hide a Fighter Base?

Our team of Glenn Frick at Nellis AFB, "DL" Smith at TAC Headquarters, Langley AFB, and me at the Pentagon realized that we had some homework to do. Before we went too far with the process of begging for money and then begging for help with construction from DoE, we needed to know exactly what we wanted to do.

The first step was nailing down our future airfield location. We initially studied a variety of possible locations and settled on three candidates – Tonopah Test Range (TTR), adjacent to the Nellis Range complex near Tonopah, Nevada; Dugway Proving Grounds, southwest of Salt Lake City, in the Utah desert; and a remote Arizona valley on the Goldwater Range south of Phoenix.

First some background on the people involved in the search. Jay Whitney was the Deputy Commander for Operations at Nellis AFB. Jay and I had become close friends during the years when he was the TAC action officer at Langley AFB for "Black Programs." I had first met him when Randy O'Neil and I were flying the MiG-17 in 1972 during the RIVET HASTE program. Jay had then been replaced at TAC Headquarters by Ralph Schneider, who had been the first Assistant Director of Operations in the 64th Aggressor Squadron (AS). Subsequently, "DL" Smith replaced Ralph Schneider and "CT" Wang replaced "DL."

By the time we were cranking up the site surveys in earnest for CONSTANT PEG, Ralph Schneider had been promoted and was stationed at Hill AFB near Ogden, Utah. Ralph was immensely helpful to us when Glenn Frick sent one of his pilots – assistant operations officer Joe "Jose" Oberle – to take a look at Dugway. Ralph Schneider was the point of contact at Hill. I think Ralph talked "Jose" out of the Dugway location without a visit, but "Jose" may have gone and taken a look for himself. In either case the result was thumbs down on Dugway.

The next candidate site was TTR. Reference to a map of southern Nevada shows TTR at the far northwest corner of the Nellis Range complex in a restricted area known as R-4809. The small mining town of Tonopah is located off the range further to the northwest. TTR is adjacent to the active Nellis ranges beyond the DoE Nevada Test Site, which is the historic location of atmospheric and underground nuclear weapons testing. DoE Las Vegas is in charge of the Nevada Test Site while the DoE office in Albuquerque, New Mexico, is in charge of TTR. The latter's mission is to test the release systems of nuclear weapons. Therefore, an aerial training mission was theoretically compatible at TTR, whereas it is unlikely that DoE could ever approve major flight operations within the boundaries of the Nevada Test Site itself.

Tonopah is a sleepy little mining town that, along with its neighbor Goldfield to the south, was a major hub of mining activity during earlier times. The major landmark in Tonopah is the Mizpah Hotel, and among other tourist attractions are the mining museum and the brothel on the edge of town. That facility was along the highway to the east of town toward Rachel, Nevada, more than 100 miles away. That stretch of highway is a tourist attraction in and of itself, being known as the "Extraterrestrial Highway" amongst those that believe in UFOs. The local high school team at Tonopah call themselves the "Muckers," a reference to the mine work hauling out mud and nonproductive mine tailings. Not much was happening in Tonopah in the 1970s, but the miners' tradition of staying out of other peoples' business, avoiding gossip, and generally keeping their mouths shut were all attractive dimensions of the setting.

A satellite photo of Tonopah clearly reveals the absence of significant local activity. It is just a little town on the highway between Reno and Las Vegas – a good place to buy gasoline or a soft drink and continue on your way. Limited motel accommodation did exist, along with a handful of bars and eating establishments. At the time our project was evolving, the Mizpah Hotel was in a transition period involving a change of ownership and restoration.

So, one day very early in the program several of us from the Pentagon and Nellis AFB boarded Cessna 207 N1592U, with Maj Chuck Holden at the controls. The destination was TTR and a meeting with the Albuquerque DoE site manager, Sam Moore. Those aboard N1592U included Chuck, the pilot, myself, Col Jay Whitney, the 57th FWW Deputy Commander for Operations, and the 57th FWW Chief of Standards and Evaluations, Maj Bill "Buffalo" Smith. While Col Whitney and "Buffalo" Smith were local officials, the trip was all about a meeting between Sam Moore and me. Col Whitney was present and fully involved but I chaired the meeting. "Buffalo" Smith had no real role during the trip, and he and Chuck stayed in the background playing out the role of the disinterested (but not really) local fighter pilots.

I had no idea of what to expect at TTR. None of us had ever been there before on the ground, nor had we noticed the facility during flight operations in the adjacent range areas. We had never even heard the name "Silverbow," the call sign for the TTR Control facility. The airfield we found at TTR was much bleaker and more remote than I had expected. It was less than 5,000ft long and posted an elevation of about 5,549ft. It was certainly no place for a jet fighter with the current runway length. It could be best described as a fairly smooth place to make a crash landing during a terrible emergency. A parking area was offset from the runway at the southeast end, and this was connected to the TTR control compound by a narrow asphalt road. The runway looked as though it had never been swept and the edges were breaking up and jagged, with grass-like desert scrub growing through the crumbling tarmac.

The DoE personnel had a Convair twin-engined airliner similar to a USAF T-29 or C-131 chocked on the parking area pad adjacent to the runway. There was no fuel or other facilities aimed at supporting flight operations.

TTR is nestled in a broad valley roughly 20 nautical miles across with mountain ridges to both the west and the east. Cactus Peak, with a summit measured at 7,476ft, is the dominant mountain in the western ridge. To the east lies the Kawich Range, about 20 miles long running roughly north and south. There are at least five peaks over 8,000ft in the Kawich Range and three are above 9,000ft. Midway down the range is Cedar Pass, a popular Red Flag route for aircraft ingressing to the range areas to the south. If one were to reference a high altitude photo of TTR, with north at the top, it would show the test range valley with the mountain ranges on either side, as well as the dry lakebed in the middle. The major axis of the lakebed served as the run-in line for the fighters and bombers conducting TTR nuclear weapon release systems range test work. The lakebed is about ten nautical miles long. There is irrigated farmland to the north of the range itself on a neighboring ranch. The ranchers turned out to be good neighbors, generating no questions or concerns.

Distances are vast in rural Nevada. The road east from Tonopah toward Rachel is 20 nautical miles north of the TTR airfield at its closest approach. I once drove my car on a family vacation on that road, stopping at a roadside park for a picnic. While able to observe the valley with the airfield through binoculars, the thermal distortion in the atmosphere made it impossible to discern specific buildings or activities on the range. The DoE compound has changed little over the years, at least outwardly.

Sam Moore met us after we landed at TTR and Col Whitney and I accompanied him to his compound office overlooking the range complex.

Sam was very cordial and respectful but almost laughed out loud when I told him we were considering seeking DoE cooperation to develop the airfield into one capable of handling jet fighters. He engaged in a litany of explanations regarding the mission conflicts and only finally came around when we discussed his Convair transportation between TTR and Las Vegas. When the idea of upgrading that Convair to a Boeing 727 or other jet service was presented he suddenly realized the enhanced efficiency that would come with cutting the commute times for his people in half – or better. He filled me in on the Albuquerque DoE leadership that would be required to agree to an airfield enhancement. He stressed they would have the final say and we left happy. Sam became a great friend and supporter, but that day I think he was pretty skeptical.

There was no fuel available at TTR, and on our way back to Las Vegas the combination of unexpected headwinds, low fuel, and extreme turbulence due to a mountain wave on the lee side of Mt Charleston just northwest of Las Vegas caused Chuck to decide to land at the air force auxiliary field at Indian Springs – this is now Creech AFB. With that decision he gave me the first of many very important lessons about flying light aircraft, especially in the mountains. The winds were 90 degrees to the runway direction and blowing in excess of 30 knots. So Chuck landed on the taxiway perpendicular to the runway, directly into the wind, and taxied right up to the flight line fence without ever turning the aircraft into a crosswind position. We got out and tied the airplane to the chain link fence and arranged surface transportation back to Las Vegas.

Jay Whitney has sworn for years that the main spar of the aircraft must have been broken due to the turbulence. It wasn't, and we flew many more trips in that aircraft before upgrading to twin Cessnas.

I was very impressed with the possibilities at TTR based on that first visit, but I had to continue my mission and survey the Goldwater Range valley. So, my next stop was Phoenix Sky Harbor Airport, with a trip to Luke AFB and then a hosted field trip to the Goldwater Range. The flight I took from Las Vegas to Phoenix was on Western Airlines. As I settled in and thought about the day at TTR, I became increasing enthusiastic about that location. The site itself was great, and it offered proximity to the Nellis range complex, the FWS, Red Flag, and the Aggressors. Naval Air Facility Fallon to the north was not that far away either. It crystallized in my mind that the other candidate locations could only satisfy the remote operations requirement.

I took a Western Airlines napkin, and in a drawing extended the runway at TTR and equipped it with turnaround pads at each end. Next, I added a parking ramp with a three-hangar complex in the center. The hangars were connected, the concept being to locate maintenance functions in one connecting bay and operations in the other. I added a Petroleum/Oil/Lubricants (POL) fuel storage facility with a refueling pit and a parking area for Sam Moore's jet to my drawing and we had an airfield! Sitting on the airliner and staring at my handy work on the napkin, I made a decision to eliminate Goldwater and focus the effort on TTR. The crowd at Luke was disappointed, but understanding, once the decision logic was laid out. We never even visited the proposed Goldwater Range site.

The napkin survived and was a part of the framed history that hung on one of the interior walls of the hangar complex for the years that CONSTANT PEG operated at Tonopah. Since then it, like so much of the historically significant memorabilia, has disappeared. Hopefully, the napkin will show up at some time in the future and find its rightful place at a future CONSTANT PEG display at the National Museum of the Air Force. Meanwhile, the drawing has been replicated on the napkin for an airline that is still operating.

How Are We Going To Do This?

Now the real work was about to start. First, the strategy was laid out in outline format from A to Z. It took several iterations and numerous consultations with the generals to get it right before launching into the Air Staff coordination process. As previously mentioned, this is called top-lining because the coordination starts at a fairly low level, and as each agency signs off or agrees to the proposal the coordination is ratcheted up a level. For this action the top line needed was the Secretary of Defense, or his representative. For "black world" projects the coordination is streamlined somewhat because only those with a must know interest are included in the coordination process.

Dan Chaney was the man in charge of graphics in the USAF Operations Center at the time, and he steered me to one of his artists for the preparation of the Briefing Book. The artist in question was Jerry Hansen, a robust man with an easy laugh. The amazing thing about Jerry was that he was missing most of his fingers on his drawing hand, but that didn't dampen his talent one bit. I briefed Jerry on the project and we went to work. My task was providing concepts and vision and Jerry's task was translating those notions into quality graphics. We stepped through the advocacy arguments generally following the emerging strategy – that we would need an operating location for the stealth fighter, assuming HAVE BLUE testing verified the concept, and the facility would also have to support a classified MiG operating location for training aircrews. The briefing book was an excellent tool for explaining the program to senior executives in tabletop format.

Before binding the book of artist's slides with a plastic binding comb, thus creating the briefing book, Gen Donnelly arranged for me to have a key to a color-copying machine. In the 1970s all the copiers were called Xerox no matter whether Xerox manufactured the machine or not. Color copiers were extremely rare, and I was one of the few majors who had a key to operate one of the Air Staff's color machines. I made copies of Jerry Hansen's book for the generals to use at their level and for my use coordinating the project through the Pentagon, and eventually the DoE and Congress. As I recall, a total of three books were prepared. There may have eventually been more copies after the approval was obtained in Washington, D.C., and coordination began in earnest with TAC and the DoE.

At this point the only officers in the Nellis community that knew what was up were Glenn Frick and his immediate staff of cleared personnel.

Interspersed with trips up and down Stairwell 94 in the Pentagon on my visits to the third and fourth floors for OSD and Air Staff coordination were numerous flights to Albuquerque to court and convince the DoE officials to support our airfield expansion and utilization plan. Fortunately, at the leadership level, the DoE vision of the future matched our hopes and Albuquerque was able to join in on our plan enthusiastically. The details of our efforts in Albuquerque involved arranging the money flow from the DoD to the DoE and the penning of the actual statements of work for the latter's sole source contractors, architects Holmes and Narver, and construction company REECo.

Relationships were formalized with the money spigot controlled by Col Murray at the Air Staff. The money was channeled both to DoE in Albuquerque for payments to the contractors and to the USAF at Nellis AFB. The money pipe going to Nellis was to support the operations and maintenance expenses, flowing to Mary Jane Smith as the spending authority. She took her direction from Glenn Frick, the spending release authority. Glenn also supervised the government contractor BDM as a part of his "White World" duties as the chief of the Red Baron project. Glenn took my napkin and from that basic concept had BDM prepare a project book suitable for submission to an architect for the development of complete plans.

Meanwhile, "DL" Smith was busy running the package through TAC. Among his tasks were the concept of operations, recruiting personnel, and organizationally arranging for a new squadron to be formed or stood up. There was no resistance at TAC because the funding was not going to come from its earmarked funds. That changed later as CONSTANT PEG matured.

In one TAC HQ meeting I attended with "DL" Smith, we briefed the TAC/DO, Maj Gen Charlie Gabriel, and his ADO, Brig Gen Jack Bennett. I'll never forget Gen Bennett sitting on the corner of a desk eating a cheeseburger while we briefed Gen Gabriel. Gen Gabriel was very attentive while Gen Bennett just shook his head back and forth in disbelief. He had been my squadron commander in the 433rd TFS at Ubon RTAB, and he was in a state of disbelief at the scheme his fighter pilots had come up with.

After the Cold War ended the TAC commander, Gen Bob Russ, shut down CONSTANT PEG due to cost and a reduced perceived need for the program as relations with the former Soviet Union normalized. I would speculate that the program ultimately failed a cost/benefit analysis in one of the never-ending budget exercises. But in the 1970s the Cold War was roaring, and my coordination sailed through the Air Staff and I was cleared to take the package to OSD on the third floor. A retired four-star admiral took my briefing and signed off on the project for the SECDEF. He had a big office and desk but worked standing up at a captain's desk as if he were still aboard a ship.

The final hurdle was the notification of Congress. To complete the approval I made appointments with the Chairmen of the House and Senate Appropriations and Armed Services Committees. As I recall it took several trips across the river to Capitol Hill to complete the task. I was somewhat disappointed because senior staffers took the briefings instead of giving me the chance to meet personally with the Congressmen. But it didn't matter, as the project was approved and funded.

By this time Glenn Frick had delivered the project book to the DoE architect and preparation of the plans for building our airfield at Tonopah was underway.

Through the entire process it was as though one could imagine events happening in a professional football context – we formed a team, we had funding, we had number one draft picks, and we won the Super Bowl the first year. This CONSTANT PEG project was enthusiastically received at every level. This was quite unlike anything I had ever witnessed in government. Everybody agreed! It was inspiring.

A CONCEPT TURNS INTO REALITY

One day I received a phone call from a Holmes and Narver official named Augie Gurrola. He asked if I could come out to their offices in Orange, CA, for a "pow-wow." Of course I said yes, asked when and booked a flight to Los Angeles. The appointed hour was 0800hrs on a Friday. I was impressed with the Holmes and Narver corporate office building when I arrived by rental car from the

Los Angeles Airport area. Augie greeted me warmly when I arrived and invited me into the building and upstairs to a large windowed conference room. It was a long room with a narrow table running the entire length. Outside there was a nice view through smoky windows overlooking the Orange County neighborhoods and commercial district.

Every seat at the table was filled except one at the end opposite from a screen. Augie ushered me into that position. I should have had a clue at that point that I was considered a special guest because the position where I was seated, unlike the other table seats, had a glass of iced lemon water and its very own plate of fruit and pastries. The remaining attendees (I later discovered that they were all engineers) had to share fruit and pastries from large platters placed at strategic points on the table.

Augie started the briefing. As it progressed I became increasingly excited about how perfectly the architects had captured the essence of our vision. The brief covered all of the essential elements from the runway and turnarounds to the tarmac and the hangar structures. Details emerged on the electrical, heating, ventilation, air-conditioning, and fire suppression systems. The fuel tank system and the refueling point located on the edge of the tarmac were also addressed. When Augie completed his brief he followed with a simple question, "What do you think?" I responded that it was perfect, exactly what we were looking for. A long silence followed. Finally, Augie said, "Well major, are we going to do this or not?" At that moment I realized that I had been invited to a decision briefing and not an information update. I considered the question for a moment and responded, "Yes, we are going to do it. It's a GO!"

Initially, there were muffled responses from around the room along with broad smiles and light applause as the engineers reacted. Then they reacted noisily in disbelief and jubilation, shaking hands with each other and slapping one another on the back. At that point I realized what I had done. I had no authority to turn the project on, but I had just done exactly that. I had to get out of there! I accepted congratulations from individuals in the group and departed for LAX as quickly as I could. I knew already that it was going to be a long flight east, and since it was a Friday the flight was going to be followed by a real long weekend before I would be able to get to generals Vandenberg and Donnelly and tell them what I had done. I was anxious about the brashness of my decision, and action. Surviving the weekend, I finally got to the generals. Thankfully, they embraced the decision. As I recall, Gen Donnelly said "You done good boy!"

In April 2007, approximately 30 years after the meeting in Orange, Chuck Holden and I were invited to come to Tonopah for the arrival of the first stealth fighters as they returned from Holloman AFB, New Mexico, to their original home at TTR for mothballing and storage. Thanks to the TTR commander in 2007, Brian Kiefer, I had the opportunity to root around through storage rooms and other facilities in a search for any of the missing archives from the MiG days. In the civil engineering map room I found a set of the original blue prints for the CONSTANT PEG facilities. One of Brian's staff helped out and we were able to use a machine in the map room and copy the plans. The originals remain in the map room at TTR. I presented the copy plans to Maj Gen (ret) Metcalf, the curator of the National Museum of the Air Force at Wright-Patterson AFB, in late April 2007.

GENTLEMEN, STAND UP THE SQUADRON!

Soon the project really got underway. One day Glenn Frick called me at the Pentagon and said "There's good news and bad news!" I humored him and asked for the good news. Glenn said, "TAC has agreed to stand up the operation as the 4477th Test and Evaluation Flight." My question right back to him was, "Why is it going to be a flight instead of a squadron." He said, it *will* be a squadron, but the feeling is that the organization will be less visible if it is officially called a flight. I said, "Okay, I guess that makes sense." It was later officially changed from the 4477th TEF to the 4477th TES.

"Glenn, what's the bad news?" Frick's response was, "I made colonel, and the colonel's group at the Air Force Personnel Center has already been in touch to tell me I am going to Egypt as the chief of the military assistance group there." Stunned, I replied, "So what does that mean for our project?" Glenn said, "That's a good question. I suggest you call Col Ron Clements, the 57th FWW commander, and discuss it with him." We hung up the telephones and I sat staring at the instrument in silence. Then it rang. I answered, and the voice on the other end said, "Peck, this is Jay Whitney at Nellis. The 57 Wing Commander, Col Ron Clements, asked me to call you and see if you would like to come out here and replace Frick and finish this project you got going?"

Col Whitney was the 57 FWW Deputy Commander for Operations or DCO. Jay was a friend from my early days as a MiG pilot during RIVET HASTE. At that time in 1970 Jay was a major or lieutenant colonel on the TAC staff at Langley AFB and was in charge of the early, but brief, RIVET HASTE MiG training opportunity. What a thrill to be working with him again.

Reality returned when he prompted me for a reply.

Stunned for the second time in less than an hour, I responded, "Yes sir, I sure would, but I'm only two-thirds of the way through a four-year tour here at the

Pentagon." He said, "I think they will let you out early to get a squadron." I had been selected for lieutenant colonel in an on-time promotion the previous fall. But my selection number was high, and I expected my pin-on date to be about a year from selection.

I told Col Whitney that I really wanted to come out there and do the job, but that I would have to run it up my chain of command and get an okay from Gen Vandenberg. My Division chief, Col Don Conway, immediately agreed to let me go and authorized me to discuss the opportunity with Gen Vandenberg. I don't recall any of the details of that meeting with Gen Vandenberg except his broad smile and thumbs up. I imagine we discussed who would take over my responsibilities at the Air Staff. I know I nominated or picked Bill Sakahara for the job and he did a wonderful job over the next few years. It was a great choice.

Things happened very quickly. It was now the late winter of 1977/78 and Peggy was very pregnant with our first child. I knew I had to get to Nellis and get checked out in the Aggressor program in time to replace Glenn before October 1978, when he was slated to head for Egypt. But we had to get a baby born, a house sold, and deal with another major relocation. Peg did her part and Jennifer was born about 15 minutes before St Patrick's Day in March 1978. Things immediately went wrong with Jennifer. She had suffered a muconium aspiration and had a life threatening respiratory problem. The medical staff at Ft Belvoir hospital in Alexandria, Virginia, quickly transferred her to the neo-natal unit at Walter Reed hospital in Washington, D.C. This happened during the pre-dawn hours of St Patrick's Day, thus avoiding the Washington rush hour.

When Peg woke up from the emergency Caesarean, the baby had already been transported and she didn't believe she had had a baby after all. I had no idea where Walter Reed was and less of an idea where the neo-natal unit was located at the hospital. Confusion raged. I finally sorted things out and made my way to Walter Reed. Jen was stable, but I will always remember her expanded chest. They had her on a canted table under a heat source with IV tubes hooked up. The charge nurse in the unit was a jewel, and over the next few days she siphoned the mess out of Jen's lungs. I bought a Polaroid camera to prove to Peggy that she did indeed have a baby. Our dear friend Stevie Henderson later shared with us a dream she had had about Peggy having a little girl and bringing her home from the hospital in an Easter Basket. That's exactly how it happened. Peg got out of the hospital quickly, and we maintained a vigil at Walter Reed until the decision was made to release Jen. That happened on Easter Sunday 1978.

Now, I could get back to work. Our moving plans gelled and soon I had orders. Another kink in the situation was that I was nearly finished with my last written paper for Air War College by seminar.

My orders first took me to Holloman AFB to get a quick jet recurrency in the T-38. This was necessary because there were no two-seat F-5s at Nellis, and my next flight as a part of the Aggressor checkout and training would be in a single-seat F-5. I next called my buddy Doc Stewart, the Chevy dealer in Clovis, New Mexico, and bought a station wagon over the phone. I had previously bought a 1974 Corvette from him in a telephone transaction, so he was accustomed to my "act." Then I completed a five ride T-38 checkout without incident. The first three sorties were simple transition with acrobatics, stalls, and traffic patterns. The final two were formation. I did find myself behind the aircraft for the first few minutes of the first ride. After that it was clear sailing.

Next, a very prophetic thing happened to me. Col Brad Hosmer, the T-38 wing commander, invited me to his office for a courtesy call. Brad was the number one graduate of the Air Force Academy. Put another way, he graduated number one in the academy's first graduating class, the Class of 1959. After graduation he went to Oxford for a Rhodes scholarship before going to pilot training. Thus, the timing was such that we both ended up as instructor pilots at Laughlin AFB, Texas, and became good friends. Brad's words to me that day in his office were chilling in retrospect.

He congratulated me warmly on getting a squadron and then he went on to caution me that I was getting into a high-risk situation. He predicted I would have no problems if all went well. But, if there were problems, he suggested that dark days would follow, and I would wonder where all my friends had gone. Our meeting ended on a warm note and I headed for an innocent rendezvous with my good friend Diane Clark, the wife of "Tip" Clark. He and I and a group of other pilots had flown F-4s across the Atlantic together a few years earlier, and Diane had become our group's ultimate tour guide in Madrid.

This time I needed Diane to give me a ride to the bus station in Alamogordo, New Mexico, so that I could make my way up to Clovis to pick up my new car. It all went without a hitch. I changed buses in Roswell, where I chatted with a very happy and friendly young man. I asked him why he was so jubilant. He replied that he had just gotten out of jail. You meet interesting people in bus stations.

Once I was at Nellis, again I was thrust into a group of great guys. Both Bill "Chops" Lamb and Bud "Budman" Bennett were classmates in the F-5E program, and became lifelong friends. Later, Bud and I were stationed together in Saudi

Arabia and then flew F-15s at Kadena. After retirement, Bill Lamb and I worked side-by-side at the FWS for many years as so-called subject matter experts, or SMEs. This whole story came full circle for me in 2007 when, as a part of my job at Nellis, I was tasked to be the MiG-21 SME in support of the Aggressors.

Meanwhile, during the summer of 1978, while I was becoming a "card carrying" Aggressor pilot, Glenn Frick was staffing up the 4477th with pilots and maintenance personnel. The aviators all came from the Aggressors unit at Nellis, and therefore split their time between the 4477th and flying Aggressor sorties. I spent a lot of time with Glenn during my checkout as an Aggressor, but in spite of our previous relationship, he was the commander and I was his replacement and, at the same time, a student. The maintenance personnel initial cadre all had unique experience. They had mostly come from Edwards AFB, in California. Two notable exceptions were MSgt Steve Hovermale, who was already stationed at Nellis, and SSgt Doug Robinson, an aerospace ground equipment (AGE) mechanic finishing his assignment at Nellis with the Thunderbirds. Both of the Nellis men turned out to be true pillars of the organization. That said, there were none in the initial cadre from any source that weren't true pillars of the organization.

SMSgt Bobby Ellis from Edwards was the senior NCO and Glenn made him the Chief of Maintenance. Actually, that translated into "Chief" of everything except flying the jets, which Bobby left to the officers.

I really enjoyed the Aggressor training syllabus. It was similar to the FWS in terms of intensity, and it was a true professional privilege to be able to attend both courses during my career.

CHAPTER 3

WHO BUILT THE AIRFIELD, RESTORED THE MiGS, AND THEN FLEW THEM?

The CONSTANT PEG project was initiated from the Pentagon in 1976, chartered by generals Vandenberg, Donnelly, and Currie, and I was the "man in charge" in the building. Maj Gen "Sandy" Vandenberg gave me the go-ahead order verbally to proceed with the MiG project that became known as CONSTANT PEG. The project location was determined to be the TTR in Nevada and Glenn Frick was the local "man in charge" of the program at Nellis AFB. TAC was the host and David "DL" Smith was the "man in charge" at TAC Headquarters, Langley AFB. The "gang of three" was in place.

It was a thrilling moment to get Glenn Frick and "DL" Smith on the phone and simply tell them, "It's a GO!" Lt Col Glenn Frick got the ball rolling and recruited an incredible team of officers and enlisted personnel. When I took over on October 1, 1978, we continued to hire the people we needed without delay. Some may remember the personnel evolution differently, and in that case I yield to those younger than me who have better memories. This is how I remember it happening;

4477TH TEF ASSIGNED INITIAL CADRE
Commander
Lt Col Glenn Frick (Nellis) – Pilot
Lt Col Gaillard Peck (Tonopah) – Pilot

Operations
Maj Ron Iverson (Nellis operations) – Pilot
Maj Joe "Jose" Oberle (Tonopah operations) – Pilot

SSgt Gary Lewellen – Operations NCOIC
Lt Cdr Tom Morgenfeld (US Navy) – Pilot
Lt Cdr Chuck Heatley (US Navy) – Pilot
Maj Gerry Huff (Airfield construction) – Pilot
Maj Don Muller (Project security) – Pilot
Maj Chuck Corder – Pilot
Maj Karl Whittenberg – Pilot
Maj Dave McCloud – Pilot
Lt Hugh Brown (US Navy) – Pilot
Capt Mike Scott – Pilot (and final CONSTANT PEG commander)
Capt Bob Sheffield – Pilot (selected by me but technically hired by
Earl Henderson)
Capt Bob Drabant – Analyst

GCI
Maj Jim Keyes – GCI Controller
Capt Bud Horan – GCI Controller

Maintenance
SMSgt Bobby Ellis – NCOIC
MSgt Don Lyon – Assistant NCOIC
MSgt Steve Hovermale – Crew Chief
MSgt Tommy Karnes – Crew Chief
MSgt Jim Richardson – Crew Chief (First Sergeant)
MSgt Jerry Baker – Crew Chief
MSgt Bob Hobson – Avionics
MSgt Merle Whitehead – Supply
TSgt Chico Noriego – Crew Chief
SSgt Tom Burzynski – Crew Chief (and final CONSTANT PEG NCOIC)
SSgt Dave Hollensworth – Crew Chief
SSgt Mike Beverlin – Crew Chief
SSgt Ike Crawley – Jet Engine Mechanic
SSgt Doug Robinson – Aerospace Ground Equipment
SSgt Jack Davis – Telecommunications

Firemen
Charles McCarty (loaned to us)
Steve Webster (loaned to us)

Ralph Payne (first fire chief)
Kermit Deitz
Louis Hinostrosa
Evan Robinson

For the record, with the exception of Frick and Iverson, who left CONSTANT PEG before flight operations commenced at Tonopah, I consider the initial cadre the group in place when flight operations began at Tonopah. Don "Devil" Muller ("Bandit 3") told me that he too left before flight operations started at Tonopah. I didn't remember the timing that way but "Devil" was adamant.

We could not have gotten CONSTANT PEG going without 150 percent or more from every man assigned, and a lot of unheralded men and women behind the scenes that helped us make things happen.

4477TH COMMANDERS AND KEY NCOS AND CIVILIANS

LT COL GLENN FRICK – COMMANDER FROM APRIL TO OCTOBER 1978

Thanks to the good work of "DL" Smith at TAC Headquarters, Glenn Frick officially "stood up" the 4477th TEF at Nellis AFB on April 1, 1978. Glenn relinquished command to me six months later on October 1, 1978. While April Fool's Day 1978 was the official start date of the 4477th, Frick had by that time already completed the essential steps necessary to create the unit at the local level.

He had worked with "DL" Smith at TAC HQ and with the Military Personnel Center to hire the right people. He had also worked with me at the Pentagon to prepare an airfield requirements statement that was used as a roadmap by the architects. Of greatest importance, Glenn had arranged for the restoration process of the aircraft to begin.

Glenn pursued his daily task list with unparalleled passion and enthusiasm and our temporary facilities at Nellis AFB illustrated this eagerness. The resistance was fierce initially, but Glenn was unwilling to take no for an answer. Nellis AFB has always been short on available operations workspace. So Glenn arranged for a pair of double-wide trailers to be temporarily positioned in the parking lot behind the fire station on the Nellis flight line road (Tyndall Avenue). This positioning was handy because in those days both the offices of the 57th FWW commander and the Deputy Commander for Operations (DCO) were located in the FWS Building 282, right next door. The wing DCO also served as the commandant of the FWS.

Glenn Frick managed to furnish the trailers and set up telephone service, including an Autovon line. In those days we were serviced by Autovon for long distance telephone calls, this being a leased line capability with a unique access switch. To use the Autovon, a Class A phone line was required. These were extremely hard to obtain, and few offices at Nellis had a Class A line. It was little short of a miracle that Glenn had been able to obtain a Class A phone line in our trailer. Class B telephone service allowed off-base calls, but no Autovon, and Class C service was restricted to on-base only. Because it was rare for an office to have a Class A line, the usual routine essential for making a long distance telephone call started with a hunting trip to find a telephone that could access the Autovon. Even when the Class A line was found, one could generally expect a near perpetual busy signal when dialing. It took some significant planning and a lot of patience to make an Autovon call. DSN is now the long distance telephone service, and access is both reliable and widely available on military telephones.

Most of our communications occurred though classified message channels that originated at and were delivered to the Communications Center on base. The Comm Center was able to handle the full range of messages, from unclassified to messages with special access required – the channel used for most CONSTANT PEG message traffic.

In spite of the availability of message communications, at times the Autovon was vital for communications, especially for coordinating meeting and travel plans.

Glenn was promoted to colonel about 15 months before the airfield was completed. Six months later he left Nellis, headed for Egypt and a USAF military training mission assignment. The Egyptians were in the process of changing over from a Soviet client state flying MiGs to becoming a US ally. Glenn was being sent to Egypt to help with the introduction of the F-4 into the Egyptian air force inventory.

Glenn once gave me a bumper sticker that I still have that reads, "Fighter Pilots are Basically Backshooters!" And in the days of our youth as fighter pilots that was an exact truth.

Frocking is the promotion ceremony when an officer is officially promoted ahead of the scheduled promotion date. The officer doesn't get paid at the new rate until the official date, but is expected to wear the new rank after the frocking ceremony. Glenn passed the flag to me and departed for Egypt in October 1978.

From JFK airport in New York, as he was preparing to board his flight to Cairo, Glenn, after consuming a few scotches no doubt, called me collect and informed me that "Frick had been frocked on Friday, and it was time for all" of us (4477th guys) "to show some respect." Expletives followed, all of which were loving but none of which were respectful.

SMSgt Bobby Ellis – Chief of Maintenance from April 1978 until August 1982

Robert O. "Bobby" Ellis was hired by Glenn Frick to restore and maintain the MiGs. Frick could not have made a better choice.

Ellis entered the arena with the same passion and enthusiasm as his boss. He steered Frick with a firm but respectful hand to ensure Glenn hired the right maintenance personnel to get the job done. Ellis surrounded himself with men that listened to him and learned and then helped and taught each other. It was as if they had all been cloned from Ellis. They were an incredible team.

These men delivered two MiG-17s and six MiG-21s in July 1979 that were the initial airworthy jets in the CONSTANT PEG program. Meanwhile, they had numerous others in various stages of restoration that were delivered later. Bobby Ellis and his mechanics and logisticians are truly the reason the program was successful.

Mary Jane Smith – Financial Resource Manager at Nellis AFB

When the CONSTANT PEG project was established at the Pentagon, Glenn Frick, "DL" Smith, and I knew that we would lose control of the program if we lost control of the money. In short, we needed a financial stream that came straight from Washington, D.C., to the MiG commander at Nellis AFB, initially, and eventually to the TTR. Col Dick Murray, the controller at the Air Staff, arranged the financial conduit to ensure this happened, and that TAC HQ didn't stick its fingers into the CONSTANT PEG money pocket.

To do this, Col Murray essentially built a pipeline for the flow of money. He arranged for his civilian financial specialist, Dana Whitmore, to operate the funnel at the Pentagon. Money was poured into the funnel and flowed through the pipeline to the desk of Mary Jane Smith at the TFWC at Nellis. The money was exclusively earmarked for CONSTANT PEG and the 4477th commander was the spending authority. It worked like a charm.

Mary Jane had a little game she played when I came into her office. She would duck behind her desk completely out of sight and then slowly emerge with big questioning eyes. She would say, "How much is this going to cost me? Tens, hundreds, thousands or hundreds of thousands of dollars?" I then rattled out the exact number and Mary Jane would rise to her chair, shake her head, sigh audibly, smile broadly, and prepare the check. I made a LOT of trips to see Mary Jane.

LT COL GAIL PECK – COMMANDER FROM OCTOBER 1978 TO AUGUST 1979

Upon Frick's promotion and reassignment I was transferred from the Pentagon to Nellis to replace him. Bill "Saki" Sakahara replaced me at the Air Staff. And "Saki" is the guy that really made the program successful because he grew the force from two MiG-17s and six MiG-21s to more than 20 airframes, all while continuing to manage the support for the program from the Air Staff.

I took command of the 4477th TEF on October 1, 1978, after completing the full F-5E Aggressor checkout program. During the checkout period I worked very closely with Glenn and his team of officers and NCOs. When the day came, I was ready to take command. With the able assistance of the initial cadre and a lot of help from non-assigned personnel, we completed the construction of the airfield while supporting Bobby Ellis and his maintenance team, who were aggressively getting the airplanes ready to fly. I was the commander at the TTR when MiG flight operations commenced in July 1979. In fact, I landed the first Soviet aircraft at Tonopah, a MiG-21, and in the process almost ran "Jose" Oberle out of fuel in his MiG-17 – after all, we had to make a few passes over the airfield. "Jose" doesn't chuckle too much when, over a beer, he reminds me of this.

One day I was sitting at my desk in the trailer at Nellis and Bobby Ellis came in and stated, "Boss, we need a truck!" I asked him, "What kind?" I continued, "A pickup or step van, or just what do you have in mind?" Ellis said, "Boss, we actually already bought the truck. We just need a check for about $70,000 to pay for it." He handed me the invoice. So, after appropriately "discussing with Bobby the need for the truck and the need to keep the commander informed" I headed for Mary Jane Smith's office to get a check. I think my counsel with Ellis fell on deaf ears as I observed no change in Bobby's lean-forward aggressive behavior. He knew what needed to be done. In his mind I was just the facilitator. Fortunately, we both understood our exact roles, and Bobby never crossed the line that got any of us in trouble.

It was simple to make hard things happen when you had a money spigot straight from Washington, D.C. Before I gave the check to Ellis to pay for the truck I felt compelled to have another, "Do we really need this?" discussion. As was usually the case when I engaged Bobby like this, I learned a lot about something – in this case over-the-road vehicles. The bottom line was that a truck like the one he bought was preferred over the less expensive cab-over configuration because the ride is much rougher in a cab-over truck. He explained that when the cab and the driver sit right on top of the front wheels as in the cab-over it was very fatiguing, and he worried about the men falling asleep at the wheel. I wondered to myself if the smooth ride wouldn't induce sleep. But, on the other hand, if the ride didn't make you tired, that was good. His explanation finally made sense to me, sort of.

What was I to do at that point? The entire discussion was an exercise in futility. The men had already bought the truck, so, Ellis got the check, the dealer in Salt Lake City got the money and we had one hell of a truck. Equipped with the new truck, Ellis and his gang became the scavengers of the west.

In the old days we called the Defense Reutilization Management Office (DRMO) the salvage yard. Any article no longer needed was disposed of at the DRMO, where it was either redistributed to another military agency, sold, or salvaged. We generated a high priority for our organization for redistribution of anything that might end up in a DRMO, and it was honored by the DRMO management. The piles of accumulated Ellis treasures grew daily in our compound at Tonopah. To the common man it would have appeared we were harvesting junk, not treasure. That giant new truck of ours became a regular visitor at every DRMO on the west coast and several points east, at least as far as White Sands Missile Test Range in New Mexico.

The men called the salvage function the "Robert O. Ellis Trucking and Salvage Company" and even had t-shirts made to identify themselves. On the front side of the t-shirts was the company pseudo name and emblazoned on the back was the politically incorrect phrase, "Slaves can't quit, they have to be sold." The shirts more or less captured the spirit of Ellis' mode of operation.

Among the first items Ellis appropriated from the various DRMOs were the trailers that you pull behind a large truck tractor, making it a so-called 18-wheeler. The truck became known to some of the men as the "K-Whopper," a name hung on it by Don Lyon, Ellis' No 2 man. As best anybody remembers the K came from Kenworth, the manufacturer, and it was a big whopper of an Air Force blue truck. There were probably several other pet names for the big Kenworth that were hung on it by the men qualified to drive it. The truck was later painted red and became known as "Big Red." Phil White confirmed that this happened on his watch as the sixth Red Eagle commander.

Soon after we got the truck I thanked Ellis for not buying a Peterbilt brand. Twice a day I drove my '74 Corvette along Interstate 15 through Las Vegas on my way to work at Nellis. I called these trips my two-a-day "combat missions" largely because of the potential conflict between the truck traffic and my little car. I was very vulnerable in the 'Vette, and more than once had to take evasive action when a truck failed to see me. Sudden truck movements caused me to react with extreme action to avoid a lane change wreck. On one such truck that I luckily avoided, I saw a bumper sticker that said, "Old truckers never die, they just get a new Peterbuilt." I was in no humor to be the butt of jokes about Peterbuilt trucks and therefore embraced the Kenworth "K-Whopper" if for no other reason than the fact that it wasn't a Peterbuilt-brand vehicle. I intended to get checked out and qualified to drive that truck, but it never happened.

I knew the men were on the road a lot, and Ellis assured me they were acquiring equipment we needed to get the MiG operation really going. I envisioned hydraulic mules and other AGE and tool equipment. One day while we were at Tonopah before the start of flight operations Ellis insisted I come down to the "Indian Village." In those early days the men had built a trailer compound they called the "Indian Village." It was later moved to our compound but the original was in a little arroyo adjacent to the road between our compound at the airfield and the DoE compound. Up until this point I hadn't been to the "Indian Village." I knew the men spent a lot of time there, but with no vehicle transportation and the fact that during the winter of 1978/79 the path to the "Indian Village" seemed to be always either muddy or snow covered, I hadn't gotten around to making that visit. I told Ellis that I didn't really want to walk down there as it had recently snowed and it was muddy and cold. He insisted so I relented and we headed out.

What I found amazed me. The "Indian Village" had matured and was now a three-sided compound made of trailers similar to the ones pulled by the "K-Whopper." Except, these trailers had the wheels removed and were set up in a U layout with a flooring between them of pierced-steel planking (PSP) reminiscent of the World War II airfields on the Pacific Ocean islands – the kind that Marine Corps ace "Pappy" Boyington and his F4U Corsairs made famous in their unrelenting pursuit of the Japanese Zeros. Overhead was a fabric roof of several layers of parachute material. The trailers had been turned into workshops, with the side loading doors of the trailers facing inward. Electrical generators hummed and the noise of an air compressor was unmistakable.

Much to my surprise, there were two or three jeep-like vehicles parked on the PSP. Up until that time, other than privately owned pickups and cars, we had no vehicles at TTR except the "K-Whopper" and an old air force tractor truck that could barely get out of its own way. Ellis made much fanfare about their current project and then presented me with the "Command Vehicle" – a World War II era Jeep that they had fabricated from scrap. There were no consistent serial numbers among the components. No VIN. Just a Jeep. The lesson here is that if you get enough junked Jeep parts together you can build up a vehicle that runs.

Bobby stated that it was no longer necessary for the commander to walk when he came to TTR by air. A closer inspection of activities during this visit revealed more vehicle parts in the shops in advanced stages of rehabilitation, along with at least one World War II era weapons carrier – a heavier truck than a Jeep, but lighter than a typical army truck. Ellis praised the genius of his men and especially of a new hire, Billy Lightfoot, our new chief of vehicle maintenance. Eventually, Billy Lightfoot built a truck on wheels with nothing but a driver's chair and an engine above the basic chassis. I believe one of the subsequent commanders had an interesting time explaining the purpose of that truck to one of his "masters." Lightfoot was an interesting character whose life ended much too young. He is a man that we all sincerely miss.

The "K-Whopper" investment was starting to pay off. Over time numerous Red Eagles mastered driving the big Kenworth. In addition to the driving instructor, Steve Hovermale, all the old guard enlisted checked out in the truck along with Richie Murphy and Ben Galloway, and others that followed. I suspect some of the pilots got driving lessons as well, but I never caught them at it.

MiG operations started from Tonopah in July 1979 – a remarkable feat in terms of the time that elapsed since approval of the concept.

LT COL EARL HENDERSON – COMMANDER FROM AUGUST 1979 TO JUNE 1980

Earl replaced me in August 1979. There was no fanfare or change of command. I had been dismissed, and after a personal interview with Gen W. L. "Bill" Creech, the TAC Commander, Earl assumed command. He led the Red Eagles for almost a year, and during that period was able to get the program established along the lines Glenn, "DL," and I had envisioned, and in accordance with the Concept of Operation we had coordinated through TAC and the Air Staff, with final approval from the Secretary of the Air Force.

Many new ideas emerged under Earl's leadership. Of most significance was the determination to mirror a Soviet fighter squadron. Earl intended to hire pilots and then "age" them in the squadron as they accumulated experience.

In the end they would earn the rating of "Sniper," a coveted level of achievement in a Soviet fighter squadron.

Lt Col Tom Gibbs – Commander from June 1980 to July 1982

Less than a year after taking command, health problems caused Earl Henderson to give up the squadron, and another good friend, Tom Gibbs, was selected to replace him. Tom had been Thunderbird Four during an earlier tour at Nellis and then came to the FWS as an instructor. He was the first commander to serve a complete two-year tour at Tonopah. And, he shared Frick, mine, and Henderson's appreciation for our Chief of Maintenance, SMSgt (later Chief) Bobby Ellis and all of the aircraft maintainers. The project could not have happened without them.

It was on Tom Gibbs' watch that Mark Postai ("Bandit 25") had an engine problem and crash-landed one of the MiG-17s in the desert. And Tom reflected to me in a February 2009 conversation that he could specifically remember two different F-4 crashes that he witnessed from Tonopah. One had been an F-4E and the other a Wild Weasel F-4G, both Red Flag participants. Such was the risk in being situated essentially at show center in the Nellis Range complex.

A lot went on in the Nellis Range complex that had nothing to do with CONSTANT PEG. The FWS was a major range customer operating F-4E, F-15, A-7, and A-10 aircraft, and a large portion of the USAF Operational Test and Evaluation mission was also flown on the Nellis Range complex. The Aggressors had two squadrons of F-5E aircraft and conducted the Aggressor training program for pilots newly assigned to those units.

This was the time during which Red Flag was maturing, and at the same time suffering a severe loss rate. Thus, it was not uncommon to see a column of black smoke rising from the desert in the Red Flag range area adjacent to the TTR. It is a credit to the USAF that the leadership recognized that Red Flag and the training it brought to the participants outweighed the risk and cost in terms of accidents. The generals in charge at the time kept the Red Flag program in place.

During Gibbs' period of command major change occurred. Following Postai's MiG-17 mishap these aircraft were retired and the unit began receiving MiG-23 "Floggers."

Gibbs' operations officers were Mike Press and Chuck Corder, both of whom did a splendid job. Mike was a very experienced Aggressor pilot, and he and Chuck under Gibbs' leadership did their part to mold the squadron into a fine operational unit. The Nellis fighter community was saddened as a group when the ever-popular Chuck Corder passed away due to natural causes years later.

LT COL GEORGE GENNIN – COMMANDER FROM AUGUST 1982 TO JULY 1984

Tom Gibbs was replaced by George Gennin, who was also a friend of mine from years before when we had ferried F-4s across the North Atlantic. He then briefly shared my house with his family when he came to FWS while he was searching for an apartment.

Along with George Gennin, the F-117s came to the TTR. They brought with them full colonels and the stealth fighter's own distinctive chain of command and method of operations. Things had to change.

With the introduction of the stealth fighter to TTR it became apparent that the MiG project had outgrown the original model. With the added security attached to the F-117 program, the Red Eagles were no longer permitted to spend nights in the town of Tonopah. Instead, they were afforded accommodation in the compound built to support the stealth operation. It was called the "Mancamp."

Thus, George had the sad task, on his watch, of re-bluing the enlisted force. That meant requiring the men to wear USAF uniforms and completely comply with grooming standards. I give him credit as an officer and commander that he was able to find the necessary toughness to get that part of the job done. It did not make him popular. But, as he has said many times publicly and privately, popularity was not a part of his task.

It is an absolute truth that there were two different organizations that flew MiGs at Tonopah – the Red Eagles before Gennin and the Red Eagles after Gennin. It would be better stated as the Red Eagles before and after the arrival of the stealth fighter community. Some really good Red Eagles from the enlisted component left the unit voluntarily, or otherwise, as a result of the generally sudden and dramatic changes Gennin brought to the unit.

And, Bobby Ellis, the Chief of Maintenance, retired and was replaced by a maintenance officer.

In spite of the turbulence and, in some cases, slumping morale, George got the job done, and at the end of his watch the unit was stronger than ever. After a full tour George Gennin passed the command to Phil White, an officer I had known since the days of my Aggressor checkout in 1978 prior to taking command of the 4477th.

Lt Col Phil White – Commander from July 1984 to July 1986

Phil White told me he struggled in the post-Gennin period with the changes that had been made. Some of the men continued to push back even after Phil took command. But there was no going back. The changes were good and "for good." On at least one occasion one of the men challenged Phil's authority and threatened to get him fired. According to Phil that individual departed the site that day, never to return.

On Phil's watch, the unit prospered in terms of accomplishing the mission and continued to grow. By the time he relinquished command, there were hundreds of personnel assigned to the Red Eagles, including a chief master sergeant for a first sergeant.

In addition to growth one major change to the concept of operations occurred on Phil White's watch. The maintenance community was overhauled to add the elements typical of a USAF maintenance organization charged with maintaining jet fighters. Maintenance experts from TAC descended upon Tonopah and pointed out the technical deficiencies of the organization and then proceeded to add manning and skill sets that in their judgment were necessary to make the Red Eagle unit compliant with USAF standards. Officers instead of senior NCOs were now firmly in charge of maintenance to the great consternation of many wonderful NCOs who deemed that personnel move unnecessary.

Meanwhile, Phil developed an excellent relationship with Brig Gen Joe Ashy, the Nellis wing commander. Phil laughed out loud when he told me, "Ashy would often fire and rehire [me] several times during the same day or week."

Phil White had been advised not to tell anybody outside the organization any more than was absolutely necessary. That wasn't his style, but during his tour as commander he came to understand why he had been so instructed. Sometimes candor brought more problems than it solved.

For a period some thought the squadron went backwards in performing its mission in that the MiGs were sometimes prohibited from flying in Red Flag. This wasn't Phil's decision but was reflective of the risk tolerance of some higher-ranking officers in the chain of command. With changes in people at senior levels, the changes in policy were sometimes good news and sometimes not. In both cases the changing rules as to which missions the MiGs could fly cascaded into Tonopah, often like tidal waves.

While he personally feels he sometimes struggled to accomplish the mission, Phil White was successful overall. He matured a changed squadron, made peace with the stealth people and had things on track when, after serving a full two-year tour as commander, Phil White turned over the squadron to Jack Manclark.

LT COL JACK MANCLARK – COMMANDER FROM JULY 1986 TO NOVEMBER 1987

By the time Jack Manclark took over the squadron, Phil White's leadership skill had become apparent in that the changeover actions including putting the men back into uniform had stabilized and the Red Eagle MiG operation was running smoothly. Jack was selected early for promotion to full colonel, and thus was required to give up the squadron short of his two-year mark.

Jack is now in the Senior Executive Service (civilian general officer equivalent) working in the Pentagon. He and Earl Henderson provided the influence and the muscle to get CONSTANT PEG declassified. Mike Scott and I, along with others, helped.

Jack passed command to Mike Scott, who was hired to run the show and then, at the direction of TAC Commander Gen Bob Russ, had the dreadful task of shutting down the whole CONSTANT PEG project.

LT COL MIKE SCOTT – COMMANDER FROM NOVEMBER 1987 TO MARCH 1988

This was Mike Scott's second tour with the Red Eagles, as I hired him as a part of the initial cadre in 1979. In the years in between Red Eagle assignments, Mike Scott was also the staff officer responsible for the Red Eagles at TAC Headquarters, a position originally held by "DL" Smith, passed on to "CT" Wang, and inherited by "Shy" Shevanik. Mike Scott, along with Bill Sakahara, probably has more intimate overall knowledge about the program than any other individual. His thoughts and opinions have been valued inputs to me.

PECK RETURNS, BRIEFLY

During the years between the end of my command in late August 1979 and the project declassification, with the exception of my visit in October 1984 to fly the F-15 against the MiGs, all details of the operation were totally closed to me. The security was that good.

The October 1984 exception occurred when I visited Nellis AFB and flew an F-15 CONSTANT PEG mission against a MiG-23. At the time I was on temporary duty (TDY) from the 18th TFW at Kadena AB, on the Japanese island of Okinawa. Our group had brought six F-15Cs to the US from Japan, and had just finished competing in the WILLIAM TELL Air-to-Air Weapons Meet at Tyndall AFB. Our Kadena weapons officers had had the foresight to arrange for the team to stop at Nellis and train for a couple of weeks against the CONSTANT PEG MiGs. In subsequent years other officers also were flown in from Kadena for this training, and it became a precedent. During the 1986 WILLIAM TELL trip Rick Tollini, a future MiG killer in DESERT STORM, traveled from Kadena to join the CONSTANT PEG deployment at Nellis.

In October 1984, during my CONSTANT PEG training opportunity, I was treated just as all other participants were. In fact when I was in-briefed, I don't think they even knew then that I was one of the officers that had helped start the whole program. If they knew that I had landed the first MiG at Tonopah, it sure didn't show. During that brief visit to Nellis in the fall of 1984 it appeared to me that the squadron was running like a "well oiled watch." I did not visit the facility at Tonopah.

As a result of the success of the security program, I still do not have detailed knowledge about the commands of each of these outstanding officers beyond what I have written. It is my hope that they will tell their own story in their own words as follow-on articles and books about the CONSTANT PEG project emerge.

BUILDING AN AIRFIELD

Gerry Huff had a strong background with light aircraft. He had been raised in Ketchikan, Alaska, and thus had been involved with fishing boats and aircraft almost his entire life. The Air Force Academy and a career in fighters liberated Huff from the north. I don't think he ever looked back. In fact at last report he had retired and was living the good life near a beach in Mexico.

Now that the project was cranking up in earnest we realized we needed transportation, and Gerry Huff arranged for us to lease an 11-seater Cessna 404 aircraft. Initially, we had two aircraft, and that fleet grew to three on my watch. It later expanded to four.

Upon being informed about the lease arrangement that Frick had agreed to, I asked Huff who was going to pilot these aircraft. "Huffer" said, "Glad you asked that. We are. And, Boss, you are scheduled for your first flight in your multi-engined prop checkout Monday morning at Terra Training at the Las Vegas McCarran Airport." He continued, "I am an FAA (Federal Aviation Administration) flight instructor. Once the guys have completed their multi-engined training and FAA check ride certifying them as multi-engined commercial pilots, I will check each one of you out in the Cessna 404." He went on to instruct me and a couple of the others to report to Mort Mortenson and take it from there. Huff told us to expect to get checked out in the Beech B-55 Baron and then take an FAA check ride. Jim Willbanks was to be our instructor. Both Mort and Jim are now deceased and Terra Training no longer exists.

The multi-engined checkout went off without a hitch, and soon "Huffer" had us all qualified as Pilot-in-Command in the Cessna 404. We parked the aircraft on the ramp just north of the Thunderbird hangar at Nellis AFB. Showtime every morning was 0600hrs, and the first ten men, plus the first pilot that showed up, took the first airplane, and the stream followed until the first 33 people were on their way for a day's work at Tonopah. The threat was that anybody that was late had to drive. Actually, we managed the workforce so that those who needed to stay overnight in Tonopah drove their private vehicles so that local transportation would be available. The men staying in Tonopah initially overnighted in the town itself. Later, trailers were added to the CONSTANT PEG compound, and they served as billets. Eventually, the men were moved to overnight quarters built to support the F-117 operation, the "Mancamp" compound located on the northern edge of TTR. "Mancamp" had both messing and recreational facilities, as well as sleeping quarters.

Gerry Huff and I had been F-4 instructors at the FWS, and he is one of the most loyal friends I have ever had. I was thrilled to learn that Glenn had brought him from the Pacific Air Forces Aggressors at Clark AB, in the Philippines, to join the 4477th at Nellis. "Huffer" was put in charge of the airfield construction and became "joined at the hip" with the REECo construction manager Del Gaulker. They were a pair to watch. Wirey "Huffer" in his flightsuit, zipper half undone, sleeves up to his armpits, and short and "kinda round" Del in his jeans and flannel shirt. Soon we had action at Tonopah. All KINDS of action!

Huff was unrelenting in holding Del's feet to the fire and insisting REECo meet the time lines, or explain why not. Gerry Huff took the task of getting the TTR airfield built as his most important life challenge. I was impressed with the depth of his knowledge and ability to anticipate the problem areas. Huff soon drew our analyst Bob "Darth" Drabant into his web, making him the assistant construction supervisor. Thereafter, Huff had the capacity to be in two places at once due to "Darth's" skill, tenacity, and dedication to the mission. "Darth" and Huff worked as a great team.

Huff was single at the time, and often spent the night in Tonopah. I wondered why. Then I had an occasion to stay overnight myself, and learned that Huff had found a girlfriend in remote Tonopah. As it turned out she was a part of the REECo team, and thus "Huffer" developed inside information channels on our project's health in terms of construction progress. His friendship with Sandy also gave us an extra finger on the benefits that DoE was attempting to harvest from the USAF project. They dreamed of things like covered parking on their compound. "Huffer" very effectively got the DoE fingers out of our cash register. Tough guy, Gerry Huff.

He loved working with the DoE people but he held them accountable. I stood back, reported upstream to our masters at Nellis, Langley, and the Air Staff and applauded the successes of Gerry Huff and Bob Drabant with the CONSTANT PEG airfield construction. Huff ultimately was very under-appreciated, and that has always troubled me. But at the time of the injustices I was out of position, and there was nothing I could do about it. I wish you well, my friend, wherever you happen to be.

We didn't have any neighbors that would come over for drinks or dinner at the site. But we did have a few that were curious, but not much for conversation. A herd of wild mustangs paid a visit to our batch plant, wandering around the unfenced area and leaving their "calling cards" everywhere. It was a pretty wild place with abundant coyotes and other desert creatures.

The initial project to support the MiG operation was finished in the early summer of 1979. It was a bare base operation, with just a runway and a compound for maintaining and securing our jets. We had abundant growing pains from the very beginning that started with our jet fuel storage and refueling equipment. These kinds of facilities must be certified to be sure the fuel is not contaminated in any way. Our fuel pit initially failed certification for man-flown aircraft. After a brief study of the problem, filters were installed and we got certified after a re-inspection.

At almost the last minute we recognized that we did not have an aircraft arresting system or jet-barrier in the plan. The MiGs weren't designed to catch a wire with a tailhook like most USAF and US Navy fighter aircraft. Therefore, a frantic search for a suitable system almost caused a delay in our timetable to commence operations in July 1979. As so often happened smart people aggressively attacked the problem and came up with a solution that led to the timely acquisition and installation of a suitable jet barrier system for the runway complex.

The runway at TTR is oriented 320 degrees and 140 degrees, and initially there was no parallel taxiway. Instead, there were turnarounds built adjacent to each end of the runway, and the runway itself was used as a taxiway. With the F-117 construction that followed, the runway was extended and a taxiway built on the eastern side of it. That smoothed out operations considerably. The taxiway to our compound was initially asphalt, and it included a small adjacent taxiway and parking area for the DoE aircraft as had been promised to the Sandia TTR site manager Sam Moore.

Our compound was fenced off and the entire paved portion initially was asphalt, except for the hangar footprints, the refueling pit, and the L-shaped concrete parking apron to the northwest of the hangars. The parking apron extended along the western and northern edges of the tarmac and could accommodate almost all of the initial force structure of MiGs.

The POL or fuel was stored in tanks adjacent to the fuel pit along the southern edge of the ramp. The original thought was that the underground fuel lines from the POL distribution point to the fuel pit would negate the need for fuel trucks. That did not turn out to be the case in the long run.

The system of trailers known as the "Indian Village" that served as specialty workshops for things like vehicle maintenance was moved from its temporary location in the arroyo, about halfway between our compound and the DoE compound, into the backyard of our compound, inside the fence on the eastern side of the tarmac. Bunks trailers were subsequently added which, until the "Mancamp" opened, enabled the men to stay overnight without making the lengthy round trip to the town of Tonopah.

We made a lot of mistakes in our design of the compound, and none was more glaring than the asphalt tarmac. These jets had old fuel bladders and other deficiencies, and like a lot of military aircraft, they leaked fuel. Not a lot, but it doesn't take much. Wherever a jet was parked, even briefly, fuel leaked onto the tarmac, softened the asphalt pavement and made a mess. We were very glad to upgrade to a concrete ramp when the F-117 construction began in earnest and money flowed again.

Another mistake was a failure to anticipate our need for other hangar-like structures to house our AGE, vehicle maintenance, specialty maintenance shops, and supply storage. To solve that problem we initially acquired inflatable hangars from the war readiness material (WRM) kits at Holloman AFB. The story about the acquisition of the WRM hangars provides some insight into the hectic and unpredictable nature of each day in our lives during this period. Bobby Ellis in his own remarkable way brought it to my attention that we had no place to work on AGE or our growing fleet of home-made vehicles. Further, we were starting to store expensive and fragile supplies outside, where they were subject to the elements. Bobby's way was appreciated because he seldom failed to bring a solution to the problems that he presented to me.

Bobby explained that he had arranged for us to visit the WRM storage facility at Holloman AFB. He had even made an appointment for us the next day. It was a simple thing for him to task his boss to load up one of the Cessnas and head for New Mexico. It made perfect sense to Bobby. After all, the pilots didn't do much anyway, in his mind at least! As so often happened, Bobby got his way, and we headed for Holloman in one of the Cessna 404s. The exact composition of the team is long since forgotten, but it must have included Bobby Ellis, Doug Robinson (our first AGE expert), and Billy Lightfoot, our vehicle mechanic. There were probably a few others on the trip with me.

The people at Holloman took a hard look at the ragged-assed militia that had invaded them and, in spite of our appearances, were courteous to the men and their uniformed commander. We looked at each and every variety of shelter they had to offer and Bobby and the men recommended to me that we take three of them. When I informed the commander of the WRM facility of our decision he laughed out loud and told us that the shelters were for precious cargo, and could only be used in the event of war in Europe. Bobby wisely counseled me not to take a firm stand and to just say thank you and leave. That's what we did and everyone was happy, even though the WRM guys were sniggering and shaking their heads as I rounded up the men and got us underway back to our Cessna. When we got home Bobby simply said, "I've got it boss" and I moved on to other issues.

Very shortly thereafter I arrived at Tonopah one day to find our men assembling the first of the shelters. It was used for vehicle maintenance. It had just been another week in the life of the Red Eagles.

Immediately prior to starting MiG sorties from Tonopah we engaged in some tactical deception activities designed to confuse the Soviet intelligence gathered from the satellites that were overhead every day. The plan was to have as many different American aircraft on the ramp at Tonopah as possible over several weeks of heightened activity. Therefore, a steady stream of visitors flowed through TTR during the early summer of 1979. One of the early jets was a US Navy QF-86 drone target. Several of our pilots and Bud Horan, one of our GCI controllers and the alternate security officer, were photographed in front of the QF-86 with our brand new hangars – with doors closed – in the background.

During this period our fire department was not yet in place. Someone, probably Bobby Ellis, made arrangements for personnel from Nellis to man our "fire station." Nellis fireman Mac McCarty remembers his role as follows:

In the summer of 1979, having been at Nellis AFB for almost two years, I was called into the Assistant Fire Chief's office and asked if I was interested in a temporary special assignment that would get me out of the fire station part of the time.

The first day the Cessna 404 pulled up in front of the station it felt really special. An airplane came expressly to take me and another airman, A1C Steve Webster, to work. When we boarded we noticed we were the only enlisted personnel in the aircraft. The rest of the passengers were all officers in flightsuits. They were all fighter pilots.

Lt Col Gaillard Peck was in charge, and he gave us a briefing on what was going to happen during our assignment. The Aggressor squadrons in Red Flag used the Northrop F-5 fighter to simulate Soviet bloc aircraft. The problem was its limited fuel capacity, and therefore the Aggressors established a forward operating base at TTR, allowing them to surprise the "friendlies" by engaging them for a longer time. The forward base consisted of a jeep with an aircraft radio, a fuel truck, a 1,500-gallon water/200-gallon foam P-4 crash truck, and a P-10 quick response Halon/Dry Chemical truck. Our facilities consisted of a two-stall fire station sitting next to the southern end of the runway. There was also a 12ft high "plane catcher" jet barrier consisting of two tall stanchions, large webbing in between, and two ship's anchor chains attached to each side of the webbing.

I liked this assignment very much. I don't know if the pilots did. It seemed every time they had something planned for the weekend, Lt Col Peck told them they were headed to the Pentagon to present a briefing. Very strange.

What Mac didn't know at the time was that we were rehearsing various events prior to beginning similar operations with actual MiGs at TTR. Steve Hovermale, one of our senior NCO maintenance geniuses, reminded me that in addition to our loaner firemen Mac McCarty and Steve Webster from Nellis, several of the Red Eagle (Air Force specialty code, or AFSC 431) aircraft mechanics were trained in how to operate the fire trucks and their equipment in basic aircraft firefighting. Our men also sat strip alert in the trucks during our initial flight operations, augmenting our emergency fire team. When our dedicated firemen Ralph Payne, Kermit Deitz, Louis Hinostrosa, and Evan Robinson arrived, ready to go to work, that problem went away. Fortunately, during those early periods of our operation, the firemen were not called upon to respond to anything more serious than hot brakes.

Another thing we didn't expect was a problem with birds. It seems the great horned lark is native to the valley. It's a fat little bird that seems to be dumber than dirt. Instead of flushing they would try and outrun the Jeeps, and lose the race, I might add. Operations were actually shut down periodically as the bird problem intensified. We had unwittingly created a sanctuary for the critters. The tumbleweed seed would blow in the wind and come to rest in between the aggregate in the runway and in every crack. Plus, there was water close by, and the heat from the black runway surface warmed the little birds. It was as though we had created a natural haven for these fellow flyers. After my watch, "Obi Wan" Henderson reported the Cessnas' windshields, leading edges, and props accounted for many bird strikes. At the height of the bird infestation problem it was unthinkable to operate a single-engined jet aircraft from the runway.

Much money and time was thus spent on bird control, with various approaches, including shotguns, loud noise devices, and a professional falconer, being tried. This particular problem was managed, at best, and never fully solved. Fortunately, the birds seemed to come and go, so the problem was not a daily occurrence for the duration of the project. However, when they showed up flight operations at Tonopah slowed to nothing but Cessnas.

SOME REALLY GOOD MEN

Ron Iverson was the operations officer when I took command. We were still at Nellis AFB and our primary tasks were gearing up for commencing MiG training operations, getting the airfield built and supporting the Aggressor squadrons in our "cover" job as F-5E Aggressor pilots. Ron and the assistant operations officer "Jose" Oberle brought a great deal of experience to the project because they had been a part of the USAF Aggressor initial cadre and had actually previously set up an Aggressor squadron. These two officers primarily provided insight and momentum to the hiring process of pilots. Both were well known in the Aggressor community and had great contacts that helped us decide who to hire to fly the MiGs.

Ron made lieutenant colonel in an early promotion (known as "below the zone") and left the unit before we started operations at Tonopah. His next assignment was at TAC Headquarters at Langley AFB in personnel, placing senior officers. His career continued to blossom and he retired as a three star or lieutenant general.

"Jose" Oberle made a close study of Iverson, as he was positioned to take the operations officer job at Tonopah. Jose was an ideas man with a stunning background in fighters, including a tour as an exchange officer with the US Navy as a carrier-based pilot. Plus he was a business major, which allowed him to grasp the non-engineering aspects of our project, especially financial.

Ron, "Jose," and I went to work with a clear vision of our goals for the day, every day. At the end of the day the activity trap called a fighter squadron caused us to look back at the accomplishments of the day and wonder how so many unexpected issues could come up and completely destroy our agendas. Nevertheless, we plugged away, and in the final assessment got the things done that had to be done. Like most activity-intense ventures, our "to do" list grew at a rate that met or exceeded our capacity.

A smart decision that we made was to put Don "Devil" Muller in charge of security. "Devil" developed a security plan that truly withstood the test of time. Even as early as the summer of 1979, when Lt Gen Tom Stafford came to visit and conduct the pre-basing F-117 stealth fighter site survey, "Devil" had the game plan laid out and our team was able to brief security in a convincing fashion. We knew we had to keep a tight lid on the program, and at the same time expose a large number of people to the MiGs. The system "Devil" set up closed doors behind people that left, cutting them off from information as though the program did not exist. Newly assigned officers and enlisted personnel were briefed with the same rules that applied to those temporarily assigned for training events actually flying against the MiGs. The importance of security was hammered home to everyone, and nobody ever let us down with a major security breach.

We can all thank "Devil" Muller for the security program that allowed CONSTANT PEG to grow and flourish. Bud "Chops" Horan (GCI) inherited the program from "Devil" and did a masterful job during the remainder of his time with the Red Eagles.

The US Navy added an entire new dimension to the CONSTANT PEG team. Tom "Squid" Morgenfeld ("Bandit 7") and Chuck "Heater" Heatley ("Bandit 8") showed up first and Hugh Brown ("Bandit 12") followed a short time later. From the days of HAVE DRILL and HAVE DOUGHNUT, US Navy pilots had been active cast members in MiG testing and exploitation. This interest and support continued throughout the USAF advocacy for the CONSTANT PEG program at the Pentagon, and when the offer was tendered, the US Navy enthusiastically accepted the USAF invitation to send pilots to fly the CONSTANT PEG MiGs.

Almost from the moment Morgenfeld showed up I had a new nickname, "The Skipper." Many of the gang still call me that when we get together for one reason or another.

Morgenfeld and Brown were test pilots from Naval Air Station (NAS) Pt Mugu, California, while Heatley was an instructor at the Navy Fighter Weapons School, better known as Topgun. All were F-14 pilots, while Morgenfeld had also previously flown the F-8. He still holds that jet on a special pedestal in his fighter pilot heart. An unknown US Navy fighter pilot once said, "When you are out of F-8s, you are out of fighters."

These three officers completed the Aggressor checkout program in the F-5E at Nellis just as though they were being assigned to a USAF Aggressor squadron, and then waded into the list of remaining CONSTANT PEG projects with great enthusiasm. It is worth mentioning that Iverson and Morgenfeld were completing the operational performance evaluation of the MiG-23 during this period of time. The program was called HAVE PAD, and Bob Drabant was performing the operations analysis element of the exploitation in addition to assisting Gerry Huff with airfield construction.

I first met Bob Drabant at Nellis when he was a captain and I was a new instructor at the FWS. Bob had the aeronautical engineering education and computer knowledge to make charts comparing the energy states between fighters. These charts helped us understand why one jet developed an advantage over another jet in high performance maneuvering. By that I mean high angle-of-attack and slow speeds. Bob's contribution to the USAF went largely uncredited, but it was certainly noticed by those of us in the business at the FWS. These charts were just the beginning for Bob Drabant. Along the way he learned to fly, and became a flight instructor in civilian aircraft. For many years we sat together every two years in the FAA-mandated Aircraft Owners and Pilots' Association flight instructor renewal seminars. The seminars are one way for flight instructors to keep their continuing education requirements up to date and their instructor license valid.

After the initial *Star Wars* film came out we named Drabant "Darth," and he is still "Darth" today in his job as a senior civilian in the Nellis test community. As he recalls the naming event, one day he rode his motorcycle to work and walked in to the trailer offices at Nellis wearing his motorcycle helmet looking every bit like Darth Vader. So it was, and has been ever since.

Throughout the Red Eagles' existence, we were very interested in quantifying the comparisons in performance between the MiGs and our fighters so as to provide meaningful debriefings to the participating pilots. "Darth" brought that analysis capability to the table. He was a valuable member of our team. Always willing to tackle a challenge, after HAVE PAD we hooked Drabant up with "Huffer," and "Darth" became a civil engineering airfield construction expert and alternate "straw boss." His help was truly valued as we worked that seemingly impossible airfield construction project.

Our squadron project list, long since forgotten in detail, wasn't the really sexy, visible stuff, but was the "meat and potatoes" necessary to assemble a fighter squadron.

Bob Drabant graciously responded to my invitation to send me his memories from those days. His input was very thorough, as is everything he does. The parts that follow help explain how "Darth" Drabant became a Red Eagle:

I left Eglin in September 1974 to go to Luke AFB to be on the Follow-on Operational Test and Evaluation (FOT&E) Team on the F-15A. I was there from October 1974 through to September 1976 after helping to write the final report at Air Force Operational Test and Evaluation Command (AFOTEC) Headquarters in Albuquerque, New Mexico.

After FOT&E I was transferred to Nellis to be a member of the USAF's Independent Analysis team for a very advanced air-to-air combat test called AIMVAL/ACEVAL, which ran from January 1977 through to February 1978. In March 1978 I became a de facto member of the 57th FWW under Lt Col Glenn "Pappy" Frick and his operations officer, Ron Iverson, to do the analytical work for project HAVE PAD – the exploitation of the MiG-23. This was a real two stage honor for me – first, to have Ron Iverson ask me to be his analyst, and second, to be on the exploitation team.

The exploitation started out slowly to find out what the aircraft could and could not do based upon the initial performance charts that I had generated previously at Eglin AFB. Those early charts were based upon data on the aircraft supplied to us by the intelligence community. Since we had not had the opportunity to fly the aircraft prior to HAVE PAD, the intelligence info was based on best guesses. Supposedly, the MiG-23 would turn very well and have reasonable acceleration capability. The early flights proved these were wrong in that the airplane did not turn well at all and, in fact, when it approached high angle of attack the MiG-23 became very unstable and was prone to depart controlled flight.

Rule one in predicting the capability of a fighter aircraft in turning flight is wing loading. The wing loading on the MiG-23 was quite high, and this should have been the first clue for us that the jet would not turn well.

The next big thing we learned was that the MiG-23 could accelerate like no other fighter we had seen, and in fact the faster the aircraft went the faster the airplane/engine wanted to go. However, as the aircraft got faster and faster the stability issues resurfaced, even in straight and level flight.

I recorded all of this info on the Air Combat Maneuvering Instrumentation (ACMI) system that we had set up at Nellis for the AIMVAL/ACEVAL test. The ACMI range was a 30 nautical mile circle centered over Dog Bone lake in the Nellis 60 series ranges. The reason this area was chosen will be explained a little later.

The F-5E was already replicating the MiG-21 as a surrogate trainer, but the performance of these aircraft was very different to the MiG-23. Early on we determined that the best American aircraft to replicate the MiG-23 would be the original A-model F-105, since its turn and acceleration capability were very similar to the MiG-23. While the F-105 was a lot larger than the MiG-23, its visual presentation was similar. Even with the size difference, we estimated a fighter pilot looking at the aircraft would only misjudge this as a range discrepancy of about 3,000ft or 0.5 nautical miles. Our proposal became a moot point because there weren't any F-105s available for this role. We were never sure whether the availability was physical or fiscal.

After the initial exploitation we got into the more operationally relevant testing which evaluated the MiG-23 against slatted wing F-4Es and F-15As. Our F-4E crew consisted of Capt Ron Keys, pilot, and Capt R. T. Newell, WSO. Our F-15 pilots were Maj Tim O'Keefe and Capt Ed Clements. All were instructors in their respective FWS squadrons.

We started out with some basic offensive and defensive basic fighter maneuver (BFM) set-ups and then progressed to nose-to-nose air combat maneuvering (ACM) set-ups and concluded with some tactical intercept set-ups. Our initial assessments were confirmed in that the MiG-23 was NOT a dogfighter and could easily be defeated and corralled by both the slatted F-4E and F-15A. The only time this was not the case was if either the F-4E or the F-15A made a head-on pass against the MiG-23 and the MiG decided to leave. By the time the F-4E or the F-15A got turned around to pursue, the MiG-23 was two to three miles away and was rapidly accelerating well outside of any missile envelope.

We decided that the MiG-23 would be good for an interceptor doing hit and run attacks, but that was pretty much it. Obviously, the Russians thought otherwise since they also made it into a ground attack platform by developing the MiG-27 air-to-ground version of the basic MiG-23 airframe.

After the exploitation, we asked how long it would take to modify the Energy Maneuverability performance charts so that they could be put into the fighter pilot's "Tactics Bible," the AFM 3-1. We were told it would take a year. I asked Ron Iverson to send me to Eglin AFB TDY for two weeks, where I would have access to first class computer equipment and I would see what I could do to speed this up. At Eglin it took me a couple of tries before I had a 95 percent match with what I had collected on the ACMI. We quickly produced the plots that then went into the AFM 3-1 tactics manual.

When HAVE PAD was over and the test reports were written, I was still assigned to what became the 4477th TEF. "Pappy" Frick had been promoted to colonel and departed Nellis. Gail Peck was the new commander, charged with finishing the CONSTANT PEG project and readying the TTR airfield for fully fledged MiG operations. Getting the TTR airfield and corresponding operations and maintenance complex up and running was a major challenge. When we first went up there, the short runway was in only fair condition and only had a small taxiway that led to the Sandia parking ramp, which was connected by a road to the DoE test support building complex.

In addition to the original airfield design we had to add barriers at either end of the runway for MiG use in the event of an emergency. Since the MiGs did not have tailhooks like US aircraft, we had to install what we called a "rabbit catcher" system that consisted of large netlike barriers capable of capturing and stopping an aircraft that was otherwise unable to slow down. We also needed basic weather instrumentation at either end of the runway so that we knew what the wind speed and direction was. It should be remembered that the airfield at TTR is at an elevation of more than 5,000ft, and in the summer time, temperatures exceeded 90 degrees Fahrenheit. This equated to a density altitude of about 9,000ft. Density altitude is important because both the take-off and landing rolls are significantly longer on hot days.

I operated a "ditch witch" from the back of our three hangars to either end of the runway so that we could run cables from there for remote weather instrumentation, with displays in the operations area of the hangar complex.

I settled into a daily routine working the airfield construction project with Gerry Huff. We never knew what would come up during any one day. Such was the situation when the Chief of Maintenance SMSgt Bobby Ellis asked me where he could get a transit to "shoot" one of the MiG-21s. Bobby had become convinced that one of the MiG-21s being restored was bent – similar to the twisted frame of an automobile after a car crash. So, I arranged for a surveying unit to be available and Bobby confirmed his suspicions.

The day that the MiGs arrived was memorable. And, I was there in the operations facility the day of Hugh Brown's accident. I could not believe it. What really got my attention was that I then heard that Hugh had been out of control in the jet the day before while out flying with the Aggressors. The latter pilots had decided to handle it in-house, and therefore did not inform anyone in the 4477th chain of command. Then Lt Col Peck got fired! Things just didn't smell right to me. So, right after Earl Henderson came on board as the new commander, I went to him and told him that I had fulfilled my contract with the outfit and needed to be reassigned. I felt comfortable approaching Earl because I had known him earlier from my days at Eglin when he was an instructor at the F-106 interceptor weapons school at Tyndall AFB.

What was my request based upon? Well, it was based upon mentoring from Col John R. Boyd, who told me if a man doesn't have his integrity, he is without anything of value. I could not live with the way things had unfolded.

MORGENFELD

Our senior naval officer Tom Morgenfeld eventually got out of the US Navy as a result of issues about command screening. Through what appeared to be a major mistake administratively, Tom Morgenfeld was not selected to be a squadron commander in the US Navy. Such an assignment should have been assured given Tom's abilities, career pattern, and overall background. By the time the problem was cleared up, Tom had decided to resign from the US Navy and had lined up a job as a test pilot with Lockheed. That move was a real loss to the US Navy but a gain for Lockheed and the USA. "Squid" worked his way up in the civilian test pilot world and became the Chief Test Pilot at Lockheed. In that capacity he was involved in maturing the F-117 stealth fighter, as well as being responsible for bringing the F-22 and the F-35 prototypes into winning configurations.

"HEATER"

US Navy Lt Chuck "Heater" Heatley was especially dramatic and intense. Early on, he originated the idea of adopting the same name and symbol used by the Soviet version of the USAF and US Navy FWSs. I was never able to actually validate that the Soviets even had a FWS, but we came to believe they did, and we thought that they called themselves the Red Eagles and wore a cool patch. "Heater" wanted to model our squadron after the alleged Soviet unit. My initial reaction was negative. We were supposed to be invisible except to those we brought into our circle. Calling ourselves the Red Eagles and sporting a patch similar to the alleged Soviet FWS wasn't exactly being subtle, and certainly would not be invisible.

"Heater" persisted with a new argument every day. I finally caved in when he pointed out that nobody had a clue about the stuff we suspected regarding the Soviet FWS, and therefore we would just be another squadron around Nellis. He turned out to be exactly right, and I'm very glad I was persuaded to call the squadron the Red Eagles. We also adopted the patch that "Heater" modified from what was alleged to be the Soviet original. As far as I know nothing was ever said about it, by anybody, other than "nice patch."

One Friday morning I was sitting at my desk in our trailer at Nellis and the phone rang. I answered it and on the other end was a gruff voice that said, "Peck, this is 'Gator.'" I said something like, "Pardon me!" and then realized I was talking to Rear Adm Paul Gillcrist, also known as "Gator," at NAS Miramar. He was the "king" of Naval Aviation on the west coast, and he later served as an advisor on the popular television show *JAG*.

"Gator" asked, "You ever write a Navy fitness report?"

I replied, "No sir."

He said, "Are you up to it?"

I said, "Yes sir."

He said, "You got a secretary that can type on one of those new fangled optical reader typewriters?"

I replied, "Yes sir, I do."

"Gator" said, "Well that's good. You know the United States Navy is charging ahead into this new electronic information age and I'm glad we will be able to work this together. In about ten minutes my exec is going to walk into your trailer and give you a package. It contains all you need to write a fitness report on Mr Heatley. My exec came up to Nellis in an A-4 this morning with the package and will be back stopping by your office at 1630hrs this afternoon to pick up the completed fitness report on Mr Heatley. Any questions?"

Another day with my priorities realigned.

The exec showed up as promised, and I spent most of the day writing the fitness report on Mr Heatley. Our secretary produced the final electronic document as I had said she would. At 1630hrs the exec showed up, took the package and headed back to Miramar. I don't remember for sure, but I imagine I then went to the Nellis bar for an adult beverage, known as "white whiskey" or "clear pop." At a civilian bar it would be Beefeaters gin on the rocks with a twist of lemon.

Bright and early on the following Monday morning the phone rang. "Peck, this is 'Gator.' I'm proud to tell you the United States Navy has promoted Mr Heatley to lieutenant commander, and I would appreciate it if you would frock him for me this morning." I was stunned. "Heater" was one of my junior captains (O-3, lieutenant in the US Navy and captain in the USAF) and he had just stepped past several officers in rank and had become my junior major (O-4, lieutenant commander in the US Navy and major in the USAF). All I could say was, "Yes sir." And then I complied.

The naval officers were all top notch, and everyone was happy for "Heater's" skyrocket elevation in rank.

"Harpo"

Karl "Harpo" Whittenberg joined the Red Eagles after completing an Aggressor tour with the 26th AS at Alconbury, England. I had known "Harpo" for many years and he was a welcome addition to the squadron. He also worked the many projects that modern fighter pilots would call "qweep." An exact definition of qweep escapes me but it can be classified generally as "little stuff." Some qweep is important and some isn't. The qweep Harpo took care of was important.

After I left CONSTANT PEG I spent nearly 30 years without any contact with "Harpo." By the time I found him in the Washington, D.C., area after CONSTANT PEG was declassified he had married, progressed in the USAF to the rank of colonel, and produced an All-American athlete son in the sport of Lacrosse.

"MARSHALL"

Dave "Marshall" McCloud was serving as a highly respected pilot in an Aggressor squadrons when we decided to hire him for the 4477th. "Marshall" came to me one day and said, "'Skipper,' I really appreciate you offering me a job to fly with the 4477th. It is an honor without equal." He continued, "but I have a huge decision to make because I have been selected to attend the air force Test Pilot School at Edwards." We chatted for a while and discussed the pros and cons of both professional alternatives. I steered the decision he was asking for help making back into his lap. After thinking about things for a few days "Marshall" turned down Test Pilot School and became a Red Eagle.

About three years after I retired I was sitting in my office in Las Vegas and the phone rang. It was "Marshall." He said, "'Skipper,' I just wanted you to know that you have had the greatest impact on my career of any officer I have worked for. This is my first call. I haven't even told my wife yet. They have just informed me I have been selected for brigadier general." I was stunned and honored to receive the call, but not surprised at his success.

"Marshall" McCloud was the F-15 wing commander at Langley AFB and went on to be a lieutenant general (three stars). He was serving as commander of Alaskan Command when he was killed while flying a sortie in his own aircraft in July 1998. Not surprising, his privately owned machine was a Russian Yak-54 aerobatic and sports competition airplane. McCloud's death was a tragic loss to his family and nation.

"BLUTO" AND "CHOPS"

We called Jim Keyes "Bluto." He was a skilled Aggressor trained GCI controller. In the Soviet system the fighter pilots relied completely on their ground controllers to give them radar vectors into positions of advantage. Jim Keyes was very good at doing this.

At the time CONSTANT PEG was cranking up we did not have dedicated GCI facilities at Nellis AFB for our controllers to use. As a result a deal was made to use the FAA radar located on Angel Peak, one of the mountain tops adjacent to Mt Charleston, west of Las Vegas. The elevation of Angel Peak is 8,891ft above sea level. In those days I was led to believe there were no microwave down-links to Nellis or Tonopah, so the controllers had to physically drive up to the radar facility on Angel Peak every day in order to give us the control required to replicate the Soviet system. The drive up the mountain wasn't too tough in the summer time, but winter reportedly offered many opportunities for Jim Keyes

RIVET HASTE TAC Aggressors Randy O'Neil and Gail Peck. (Gail Peck)

The original 4477th Test and Evaluation Flight Red Eagles logo. The unit was later upgraded to a squadron. (Gail Peck)

Peck's Fighter Weapons School Class (Class 71-B3), which graduated in December 1970. These men are, front from left to right, captains Bill Stearns, Dick Swope, Bob Lodge, and T. C. Skanchy, Maj D. J. Adams and ains George Branch, John Rahn, and Rex Cloud. In the back row, from left to right, are captains Larry Faison, . Johnson, Rich Montague, Gail Peck, Joe Hicks, Mike Ryan, John Madden, J. D. Allen, and Capt Steve Comb (US Marine Corps). (USAF via Gail Peck)

Official Photo: Colonel Peck while the wing commander of the 26th TRW at Zweibruecken Air Base, Federal Republic of Germany (summer 1985–summer 1987). (Gail Peck)

Cessna 207 N1592U – the transportation for the first trip to TTR. (Earl Henderson)

An aerial view of TTR airfield prior to 1977. (TTR Archive)

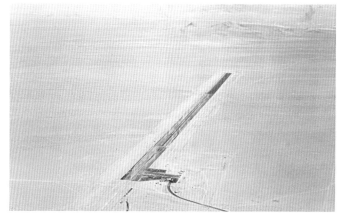

Below: TTR airfield after it had been expanded into a home for the Red Eagles and the F-117s (background). DOE range compound is in the foreground. (Gail Peck)

HAVE BLUE was Lockheed's prototype for the F-117 stealth fighter, the arrival of which at TTR in the early 1980s had a significant impact on the way the Red Eagles operated from the airfield. (Lockheed Martin via Paul Crickmore)

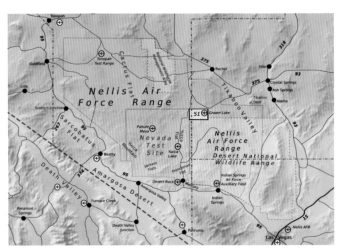

The Nellis AFB Range Complex, including the TTR. (Gail Peck)

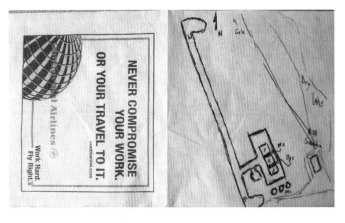

A replication of the initial sketch for the CONSTANT PEG airfield at TTR, as drawn on the back of an airline napkin by Gail Peck. (Gail Peck)

eggy Peck (1945–2002), the "Peg" in CONSTANT PEG, photographed with the author in June 1985. (Gail Peck)

j "DL" Smith in an original Aggressor photo. He was r CONSTANT PEG" at TAC HQ, Langley AFB. ;AF via Earl Henderson)

Lt Col Gail Peck in the cockpit of a Cessna 404. He was "Mr CONSTANT PEG" at the Pentagon and later the first commander of the Red Eagles at TTR. (Gail Peck)

Lt Col Frick in the cockpit of an F-100. He was "Mr CONSTANT PEG" at Nellis AFB and he was the first commander of the 4477th TEF at Nellis. (Gail Peck)

The TTR Red Eagles compound under construction in the late 1970s. (USAF via Gail Peck)

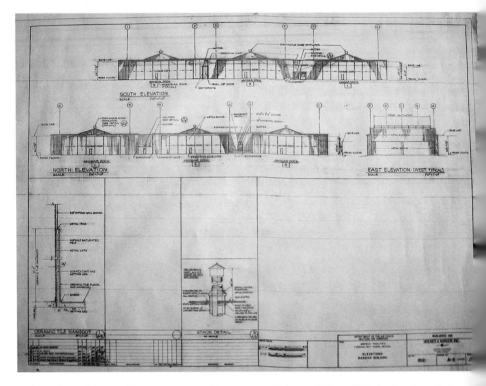

A photo of one of the TTR blueprints as prepared by contractor Holmes and Narver. This drawing shows the layout of the first three MiG hangars to be erected at the TTR. (Gail Peck)

Above: Wild mustangs (leaving their calling cards) visit the batch plant during construction of TTR airfield. (USAF via Gail Peck)

Right: The initial CONSTANT PEG compound and runway threshold at TTR as it looked very early on in the program. The trailers in the semi-circle at bottom right were known as the "Indian Village," and they served as overnight bunks until the F-117 Man Camp facility was completed. The original "Indian Village" was off-site, and consisted of 18-wheel trailers converted into specialty workshops in which vehicles and other equipment was built. (USAF Gail Peck)

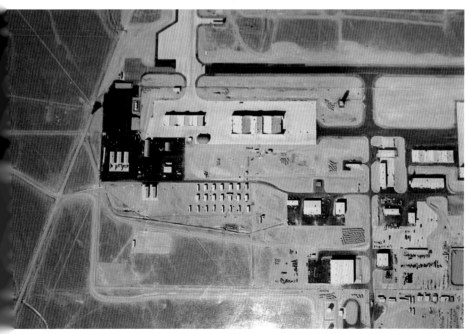

e CONSTANT PEG compound after major reconstruction had been completed, this adding two large hangars, a crete ramp, a parallel taxiway, and a control tower to the original site. This upgrade was completed to support the down of the MiG-23s in the early 1980s, which coincided with the introduction of the F-117 to TTR. The ginal three MiG hangars are at the left center of the photo on the left end of the white concrete aircraft parking on. (USAF Gail Peck)

The initial cadre used this Kenworth truck for Red Eagle logistic support. Bobby Ellis is at far left and Don Lyon is sixth from the left. Others in the photo, from left to right, are Richarson, Hollensworth, Robinson, Crawley, Lyon, McHenry, Hovermale, and Ealey. (Earl Henderson via Gail Peck)

The "K Whopper" became "Big Red" after the 18-wheel tractor-trailer truck was overhauled and repainted while Phil White was unit commander. (Bob Breault via Gail Peck)

Rich Murphy at the wheel of the "K Whopper" before it was repainted. (Hope Murphy via Gail Peck)

A Red Eagle MiG-17 leading two Aggressor F-5Es, with a Red Eagle MiG-21 in the diamond formation slot position. (USAF via Steve Davies)

MiG-21F-13 "Bort 85," which was flagship of the Red Eagles during Lt Col Jack Manclark's watch. (USAF via Steve Davies)

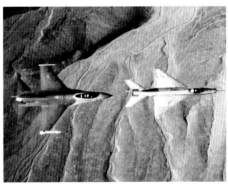

A Nellis-based F-16 sits astern a CONSTANT PEG MiG-21F-13 in trail formation. (Rich Samanich via Gail Peck)

Above: The somewhat obstructed view through the combining glass and windscreen of a CONSTANT PEG MiG-21F-13. (Rich Samanich via Gail Peck)

Left: A CONSTANT PEG MiG-21F-13 climbs vertically high over TTR. (USAF via Steve Davies)

Looking pristine, this MiG-21F-13 was parked on purpose in front of the flagpole within the TTR compound so that a series of official photos could be taken for the 4477th. (Rich Samanich via Gail Peck)

A 4477th TEF MiG-21F-13 returns from an early training mission at TTR in 1979-80. (USAF via Gail Peck)

The pilot of this strikingly camouflaged MiG-23MS "Flogger E" is preparing to land at TTR following the completion of yet another Red Eagles mission. (USAF via Gail Peck)

A Red Eagle MiG-23MS "Flogger" interceptor on the ramp at Tonopah. (USAF via Steve Davies)

apt Rob Zettel ("Bandit 39") standing next to a Red Eagle MiG-23MS. (USAF via Steve Davies)

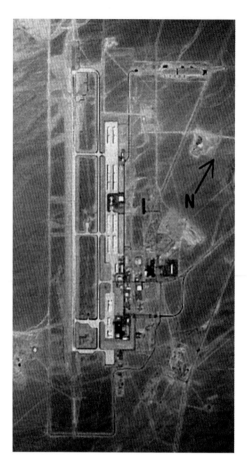

Above: Wall plaque made by MiG pilots Capt Rob Zettel and Lt Cdr Guy Brubaker (US Navy, "Bandit 48") to chronicle the Red Eagles by their "Bandit" number. The latter were allocated in the order pilots were assigned to the 4477th. Bandit numbers do not predate the CONSTANT PEG concept. The original plaque contained a ceramic disk image of the Red Eagles logo at the center top. (Gail Peck)

Above: TTR airfield after construction of the F-117 facilities had been completed. (USAF via Gail Peck)

Below: Static displays of a MiG-29 (foreground) and a MiG-23 (background) in the Threat Training Facility at Nellis AFB. (Gail Peck)

Above: A USAF F-15 flies in formation with a CONSTANT PEG MiG-23MS over a snow-covered Nellis range. (Rich Samanich via Gail Peck)

Nellis A-10s flying formation with a CONSTANT PEG MiG-23MS in the early 1980s. (Rich Samanich via Gail Peck)

An F-117 parked inside an individual aircraft hangar at TTR. Each stealth fighter was provided with such a shelter. (Gail Peck)

early Red Eagles pose in front of a US Navy QF-86F visitor at the TTR in the early summer of 1979. They are, from t to right, Lt Cdr Charles "Heater" Heatley (US Navy, "Bandit 8"), Capt Bud "Chops" Horan (GCI), Capt Karl larpo" Whittenberg ("Bandit 11"), Maj Gerry "Huffer" Huff ("Bandit 6"), Capt Dave "Marshall" McCloud 3andit 10"), Lt Cdr Tom "Squid" Morgenfeld (US Navy, "Bandit 7"), and Maj Don "Devil" Muller ("Bandit 3"). ud Horan via Gail Peck)

Capt David "Marshall" McCloud and two female friends admiring a MiG stick grip that was presented to Maj Don "Devil" Muller at his leaving party. (Gail Peck)

Senior MSgt (later Chief MSgt) Bobby Ellis, the initial cadre Chief of Maintenance. Bobby was also in charge of logistics and was the leader of the enlisted team of geniuses that restored our aircraft from marginal museum displays into safe flying machines. (Earl Henderson via Gail Peck)

Some of the original CONSTANT PEG cadre at a favorite saloon in Las Vegas. Included in this photo are Ralph Payne (fire chief), Doug Robinson (AGE), Jack Davis (telecommunications), Kermit Deitz (fireman), Gary Lewallen (Operations), Bill McHenry (crew chief), Don Lyon (Assistant Chief of Maintenance), Gail Peck (commander, centre, in brown shirt), Mariel Ellis (center, hugging Gail Peck), and Bobby "Daddy" Ellis (Chief of Maintenance, standing at far right). (Gail Peck)

Lt Col David "DL" Smith, photographed while serving as the commander and flight leader of the USAF aerial demonstration squadron, The Thunderbirds. (Gail Peck)

Red Eagles (from left to right) Bill McHenry, Gary Lewallen, and Ben Galloway on the TTR ramp receiving Air Force Commendation Medal decorations from Brig Gen Charles Cunningham, 57th WW Commander. (Ben Galloway via Gail Peck)

This Royal Air Force Jaguar GR 1 from No 54 Sqn was "captured" by Don Lyon and Bill McHenry following the jet's emergency landing at TTR. Security was not breached during the incident. Don Lyon holds the pilot's Jaguar flightsuit patch, which he obtained as a souvenir. (Don Lyon via Gail Peck)

5th Aggressor Squadron pilot Lt Col Phil White next to the squadron F-5E flagship prior to his assignment as the commander of the Red Eagles. (Gail Peck)

Assistant Chief of Maintenance MSgt Don Lyon poses on the wing of a VA-127 TA-4 prior to taking his final retirement flight. (Don Lyon via Gail Peck)

Lt Cdr Chuck "Heater" Heatley arranged for two TA-4s to come to TTR for the final flights of Don Lyon and Steve Hovermale, two of the initial cadre of maintenance personnel that restored and maintained the MiG aircraft. (Don Lyon via Gail Peck)

Capt Mick Simmons ("Bandit 57") after giving a T-38 incentive ride to a visitor from the F-117 maintenance community, who is wearing his lunch on his flightsuit. (Rich Samanich via Gail Peck)

and our other controller, Bud "Chops" Horan, to learn the skills of winter mountain driving. "Chops" recently confessed that they never drove to the mountain because the radar WAS down-linked to Nellis by microwave. Keys confirmed this. And I thought I knew what was going on!

The real truth is that GCI radar is strictly line of sight. If a mountain is in the way, the radar does not see a target lurking in the shadow behind the mountain. The FAA radar on Angel's Peak was essentially blind below about 12,000ft MSL (mean sea level) in the areas around Tonopah because of the numerous mountain ridges in between the radar and our site.

At the same time we were working together to build an airfield, the GCI team was working to get us a forward deployed radar in the vicinity of Tolichi Peak, just south of TTR. It was even hoped that a Soviet radar like a "Barlock" or "Spoon Rest" could be acquired and set up to heighten the realism of the CONSTANT PEG product. At least that's the story "Bluto" and "Chops" tell. I have no reason to doubt them, and I don't know if it ever happened because the security door hit me in the back before anything could happen.

"Bluto" and "Chops" just pressed on, working their own agenda while also performing their assigned jobs, happy to be a part of the project. When we flew they gave us a great air picture from their radar scopes as long as we didn't get too low. We soon added Dan "Truck" Futryk to the GCI controller team, and he was also a good fit. A stream of other controllers followed this initial cadre of outstanding officers. I can't say enough about these GCI controllers, they were the essence of our success, vectoring us around the sky so that we showed up in the right place at the right time. I can truly understand why the Soviets used close control for the interceptor mission for these short legged (in terms of fuel) fighters. With a properly trained controller on the scope, the pilots in the single-seat jets really did have a "wingman" and, as a result, enjoyed great situational awareness.

"ADMIRAL" NELSON

This story focuses on the jets and the men that built them, maintained them and flew them. But, like so many other successful endeavors, the team that operates "under the radar" or behind the scenes is often the glue that holds things together and allows the operation to work. Such is the case with "Admiral" Nelson.

John Nelson was called the "Admiral," and to this day includes his nickname in his email address. I had never met "Admiral" Nelson before May 7, 2009, but because of his wonderful reputation with the unit members I felt like I knew him. John Nelson was one of the most effective and revered of the Red Eagles. And he neither flew jets nor worked on them. I was stunned to learn that the "Admiral" had retired as a major. Before I learned of his final rank in the air force, I had heard the story of "Obi Wan" Henderson's experiences while hiring John.

The "Admiral" was a career logistician in the USAF. That means he was an expert at planning mobility of personnel and equipment. He was also credited with being good at civil engineering records keeping and financial analysis and procurement. It soon became apparent to "Obi Wan" Henderson that he needed a man with these talents to help take some of the daily business of operations off the shoulders of the pilots that had gotten things going at TTR and were now very busy flying and training the good guys. Nelson was identified as the man to take over the daily business of supporting the Red Eagles. "Obi Wan" made some phone calls and pretty much got stone-walled by John's chain of command. Nelson was too valuable to their mission, and it would be impossible for them to release him for an undefined classified job. "NO WAY" was the response.

As "Obi Wan" ratcheted up the pressure on hiring John, his leadership's resistance to letting him go also intensified until the final trump card was played and the realization set in that Nelson was in fact going to be reassigned to the classified job. Suddenly the tune being played by John's immediate supervisor changed. He contacted "Obi Wan" and discouraged him from hiring the "Admiral" because, in the words of the supervisor, Henderson would be disappointed in the product. The boss went on to bad-mouth Nelson in what became a clear attempt to keep "Obi Wan" from going forward with Nelson's reassignment to the Red Eagles.

The last minute ploy to keep John Nelson didn't work and the assignment went forward. The last great act of defiance came when the supervisor wrote an effectiveness report on John that basically terminated his career and led to his retirement as a major. This was a vindictive act taken upon an extremely competent officer because his boss' nose was bent out of shape and, John's superior realized, he might not be able to win but he could get even by hammering the "Admiral" on his effectiveness report! This was a cowardly and unprofessional act that was sad but true.

John was ultimately able to cause the effectiveness report to be removed from his record, but it took a couple of years and numerous letters from general officers. By then it was too late. John Nelson had been done in professionally by a "weak sister" bent on revenge.

While such a tale might cause one to expect that Nelson would cash in and wait out retirement with minimum effort, the exact opposite happened. "Admiral" John Nelson embraced the Red Eagles and they in turn embraced him. He became one of the most effective and influential members of the team, working for Henderson, Gibbs, Gennin, and White. During that five-year period he became a fuel cell for the entire operation, from simple logistics to financial management and procurement. He even served as a de facto chaplain on one happy and two sad occasions.

The latter involved his liaison with the Nellis chaplains, and the trust that they placed in him. One was counseling for a family following a sudden infant death and the other was a similar story with a sad ending involving another child in the Nellis community.

The happy story happened one evening when the men had all returned to Nellis and some were enjoying a cold beer. The phone rang and it was the emergency room doctor at the Nellis hospital. The medical community had a critically ill child that needed to be rushed to San Diego for a surgical procedure only available there. John put the word out to the pilots and two US Navy officers responded that they were sober enough to make the flight. John got the wheels moving to remove seats from one of the Cessnas to make room for the litter. The hospital was alerted that all was a go. Gen Mike Kirby, the 57th FWW commander, was notified and concurred with the plan.

The medical ambulance arrived at the flight line for the air transport of their patient. Nelson was present and witnessed the child being loaded, the mother boarding, and the father kissing everyone goodbye and then returning to the ramp. The "Admiral" said to the father, "Aren't you going?" The airman replied, "No sir, I've gotta work. They would never let me go. I'd be AWOL." Nelson said, "Okay, but get back on board and give them another hug." The airman complied and Nelson shut and locked the door behind him, essentially kidnapping him so that he could accompany his family. By then the engines were being started and no one was going to open the door. Nelson called Gen Kirby and told him what he had done, and Kirby responded, "No sweat, good work. I've got it." Those are always good words to hear from a general. Nothing was ever said about this emergency airlift, or the fact that the little girl's life was saved by these men. But, the truth is that the 4477th logged a SAVE that night, and "Admiral" Nelson was the key coordinator of the event. The US Navy pilots and the accompanying medical team were heroes as well.

When I talked to "Tonopah Tommy" Karnes in Knob Noster, Missouri, in the spring of 2009, he blurted out that once Nelson showed up he never had to battle the finance office again over per diem. The "Admiral" was always there for the men.

One day he took a handful of travel vouchers to the finance office to be processed and was informed by a prissy person in finance that the men would be required to bring in their own travel vouchers before she could process them. He responded, "No, not my men." She dug in her heels and eventually John made a phone call and someone spoke to her and suddenly everything was okay. Nelson was good on the phone and was willing and able to call in top cover when he needed it. The chain of command never let him down.

One time during a TAC Inspector General (IG) inspection at Nellis, a number of purchase orders were missing at the finance office. When pressed, the finance personnel told the IG inspector – an air force captain –that Nelson had the POs in his office. After getting directions, the captain presented himself to the "Admiral" in his Nellis office and demanded the POs. Nelson refused to turn them over to the IG and the conversation heated up. John explained to the captain that he had no need to know about the POs, and that the information was classified. Next, the captain threatened John, telling him that the IG inspecting officer had every possible security clearance. John explained that might be true, except for one. And, he wouldn't be getting access to the POs.

When the captain threatened to go to his boss, Gen Craig, John picked up the phone and called TFWC commander Gen Jack Gregory. His secretary answered and the "Admiral" asked to speak to the general. When the Gen Gregory picked up the phone John explained that he had an IG captain in his office demanding to have access to documents that were in John's mind classified beyond the IG's need to know or see. As it turned out Gen Craig was in Gen Gregory's office and the phone was duly passed to him. Nelson in turn handed the phone to the captain, and the resulting dialogue from the captain's end was, "Yes sir! Yes sir! Yes sir!" The phone was hung up and the captain departed Nelson's office without a word, never to be seen again.

A very vital tool for a commander at any level is a warrant, which is an authority bestowed upon an individual that permits him/her to commit the US government to a legal contract. The Red Eagles by this time had progressed beyond the days when Mary Jane could write a check for what we needed on a daily basis, and had become dependant on the procurement office at Nellis to issue contracts. Getting simple contracts through procurement at Nellis AFB became a nightmare. Contracts were needed for engine maintenance at Wright-Patterson AFB and brakes and fuel bladders at Hill AFB and numerous other propositions vital to keeping the MiGs flying. Operations were grinding to a halt due to delays in the Nellis procurement office.

As an aside, let me say that later, when I was a wing commander at Zweibrücken AB, Germany, no one on my air base had a warrant. We were totally dependent on the centralized procurement office at nearby Kaiserslautern. It was so frustrating that I was eventually forced to take advantage of a unique situation. A female master sergeant in my front office was married to a chief who was on joint duty with the US Army at the post across the valley from the air base. The chief had a warrant, and we actually used it for petty cash purchases for the entire 26th Tactical Reconnaissance Wing. Once the PO was completed, finance paid the bills.

Back to the Red Eagles story, the absence of anyone at Tonopah with a warrant caused untold grief in terms of delays for important supply and support items needed to keep the MiGs flying.

One day the general in charge of logistics at TAC was visiting and John Nelson rode on the Cessna 404 with him on the trip from Tonopah back to Nellis. The "Admiral" got in the general's ear about needing a warrant. The general promised to look into it, and within a few weeks Nelson had a warrant authorizing him to enter contracts for up to $100,000. Life improved for the Red Eagles after that.

The men worked long hours at the remote location and were entitled to a $150 monthly extra allowance. The money was paid to them out of classified or black accounts and was distributed by "Admiral" Nelson to the men in cash. As such he was often in possession of large quantities of money. Once he arrived home with about $25,000 in cash, only to be told by his wife that they HAD to go shopping at the mall and they HAD to go right now. He held her off long enough to find an empty plastic Kool Whip container in the cupboard. He wrapped the cash, secured it in the Kool Whip container and put it in the freezer. Then he went to the car to join his wife for the trip to the mall.

He distributed what the men called the "Dirt Money" personally to each individual every month. Even when he fell sick and was confined to bed after picking up the money, the distribution was made to the men who came one at a time to his house and were then ushered into the bedroom for the payoff by the totally bewildered Susan Nelson. She had no clue as to what was going on.

One time John asked her to be sure his airline ticket was in his briefcase. She knew the combination and quickly complied. Still in the shower, he heard her scream and remembered that the briefcase was filled with cash, like something out of a James Bond film or a spy novel. She demanded to know what the money was for. His reply was, "Enough to get the job done, but not enough to go to jail for." And, that was that.

Maintenance

When we set up the program Glenn Frick basically "bought" a maintenance package. His first hire was MSgt Steve Hovermale, an F-5E mechanic who had been with the Aggressors for a long time. He had initially worked with the T-38 and then moved on to the F-5E and finally the MiGs at Tonopah.

A large contingent of the maintenance team came from Edwards AFB. They possessed extraordinary skills, worked well as a team, and had the ability to think and perform "outside the box." The group, led by SMSgt Robert O. Ellis, was anxious to take on the task of restoring the MiGs and then supporting the flying operations as members of TAC. Ellis, as the senior NCO, was both the official and charismatic leader of the enlisted people assigned. He was hired as the Chief of Maintenance and served in that capacity until he retired, whereupon he was replaced by Capt Dave Stringer (who retired as a brigadier general).

"Bobby O.," as we called Ellis, worked alongside other great senior NCOs like his assistant Don Lyon, as well as Steve Hovermale, Tommy Karnes, Jim Richardson, and Chico Noriego. All were master sergeants except Chico, who attained this rank soon after being assigned.

In the CONSTANT PEG archives only a few photos are known to exist of the initial cadre of personnel at TTR. One is a shot of some of the pilots and one of our GCI controllers clustered around a US Navy QF-86 drone outside our original hangars. Another photograph from the early days is a Polaroid picture of SSgt Doug "Robbie" Robinson reenlisting. In the photo, taken inside one of our hangars at Tonopah, one of our MiG-21s can be seen in the background, and the folded pitot boom of another is shown in the foreground, with the vanes right above the head of SSgt Robinson. It was an honor to reenlist "Robbie." Soon after we started operations we added another Robinson to our team. That would be Evan Robinson, one of the firemen. Thus, we had "R-1" (Doug) and "R-2" (Evan).

Doug Robinson worked for us as an AGE mechanic. His job included maintaining starting units, hydraulic mules, and other machines and equipment that supported the aircraft maintenance and ground operations processes. Our men were all multi-talented when it came to mechanical tasks. "R-1," like most of his contemporaries, was able to perform many of the duties of the other specialists as a result of his mechanical aptitude and ability to work with his hands.

All of our enlisted personnel were required to wear civilian clothes and were exempt from compliance with AFR 35-10 (the air force uniform and appearance standards regulation) for haircut, mustache, and beard grooming standards. This exemption was necessary from a security standpoint to ensure our men appeared to be just additional civilians in the highly transient mining community of Tonopah. In the early days the men spent a lot of nights in town, avoiding the daily commute to Las Vegas. Hence at Doug Robinson's reenlistment ceremony, he wore an unorthodox uniform combination of blue jeans with holes while I wore a flightsuit. The only thing conventional about the reenlistment was the American flag and the oath.

Don Lyon

Don Lyon remembers details about the early hiring criteria. "If I recall correctly, Chico Noriego was hired as a technical sergeant. I don't remember hiring anyone above technical sergeant while I was there, but I'm sure Chico later made master sergeant."

When an enlisted person comes on active duty they first attend basic training and are then usually sent to a tech school, where the basics of a technical skill are learned. These tech schools cover the full spectrum of air force work, ranging from medical and administrative to flight line crew chiefs, avionics, fuels, hydraulics, AGE, vehicle maintenance, jet engine repairs, etc. Graduation provides them with an AFSC, with crew chiefs awarded the AFSC of 431 and a clerk typist given an AFSC of 702, etc.

After tech school the young person is awarded an entry level certification in their specific AFSC and is assigned to a "real air force" unit. The first step or entry point is a 3 Level, and increasing skill brings awards of 5 Level, 7 Level, and 9 Level. Thus a crew chief would begin his or her real USAF job as a 3 Level 431. An on-the-job training (OJT) program would start at this point too, and as progress is made in the OJT they are awarded skill level advancements that progress through 5 Level to 7 Level. Skill level advancement parallels advancement in rank, and a 7 Level is typically a technical sergeant. Upon selection for promotion to master sergeant, the NCO is expected to attain the 9 Level after demonstrating such performance in their job for a specified period of time. No one knows what happened to the 1 Level, 2 Level, or the even numbered levels. These simply do not exist. A 9 Level is fully skilled in his/her technical area of expertise.

Therefore, Don Lyon's point is that the Red Eagles did not hire young people fresh out of tech school or even after they had achieved a 5 Level. Getting hired required a 7 Level of technical skill, and NCOs with this kind of experience were typically staff or technical sergeants. After getting hired to be a Red Eagle, the master sergeants were able to bring the 7 Levels up to a 9 Level, the highest skill level in the AFSC. For a master sergeant to make senior master sergeant, completion of the NCO academy at major air command level was required. This could be done with attendance in residence or by correspondence.

Lyon continued:

> Mostly, in the initial hiring, we looked for staff sergeants and technical sergeants. Staffs had to have their 7 Level for consideration and selection to become a Red Eagle because we had no formal on-the-job training program to provide skill level advancement below 7 Level. And we were not administratively set up to maintain the training records vital for tracking the progress of an individual below 7 Level. I'm told that changed later on.
>
> Another unique aspect of the Red Eagles was that most of the enlisted force were not only at the top of their skill level, but were also able to perform at a very high skill level in most of the other flight line and vehicle AFSC functions that were outside their 9 Level skill. Jet engine mechanics could perform crew chief functions and AGE specialists could handle fuels and other tasks. Even the vehicle mechanics were able to cross over and perform aircraft related tasks and vice versa. Accordingly, over time our people became a team of multi-task capable individuals. This was vitally important, especially at the beginning of the program because of the shortage of manpower and the fact that many tasks required help from another person.

The USAF later embraced this concept to a limited degree in a skill cross-training program that widened the horizons of the participants. But, even with cross-training, aircraft maintenance in the air force still requires a very skill specific set of tasks.

HOVERMALE

MSgt Steve Hovermale was technically the first aircraft mechanic hire made by Frick, and he embraced his new challenges with the enthusiasm typical of the initial cadre. Steve laughed about the initial proposed name for the unit, the Tonopah Integrated Training Site. One official message to higher headquarters squashed TITS as the official name.

Hovermale was the only truck-driver certified individual assigned to the initial cadre. As such Ellis had despatched him to find a suitable vehicle for the long haul trips to the salvage yards that he already envisioned. Steve agonized over make and model. He knew he did not want a cab-over configuration because of the harshness of the ride, with the driver literally sitting almost right on top of the left front wheel. He settled on a Kenworth and found the deal in Salt Lake City. At the time I had not yet been informed that a truck search was underway. The financial aspects that consummated the purchase have already been reported. Mary Jane Smith came through for us again. The missing link was that Hovermale was a part of the conspiracy that led to the search and the acquisition of the "K-Whopper."

Hovermale was also trained as a firefighter, and he became a part of the temporary fire department that sat strip alert during the period of deception prior to MiG operations commencing, and also during the early stages of proper Red Eagles operations. He shared this duty with Ralph Payne, prior to arrival of dedicated firemen Kermit Deitz, Evan Robinson, and Louis Hinostrosa.

In addition to the seemingly continuous road trips to the west coast and White Sands salvage yards, Steve went on numerous overseas trips in the never ending quest for parts. It was one of those Kenworth road trips to White Sands that harvested the components that enabled the television station to be completed at Tonopah.

While Lyon doesn't remember this aspect of the story, Steve recalled that golf clubs and toolboxes were sometimes taken on the overseas extraction trips for use in trade and bartering with the host nation's enlisted personnel.

Steve was also involved in more than a fair share of the pranks that characterized the unit. Nothing was ever damaged or anyone hurt, but there were a few close shaves. One CONSTANT PEG initiation almost went wrong during a mock lynching when Steve inadvertently fired a shotgun inside one of the hangars. Fortunately, the round that fired had been disarmed and all that was projected was the wad, which harmlessly ricocheted off the hangar ceiling.

Steve was in many instances the mobile base operations officer responding to the needs on the transient ramp with the stream of visitors that obtained site clearance and showed up at Tonopah for orientation. He also traveled with the Cessna 404s and Mitsubishi Mu-2s when those aircraft were taken on road shows. The Mu-2 was cranky about engine restarts during short stopovers. Steve knew that by keeping the prop turning after engine shutdown, the engine would restart without difficulty. He was often seen on other people's transient ramps keeping the props in motion on the Mu-2 while the others hurried through their business.

THE REST OF THE GANG

The core enlisted cadre consisted almost entirely of aircraft mechanics or crew chiefs. The AFSC was 431 for crew chiefs. MSgt Bob Hobson, who was our avionics specialist or "spark chaser" as Ellis called him, was one of the exceptions to the heavy manning of aircraft crew chiefs. Others that were not crew chiefs were the supply specialist Merle Whitehead and AGE mechanic Doug Robinson. And, of course, the firemen. Many other specialists quickly came along too, like vehicle mechanic Billy Lightfoot, jet engine mechanic Ike Crawley, and the communications specialists. Several junior NCOs that had attained 7 Level were included, and they were actually the men that restored most of the aircraft. These individuals were natural mechanics in their own right, but Ellis and the other senior NCOs raised them to the higher skill levels required for the program by sharing every trick of the trade.

Karnes once said to me, "Watch out if Ellis comes over to help you do something dangerous. It sure as hell won't be Ellis that gets hurt performing the secret Ellis fix."

The men were amazing to watch. They were actually operating as cross-trained specialists before the USAF ever thought of the concept. Doug Robinson, our AGE guy, could service the hydraulics on the airplanes as well as perform other crew chief maintenance functions. And our crew chiefs – Burzynski, Hollingsworth, Beverlin – and the others could build Jeeps and other vehicles out of scrap parts. I will always treasure these men, as they are the finest group I have ever known – a true band of brothers that have stayed in contact with each other and with me. I wish I had pictures of all of them to include in this book.

THE LEADERSHIP STYLE OF BOBBY ELLIS

Bobby Ellis could be controversial, and he ruled the enlisted personnel with a gentle fist made of steel. According to Karnes, Ellis dispatched Don Lyon in one of the older USAF trucks to pick up a load of rebar and steel in the Sacramento, California, area. Don picked up the load and had just crested Donner Pass on Interstate 80 between Sacramento and Reno when he was pulled over by the California Highway Patrol. The highway patrol officer was concerned over the tie down on Lyon's load. After a careful inspection the officer informed Lyon that the load was inadequately secured and that he would be unable to proceed until that problem was fixed.

Lyon looked down the hill and spotted an exit with a motel, a restaurant and a bar. He proceeded to negotiate with the officer the necessary authority to cautiously continue to the exit, where he would be able to find an overnight billet (and an adult beverage) and make a phone call to his boss, Bobby Ellis. The cop agreed. When Don got Ellis on the phone and told him the problem he was having, and requested help, Ellis exploded and asked again where Lyon was. Don explained and Ellis bellowed into the phone, "Goddammit, if you're that close to Nevada why didn't you just make a run for the border?" Lyon was rescued in spite of Bob's outburst.

After Ellis retired from the USAF he went into business with Red Eagle pilot Gerry Huff and a retired 1959 graduate of the Air Force Academy named Bob Fay, now deceased. Bobby became their outside man and deal maker. I was never certain about the exact nature of their business, which was called IMI, but it was defense contractor related. In 1986 Bobby and his family visited me and my family in our home at the Zweibrücken AB, where I was the wing commander. Peggy made the summer visit a cordial and memorable event for all of us. We drank, ate, and remembered the good times at Tonopah. Bobby had been in Switzerland as I recall working on a business deal.

I had no clue that storm clouds were on the horizon for the Ellis family. As I learned later, Bobby had met a younger women who, according to the word on the street, was an Israeli. He eventually divorced his wife Mariel.

In an apparent fit of jealous rage Mariel shot and killed Bobby with a high powered pistol in the parking lot of the apartment he shared with his friend in Las Vegas. Rumors were rampant that one of their daughters had actually killed Bobby, and that Mariel had taken the rap for her child. Bobby and Mariel Ellis' daughter Patti posted a blog on the CONSTANT PEG website set up by Steve Davies, the author of *Red Eagles – America's Secret MiGs*. Patti's blog, titled "Daddy," casts some light on a very sad event. Her despatch follows an introduction by her husband John Sanders who, incidentally, was also a Red Eagle from 1986 to 1988, specializing in non-destructive inspection – an x-ray/ultrasound type system used for finding cracks in metal:

As fate would have it I met "Daddy's" older daughter, Patricia Ellis, in October 1992 and married her in December 1993, and we are still going. She went on to work for the police department here in Vegas, and was similarly employed when we were stationed at Ellsworth AFB, then moved on to social work. She never said a word about "Daddy." Later, I discovered who I had married. I recently told her I had joined this network and she told me about some of the rumors that were around. Today she offered this reply:

Hello, this is Patti, daughter of "Daddy." Here's just a bit of the background. I was 22 at the time and my younger sister was 16. My mother did kill my father on February 8, 1987, at his apartment off of Flamingo and Arville, in the parking lot, by herself. My mom, Mariel, was not dealing well with the divorce and had discovered that I had been out of the country with my dad and his girlfriend just a few weeks prior. She took the opportunity, after my younger sister mentioned she just got off the phone with my dad who had just returned to his apartment from a trip, with his girlfriend. She took a gun she had purchased, told my sister she had to go somewhere and left.

At the time, I resided with my boyfriend, a Las Vegas Metro Officer, up the street. She took the life of my beloved father that evening, then left me with the remnants of that deed, as well as a lifetime explaining the situation many times over basically alone. Ike (Crawley) and Mike (Beverlin) came to my rescue, eventually providing me a room to stay with until I went back into the world. My cousin Randy Horsely would be there two years later to help. My sister, 16 and pregnant at the time, would end up marrying an older guy by the name of Jeff Glover who would join the outfit later as a maintainer.

In the end my father's family, most family friends, and just about anyone else disappeared too. A family-involved murder was new and "hush-hush" to the world then. Unfortunately, having worked police despatch years later, it would become an all too common occurrence.

My mom Mariel served a short time, three years I believe, and has assimilated back into the world, remarried, and goes about her life.

I worked law enforcement, got an advanced degree and have an extraordinary memory of an excellent father, my Daddy, who will always be missed. I am open to any questions or any inquiries I can answer. Most of all, please tell me about YOUR memories of all the things I missed, while I was younger and he was being your "Daddy."

Thank you.
Patti

AND POPULATE IT WITH MiGS, AND MORE

We took full operational control of the facility in the early summer of 1979 and started the tactical deception operations. In July 1979 we introduced our two MiG-17s and six MiG-21s. We were ready to roll. The MiG-17s were retired a few years later and the MiG-23 was introduced. At the peak of the CONSTANT PEG operation, the MiG inventory numbered 27 jets in total, although not all of them were flyable at the same time.

Shortly after I left the 4477th, the unit took control of the first T-38 – the Red Eagles would eventually have five of these two-seat trainers. They were used as chase planes and for a variety of other essential support work, as well as for incentive flights for our non-pilot personnel. Sometimes the density altitude combination of airfield elevation and outside air temperature limited the use of the T-38. Operating with less than a full fuel load offset this problem to some degree, giving the T-38s about the same endurance as the MiGs.

One day during the early summer of 1979 I received word that Lt Gen Tom Stafford would be arriving for a short-notice visit. While I never discussed HAVE BLUE with the 57th FWW commander Brig Gen Tom Swalm, I informed him of Gen Stafford's impending visit and asked our security experts to be ready to brief the general on our arrangements. I knew intuitively that the general and his executive officer, Col Duke Johnston, were coming to TTR to take a look at it prior to making a basing decision for the operational version of HAVE BLUE, but this sensitive subject was never discussed during their visit. The operational derivative of HAVE BLUE was destined to be called the stealth fighter, or more properly, the Lockheed F-117 Nighthawk.

Duke and the general arrived as scheduled in a light twin aircraft. Both were dressed casually in jeans. Gen Swalm arrived at TTR in an F-5 shortly after Gen Stafford. We sat down in our conference room and briefed Gen Stafford on our security plan and then took him on a comprehensive tour of the facility and the near local area. Of particular interest to him was a hill just off the range to the north of the airfield. It was stark desert with small sagebrush and nothing else. There was no access to the hill except by transiting the desert. Gen Stafford was exuberant and thanked us very sincerely. Then he and Duke were gone.

Gen Swalm stuck his finger in my chest and told me that I had "failed VIP." He elaborated by saying that if I valued my job I would not fail VIP during the impending visit of TAC commander, Gen Creech. That was the first I knew about the impending Creech visit. Gen Swalm left and I gathered the men and jokingly told them they had failed VIP. This led to a more comprehensive discussion with "Jose" Oberle, the operations officer. "Jose" said, "Boss, we need an 'imprest fund.'" My response was, "What's that?" which was a standard question from an engineer to a business major. "Jose" explained, and we had Mary Jane Smith set up the petty cash account complete with a credit card. At that time "Jose" said, "Boss, I've got it!" As always, when that was said, I got out of the way. In fact I have a treasured plaque that I had made in the Philippines years later to remind me of those guys. The plaque reads, "There they go, I must hurry after them for I am their leader!"

"Jose" went to Dillards Department store in Las Vegas, and with his petty cash account credit card he purchased a nice linen table cloth for our conference table, a set of dishes and stemmed crystal. During his visit Gen Creech had lemon water in a crystal stem, as was his preference, and he nibbled on pastries "Jose" had ordered from the bakery in the DoE compound in Mercury, Nevada. Desert Rock airfield is located adjacent to the nuclear testing range at Mercury, and "Jose" had landed one of the Cessna 404s there that morning and picked up our catered snacks from the bakery. The cost was billed to the USAF.

"Jose" Oberle is a man that gets things done. He also arranged for the carpentry shop at Mercury to make several dozen very nice picture frames, complete with glass. When Gen Creech arrived at our compound at the Tonopah Test Range, the hallway and conference room of our brand new facility was completely furnished with art lithographs from the USAF art collection. We shined during Gen Creech's visit and he was obviously impressed and pleased with what he found. While Tom Swalm never said anything to us, one way or the other, our conclusion was that we had passed VIP with Gen Creech, according to our boss' criteria.

The success of the brief to Gen Stafford resulted in our $10 million facility enhancement blossoming into a $100 plus million airfield development project to house MiGs and the fleet of F-117 stealth fighters. We were very happy to get some much-needed upgrades to our facilities.

THE SUDDEN END TO "MY WATCH"

Very soon after flight operations commenced the MiGs began using the call sign "Bandit" plus a number. A number was assigned to each pilot, and it matched the order in which he had been assigned to the Red Eagles. While there are some inconsistencies and omissions, the numerical sequence is generally accurate, especially from 1979 onward.

My tenure in place at Tonopah didn't last very long. In August 1979 Lt Hugh Brown was killed in the crash of our MiG-17 known as "002," and as the unit commander I was held accountable and relieved from command. In spite of great words of encouragement from many, including general officers, assuring me that Gen Creech was in my corner and telling me to "hang in there and keep things going," Maj Gen Bob Kelley elected to relieve me. That was a bitter pill for me to swallow after all that had gone into making the project happen. While I truly grieved his loss, I didn't in my heart feel responsible for Hugh's death.

Lt Cdr Tom Morgenfeld, who was the senior naval officer assigned to the 4477th TEF at the time of Lt Brown's death, had been a squadron mate of Hugh's and a fellow F-14 Tomcat test pilot in the naval test squadron VX-4 at NAS Pt Mugu. Lt Brown had not been hired by the USAF to participate in the program, but instead he had been sent by the US Navy to fill the third of three US Navy/Marine Corp pilot manning positions as designated in the Concept of Operations.

As with the other initial cadre naval officers, Hugh Brown came to the 4477th fully qualified to fly a MiG – in this case the MiG-17. To be sure of this fact regarding Hugh's qualifications, several years after the declassification of CONSTANT PEG, at my request, Tom Morgenfeld verbally confirmed Hugh's qualifications in the aircraft. This occurred in a discussion Tom had had with Lt Col (ret) Dave Ferguson (now deceased), a USAF test pilot who subsequently became the chief test pilot for Lockheed in Burbank, California. The conversation between Morgenfeld and Ferguson confirmed the fact that the latter had indeed checked out Hugh Brown and certified him fully qualified to fly the MiG-17 prior to his assignment to the 4477th TEF. Hugh had also completed the Aggressor checkout in the F-5E at Nellis.

Considering Hugh's background as a carrier-qualified F-14 pilot and a test pilot with VX-4 at Pt Mugu, there could be no question about his flying skills or overall ability. He was a top officer and Naval Aviator.

Sometimes, there are bad days and August 23, 1979, was one of them for both the Brown and Peck families. I never saw the mishap report so I don't know any details relating to cause or culpability. But I personally and professionally survived that tragic incident, unlike my friend and colleague Hugh Brown.

AIRFIELD EXPANSION FOR OUR NEW RESIDENTS

As part of the initial expansion in support of the future F-117 basing, the TTR airfield got a parallel taxiway, a fire station, and a control tower out of the deal. Additionally, with the introduction of the MiG-23, the Red Eagles got two further hangars and new POL facilities, and our ramp was changed from the original asphalt to concrete. The ramp and hangar facility to the north of our compound consisted of individual hangars for each F-117. While not exact duplicates, the hangars appeared basically to be modeled after our small hangars, with separate hangar sets connected with office and workshop space between each hangar bay. The taxiway between the hangars was long and fairly narrow, and it was referred to as the "canyon."

In August 2009 I received an e-mail from John Pollet, the now retired Vice President of Holmes and Narver in Orange at the time the facilities for both the Red Eagles and HAVE BLUE projects were designed. John confirmed that the new F-117 facilities had also been designed by our old buddies from Orange and built by REECo under the supervision of its headman, Dale Frazier. Several iterations of construction followed, and the final expansion at the TTR airfield added a second and third set of F-117 hangars, along with a very large parking ramp. The latter was located in between the two northwestern hangar sets, and these additional hangars added to the F-117 taxiway "canyon" at the airfield complex.

The F-117s operated in total secrecy for many years from the base at the TTR. Thus, the idea of MiGs by day and stealth by night became a reality, adding to the national wealth that had become the Tonopah investment.

The MiG operation shut down in March 1988 after the Cold War had ended. Soon after the F-117 was declassified and came out of the closet for the first time. Eventually the F-117 unit was moved from the TTR to the 49th FW at Holloman AFB, leaving Tonopah in a caretaker status. In April 2007 Brig Gen David "Fingers" Goldfein, 49th FW commander, led the first of two flights of three F-117 stealth fighters into retirement at the TTR airfield. The April 2007 redeployment was the initial increment of the F-117 fleet's return to Tonopah after several years of operations at Holloman and numerous combat campaigns in Panama, Iraq, and the Balkans.

The original plan was to remove the wings and store the jets indefinitely at TTR in their original hangars. This alternative for retirement was selected allegedly because the stealth technology could not be adequately secured at the "Boneyard" storage facility at Davis-Monthan AFB in Tucson, Arizona.

Prior to the redeployment of the F-117s to Tonopah, the interior of the weapons bay doors of the aircraft were artfully painted in a farewell gesture by the load crews at Holloman AFB. When the weapons bay doors were opened as a part of the engine shut down procedure at Tonopah it appeared that the jets were carrying bombs. On closer examination the bomb-like devices in the weapons bay turned out to be travel pods that the pilots use for their cross-country clothes bag and other aircraft support items. The pods had been manufactured from empty napalm canisters.

CHAPTER 4

THE AIRCRAFT WE FLEW

For anyone that loves fighters and aviation, the TTR flight line was a thrilling place to hang out during the operational years of the Red Eagles. I am reminded of Ernest Hemingway's great observation about fighter aircraft:

> You love a lot of things if you live around them. But there isn't any woman and there isn't any horse, not any before nor after, that is as lovely as a great airplane. And men who love them are faithful to them, even though they leave them for others. Man has one virginity to lose in fighters, and if it is to a lovely airplane he loses it to, there is where his heart will forever be.

CONFIGURATION

The MiG-17 and MiG-21 variants that we had were pretty much stock export models of these great Soviet fighters. Both were early models of the "Fresco" and "Fishbed," to use NATO terminology.

Our fuel was measured on the fuel gauge in liters and most of the flight instruments were the Soviet originals. We did have trouble judging speed in "kilometers per fortnight" or whatever the measure was on a Russian aero-speedometer, and so we replaced them with American airspeed indicators that measured speed or velocity in knots, like all US-built aircraft. The same was true with the altimeters. We needed to think about altitude in feet instead of meters because of our historical training. Those were the only modifications made to the jets, except for the fitment of an air traffic control transponder and a tunable UHF radio, both of which were added to the avionics stack.

We didn't fly the jets in poor weather or at night so Instrument Flight Rules equipment for in-weather operations and night lighting were not needed, even though the Soviet jets had the capability.

We also had no VOR (VHF omnidirectional radio range) or TACAN (tactical air navigation) equipment, and therefore relied on map reading and visual pilotage techniques during operations. Our navigation was also facilitated by radar tracking and the outstanding vectors offered by our GCI controllers on the ground. The MiG pilots also knew the Nellis and Tonopah ranges like our own backyard, so pilotage navigation was never an issue.

The MiG-17 could carry fuel in two external wing drop tanks and the MiG-21 could carry a centerline fuel tank, but we seldom used them because they didn't offer much in terms of endurance and they restricted our maneuverability and g-limitations.

We began training USAF and US Navy/Marine aircrews using the MiG-17 and the MiG-21 as adversary aircraft in July 1979. The early sorties were flown in support of the Aggressors and their F-5E syllabus of instruction for newly assigned pilots. In that syllabus every effort was made to teach air-to-air tactics to a very high skill level, with an emphasis placed on the pilot's ability to debrief the engagement accurately so that maximum learning value could be extracted from the debriefing. To do this professionally Aggressor pilots had to be masters of both US and Soviet tactics, techniques, and procedures. After all, the mission of the Aggressors was to train the tactical fighter forces of the USAF, US Navy, and US Marine Corps.

To prepare the F-5E Aggressor pilot for this task, each completed a rigorous academic and flying training program that lasted several months. The syllabus was based on a building block approach, and each pilot was required to perform well in each level in order to progress through the course. The goal of the Aggressor syllabus was primarily to hone a fighter pilot's basic air-to-air skills to a razor sharp edge and then to teach him the tactics, techniques, and procedures employed by his Soviet counterparts. This was not just academic training, as each pilot had to master the execution of enemy tactics. By that I mean this "was not training about the mechanics of a piano." It "was training to be a concert pianist." The baseline for the enemy was a run of the mill Soviet fighter pilot and his approach to combat operations.

Since the Cold War was still raging and there was no Internet to explore difficult subjects, Aggressor units depended very heavily on the intelligence community to explain to their leadership, and the writers of the Aggressor training syllabus, the various formations and tactical employment techniques being used by the Soviets and taught to their client states. The latter were, like the Red Eagles, flying export models of Soviet fighters.

This information on how the enemy conducted fighter operations came to the Aggressors from many sources behind the "green door" of the US intelligence gathering and interpreting community. In the beginning information provided was accepted as the gospel truth by the Aggressors. Over time the "green door" opened to some degree, and the Aggressors were allowed inside the so-called intelligence room of knowledge. Once there, the Aggressors were able to review raw intelligence and make their own, often differing, conclusions about how the enemy could be expected to do business in an air combat scenario.

The Red Eagles were simply an extension of the Aggressors, and there was a notion – especially within the leadership at Nellis – that the Red Eagles should also replicate the "bad guys." Eventually, this did indeed happen. Initially, however, the Red Eagles didn't have the opportunity to replicate tactics because we only had a few MiGs, and our tasking had us totally engaged in the basics of exposing the Aggressor pilots to them in brief "look and see" sessions, followed by comparative performance profiles, and, finally, in one-versus-one maneuvering or dogfighting, to use a commonly understood term.

The comparative performance profiles weren't drag races or comparisons of that sort. Instead, after an initial join-up, the Aggressor pilot was cleared to fly close formation and to cross under and over the MiG to take a good hard look at the Red Eagle jet, whether it be a MiG-17 or a MiG-21. With the "look and see" satisfied, typically, the next step was to direct the Aggressor pilot to move to an extended trail position and follow the MiG though a series of climbing and diving turns or "Lazy-8" type maneuvers. Each repetition brought increasing g-loading and roll rates. The MiG instructor would eventually make a "knock-it-off" call over the radio and signal for a join-up. With the F-5 tucked back in close formation, the MiG instructor would direct the Aggressor pilot to take a "perch." The fun then began with a full up offensive attack on the MiG.

Usually, in spite of the F-5 pilot's best effort, the Northrop fighter would transition from offensive to defensive in the first try. After that the learning curve started to take over, and the F-5 pilot usually began to prevail, maintaining the offensive. The Red Eagles had pre-briefed the Aggressor pilots in how best to defeat the MiG, but it typically took a couple of attempts for our F-5 pilots to grasp the situation fully and implement the "school solution." After two or three perch attack engagements, the MiG pilot would take the perch and let his opponent in the F-5 experience defending against the Soviet jet. With this profile completed, fuel was usually the deciding element as the MiG pilot raced back to Tonopah to get the jet back on the ground with adequate fuel reserves still in the tanks.

To keep the daily schedule unclassified the MiG-23 was posted as an F-4 on the schedule and the MiG-21 was posted as an F-5. Also, the daily call signs were "Bandit" plus a number. These numbers were simply daily flying schedule numbers and not the Bandit numbers assigned to the pilots in the order they joined the Red Eagles.

THE LAST SORTIE

The news that the Red Eagles program was shutting down was a devastating blow to those assigned to the unit in early 1988. One such individual was pilot Capt Mick Simmons ("Bandit 57"):

> Being good "soldiers" we all took the decision in our stride and prepared to make the last sortie memorable. It turned out to be my job to make it so. For the last sortie all the pilots were matched to the jets with their names on the canopy rail. The aircraft's designated crew chief, who had his name on the other canopy rail, stood alongside "his" jet for the last time.

Mick described the final mass flight as a thing of beauty. He continued by describing the moment when he looked down the line of the MiGs, all waiting to take-off. There were 13 MiG-21s and four MiG-23s all lined up, engines running, with the exhaust heat shimmering behind each jet. Each pilot was ready to go and give Red Flag one last aerial engagement to remember for all time. I asked Mick how the final sortie went. He grinned and responded, "Who cares? We really looked good on the ramp!" Turning serious for just a moment, he added, "We sent the MiG-21s up the middle and set a little bracket with the MiG-23s. I don't know if anybody got a shot off at the Red Flag warriors or not, but we really looked good on the ground getting ready to go. When it was over the guys all came home and landed, taxied in to our compound, shut down the engines, got out of the jets, shook their crew chief's hand and that was that!"

THE MiG-17

The HAVE DRILL MiG-17F aircraft, call sign "Patty 02," was assigned to CONSTANT PEG, and most of my MiG flying time was accumulated in this aircraft. We also had a later model MiG-17PF with a radome mounted on the intake lip that we called "08." This machine was the MiG design bureau's attempt at producing an all-weather aircraft for the interceptor role. The radar didn't work in this aircraft during my watch at Tonopah, and as a result we used the two MiG-17s interchangeably. In NATO nomenclature these MiG-17s were "Fresco C" (MiG-17F) and "Fresco D" (MiG-17PF) models, respectively.

During the HAVE DRILL/HAVE FERRY exploitations, the jets wore a camouflaged paint scheme. However, before the aircraft were assigned to the 4477th TEF, the paint was removed and the aircraft flown by the Red Eagles at the onset of the CONSTANT PEG program were all highly polished aluminum.

Lt Hugh Brown was killed when "02" crashed in August 1979. A third MiG-17, numbered "5," was then acquired by the squadron. This happened after I was fired and left the unit. It is possible that I have "5" and "8" reversed in terms of assignment, but that really doesn't matter. We had two MiG-17s available for our training program from the beginning through to the time when the "Fresco" was retired.

Let's take a look at the aircraft parked on the ramp and then, starting at the aft end, conduct a walkaround so as to get acquainted with some of the jet's external features. Then we will hop in the cockpit for a fit check, talk a little bit about the switches and controls, and then take her up for a flight.

The MiG-17 is a very small, single-engined jet aircraft with a highly swept wing. The wing is mid-fuselage mounted and attached well forward on the fuselage. The cockpit is also very near the nose, and the leading edges of the wing obscures the pilot's view on the belly side of the jet. Thus, he must, in some cases, roll the aircraft onto its back in order to clear the airspace below him.

The airplane has short landing gear struts, which in turn mean that it is very low to the ground. When parked, the MiG-17 almost appears to be squatting on the ramp, especially if observed from a distance. Sitting on the ramp and in flight, the MiG-17 closely resembles its older brother the MiG-15 that was used by the communists in the Korean War. The most obvious visual cues revealing whether the aircraft is a MiG-15 or MiG-17 are the wings and the aft section. There are three fences on each wing of the MiG-17 to reduce the span-wise flow of the air over the highly swept wing. The MiG-15 has only two. Without these wing fences the air would slide down the wing toward the wingtip instead of flowing over the camber parallel to the aircraft fuselage. The wing on the MiG-17 is also more highly swept than the wing on the MiG-15. My best guess is that the increased sweep angle of the MiG-17 wing mandated the installation of the third wing fence.

There are several versions of the MiG-17, and the earliest variant has the same Klimov VK-1 engine as fitted in the MiG-15. This aircraft is called a "Fresco A" and it does not have an afterburner. The engine in the MiG-17F/PF "Fresco C/D is a Klimov VK-1F, which has an afterburner with a variable exhaust nozzle. The tailpipe of the MiG-15 is a slim cylinder similar to the tailpipe in a T-33. The afterburner nozzle section of the MiG-17, however, protrudes slightly aft of the skin of the aircraft. The actuators that position the expanding and closing nozzles of the afterburner give the aft section a slightly bloated look when compared to the MiG-15.

Just forward of the exhaust on either side of the aircraft are hydraulically actuated speed brakes. These are easily operated by the pilot via an electrical switch.

Noting the left wing, there is a long pitot boom mounted on the wingtip. There are actually booms on both wingtips, but the one to the right is a dummy that was evidently installed to balance the aircraft aerodynamically. The working pitot boom services the aircraft's pitot-static instrumentation in the cockpit. Pitot-static systems provide the pilot with airspeed, altitude, and rate of climb and descent information.

Under each wing is a hard point capable of carrying either a bomb of up to 1,100lbs (500kg) in weight or an external fuel tank. I only flew with external tanks a few times, and never with a bomb attached. My impression was that the external tanks provided only a nominal amount of extra endurance. In a real combat dogfight the pilot would almost certainly jettison the tanks. During CONSTANT PEG operations we never exercised the bomb carrying capability, instead focusing on the air-to-air mission. External tanks did not fit into our configuration needs either because our goal was to train the Blue Force in the best techniques for a dogfight with the MiG.

On the top of each wing just inboard of the middle wing fence is the main landing gear indicator. The landing gear indicator is a metal rod several inches long. The rods on our jets were painted red and white like barber poles. When the landing gear is down and locked the metal rod sticks up above the surface of the top of the wing almost as high as the wing fences. When the gear is retracted the rods retract and are not visible. There is a similar indicator for the nose gear on the left side of the fuselage at the "ten" to "eleven o'clock" position just forward of the windscreen.

The engine intake is a large round opening which splits into two ducts just inside the intake lip. The ducts go around the cockpit and rejoin just in front of the inlet stage of the centrifugal flow jet engine. There is a fuel tank between the cockpit and the engine. On the upper lip of the intake of "Fresco C" is a small glass window aperture for the gun camera – the latter never worked very well for us. The film for the camera was quite wide (35mm as I recall), and it was supposed to provide a motion picture when the gun trigger was squeezed. During my time with the jet our avionics specialist Bob Hobson made numerous attempts at getting the camera to work. It was never clear to me whether the problem was with the camera or our photo-lab processing. When we did get an image it was grainy and of little or no value.

The MiG-17 can be equipped with either three 23mm cannons or with two 23mm and one 37mm cannons. The guns are located under the intake on the chin of the fuselage. The guns and ammunition are mounted in a cradle that is lowered on cables for loading and servicing. Later radar-equipped models of the MiG-17 could reportedly carry up to four AA-1 "Alkali" radar guided air-to-air missiles. We made no attempt to replicate this alleged capability in our training program.

The MiG-17 is equipped with a periscope in the canopy directly above the pilot's head when the canopy is closed. The canopy operates by sliding forward and aft on rails, and when it is closed the pilot can glance up and see directly behind the aircraft through the periscope. The image is focused at infinity, and learning to use it is as simple as adapting to a different rearview mirror in an automobile. It is very helpful as the canopy is narrow and tends to restrict the pilot's head movement. The canopy is operated manually. When open, it is held in this position by a pin that locks into the rail mechanism. To close the canopy the pilot lifts up on a knob on the right rail of the canopy itself, disengaging the pin, and allowing the canopy to be pulled forward. It is necessary for the pilot to duck his head slightly to permit the forward canopy bow to pass over his helmet. Once the canopy is closed and locked the pilot is able to resume a normal head posture within the crown of the canopy.

Continuing our walkaround of the aircraft, several antennas would be noted. These were of little interest to us because there was no functional on-board navigation system and the MiG-17 radio communication system had been replaced with a tunable UHF transceiver with its own unique blade antenna.

Finally, returning to the tail of the aircraft, one would note the horizontal stabilizer mounted at about the midpoint on the vertical stabilizer, as well as ports for four flares on the right side of the vertical stabilizer. The flare ports were color coded with four different colors. Fighter aircraft in the 21st century use flares as defensive measures against infrared heat-seeking missiles. In the case of the MiG-17, the flares are not thought to have been for defensive purposes. Instead, they were probably installed to permit the pilot to communicate with the control tower or other ground personnel in the case of radio failure, or during forward operations at remote airfields not equipped for two-way radio communications.

Next, let's climb aboard. One distinctive feature of every MiG-17 or MiG-21 that I have either flown or sat in is the aircraft's very pungent and distinctive smell. I have never been able to isolate the source of the odor, but all that I have been in smell the same, and it is memorable. Perhaps it comes from the insulation on the wiring or some standard cockpit material. I visited one of the national aviation museums that had the open cockpit of a MiG-21 on display. The nose, tail, and wings of the jet had been cut off, leaving just the cockpit. The cockpit section was mounted and stabilized on a pedestal platform, and steps had been fabricated allowing the visitor to climb up and lean into, or even climb into, the cockpit for a good look. I mounted the stepladder and leaned into the cockpit, and immediately noticed the same odor that had characterized the MiGs I had flown.

We didn't preflight the aircraft. The crew chiefs had already done that, and our confidence in them was so high that it was traditional for the pilots to show up, be sure that the seat cushions were the correct height and get in. Getting fitted properly into the cockpit, getting the engine started, managing the pneumatic system, and keeping track of the available fuel on board were major challenges for American pilots.

Seating height is tricky. The ejection seat in the MiG-17 is not adjustable in height so cushions are used to obtain the correct seating height for the pilot. It is desirable to sit as high in the cockpit as possible, without having one's helmet interfere with the periscope or other elements of the canopy. All pilots have different sitting heights, so much time was spent obtaining the right combination of cushions that would provide the correct seating height for each pilot. It was always a worry I had that a critical cushion would disappear and I would go out to fly the jet and not fit properly in it.

Looking around the cockpit before we crank up the engine will reveal other areas of interest. We wore American anti-g suits and backpack parachutes. Our other life-support equipment had fixture modifications to enable us to plug into the oxygen, communications, and anti-g suit aircraft systems. The anti-g suit we wore was a waist down garment that consisted of a belly bladder and bladders over each thigh, all fabricated within the garment. The anti-g suit was donned by first hooking a waist zipper on the left side and then reaching down and zipping up the chaps-like leg components from the inside of each ankle up to just below the crotch. The back of the waist (opposite the belly bladder) and the backs of the legs had strings that could be laced tight to ensure a proper and snug fit. When the bladders inflated the pilot felt an immediate squeeze. The anti-g suit hose plugs into an aircraft hose that supplies high-pressure air from the engine through a valve system. The more g the pilot pulls, the further the valve opens and inflates the bladders in the anti-g suit.

The purpose of the anti-g suit is to help the pilot maintain consciousness during long-duration aircraft maneuvers at up to 6 or 7 g. The combination of the pressure from the anti-g suit and the pilot flexing gut and leg muscles helps keep the blood from pooling in the lower body extremities. This pooling, if not checked, can lead to loss of vision and even unconsciousness.

With increasing aircraft g and without the anti-g suit and the muscle straining effort (called an M-1 maneuver) the pilot will gradually begin to gray out. This means blood loss in the head (due to pooling in the lower body), which causes the pilot's peripheral vision to gradually become increasingly gray, starting on the outside edge of vision. Then, as the g forces continue to pool blood, the pilot's vision will narrow like a doughnut of decreasing size until there in only a point of light followed by black. We call that final event blacking out, and when blacked out the pilot is blind. Gray-out is the onset period and black-out is the final event short of unconsciousness. The pilot is fully awake when blacked out and can continue to fly the aircraft even though blind. The pilot just can't see because blood loss to the eyeballs has a more dramatic effect than blood loss to the brain.

If the high-g event continues, it is possible for the pilot to suffer GLOC (g-induced Loss Of Consciousness), which is a very serious condition because when this happens the pilot relaxes, releases the controls, and runs the risk of hitting the ground before recovering from the unconscious state. It is important to note that the pilot is fully conscious when graying out or even when blacked out.

During gray-out the pilot can usually stop or even reverse the gray-out/black-out process by bearing down on the gut muscles while maintaining aircraft g. Most aircraft have a button that the pilot can push to inflate the anti-g suit manually. When flying an American fighter, it was routine for me to bear down and also push that button with my throttle hand so as to get the suit inflation process started before pulling back on the stick and increasing the aircraft g load to 6 or 7. I viewed this procedure as anticipating and preparing for what was about to happen. I cannot recall whether the MiGs had such a button.

The oxygen system in the MiG-17 is a conventional diluter demand system whose operation is unremarkable. We always wore hard helmets and oxygen masks, with communications equipment built into both.

We strapped in snugly in case of negative g, but not as tightly as an aerobatic pilot.

Among the unfamiliar gauges on the instrument panel are three that are very important. Firstly, the fuel remaining gauge. It bounced around a lot during light turbulence but was generally considered accurate and reliable. Secondly, the engine RPM indicator measured true RPM instead of percent of RPM, and this required a little memory work to set in one's mind the RPM at full Military Power, idle RPM, and other power settings required for safe operation. For example, of special interest to the pilot was the RPM required to ensure that the aircraft was flying at approximately 300 knots of indicated airspeed during the initial approach (prior to the pitch-out for landing). Thirdly, the exhaust gas temperature (EGT) gauge. This was of vital importance, especially during engine start and when the powerplant was being run during ground operations such as routine maintenance.

On the cockpit side panels are various switches and red valves. The latter have a little lever that pops up and serves as a crank for metering emergency air to deal with various systems malfunctions. There are also red-handled lanyards to unlock the landing gear in an emergency. On the left console adjacent to the throttle quadrant are the buttons to push when dialing in the original crystallized radio frequencies.

The trigger for firing the guns is a red lever that lies flush on top of the control column. There is a hinge at the forward end of the lever (closest to the instrument panel). To shoot the gun, after gun switches are properly set, the pilot lifts the red lever and moves it up and forward around the control column to the very front. There is a button on the front of the column, and continuing to squeeze the red lever against the column depresses the button and fires the guns.

Looking straight ahead when sitting in the cockpit, there is a windshield that suffers from distortion due to its thickness and the deteriorating pale orange coating on the glass. Just above the instrument panel is the combining glass that displays the aircraft's gunsight when the proper switches are selected. A set of crosshairs is positioned in the center of the gunsight, with a spanner circle surrounding the crosshairs. The adjustable gunsight spanner is controlled in diameter by twisting the handle on the throttle. It provides the pilot with target range information when set to a specific setting for a known aircraft's wingspan. For example, the spanner would be set to a very large diameter to indicate firing range against a large bomber like a B-52. On the other hand, the spanner circle would be adjusted to a much smaller diameter against a fighter-sized target, cueing the pilot to open fire when he was at the correct range. We did not find much use for this tool, instead preferring to rely on our range estimating judgment.

There are ejection seat foot stirrups designed to prevent leg flailing during ejection. We did not have confidence in the ejection seats and neither thought nor talked much about the possibility of ejection. The need would never happen, we silently told ourselves. The ejection seat had an armrest handle that could be raised, revealing triggers designed to fire the seat. The pilots' thinking about ejection eventually matured, but not before there were some real jolts to the operation starting with the loss of Lt Brown.

To the best of my knowledge, having never seen the accident report, Hugh Brown never attempted to eject during the incident that claimed his life. It is widely believed that he experienced multiple stall/spin/recover events, with the last of these happening at too low an altitude for recovery. Because of security classification and range access restrictions, the men of the Red Eagles had the sad task of reclaiming Lt Brown's remains from the wreckage. This was to be repeated on other occasions.

Eventually, the Red Eagles did have an engine failure in the MiG-17 (on April 8, 1982), resulting in Capt Mark Postai having to belly land the jet in the desert near the TTR airfield. He was not injured, but reported later to a friend that it was a really rough ride, and that he would not do it again. He was later killed upon ejecting from a MiG-23. The belly landing mishap led to the end of MiG-17 flight operations in the CONSTANT PEG program.

Each sortie in the "Fresco" was a memorable experience starting with ground operations. An aircraft maintenance stand positioned next to the aircraft and adjacent to the cockpit was always occupied by a crew chief while we were starting the engine. Because the early Red Eagle pilots did not initially have a lot of experience with the MiGs, our crew chiefs closely supervised the critical steps in getting the engine going. They were furiously protective of their jets, and this was perfectly understandable as they had essentially built them through an extensive restoration process. Like all crew chiefs, they insisted that they only loaned their jets to the pilots to fly, and they expected them to return the MiGs in good shape.

The engine starter is engaged electrically, powered by an external power source upon a signal from the pilot. At that time the engine starts to rotate the throttle is advanced slowly, with the fuel control unit metering fuel into the engine. Ignition is then selected and light-off occurs. The engine slowly accelerates to idle, prompted by slight throttle movements. During the acceleration from light-off to idle there is a great tendency for the engine to overheat, and delicate movement of the throttle fore and aft is required to cause the engine to continue to accelerate, but not exceed the maximum allowed starting temperature even in a brief transit. That would be called an over-temp. The temperature rise can be sudden, and it is detected by the pilot as a sharply increasing temperature trend on the EGT gauge. When that happens the throttle has to be retarded somewhat. The EGT must be kept below the maximum permitted starting temperature to prevent damage to the engine.

Often the crew chiefs would take over the modulation of the throttle during the engine starts, especially during initial pilot checkouts. Like everything else, experience counts, and eventually the pilots got the hang of it and the crew chiefs just watched.

There is a noticeable rumble when the engine lights off and during the initial acceleration toward idle. This is similar to the engine start in a T-33, which also has a centrifugal flow engine. The surface wind is also a factor with a tail wind blowing up the tailpipe tending to exacerbate the over-temp propensity.

So, the crew chiefs always monitored our starts to be sure we weren't too aggressive with the throttle, inducing a hot start and over-temping the engine. Even after the engine is running in idle, advancing the throttle out of idle must be carefully accomplished with one eye on the EGT until about 90 percent of full Military Power RPM is achieved. We were used to gauging power by referring to instruments calibrated in percent of RPM instead of actual engine RPM. Thus, looking at and correctly interpreting power from the actual engine RPM took a little bit of practice.

After a few system checks it is time to taxi. The pneumatic system in the MiG-17 does not have an on-board compressor. A part of the ground crew preparation of the aircraft for flight is to recharge the pneumatic bottles to full capacity. As a result of this non-replenishable supply of compressed air, the pneumatic brakes have only a limited number of applications. I never ran out of compressed air, but I was always conscious of the possibility, and therefore used the brakes as judiciously as possible.

The very long control column is topped with a grip which is big enough for both hands. The column has a brake lever at the "ten o'clock" position if you look down on the column from above. The brakes are applied when the lever is squeezed. To turn the aircraft while taxiing the brake lever is squeezed, applying braking to both main wheels. The brake opposite the intended turn direction is then released, allowing the aircraft to pivot around the other wheel. The pilot releases the brake by pushing the rudder pedal in the direction of the desired turn. So to turn right the pilot squeezes the brake lever and applies right rudder pedal, which releases the left brake and allows the aircraft to turn to the right. The nose wheel just castors. Balancing the power needed to keep the jet rolling along with enough brake to make the turn takes some practice.

This system is a far cry from the electrical nose wheel steering in both modern American aircraft and later models of the MiG (starting with the MiG-23). Even the direct steerage (rudder to the nose wheel) linkage in a Cessna 172 is simpler.

Before the days of nose wheel steering in American jets, aircraft like the T-33 also used a fully swiveling nose gear and individual main gear hydraulic brakes with toe brake control pedals on the top of the rudder pedals. Thus, the jet could be steered on the ground with differential braking.

When new pilots checked out in the MiG-17 they looked like little fish swimming up a trout stream, zigzagging along the taxiways as they proceeded. But, taxiing the MiG-17 is a skill that has to be acquired, and pilots quickly mastered the techniques needed to taxi in a straight line. The slow learners just taxied fast and used the rudder for steering.

Fuel was another issue, as the jet only carried 375 gallons. There just wasn't much on board, and the gauge measured in liters. It took some time to learn how to correlate fuel remaining in liters into flight time remaining in minutes as our brains were calibrated in fuel burn rates measured in pounds of fuel per hour. Liters per minute required some mental adjustments.

Any time a pilot has the chance to fly a high performance single-seat airplane for the first time alone without a preceding checkout in a two-seat model, it is a thrill never forgotten. We had no two-seat MiGs at Tonopah, so every first trip was one of those memorable experiences. I did this twice, once in the MiG-17 and then again in the MiG-21. Before we got to fly the first time we conducted the supervised start and taxied to the runway, closed the canopy, and powered up to full afterburner, rolling 1,000ft or so down the runway prior to selecting idle power and braking to a stop. It was a great warm-up for the next event.

There is one thing I learned about flying the MiGs by myself on the first flight that I have never forgotten. In the years since, I have instructed others to pay attention to this same lesson. That lesson is to ensure you absolutely capture the visual situation at the moment the aircraft lifts off the ground because that is the exact picture the pilot will be looking to see at the moment of landing the first time. At the exact moment of lift-off, note the vertical height above the runway, the location of the horizon on the canopy windshield or relative to the nose of the aircraft, etc. Even minor differences in flap settings do not negate the importance of this lesson when checking out in a new airplane, whether alone or with an instructor.

Let's take this jet for a "spin" around the local area. Supervised start followed by taxi clearance. It is very important to focus on pneumatics on the ground and fuel in the air. Canopy closed and locked, transponder set, power gently up to full throttle, initially keeping one eye on the EGT until the engine is well above idle (about 80 percent power, except we don't have a percent of power indicator). What is the true RPM for 80 percent? Doesn't matter, as I can hear the engine now and I have enough RPM to be more aggressive with the throttle. Okay, I'm at full throttle. Quick check on fuel, EGT, oil, and hydraulics – all good. Let's go.

Release the brake lever. The jet lurches a little off the centerline, so make a tap on the brake to center up on the runway again, throttle forward to full A/B (afterburner), feel the push as the A/B lights, check the EGT – all good, with airspeed building nicely. Rudder is now effective for steering, with a slight adjustment to the centerline using rudder. Control column is "waking up." I can feel the airflow over the elevator. Take-off trim is set so let it accelerate. Nose is lightening and now coming up. A little pitch decrease on the control column to hold that take-off attitude.

STOP! Take a mental snapshot of what it looks like because this little jet is about to fly. Where is the nose relative to the sides of the runway and the mountainous horizon? GOT IT! Now how high am I above the runway? This is where I want to be when I come back to land. GOT IT!

Airborne, little wing waggle as the aileron sensitivity registers. Nice gentle climb attitude. Safely airborne, gear handle UP. The hydraulics are clearly audible as the gear unlocks and retracts. Now, check the little gear indicators. Left wing FLUSH, right wing FLUSH, nose gear FLUSH. Gear handle back to NEUTRAL.

Approaching afterburner termination airspeed. Okay, A/B off NOW! Engine RPM and EGT steady.

Where's that trim lever? Ah, got it. Little nose down trim to deal with the acceleration and we are approaching climb speed. Nose up to zero out the acceleration and climb at the constant airspeed with full Military Power.

WOW!

Visibility out of the aircraft is less than I expected. A lot of head movement is required to look around the windshield superstructure and scan every segment of the sky ahead. I feel like I'm sitting in a hole because the canopy rails are so high. Just my head is above the rails. But the visibility over the nose is good. That's a plus. Let's figure out this periscope. Where is my T-38 chase aircraft? Looking back over my shoulder, I spot him about 1,000ft back and just offset to the left. I'm going to make a slight right turn and then look into the periscope and see if I can find him. Holy smokes, there he is. No eyeball focus adjustments or anything. The periscope is focused at infinity and it is working just as advertised. That's nifty because it sure is hard to turn my head around and look directly behind me. In fact I can't really see the area between "four" and "eight o'clock" without using the periscope.

I don't like that but my helmet bangs the canopy if I try to twist around. Maybe my seating height is too high. No, if I were lower I would not be able to see over the canopy side-rails. I'm going to lean straight ahead as far as I can and then twist at the shoulders and see if that works. It does. I have now figured out how to look back at my "six." Why is that important? It is important because if I am under attack and in a defensive turn I may be able to force the attacker to overshoot. If we are in a left turn, he will go from my "eight o'clock" through my "six" to my "four o'clock" or to line abreast, or even ahead of me. I must be able to follow that event visually so as to time my reversal, taking away his attack advantage and putting me on the offense.

Let's try some turns. Roll response is crisp and easy to stop and start precisely. I wonder how it is without the hydraulic boost on the ailerons. BOOST OFF! Roll now. Hmmm, that is going to take some muscle and maybe require both hands on the control column. Really sluggish with the boost off. Okay, enough test pilot work – BOOST ON!

Fuel is noticeably lower and I've only just gotten airborne.

I need to do some "Lazy 8" climbing and diving turns to get the feel of the pitch and roll at various airspeeds. Okay, there's a good entry airspeed. I have a visual reference point 90 degrees to my left, nose coming up, gentle roll, looking for about 45 degrees nose high at the 45 degrees of turn point. There we are. Roll is continuing, with nose dropping smoothly. Now add some back pressure on the control column to coordinate the turn and allow the nose to drop through the horizon after 90 degrees of turn and at 90 degrees of bank. Very nice if I do say so myself.

Let's knock this off and try a stall, but first note that a stall in an airplane is different from a stalled car. The stalled car stops moving usually due to an engine or transmission failure. A stalled airplane simply does not have enough speed to generate lift over the wings. When an airplane stalls the nose usually drops, and if there is sufficient altitude below the airplane, speed builds and the wing starts to generate lift again. People that don't fly fear the dreaded stall. Aviators want to be able to recognize the approach to the stall and ensure the airspeed is enough to keep the wing flying.

Now our MiG airspeed is pretty slow so the stall should come quickly as we slow down. Aircraft configuration is clean, nose is coming up to make things happen a little faster, a little wing rock, but okay, and now the nose shutters and drops as the wing loses lift. Now, power up, release back pressure, and, as airspeed builds, smoothly pull the nose up to the horizon, avoiding a secondary stall. If the recovery is too aggressive the jet might dissipate airspeed needed to fly and enter another stall situation. We call that a secondary stall.

Okay, that stall was about what I expected. Let's try it again with a little more power and in a bank. Here we go. Nose is coming up to 25–30 degrees above the horizon, airspeed is dropping, WOW, sharp nose drop with an associated wing drop that was dramatic. That got my attention. Leveling the wings with rudder while adding power, I release back pressure and all is well.

Next, gear handle down, check the gear indicators, gear handle neutral. Lower the wing flaps to simulate landing and now let's slow down and see how the stall feels with the gear and flaps extended in the landing configuration. Airspeed slows, and light burble can be felt through the control column due to the turbulence of the air over the flight controls as the wing loses life. Nose drops, power up, milk the nose up to the horizon with back pressure, avoiding over control in pitch. That makes for a smooth, powered recovery.

Now let's do slow flight. Obtain final approach airspeed, level flight, and stabilize the altitude and airspeed. Make some gentle turns each way, power back slightly, lower the nose, and attain a final approach attitude with a stable airspeed and a gentle descent. Now nose up until the stall approach shutter. Rudder to keep the wings level. Power to recover. Positive climb as in a go-around, gear up. Check indicators, gear handle neutral. Flaps up.

If I wasn't just about out of gas I'd be ready to take a perch on my chase plane and do some BFM. However, the last bit of gas is best used shooting a couple of traffic patterns and low approaches before the red light comes on, indicating low fuel and time to land. So BFM will have to wait until the next sortie.

Remember to grab that landing attitude site picture that was taken during take-off. Note the nose relative to the end of the runway and to the runway edges and judge the height above touchdown. A gentle squeak as the rubber meets the runway and that trip is behind me.

In flight the throttle wasn't quite so sensitive, but as a group the Red Eagle MiG-17 pilots always respected the engine and treated it with care. After all, it was the only one we had.

The landing gear handle is located on the left side of the instrument panel. The handle has three positions – down, neutral, and up. Reviewing the landing gear operational sequence, the handle is always in neutral, except when the gear is being raised or lowered. After take-off, to raise the landing gear the handle is moved to the up position until the undercarriage is up and locked. Then it is moved to neutral. A similar sequence follows for lowering the gear – handle is moved from neutral to down, and then back up to neutral after the gear is down and locked. This procedure required some thought for US pilots whose experience was limited to the up-down gear handle of American aircraft. The reasoning for the gear handle being returned to neutral related to removing the hydraulic pressure from the system once the gear was locked up or down.

There is no elevator trim switch on the control column. Instead, there is a lever on the left canopy rail which operates the trim. The electrical switch is spring loaded to the horizontal position, with the handle pointing aft. Trim is adjusted by momentarily pushing the lever up or down with the throttle hand until control pressures are neutralized on the control column.

When in flight the MiG-17 is very difficult to see from the direct front or rear, but it becomes very visible at close range as soon as it initiates a turn. Indeed, the MiG provided a distinctive visual planform.

The MiG-17's wing loading is low, giving the jet excellent turn performance. In fact it turns more like a Cessna than a jet fighter. Combat gun camera photographs taken over Vietnam reveal that F-105 pilots engaging MiG-17s were only able to drag the gunsight through the VPAF fighter by pointing initially well in front of the MiG. As the enemy pilot increased his defensive turn, his USAF opponent was unable to match the turn rate and was forced to make a slashing gun attack.

The MiG-17 was a lot of fun to fly once you were airborne. It could be a challenge to taxi, however.

The jet's pitch performance was very good, and airspeed could generally be maintained in a 4 to 5 g hard turn at or above 300 KIAS if afterburner was selected. While the aircraft turned well at low and moderate airspeed, the faster you flew the more muscle it took to move the control column. This was especially true with roll commands to the aircraft, even with the hydraulically boosted ailerons. The long control column had an elongated grip, which offered significant leverage when compared with US fighters and their hydraulically actuated controls. I often used both hands on the MiG-17 control column, usually with the throttle locked forward in full afterburner.

We found that the aircraft was very honest overall. When the control column was pulled back aggressively and the aircraft was forced into a high angle of attack as in a hard defensive turn, it had a tendency to snap roll in the opposite direction of the turn if any aileron was applied – a classic adverse yaw reaction. This characteristic was used by VPAF pilots to secure a tactical advantage when they were under attack by F-4s. The hard turn would force the Phantom II to overshoot the MiG's turn circle. The snap roll could easily be stopped after about 90 degrees of roll by releasing back pressure on the control column, resulting in the MiG pilot achieving a near perfect position to get off a gun shot at the overshooting F-4. This was a major learning point as we taught the American pilots how to fight the MiG-17 and win.

The white stripe down the center of the instrument panel existed on all three MiG types that we had at TTR. Its purpose, according to Soviet literature associated with the jets, is to provide a visual reference for centering the control column fully forward should an out-of-control flight situation occur. I never used it in the MiG-21, but an outside rolling departure was a regular event in the MiG-17, and the airplane always recovered when I centered the control column on the white stripe.

To sum the MiG-17 up, the little jet is honest and fun to fly. It turns well horizontally and can be hard to see visually, but it doesn't have much sustainability in a climbing situation, with the airspeed dissipating rapidly when the nose is pulled up. In a dive the control column gets very stiff in both roll and pitch as airspeed increases above 400–450 knots. Indeed, it becomes necessary to use two hands on the control column either to roll or change the pitch with added g.

MiG-17 TACTICS AND COUNTERTACTICS

I loved flying this little airplane once I learned to taxi it with confidence. I would take off and climb out, and the jet would just zoom along and do whatever I asked of it. It made its own sounds and had its own smell, but that gradually became a part of the love affair. There was a noticeable wallow or Dutch Roll tendency that could have been eliminated with a yaw damper. But, the MiG-17 didn't have a yaw damper so we just wallowed along. Rudder was effective to some degree in dampening out the wallow, but unless engaged in a dogfight and in a shooting position, I usually didn't worry about the wallow and let the jet do its thing.

The MiG-17 was similar to a light aircraft in that the roll into a turn was noticeably more crisp if it was led slightly with a touch of rudder in the direction of turn. This overcame the initial adverse yaw from the drag on the aileron on the rising wing.

The gunsight was another story, and I can absolutely understand why gun attacks by the MiG tended to be at very short range. If the control column was pulled back in an effort to match a defender's turn, the gunsight would move lower and lower on the combining glass above the instrument panel until, with 4 to 6 g on the jet, it completely disappeared, masked under the nose of the aircraft.

I have often read about World War II pilots driving in for the kill, opening fire, and then adjusting their aim based on the tracers, with little regard for the gunsight. I think the MiG-17 was a similar challenge. So, to kill with the gun fitted in the "Fresco" the name of the game was to get close, let her rip, and adjust from there. Our TAC training rules specified a minimum of 1,000ft behind the adversary in a gun attack, and this would probably have been out of range for an accurate gunshot with the 37mm or the 23mm cannons fitted in this aircraft.

THE MiG-21

Like the MiG-17, all of our MiG-21s at the beginning of the CONSTANT PEG program were silver. The US star and bar on the nose of the jet was only seen during the HAVE DOUGHNUT exploitation program. Later, in the early 1980s, the fighters were painted to replicate Soviet client states' camouflage schemes, and a great variety of different paint jobs resulted.

Airspeed in an aircraft is determined by the pitot-static system. The pitot tube is pointed straight into the wind stream, which is the source of ram air. The pitot tube port measures the ambient air pressure, and by comparing readings the cockpit instrumentation reports the aircraft's speed through the air mass. As the jet climbs to higher altitude the air is less dense and, therefore, the indicated airspeed decreases even though the speed across the ground is the same.

Pilots learn the airspeed sequence early on in their training, and most use the mnemonic crutch ICE-T, or phonetically "ice tea," to keep it all straight when they are learning. Indicated (I) is the speed read on the airspeed indicator in the cockpit. Calibrated (C) is the adjustment for installation errors associated with the pitot-static system. There is a chart for each different aircraft to convert this speed. Equivalent (E) is the adjustment for transonic airflow during flight near the speed of sound. Another chart makes this conversion. Finally, True (T) airspeed is the speed of the aircraft across the ground in a no-wind situation.

Pilots fly indicted airspeed for take-off and landing and calculate an indicated airspeed for climbs and cruise. For navigation purposes the airspeed is converted to true airspeed and the wind effect is added. At higher speeds pilots also use the Mach number as a reference. Mach 1 is the speed of sound. Airspeed at less than Mach 1, for example 0.9, is subsonic. Airspeed at and above Mach 1 is supersonic. Both indicated airspeed and Mach number were displayed on the instrumentation we put into the MiGs.

So, the airspeed interpretation process starts with the ram air coming in the pitot tube of the aircraft. In our MiGs, the pitot tube was mounted in a boom on the wingtip of the MiG-17 and under the chin of the intake opening in the early-model MiG-21. Close examination of the pitot boom on the MiG-21 reveals little horizontal and vertical vanes that provide pitch and yaw errors from flight straight and true through the air. These inputs are converted into electrical signals, which are then sent to the aircraft's gunsight. On our "Fishbed C/E" aircraft the pitot boom was mounted on the engine intake at the "six o'clock" or chin position. In the later versions of the MiG-21 the pitot boom was moved first to the "twelve o'clock" position above the intake, and then in the newest aircraft to the "two o'clock" position.

Because of the location of the pitot boom on the chin of the intake it was in the way when the aircraft was towed during ground movement operations. This made the boom vulnerable to damage. As a result the pitot boom has a lockable hinge point under the chin that can be unlocked to allow the boom to tilt up and out of the way of the tow equipment for ground operations. This tilted pitot boom position is evident in some of the ground operations photographs, and should not be confused with the locked down straight ahead position. When locked down the boom is parallel to the longitudinal axis of the aircraft, which is obviously necessary during flight operations.

The early MiG-21 had guns, the mid-life version did not, and a new gun made a reappearance in the final variants. So, the pitot tube was out of the way of the gunsight in early versions of the aircraft because of the chin mounting. The mid-life MiG had the pitot boom at "twelve o'clock" on the intake, but that didn't matter since the jet had no gun. With the later model the pitot was moved to the "two o'clock" position, and thus the pilot was able to use the gunsight without visual interference from the pitot tube.

The nose cone in the center of the intake moves in and out to control the position of the shock wave during supersonic flight of the aircraft. Obviously the air is not supersonic. Instead, it is the aircraft flying through the air at supersonic speed that creates a supersonic bow wave. To analyze the airflow when the aircraft is flying at supersonic speeds, it is both convenient and accurate to imagine the aircraft to be still and the airflow supersonic. Supersonic air is incompressible like water. So, when supersonic air slows to a lower speed an oblique or angled shock wave is formed, with the faster supersonic air in front and the slower supersonic air behind the shock wave. It is a sudden change in velocity at the physical point of the shock wave. The supersonic air encountering the angled intake cone causes the air to slow and a shock wave forms.

On the other hand subsonic air is compressible and changes in velocity are smoother and without a shock wave. Typically, supersonic air will slow first through a series of oblique shock waves as it moves up the intake cone and slows down. The air is still supersonic on both sides of the oblique shock wave as the air decelerates. Each successive shock wave is closer to vertical. The final shock wave, with supersonic air on one side and subsonic air on the other, is 90 degrees to the airflow and is called a normal shock wave (versus an oblique shock wave).

A complete science exists for predicting the angle of oblique shock waves, and the difference in air velocity on each side. Aeronautical engineers can measure the angle of the shock wave and make determinations about the change in speed.

The reason for the moveable cone in the intake is to ensure that the normal shock wave is outside the intake because the engine is not capable of accepting supersonic or incompressible air. That makes sense when you think about it because the roll of the compressor stage of a jet engine is to compress the air. You can't compress incompressible air. And, if a turbojet engine "swallows" the shock wave and supersonic air enters the engine compressor, a compressor stall will follow, usually accompanied by a flameout of the engine. This can be an unsettling event for the pilot because the compressor stall is accompanied by a very loud bang and, typically, fire from the intake, even when the aircraft is flying at supersonic speeds. Pilots have reported the violence of the compressor stall knocking their feet off the rudder pedals. Usually the event does not damage the engine, and if the engine does flame out, it can generally be restarted.

These are aeronautical facts about the physics of airflow, and the MiG-21 design engineers took them into account when they created the moveable cone in the center of the jet's intake. Practically speaking such issues were of little significance to us during our time flying the "Fishbed" from TTR. The nose cone movement is generally automatic, but it has a manual feature. The nose cone is fully activated at 1.5 Mach in this model of the MiG-21. We seldom ever flew at speeds even close to Mach 1.5.

The landing gear indicator on the MiG-21 is similar to that on the MiG-17. The undercarriage indicator is silver on the static display aircraft outside the Aggressor Squadron building at Nellis AFB. Someday we will get the gear indicator painted correctly in a red and white barber pole design. That particular MiG-21 is the jet we knew as "04" at Tonopah. It was restored to flyable status by MSgt Tommy Karnes, with a lot of help from his brothers. When the jet was put on static display in front of the Aggressor Squadron, the touch-up paint efforts spread to the landing gear indicators, and they came out silver instead of red and white.

The early MiG-21 has a very busy cockpit. I remember strapping into it for the first time and turning to my crew chief, Don Lyon, and jokingly said, "Don I'll never be able to fly this thing." He asked, "Why not Boss?" I responded, "Look at all those switches (on the right side panel of the cockpit). They aren't marked in English and I'll never be able to remember which ones go where." Don responded with his own joke, "No sweat Boss. They all go either up or forward!" That took a weight off my mind. In fact most of the switches were for the largely inoperative weapons system and had been disconnected from electrical power.

As with the MiG-17, the airspeed indicators and altimeters in the MiG-21 had been replaced with instruments calibrated in knots and feet instead of kilometers per hour and meters. The four- or five-channel original crystallized radio was also swapped out for a tunable UHF transceiver set. Finally, the jet was equipped with a 4096 code transponder, making it compatible with western air traffic control radars.

The three most notable non-instrument related features of the cockpit include the thick combining glass component of the windscreen, the head bumper, and the white stripe down the middle of the instrument panel.

The combining glass in the windscreen actually consists of several layers of glass. The major component is several inches thick and is said to be bulletproof, having been designed and manufactured specifically to protect the pilot when attacking bombers with tail guns. The thick windscreen coupled with the superstructure around the glass severely restricted forward visibility.

The head bumper is a black padded component on the gunsight at the top of the instrument panel. It is there in case the pilot is thrust forward in the cockpit, at which point his head would hit the bumper rather than the metal of the gunsight.

The control column in this aircraft, like the one in the MiG-17, was longer than the western fighter aircraft that I had the opportunity to fly – the F-4, F-5, and F-15. The leverage afforded by the extra length allowed both hands to grip the control column. This proved handy when flying at high speeds, when extra muscle was required to move the controls.

The early MiG-21s also had a helmet protector at the top of the ejection seat in the form of a curved metal flap hinged at the back. It could be lifted up to facilitate the pilot entering the cockpit. Once he was strapped in, the helmet protector was lowered, and it remained attached to the ejection seat between the helmet and the canopy itself. The canopy is hinged at the front of the cockpit in this model of the MiG-21. Others models had canopies that were either side-mounted or aft hinged.

The ejection sequence commences with the pilot raising one of the red handles adjacent to the seat and squeezing the trigger. As the seat goes up the rail the aft part of the canopy attaches to the ejection seat while the forward part of the canopy detaches from the aircraft. Therefore, the pilot is ejected in a cocoon-like contraption, with the canopy protecting him from the windblast. Subsequent events jettison the canopy and separate the pilot from the seat. Seat separation is followed by parachute deployment and descent under the parachute canopy.

The gear handle operates in a similar fashion to the MiG-17, with a neutral position as well as up and down. To raise the gear move the handle up from neutral. When the gear indicates up, return the gear handle to neutral. Lowering procedure is similar.

There are buttons that electrically control the wing flaps when pushed.

The aircraft can also be configured with a centerline fuel tank, but it doesn't hold much fuel and only nominally extends the range and endurance. Taxiing the MiG-21 is very similar to taxiing the MiG-17 in that the "Fishbed" also has a fully castored nose wheel and a pneumatic braking system. Steering the aircraft requires the same technique as used in the MiG-17 – to turn right, squeeze the brake lever mounted at the "ten o'clock" position on the control column and push the right rudder. There is also a nose wheel brake that is switch selectable. It is only used during the landing rollout.

I had a chance to fly a Yak-18-inspired Chinese-built Nanchang CJ-6 in the summer of 2008. This prop aircraft had the same braking system, and the instructor I flew with was amazed that I could taxi the aircraft accurately. He had no idea about my background with the MiGs!

The stabilator or "stab," as it is known to fighter pilots and jet mechanics, is hydraulically operated. It includes a ratio controller to manage control authority below 16,000ft, above 32,000ft, and at very high velocity or airspeed. High speed is often called high-q.

The rudder is manually operated, while the ailerons are also basically manual but with a hydraulic boost similar to the system fitted in the T-33.

The axial flow engine in the MiG-21 is slow to spool up, requiring about 15 seconds to accelerate from idle to MIL (Military Power) or full throttle without afterburner. Afterburner light-off requires another three to five seconds after reaching MIL.

At about 30 knots the rudder becomes effective for directional control. To conserve compressed air for the brakes most MiG pilots taxied the aircraft fast enough for the rudder to become effective for steering.

On take-off the engine is run up to MIL power, brakes are released, and the afterburner is selected. The jet accelerates rapidly and back pressure is applied to rotate the aircraft at about 140 knots. The jet becomes airborne at about 170 knots, the landing gear is raised, and the MiG-21 is accelerated to about 300 knots, at which time afterburner is deselected. Acceleration continues in MIL power until reaching 400 knots, at which time the pilot increases back pressure on the control column so as to climb at a constant 400 knots IAS to 0.88 Mach, which is then maintained all the way to altitude.

When CONSTANT PEG was originally declassified the only photographs immediately available were from HAVE DRILL/FERRY and HAVE DOUGHNUT. Since then many images of CONSTANT PEG MiG-21 operations have been located, and some are included in the photo section.

IKE CRAWLEY TROUBLESHOOTS A MiG-21 ENGINE

Ben Galloway, one of our AGE specialists, told me a wild story about a Spiderman-like moment in the life of Ike Crawley, the first Red Eagle jet engine mechanic.

Ike and another Red Eagle had the MiG with the cranky engine on a makeshift engine trim pad, where they were troubleshooting the problem. The jet was tied down, with one Red Eagle in the cockpit and Crawley outside the aircraft checking various open panel accesses to the engine. Ike was wearing googles and a headset and microphone assembly on so that he could talk to his compatriot in the cockpit. Evidently the problem was a malfunction in the afterburner section of the engine, and to isolate the problem Ike determined he needed to look up the tailpipe of the jet with the engine running in full afterburner.

Some distance behind the jet was a chain link fence. Ike positioned himself up against the fence and instructed the Red Eagle mechanic in the cockpit to select afterburner. Ike inched himself directly into the jet exhaust while continuing to lean against the fence. As the engine developed afterburner thrust the jet exhaust blast literally pinned Crawley to the chain link. Free from the effects of the earth's gravity due to the overpowering jet blast, Ike was able to maneuver himself on the fence as though he were a spider on the wall. He worked his way up the fence with his feet completely off the ground in an effort to get a better view up the tailpipe.

Deciding that there was some asymmetrical problem with the way the afterburner was operating, Ike then slowly worked himself around in a circle while pinned to the fence. At one point he was inverted, and he would have crashed to the ground on his head but for the jet blast of the engine, which continued to pin him to the fence.

The original Spiderman, Ike Crawley.

"Thug" Matheny ("Bandit 27") and the Canopy Implosion (crosshead)

Jim "Thug" Matheny was one of our most experienced MiG pilots thanks to the high number of sorties he flew in both the MiG-21 (240) and the MiG-23 (142).

Among "Thug's" most memorable experiences during his CONSTANT PEG flight operations is the day a MiG-21 canopy imploded on him at more than 500 knots. The mission was scheduled to be one-versus-one with an F-15 from the FWS. As best anybody can remember the assigned area was probably Range 71 N in restricted area 4807A – due west of TTR, with Mud Lake in the northwest corner. "Thug" recollects that the mission was east of TTR, but he can't explain how he could have gotten to a location that would tempt him to land on Mud Lake. He reflected with a smile, "Maybe I got there after the main event when the airplane was taking me along wherever it wanted to go."

This is what happened. He and the Eagle joined up and "Thug" directed his opponent into fighting wing for the first demonstration maneuver. With both aircraft at about 550 KIAS and the MiG in full afterburner, the plan was for "Thug" to execute a 6 g 180-degree level turn in full afterburner to show the F-15 pilot the comparative airspeed bleed rates of the two aircraft. The Eagle driver was briefed to expect to need to retard power out of afterburner, and judiciously manage the F-15 power and perhaps even use the speed brake to keep him from overshooting the MiG. "Thug" knew that the MiG would slow to just over 200 KIAS in this turn – a loss of more than 300 knots of airspeed.

The Eagle pilot called "Ready" when he was in position and "Thug" sharply banked the MiG and applied back pressure on the control column to increase the g. As the g forces built "Thug" banked the MiG as necessary to maintain the level turn. All was going as planned, and briefed. Suddenly, the MiG-21's canopy imploded with a thunderous crash, nearly impaling "Thug" with shards of Plexiglas. To say he was dazed momentarily would be an understatement. Regaining his faculties after a few seconds, he realized that his helmet was battered and his oxygen mask and communications microphone were gone. "Thug" was riding a high-speed convertible that was taking him wherever it wanted to go. As the fog started to clear in his head, he realized he was pointing straight down with the engine still in full afterburner.

"Thug" was bleeding heavily from the canopy shard wounds to his head and upper body. He continued to be distracted further by the need to grasp pieces of the canopy that were all around him in the cockpit and throw them overboard. Realizing that sudden death due to collision with the ground was imminent, he considered ejecting, but quickly dismissed the idea due to uncertainties in his dazed mind. Did he have enough altitude to eject safely and would the seat work? He didn't have confidence in its operability, so he grasped the controls, pulled the throttle out of afterburner and hammered on the g necessary to recover from the high-speed dive.

Following the implosion the jet had started to vibrate violently, and this was causing severe pain in "Thug's" arms and shoulders. It was like a thousand needles being jammed into him over and over and then being extracted. When the imaginary needles were extracted they felt as though they had grown fishhooks on their ends. This excruciating pain only subsided when the jet was eventually slowed to under 200 knots.

Meanwhile, the Eagle pilot had lost sight of the MiG and the GCI controller was becoming frantic, knowing that all was not well but being totally ignorant as to what had happened. GCI was still talking to the F-15 pilot, and together they were trying to find "Thug" and his MiG-21. By this time "Thug" had recovered from the screaming dive, but was dealing with other issues. Moving his head only inches left or right subjected him to the violent slipstream. With blood in his eyes and pretty much all over his upper torso, "Thug" continued to heave large chunks of the canopy Plexiglas overboard after extracting each piece from various locations in the cockpit. In some cases the pieces were interfering with the flight controls and electrical switches.

At this point "Thug's" decision making process was still severely inhibited, and upon seeing Mud Lake he decided to land the jet on the dry lakebed. The undercarriage came down and he suddenly realized he could not see out of the aircraft straight ahead because the bulletproof combining glass of the gunsight had completely crazed and was opaque. As he tilted his head left and right to look around the combining glass the wind blasting around the shattered canopy remnants battered his head.

Determined to get the jet on the ground safely, his head suddenly started to clear and he realized that the engine was running fine. With the intake well ahead of the canopy, the engine had thus experienced no debris ingestion damage. Then "Thug" saw that there was only a low mountain ridge separating him from the TTR airfield. "Why land on the lakebed?" he asked himself. "Let's just turn in the other direction and land at the TTR airfield." That decision made and the turn reversal complete, the Eagle suddenly zoomed past him. The F-15 pilot was now badly overshooting the GCI rendezvous that he and the radar controller had so frantically put together.

Ignoring the Eagle, "Thug" concentrated on landing the aircraft. He was now lined up with the TTR runway, landing gear and flaps were down and he was able to cheat a quick peak at the touchdown zone around the combining glass before the slipstream blast battered his head back into the relative calm behind the windscreen. The Eagle was joined up now and the pilot radioed to base that the MiG was inbound without a canopy. "Thug" landed without fuss and deployed the drag 'chute, braking to a halt.

Nobody on the ground really knew what had happened or had had much warning that "Thug" was inbound. Rushing to the aircraft, the ground crew found that the jet's cockpit was covered in blood and small pieces of Plexiglas. It appears that "Thug" didn't look too red hot either, but he was alive and the jet was spared.

The MU-2 airlift aircraft became an air ambulance, taking "Thug" back to Nellis. The doctors looked him over and cleaned him up, and the remaining Red Eagles headed for the bar. The rest of the story of what happened next is lost in the fog of alcohol.

We later learned that the Russians changed canopies every few hundred hours in their MiG-21s – this jet had a lot more flying hours than that with the same canopy. Thankfully, we had unnamed, but much appreciated, craftsmen that were able to make us new canopies.

Bob "Bro" Breault added the following footnote to Jim Matheny's wild experience in the MiG-21:

Danny Nichols, a Non-Destructive Inspection specialist, was assigned the task of finding a defense contractor to manufacture replacement canopies (and frames) made of Lexan so they would be safer and last longer. He worked with several agencies and accomplished the mission with outstanding results. For this, I wrote him up for a Meritorious Service Medal, which he received. To my knowledge he is the only Red Eagle to receive an MSM.

FIGHTING THE MiG-21

I was sent the following first-hand account by Marine Corps F-4 pilot Mike "Wassa" Mattimoe, who fought against the MiG-21 during his unit's deployments to Red Flag in the early 1980s:

My second trip out to Nellis was an interesting time. It was my last deployment in the F-4, and the schedule was CONSTANT PEG one week, then into Red Flag. I was fighting HQ Marine Corps to get my orders changed so that I could get into the then brand new Hornet as quickly as possible, but had had little luck throughout the time I was in Nevada. On Friday – the last day we were there – I was on the schedule to finally go up north, but only as a lead for a first lieutenant, who was to get the entire period with the MiG-21 flown by Maj George C. "Cajun" Tullos ("Bandit 37"), an old F-4 IP buddy of mine from MCAS Yuma, Arizona.

Before stepping to the jet, I finally found out that my orders had been changed and I was heading for the Hornet.

After startup, my wingman's jet went down. I asked ops if I should give him my F-4 or just cancel. They consulted all the satellite overflights and whatever else they look at and told me to go solo and take the whole period. When I checked in with "Cajun" he said that since I had been there before we would skip all the performance comparisons and perches and the fight was on! I actually flew as well as I would have expected, getting away clean in one neutral fight and going what I thought was slightly offensive on the other. At that point "Cajun" called that he had a flame out and, as had been briefed, he did not make any other calls in order to save the juice (electrical power) to restart. I drifted down with him in silence, calling out an occasional altitude until I saw a puff of smoke at around 7,000ft and he said he was relit and returning to base.

When I landed at Nellis, I knew that I had two months left in the squadron (one of which would be at Tactical Air Control Party school for my new assignment with the grunts) and that I would never fly the F-4 again – I had decided to make this memorable sortie fighting a MiG-21 my last ride in the "lead sled." When I got back into the ready room I announced that I was buying at happy hour, and to my surprise the entire squadron showed up at 1630hrs sharp. Before closing my tab out 90 minutes later, I had ordered a round of 32 kamikazes, which were made on a large tray. Starting a long-standing tradition, the buyer had to also drink the spillage on the tray. Later that night it was "no autopsy, no foul" game of crud (played on a snooker table) with the air force that eventually led to toilet paper mascots and a mild attempt at a bar fight.

I don't know how they are training the young fighter pilots in America today with no strippers at happy hour, no Clark AFB, and no NAS Cubi Point, but I know there was no better training to be had than the training I got that day!

A few years later, I had a 1963 Pontiac Catalina whilst at El Toro (Naval Air Station, CA). When the 4477th bogey drivers found out they were being shit-canned (in 1988), a group of them flew over to El Toro to drown away their sorrows. There were somewhere between ten and twelve of them – not happy campers. Not only were they getting shut down, but the orders the boys were getting were not pretty either. I tossed them the keys to the big Catalina and off they went with two in the trunk. The car made it back the next day, but it did not smell very good...

This unnamed veteran pilot also engaged the MiG-21 in the Phantom II during the 1980s:

While flying F-4s from George AFB, California, I had the opportunity to go against a MiG-21. Part of a recently declassified project, some folks were allowed onto the Nellis range that housed MiG-17s, MiG-21s, and MiG-23s. I led a two-ship, with George AFB's wing commander as my observer and No 2 man. "Lucky me" as it turns out.

After a rendezvous with the MiG-21, so as to gain an appreciation of its performance, we proceeded on our briefed plan that included my No 2 going high to observe a one-versus-one set-up. I was to be on the receiving end. Naturally, the MiG-21, due to his size and slim profile, disappeared from sight. But we quickly regained a tally as he came in from about "five o'clock," with good overtake. I put a moderately high g turn on him, moved him out to "four o'clock." And as he reached a range of about 1,500ft behind me, I laid all the g I could legally muster from the F-4. The MiG-21 appeared to overshoot.

At this point I should have recalled those g maneuverability charts that I regularly instructed to the young lieutenants in the squadron. If I had done that I would have dropped my F-4's nose and started a "jinking extension" so as to get out of the MiG-21's gun range, and later re-enter on my own terms. Instead, my "fangs punctured my oxygen mask."

With the mindset "I can do this!" I kept gs on the F-4, stomping its top rudder to reverse nose high. But I soon found the MiG-21 not out in front of me but 100ft line abreast off my left wing in loose formation. I eased the F-4 into as "pure" a vertical move as I could. I thought I really had him now!

Hah, not so fast! The MiG-21's nose dropped slightly instead of falling off, but "Big Ugly" (F-4) was slowing below 200 knots, and I knew I wouldn't be able to control the jet's nose direction much longer. And in that energy state the F-4's nose will drop and the jet will then dive for the center of the earth – it may even go end-over-end in a tumble, if the pilot mistakenly moves the stick left or right, introducing a touch of aileron.

What happened next made my eyes water.

The MiG-21 wasn't falling off! The pilot simply altered trajectory, leisurely drifted back to my "six," where, slowing down through 120 KIAS, he had enough stick authority to ease his nose back up and "gun out" my few remaining brains.

MiG-21 Crew Chief John "JD" Dvorachek

The following are extracts from a seven-minute talk that John Dvorchak gave at the Evergreen Air and Space Museum in McMinnville, Oregon, in August 2009. The talk was given on the occasion of the dedication of a MiG-21 restored to replicate the CONSTANT PEG "Fishbed" known as "Red 84." The jet's assigned pilot was Maj Charles E. "Smokey" Sundell ("Bandit 58") and "JD" was his crew chief:

I was a late arrival at the Red Eagles. By that I mean, unlike in the early days, by the time I got there everyone wore uniforms, had haircuts and was in compliance with air force grooming standards. I came from the Thunderbirds, and some referred to the Tonopah operation as a Thunderbird retirement home because we had found some place to go after the Thunderbirds that allowed us to stay in Las Vegas.

While on the Thunderbirds I didn't know what happened at Tonopah, but I knew it was a tight-knit group that worked hard and played hard. I knew it was something special and I wanted to be a part of it. I was never disappointed.

The unit had terrific corporate knowledge that was passed from the old guys to the new guys. The MiG is a simple little airplane, especially the MiG-21. With a set of metric tools you could buy at Home Depot and a set of four-way screwdrivers, you could get a lot of maintenance completed on the little jet.

It always amazed me that my pilot, "Smokey" Sundell, could be in a fierce dogfight at 40,000ft one minute and the next we would be refueling the jet and pushing it into the barn, as we called the hangar, for the night. Once it was put away we would jump on an airplane and head home for the night, but we couldn't talk about our day at work once we got home. It just seemed like things happened so quickly.

We had good duty – far better than the guys working on the rubber jets (F-117 stealth fighters) at the northern end of the airfield. They worked all day and then got to work all night too. We got to go home most nights. They didn't like us very much.

When I left the Thunderbirds I ended up with an extra pair of deerskin gloves, and when I was assigned as "Smokey's" crew chief I gave him the gloves. He was really proud of those gloves. "Smokey" never forgot who was responsible for ensuring his jet was safe to fly, and he always was respectful and appreciative toward the maintenance team.

Among those of us gathered here today at the Evergreen Air and Space Museum I see my old friends Ike Crawley and Ben Galloway. Ike was a jet engine specialist and Ben worked the AGE, including the aircraft starting units and other devices necessary to either operate the jets or work on them. We all really enjoyed our jobs and working with the officers that flew the jets.

To this day my interest in aviation has continued. I am working as an FAA safety inspector in Fort Worth. As they say, like father, like son. My son just completed training as an air force aviation mechanic and was an honor graduate. He will be working on KC-10 aircraft for his initial assignment. So, like those that taught me to work on MiGs, I passed down my profession to my son. The training on the MiGs was also passed down through the generations, and for the most part guys stayed there and worked on the jets for a long time. It would have been wrong to just have them there for two years and then post them way to do something else.

I got to fly in the T-38 with "Smokey" one day and was very proud that I didn't get air sick. I kept the barf bag close and my cockpit temperature as cold as I could get it. That did the trick. "Smokey" and I had our picture taken together in front of our MiG after the flight. It was really special.

After the dedication and talk, "JD" and "Smokey" posed for a picture in front of the replica of MiG-21 "Red 84" approximately 21 years after the original photograph was taken.

"Tonopah Tommy" Karnes Rebuilds a MiG-21

I visited Tommy Karnes and his wife Sarah in Knob Noster, Missouri, in April 2009. At the time Tommy and Sarah lived in Herculaneum, Missouri, near St Louis. I alerted them that I had an upcoming trip to Whiteman AFB in Knob Noster, and they decided to drive over and meet me for dinner and a chat. I was at Whiteman with the F-22 Weapons School instructors working with the USAF's other low observable platform, the B-2. We all stayed in the Econo Lodge on Route 50 in Knob Noster. We sat down in the motel for a couple of hours and then had dinner in nearby Panther's restaurant. Dinner was good, but don't look for the restaurant on any of the big name websites. Fortunately, I had a cocktail prior to leaving the motel, as sweet tea was as good as the beverage menu got at Panther's. The salad bar and steak were agreeable, however.

Tommy and Sarah had been married, had children, and then got divorced. Later in life they remarried, and that is why I didn't know Sarah during my time at TTR. Tommy had been married to Valerie during the Red Eagle days. My observation is that Tommy finally showed great judgment by getting back together with Sarah, as she is one super lady!

We chatted about old times and where we had all been living since the Red Eagles. Tommy and I had run into each other again at Kadena in 1983. By then he had retired and had taken a job as a crew chief for the F-86s that were towing the air-to-air Dart targets. His company was on contract to tow the targets for the F-15-equipped 18th TFW at Kadena and other air-to-air units in the western Pacific. I was amazed to find Karnes, Hovermale, and Lyon working that contract when I showed up at Kadena as the deputy commander for operations in 1983.

In the motel in Knob Noster, Tommy offered me a beer and we started to chat. I asked, "How did you build a MiG-21 from whatever you started with? Was it a wreck or in pieces or what?" Tommy, always humble, replied that it wasn't too hard. The jet was pretty simple, especially by current standards. I pressed the question. He went on to say that he was originally assigned to the MiG-21 known as "04." It had been a flyable aircraft but had experienced a catastrophic fuel cell failure. When he first started to get acquainted with the aircraft it was in the back of the hangar, and crew chiefs assigned to other MiG-21s were stripping parts off the jet to help them rebuild their machines.

I asked again, "So how do you build up a MiG?" Tommy said that the first step was to take it apart and have a hard look at every component. Then, you fix the broken parts and reassemble the aircraft. Simple!

As it turned out Tommy was involved in actually getting the fuel cell for MiG-21 "04" rebuilt by a contractor in Dayton, Ohio. Once he had the fuel cell in hand the restoration of the MiG began in earnest. MSgt Tommy Karnes took "04" apart and got started on repairing or replacing the needed parts that were either missing or in a state of disrepair. He also reclaimed a lot of parts borrowed from "04" for the other jets at TTR.

Every step of the way Tommy was assisted by Ellis and the other crew chiefs that had experience on the MiG-21. It was a mutual quality assurance system between the men. When they needed help they called on one another, and when it was time for a quality inspection, this was conducted by a colleague qualified to make the critical decision. The process was recorded in great detail in the Aircraft Log, which is known as an Air Force Form 781.

When parts were missing the drama increased. In some cases the vast supply of undocumented and non-inventoried parts that were in storage at TTR would yield the needed component. Sometimes our machinists at Tonopah, or others at Edwards AFB and other air force facilities, were able to fabricate the parts. In other cases contracts were let to have major aerospace companies fabricate the parts. The job got done, but it wasn't inexpensive.

As the airframe came together avionics and engines became the key issues. We typically left all the Soviet instrumentation and avionics in place, substituting only the airspeed indicator, altimeter, transponder, and UHF radio. Many of the systems and switches were simply disabled because we were either unwilling or unable to make everything work. Instead, we wanted a safe airplane to fly. Our mindset was for visual training and not training requiring advanced avionics.

As the CONSTANT PEG program matured over the years, radar systems in the MiG-21 and MiG-23 were restored and then maintained. But in the early days at TTR the requirement was for a safe, flyable airframe. To that end pilots needed to have radios that could select different frequencies, as opposed to the Soviet equipment which usually only had five frequencies that were hard crystals instead of tunable. The pilots also needed airspeed and altitude instruments that indicated airspeed in knots and altitude in feet instead of meters. We joked that airspeed in kilometers per fortnight just wouldn't work for us.

The engines were routinely torn down and inspected, with parts replaced as necessary and available. Then they were run in the test cell. We can thank the engine magicians at the General Electric facilities at Edwards AFB, Wright-Patterson AFB and other locations for their assistance in keeping the MiG engines operable for almost a decade at TTR. So, Tommy knew he had a good engine when it was installed in the jet. As pilots we had total confidence in the powerplants.

I asked, "What about electrical power and hydraulics? Was it exciting the first time the jet was electrically or hydraulically powered up?" Tommy explained that the electrical units we had in our USAF inventory were generally compatible with the MiGs. Sometimes the men had to fabricate the plugs on the end of the power unit cables to make them fit the MiG receptacles, but as long as the power unit put out a lot of power everything worked well. Some of our older units could not sustain enough output to satisfy the MiG, especially for engine starts, but Doug "Robbie" Robinson, our original AGE mechanic, and Ben Galloway, who came later, managed to mate the correct ground power unit with the aircraft in question and make things work.

I pressed the question and Tommy elaborated that the hydraulic actuators were put on a test bench and powered up. Hydraulic pressure was gradually added and the actuators were validated. If they failed they were dismantled and repaired, usually with new seals. So, when power was applied to the aircraft there were not many electrical or hydraulic surprises.

"Robbie" also kept our hydraulic units, called MULEs, working. He and the men had to fabricate fittings so that the hydraulic output from the MULE flowed into the MiG without leaks causing a drop in pressure. The men got these seemingly complicated tasks taken care of as if they were no major issue. With good electrical and hydraulic systems and a serviceable engine, the MiG was ready to go.

I flew Tommy's "04" many times, and I always felt close to him and the others that had made the jet airworthy. I never preflighted one of the MiGs. I went to the jet and got in and flew it. I had no issue with trusting my life to these men. They were that good!

"CATFISH" SHEFFIELD'S ("BANDIT 16") MiG-21 MEMORIES

Pulling gs

Before I get into describing my favorite memories of flying the MiG-21 with the Red Eagles, I have to tell you about what an incredible feeling it is to pull 7gs, and what it's like to zoom around in a high-performance fighter aircraft. Gs is the common expression for the centripetal force exerted on a pilot's body when the aircraft is turning hard, and is expressed in multiples of the 1g we all feel in everyday life. If you've ever been on a rollercoaster or other amusement park ride that rapidly changes direction, you know a bit about what it's like to experience more than 1g.

Fighter pilots talk about "pulling gs" because the centripetal acceleration they describe as "gs" results from pulling back on the control column. Few amusement park rides create more than 2gs. When you pull 7gs, your head weighs seven times as much as normal, and it takes a great deal of effort to move it around. Fighter pilots must move their heads around very actively during aerial combat to look out for unseen aircraft and to keep sight of the ones they are battling. Consequently, most fighter pilots have relatively big and very strong necks. The neck size on my shirts increased two inches from the time I joined the USAF until I left.

The ability to "pull gs" and keep sight of other aircraft in aerial combat is essential because fighters, especially the latest designs like the F-22 Raptor, can really move in all dimensions. Even in the relatively old technology types I flew, which included the F-4 Phantom II, the F-5E Tiger II, and the MiG-21, we could easily accelerate to supersonic speed, zoom at initial climb rates of well over 20,000ft per minute, and, at low altitude, sustain high g loads. Cockpit tape recordings of fighter pilots engaged in "dogfights" are filled with heavy breathing and grunting. Though some would claim the experience is comparable to other activities associated with heavy breathing and grunting, the physical stamina demanded for dogfighting is far less pleasurable.

Crossing Ridges

One of my most vivid memories of "pulling gs" is of flying in the back seat of a T-38 Talon, with Dave "Marshall" McCloud ("Bandit 10") in the front practicing ridge crossings on our way from Nellis up to the Red Eagles' airfield at the TTR. The Red Eagles used the T-38 as a chase plane for test flights in the MiGs. The T-38's primary use in the USAF has been as a supersonic jet trainer in undergraduate pilot training. The F-5E is a "beefed up" fighter derivation of the T-38's design. McCloud was flying very low up the western side of the Nellis range complex, practicing maneuvers to present the least possible opportunity for an adversary to get a "blue sky" background for a heat-seeking missile shot.

To avoid giving a "blue sky" background for a heat-seeking missile shot, fighters and fighter-bombers at low altitude seldom approach a ridge head on. They first turn about 30 degrees to approach the ridge obliquely, then reverse the turn for about 60 degrees as they first pull up to the ridge crest and then dive back down on the opposite side. It is exhilarating, to say the least, to cross the top of a ridge at less than 500ft and more than 500 knots while nearly inverted and pulling with a force of at least four times normal gravity. McCloud was really pulling hard and coming very close to the rocks at the top of each ridge we crossed. When I complained, he said, "Come on Sheffield, you don't want to die all tensed up. Just imagine you're watching a movie."

Chasing Clouds

One of the other vivid memories I have of pulling gs is of the day I took one of our crew chiefs up for a joyride as a reward for his being named Crew Chief of the Month. All our crew chiefs were real characters with extreme personalities, but Roy Miller was a special case. He always had a childish glee about everything he did. He wore a baseball cap featuring a pinwheel that was usually spinning madly on our windy flight line at the TTR.

Roy and I took off from Tonopah in the T-38 in mid-afternoon when cumulus clouds were forming over the Sierra Nevada mountains to our west. They were popping up in rows and drifting in lines like rows of corn across the airfield and the ranges to the southeast. The cloud bases were around 10,000ft, with tops at around 30,000ft. Running through a channel between the rows of soon-to-be thunderstorms, I selected afterburner, accelerated to more than 400 knots and smoothly pulled up the side of one of the cumulus clouds, rolling gently across the top of it at less than 200 knots. We fell down the far side into another gap in the rows of clouds, then zoomed up and did the same thing over and over again until we ran low on fuel. Passing so close to the slow-moving clouds gave a full appreciation for our speed and made these maneuvers every bit as exhilarating as McCloud's ridge crossings, but far less frightening. Unlike the rocks at the top of ridges, we could skim through the misty cloud tops without harm. Roy Miller was grinning for days.

Truth of Dogfighting

Although fighter pilots, much like many fishermen, are prone to exaggeration, gun camera film tells the true story. Hence, fighter pilots can almost always establish who really won the fight and, hence, there was a fairly well established hierarchy of who was the best among us. Some of the best loved to rub it in when they got into a kill position behind their adversaries. Fighter Weapons School instructor Clyde "Joe Bob" Phillips was famous for getting into a guns tracking solution behind his opponent and then calling over the radio demanding that the defeated pilot "squeal like a pig." For those of you who saw the movie *Deliverance* you know what that suggests.

A guns tracking solution is a stable, relatively low-angle gun-firing pass, usually from no further behind the target than 1,500ft, wherein the attacker is able to stabilize the gun-aiming device (the "pipper") on the target for at least a half-second, during which time up to 25 bullets from my MiG-21 (up to 50 from the faster firing M61 cannon fitted in US fighters) could pass through the target. The term "guns tracking solution" is used here in distinction to a high-angle gun-firing pass, wherein the attacker is only able to rake the "pipper" through the target as it passes, which would be called a "snap shot."

First Flight Solo

My first flight in the F-5E Tiger II was solo, but that wasn't such a big deal because the F-5E was just a T-38 on steroids and had very similar flying characteristics. My first flight in the MiG-21 was also solo, and its success was due to the training I'd had and the trust of people like Earl Henderson, who hired me for the job and allowed me to fly the MiG. Gail Peck had originally identified me as the next pilot to hire.

The cockpit was 90 percent Russian – that is the labels on most of the switches and instruments were in Russian. Unlike the F-5E and everything else I'd flown in the USAF, the MiG-21 didn't have nose wheel steering. You steered it with differential braking, and the brakes weren't hydraulic – they worked off pressurized air, and you only had so much of it. If you were sloppy with your brake use while taxiing out for take-off, you depleted the air pressure you'd need for braking on landing. One of the key checks on turning from downwind to base leg for landing was to assure that the air pressure was sufficient to stop and taxi in after landing. Taxiing, especially at first, was a weaving affair.

In the F-5E, the control column height was such that I rested my forearm on my thigh and controlled the bank angle with very light pressure on the stick, and just bumped the trim tab to adjust my pitch in normal flight. In the MiG-21, the top of the control column was several inches higher than in the F-5E, so my forearm was suspended in the air and my hand forced to hold on with a bit more pressure. I suspect this design was a carryover from the MiG-15 and the MiG-17, where control forces called for a bit more leverage. I found the MiG-21 very easy to fly and wonderful to maneuver, especially at slow speed, where the nose could be controlled and held up well below stalling speed.

Landing the MiG-21 was much like, but easier than, the T-38. The aforementioned ability to hold the MiG-21's nose up made aero-braking after touchdown very effective. So my first solo in the MiG-21 was uneventful.

MiG-21 versus Harrier II

One of my fondest memories of flying the MiG-21 is of a day when I got to fight a Marine Corps pilot in an AV-8B Harrier II. As stated in the Defence section of *Flight International's* February 17, 1972, issue, the Harrier should be able to beat a MiG-21 in a subsonic dogfight at sea level. "In fact it has been shown – though not in operational service – that the Harrier is capable of out-turning the MiG-21F by a substantial margin, assuming a sea-level combat at Mach 0.9. Coupled with turning performance is the Harrier's high specific excess power (SEP) figure – both positive and negative by virtue of thrust vectoring – which gives it a unique opportunity in evading air-to-air attacks and in turn becoming the attacker."

In aerial combat, Harrier pilots loved to draw their opponents into a slow-speed turning contest. If they needed to cause an attacking aircraft to overshoot, they could use their vectored thrust to generate higher turn rates and sudden deceleration – a technique called "VIFFing" (Vectoring In Forward Flight).

I did my homework on the Harrier II before I first engaged one in the air over the TTR. I knew not to go low and slow and planned a vertical fight instead.

Before I describe that fight I must state some caveats. Whereas the tactics I used were successful in this one-versus-one air-to-air combat training engagement, they would not be healthy in a many-versus-many environment where an adversary with higher energy at the high-altitude parts of my maneuvers would have easily killed me. Secondly, the tactics I used would not be valid against today's all-aspect heat-seeking missiles. The rules of engagement for the dogfight I'm about to describe required the shooter to be within a 30-degree angle of his opponent's tail for a valid "Fox 2" or "Atoll" shot – i.e., you had to get behind the other guy to kill him.

The Harrier II's only air-to-air weapons were heat-seeking missiles (AIM-9 Sidewinders) and a 25mm Gatling gun. My MiG-21 also had only "heat" and guns.

We set up the first engagement at about 18,000ft and 0.9 Mach, heading in the same direction in a line abreast formation with me on the left and about two miles between us. At the call "fight's on!" we both turned aggressively into each other at maximum thrust. I descended slightly during the first part of my turn and then pulled up into the Harrier II as we passed nearly head on. I'd deliberately allowed the Harrier II to get his nose slightly in front of me as we passed so as to lure him into a hard turn to gain more advantage.

As the Harrier II passed by, I smoothly pulled my MiG-21 straight into the vertical. With the attitude indicator on the "bulls-eye" indicating straight up, I watched the Harrier II over my left shoulder, keeping one eye on him and the other on the airspeed indicator. My rule was to start pulling toward the Harrier II's extended "six o'clock" at either the point when the pilot got his nose within 45 degrees of me or the airspeed dropped below 200 knots. While the pull into the vertical was very smooth, the pull off the top of the climb was at maximum angle of attack, rolling left toward the Harrier II as I pulled to meet him at a high crossing angle.

The MiG-21 gave lots of "burble" (the aircraft shuddered) to forewarn of a stall. Low speed roll and directional control could be exaggerated by rudder use. You could do something very close to a hammerhead stall from vertical flight by standing on the rudder and unloading the aircraft with forward stick pressure as the airspeed fell through 150 knots. You could do a similar maneuver in the T-38, but the inside engine would often flame out. The MiG-21's Tumansky engine never faltered during such maneuvers.

As I had zoomed above him, the Harrier II pilot went for my opening gambit in a big way. He kept turning very hard as he pulled into the vertical to point at me. With my MiG-21 on its back pulling down, I easily kept us nearly head-on as our turns merged. As we passed I immediately unloaded, continuing to turn only hard enough to keep the Harrier II in sight as he "bat turned" for my "six o'clock." As I gained enough airspeed to go vertical again, I kept the smooth pull going, keeping my cone of vulnerability to a Sidewinder beyond the Harrier II's position.

The Harrier II had burned up so much energy in his first attempt to go after me in the vertical that he could not follow me up the second time. Pulling and rolling off the top of my maneuver toward his "six o'clock" put me well behind his wing line and on the offensive. With the MiG-21 on its back I pulled maximum angle of attack and got my nose in front of the jet. The Harrier II pilot probably "VIFFed" to cause me to overshoot, bleeding even more of his precious airspeed. He then reversed, expecting to find me squirting out in front of him in a horizontal turn. Instead, he found me pulling smoothly into the vertical again while holding him outside my cone of vulnerability for a heat-seeker. A vertical loop to the outside of his turning circle got me into a position of a valid heat-seeking missile ("Atoll") launch shot and then to a guns tracking solution for the kill and this engagement's end.

We had fuel for more, so we climbed to 18,000ft or so and accelerated to good speed before calling "fight's on" again. The first turns and near-head-on passing were identical to the first engagement, as was my zoom into the vertical after passing the Harrier II. This time, however, my opponent didn't follow me up as aggressively as he had the first time.

When flying fighters in air-to-air combat, one of the fundamental principles is to use the maneuvering "egg." It's called the "egg" because that's the shape that a well-flown fighter creates in vertical space by recognizing that gravity opposes the turning force when pulling upwards and assists the turn when pulling downwards. Hence, a turn at the bottom of a vertical maneuver will have a much higher radius than the turn at the top of a vertical maneuver. Most importantly, it wastes energy to turn too hard at the bottom and it squanders turning opportunity to turn too gently at the top of vertical maneuvering.

I'd chosen the vertical fight with the Harrier II because of my MiG-21's superior speed capability and better energy maneuverability in the vertical. Winning a dogfight against a comparable aircraft and pilot often requires patience for such features to create a decisive advantage.

In this second engagement I had to pass near head-on, zoom to the vertical and roll off the top toward the Harrier II's tail three times before he'd spent sufficient energy for me to get an "Atoll" solution, followed again by a guns tracking kill. The moral of the story is that even with the ability to use vectored thrust to generate high rates of turn, the Harrier could not beat the MiG-21 in a high-energy vertical fight.

Supersonic F-111s

With the Red Eagles having only a few assets, I often flew alone, even in the Red Flag exercises when there were usually a dozen or so "Blue Force" fighters converging on the target area at any given time. There was usually a "Blue Force" attack group of fighter-bombers with fighter cover to fend off the "Red Force," of which I was a part.

On one such day my GCI controller vectored me from the airfield at the TTR to intercept unidentified attacking aircraft. As I crossed the mountain ridge just over 20 nautical miles east of my home base, I immediately caught sight of two "rooster tails" streaking across the desert floor toward me. The F-111s probably thought they were invisible and invincible going supersonic at less than 500ft, and didn't realize that the dust being kicked up by their shock waves made them easily visible from

15 miles away. While their low altitude shock waves kicked up sand spray that gave their position away, their speed was not enough to prevent me from swooping down from 20,000ft, also supersonic, to catch them. Worse, they'd outrun their air cover, which was still ten miles behind them. As they crossed a ridge I was able to get a "blue sky" background for a valid "Atoll" launch, close to a tracking solution for the gun on the one on the right and then switch to the other F-111 for a confirmed gun kill.

As I pulled away from the F-111s and headed back east to engage the rest of the attacking "Blue Force," I caught sight of a US Navy A-7 flying very low along a path just north of where I'd attacked the F-111s. I had zoomed back up to 20,000ft or so by then, and I looked carefully all around the A-7 before attacking it. I expected at least a two-ship with a wingman line abreast or a four-ship in a "box" with another flight of two either in front or behind the one aircraft I saw. My GCI controller said he didn't see any other aircraft around and I didn't see any either, so I went down after him.

Despite a beautiful ridge crossing maneuver by the A-7 pilot, I anticipated which way he'd turn and was able to get a valid "Atoll" shot as he popped up over the crest of the ridge. As he leveled off at low altitude over a salt flat just southeast of our airfield at Tonopah, I closed for a guns tracking solution and called a "kill" in through GCI. From the guns tracking position, I slowed down and joined on the A-7's right wing, closing to the point that our wingtips were only a couple of feet apart. As the radio relay of the kill reached the pilot, his head swiveled frantically in search of the bandit. When he saw me in "fingertip formation" on his right wing his head slumped forward and he slapped both sides of his helmet with his hands. I can imagine what a sight it was for him to see the MiG-21 up close and eye-to-eye. I can also imagine how glad he was to have had this experience in Red Flag rather than for real.

"Hamburger in any wrapper is still hamburger"

On one great afternoon before the end of my time in the Red Eagles I had the opportunity to fight a two-seater F-15 flown by Maj "Buzz" Buzze of the F-15 FWS, who had a fellow Aggressor pilot in the back seat. To avoid any further embarrassment for that fellow Aggressor pilot after all these years, he shall remain anonymous in this story.

I knew "Buzz" had been one of the best air-to-air fighter pilots in the F-4 FWS (414th FWS) and he was unbeatable in the F-15, which has far better maneuverability and power than the F-4. I did my best to lure "Buzz" into a slow-speed "knife fight" where, if he were impatient, I could use the MiG-21's great slow-speed nose-positioning ability to flush the F-15 in front of me. "Buzz" flew two successive, wonderfully executed, fights, where he exploited his aircraft's turning capability and its superior thrust-to-weight ratio. I heard "Fox 2" (heat-seeking missile launch) and "Fox 3" (guns tracking solution) in both fights, with the latter call bringing an end to this mismatch. Having fought many, much better, fights with other F-15s, I was feeling absolutely humiliated.

Then "Buzz" announced that he was going to let my fellow Aggressor pilot fly the next engagement from the back seat of his F-15. I feared the humiliation was only going to get worse, as he had clearly seen how "Buzz" had maneuvered the F-15 to thoroughly kick my butt.

With my first two attempts to draw the F-15 into a quick knife fight having failed utterly, I was a little more patient in preserving my energy through the first two, near-head-on passes that ensued after the back-seater gave the "fight's on" call. My patience must have frustrated him for he went for the quick kill very aggressively. Since "Buzz" had killed me so quickly in the first two engagements, perhaps my Aggressor friend felt some pressure to do the same. Whatever the motivation, he squandered the F-15's superior energy-maneuverability by pulling very hard, continuously.

As I pulled into the vertical after our third pass, with both of us turning right, I sensed that I had more energy. Rather than continuing a climbing turn to the right, I rolled left as I pulled straight up through the vertical and down into a barrel roll to the outside of the F-15's continuing right turn. Rather than the usual hard pull from the top, I unloaded the aircraft to accelerate as I more or less "fell" off the top of my climb toward his extended "six o'clock" (the airspace directly behind his tail). As I barrel-rolled to the left, I slid under his turning circle and then outside it at a point about 6,000ft behind him. To keep from losing sight of me, my Aggressor friend turned even harder, this time from the horizontal to the vertical – the wrong part of the "egg" for maximum "g" turns.

Coming out of my barrel roll to the left, I followed the F-15's hard right turn from a lagging position (my nose was pointed at least 30 degrees behind his). My Aggressor friend in the F-15 must've thought I'd overshot his turn badly as he reversed his turn from the right to the left and pulled into the vertical, almost replicating the maneuver I'd just done. As he tried to slide into my extended "six o'clock," I pulled smoothly into the vertical then hard down into a repeat barrel roll to the left. By now our energy difference was substantial, and as I slid into his extended "six o'clock," I was able to get the right angle and tone for an "Atoll" solution, followed by guns tracking.

Unfortunately, I was by now low on fuel, so I couldn't give my friend a chance to redeem himself. Gloating on the speed of my recovery after the beating that "Buzz" had given me, I couldn't resist firing a little of humor in the F-15's direction as it headed back to Nellis and I turned for the runway at the TTR. I quipped "hamburger in any wrapper is still hamburger" over the radio – a comment that I'm sure must have stung my Aggressor friend, and left "Buzz" feeling like he was Superman.

In an e-mail exchange with Bob Sheffield I asked about the nickname "Catfood" versus "Catfish." His reply read as follows:

> Yes, "Admiral" Nelson is a great guy, despite the fact that he may have called me "Catfood" instead of "Catfish." Actually, I recall very clearly that it was not the "Admiral" but Dan "Truck" Futryk (GCI) who invented the alternate nickname of "Catfood," which he used constantly to humble me. You may remember at the time there was a baseball pitcher called "Catfish" Hunter (Oakland A's I believe) who had a funny television commercial where one of his critics called him "Catfood." "Truck" picked up on that and applied it to me.

THE MiG-23

The MiG-23 was added to the CONSTANT PEG inventory in 1983 at about the same time the MiG-17s were being retired. Some of the MiG-23 photographs included in this book were taken in the Threat Training Facility (TTF) at Nellis AFB, Nevada.

Like the exploitation projects for the MiG-17 (HAVE DRILL/HAVE FERRY) and the MiG-21 (HAVE DOUGHNUT), a MiG-23MS export variant (fitted with a "Jay Bird" radar) of the Soviet fighter interceptor was acquired and exploited by the US in the late 1970s. The project was called HAVE PAD and the report dated November 1, 1978, was initially classified secret. In the opening paragraphs of the document it is stated that the information in the report is based on data made available to the Foreign Technology Division of Air Force Systems Command as of September 1, 1978. HAVE PAD was declassified on December 8, 2002, according to dated markings on the document.

Test pilots flew the HAVE PAD article on a total of 115 sorties accumulating 87 flight hours. Both USAF and US Navy pilots participated in the project. The operational evaluation findings were labeled as preliminary. It was further reported that final analyses and reporting may affect some of the findings. The final analyses were not included in the declassified report.

Overall, the operational evaluation stated that the MiG-23MS, known to NATO as the "Flogger," "should be considered a serious threat in the air combat arena because it represents an excellent blending of airframe and avionics capabilities."

The performance evaluation listed the good and bad points of the aircraft as follows:

GOOD FEATURES

1. Low altitude transonic/supersonic acceleration. All US aircraft flown against the MiG-23 were inferior in level accelerations below 10,000ft (3,000m) MSL from Mach 0.95 to 730 KIAS (maximum handbook airspeed).
2. Engine/afterburner response. Engine acceleration is excellent, with three to four seconds from idle to intermediate (full military, non-afterburner) power. Afterburner ignition time is nearly instantaneous, less than one second to full ignition.
3. Basic airframe stability. The aircraft can be flown without stability augmentation to Mach 1.8, attesting to the excellent basic airframe design.
4. Radar/ECCM capability. The "Jay Bird" radar has excellent ECCM features.
5. The cockpit layout is a vast improvement over the older Soviet aircraft evaluated. Human engineering factors are abundant.
6. The small size of the aircraft will make it very difficult to acquire visually.

BAD FEATURES

1. The turning performance is inferior to the later US fighters and comparable to a "Hard Wing" F-4E aircraft.
2. The engine smokes at non-afterburner power settings, comparable to a J-79 engine (F-4).
3. The cockpit visibility is somewhat poor, particularly in the rearward area.
4. The natural stall warning of the aircraft is poor. In a hard maneuvering flight, it is easy to exceed the stability limits of the aircraft.
5. The control forces are much higher than US aircraft and mask any natural stall warning that would be present.

While the MiG-23 performance and operational evaluation reports provide great initial insight into the aircraft, the content is not satisfying to a fighter pilot endeavoring to learn as much about the enemy as possible. The follow-on reports created by the Air Force Flight Test Center, TAC, and the US Navy may well provide additional information of value to the inquisitive fighter pilot, but these documents presently remain classified. This was one of the problems fighter pilots faced prior to recent times. In many cases information existed, but this was not made available to those that needed it most primarily because of security considerations related to sources.

The drive to create the CONSTANT PEG training program was fueled by just these kinds of reports, and the difficulty pilots had finding the information they were searching for. If and when the weapons officers found the information, typically it couldn't be shared with other pilots due to the compartmented nature of the access requirements needed to view it.

Nevertheless there are many other interesting aspects relating to the MiG-23 that can be gleaned from a close visual inspection of the jet on display in the "Petting Zoo" Threat Training Facility at Nellis AFB.

The aircraft also has a periscope embedded in the middle rail of the canopy that provides a view of the region directly behind the jet like the MiG-17.

The speed brakes on the MiG-23 are located near the aft end of the aircraft under the horizontal stabilizer. In addition, there is a dorsal fin on this aircraft which is apparently needed for stability at very high airspeed. To provide clearance from the runway and tarmac, the dorsal fin folds 90 degrees to the right any time the landing gear is extended.

The slot in the fuselage adjacent to the trailing edge of the wing houses the wing when it is swept.

The landing gear is heavy duty, and thus the aircraft is able to operate from a variety of unimproved surfaces.

Peering into the cockpit reveals that the jet is also "very busy" in respect to switches. The throttle is a modern design when compared to the device fitted in the MiG-21. It is actually a handhold, with various buttons to control avionics and other systems. The throttle handhold slides on a rail, and moving it changes the selected engine power setting. When in full afterburner the MiG-23 made a frighteningly loud noise, as AGE specialist Ben Galloway recalled. He had been sent out to pick up drag 'chutes just as a "Flogger" was preparing for take-off. Ben said he had no idea how loud a MiG-23 was when sat in the cockpit, but he remembered that it was so loud standing close to the aircraft as power was advanced and afterburner selected that it almost made him physically sick.

When sitting in the cockpit of the "Flogger," visibility straight ahead is better than in the MiG-21. In fact it is comparable to an F-4, with about the same amount of windscreen superstructure masking forward vision. The thick combining glass tends to inhibit the forward vision. Forward visibility is far superior in the F-22, F-15, and F-16.

The brake system is similar to the previous MiGs in terms of operation. However, the MiG-23 has nose wheel steering that is managed by pushing a button and steering with the rudder pedals. Braking is achieved through a brake lever on the control column, as in earlier MiGs.

The control column has an electric trim button for the horizontal stabilizer, along with numerous other switches. As with the MiG-17 and MiG-21, the white stripe on the instrument panel in the MiG-23 is a visual helper for centering the control column forward in an out-of-control situation.

The bottom line on the MiG-23 is that the aircraft is a very capable adversary in the hands of a skilled pilot. It is fast and small, and that can be a winning combination in spite of performance limitations when the engagement becomes a turning dogfight.

The MiG-23 carried fuel in the fuselage wing box for the swing-wing. The boxes would develop hairline cracks and fuel would seep out. We researched old intelligence reports and found that the Soviets had suffered a similar problem eight years prior to the "Floggers" joining the Red Eagles, especially on the older model MiG-23s like the ones that we were flying. The Soviets fixed the crack problem by welding a plate to the inner surface of the box and a stiffener on the outer skin. We did not have that capability. The decision was made to weld over the crack on the outer skin and reduce the allowable g-loading during flight operations.

The CONSTANT PEG pilots respected the aircraft and, in most cases, flew the MiG-23 less aggressively than when flying an F-5E or a MiG-21. One pilot quipped to me that he never flew the "Flogger" when it didn't try to kill him at least once. Others were less critical, especially those with a lot of flying time in the F-4C, D, and E (before the latter model was fitted with leading edge slats) and perhaps the F-100. These aircraft could bite the pilot severely if he wasn't paying adequate attention to flying the aircraft.

On August 28, 1987, Capt (now Lt Gen) "Hawk" Carlisle ("Bandit 54") departed a MiG-23 from controlled flight, entered a spin, and made a low altitude ejection that nearly cost him his life. It is alleged by those that should know that the barometer in the seat that triggers man-seat separation and parachute opening should have been adjusted to account for the high desert elevation and mountainous terrain in our flying area. I've been told that "Hawk" would have hit the ground still in the seat and not have survived if he had been over a mountain instead of a valley due to the seat barometer setting.

The following are additional details about the ejection, and the aftermath, that I gleaned during a face-to-face conversation with Lt Gen Carlisle during the summer of 2009 at Nellis AFB. "Hawk" was airborne in a MiG-23 and Capt Mick Simmons ("Bandit 57") was flying a MiG-21 when "Hawk" got his jet into a spin that he could not recover from. "Hawk" tried several times to eject once the decision was made, but nothing happened when he squeezed the trigger. Finally, he manually jettisoned the canopy and tried one last time. It worked and he was ejected from the aircraft.

What followed was a seemingly very long ride in the seat waiting for man-seat separation. At very low altitude he parted company with the seat just as he was deciding to separate manually. His parachute opened immediately. After about a swing in the parachute he landed in the desert without injury. Soon he was in desert survival mode, wondering why nobody had showed up in a helicopter to pick him up. As it turned out the alert helicopter crew wasn't cleared on the MiG project, so a land team was sent out in a vehicle to pick him up. The land team finally arrived and picked up the shaken, but unhurt, pilot and headed back to TTR, or so they thought.

"Hawk" argued briefly with the driver over the best way to go to get back to base, but the driver was determined he knew the best way and "Hawk" finally relented. As the chosen road deteriorated into a trail and then an animal path, the driver attempted to cross a dry creek bed and ended up rolling the vehicle. "Hawk" had now been in two vehicle accidents all in the same day. A helicopter was finally despatched and "Hawk" was rescued from the road vehicle accident about eight miles from where he landed after ejecting from the "Flogger."

The "post mortem" investigation of the accident revealed that the Red Eagles had a lot to learn about the ejection seat in the MiG-23. It was determined that an interlock-like block (F-4 pilots and WSOs will understand) between the canopy and the seat was out of place. The purpose of the block was to prevent the seat from being ejected through the canopy. Once "Hawk" manually jettisoned the canopy, the seat was good to go. Added to that, the barometer in the seat had not been adjusted correctly for the high elevations of the desert valleys and the adjacent mountains around TTR. Evidently, the seat "thought" it was over land that was coastal, or at least of very low elevation. All of this is a part of the "curse" of operating a complex weapons system without thoroughly understood technical data and manuals.

In this particular case it was better to be lucky than good. It had been a close call – twice!

THE T-38 TALON

Built by Northrop as a Mach 1 capable two-seat advanced trainer, the T-38 was a wonderful little training command white rocket that we painted up in shades of blue and brown and drove like a second car. A beauty to behold, the Talon is a dream to fly. The cockpit configuration is like a fighter with one seat behind the other. The aircraft can climb to more than 40,000ft in a minute or two, and rolls crisply and at a high rate. It is able to routinely pull up to 7.33gs. If a pilot is planning a loop he will start the maneuver by accelerating to 500 KIAS at the bottom of the loop, select Military Power (100 percent power, but without afterburners) and pull at least 5g's in the initial pull to the vertical. The T-38 is a high-performance machine.

As stated earlier, the Red Eagles primarily used the T-38 to chase new pilots checking out in the MiGs. Since the latter were flown only during daylight in visual meteorological conditions, instrument proficiency flying and instrument check rides were secondary uses for the T-38s. The little jets were also used for airborne photography, VIP orientation, and incentive rides for the assigned personnel that were not rated pilots. Other than the transport Cessnas and Mitsubishi aircraft, the T-38s were the only aircraft assigned to the unit that had more than one seat.

All of the men assigned to the Red Eagles felt a need to fly because it was the unit's mission. Some really loved to fly and did so at every opportunity. Others approached the opportunity with a happy face covering a deep dread inside. The MiG pilots weren't always gentle with their passengers, especially if the incentive flight was for one of the new men or one known to be apprehensive or tentative. As a result the men that really dreaded the feared incentive flight had nicknames for the pilots. One pilot was known as "Dr Puke."

The pilot scheduled to fly the incentive flight is responsible for briefing and conducting the necessary training for his passenger. A favorite story about "Dr Puke" is the effect he had on one man being briefed for his incentive flight. It was the day before the flight was to take place and the briefing related to the ejection seat and the overall emergency egress process. The man got physically sick and threw up during the briefing on the day before the scheduled flight as "Dr Puke" went over the details. No one can remember how, or if, the flight actually happened the next day.

A report on an incentive flight that did indeed take place (for an unnamed individual) read as follows:

> I was scheduled for a T-38 incentive flight with "Smokey" Sundell. We were in a flight of two, as another Red Eagle was also getting an incentive ride. "Hawk" Carlisle was the pilot of the other T-38.
>
> I was anxious about g forces and all the perils of high performance flight. I was determined not to get airsick, no matter what. One of our colleagues advised me to watch the pilot's shoulders instead of gazing around. That way I wouldn't be suddenly surprised.

We had a great flight, which included an aerial tour of Yosemite National Park. I was totally disciplined watching the pilot's shoulders and only occasionally looking at the scenery. As the flight was coming to a close I knew that one of the final maneuvers would be a loop over the airfield. As we approached I closed my eyes and tightened my gut in anticipation of the g forces. When the gs eased off "Smokey" said, "Look at that!" I opened my eyes and we were inverted, with the airfield straight down below us. I came really close to heaving at that point!

We landed and all the maintenance guys came rushing over to see if we had puked. It was reported that I was white as a sheet, but I didn't throw up! "Hawk" Carlisle's passenger was not as fortunate, and he either missed his bag or was too late. All "Hawk" could say to him was, "If you puke in an airplane, YOU clean it up."

We had five T-38s, which were painted shades of blue and brown. Each one had an assigned crew chief, and his name was painted on the canopy rail of the rear cockpit. Red Eagle pilots' names adorned the front canopy rail. As people transferred out of and into the squadron the names on the T-38s also changed.

CESSNA 404

Crew Chief Jim Richardson "inherited" a slot machine that caused one of our Cessna 404s to give the pilot, "Devil" Muller, some trim problems on take-off one afternoon. The slot machine was being "relocated" that day, but Jim forgot to tell the pilot or anyone else that he had stowed the gambling device in the aft section of the airplane. Those things weigh a lot, and he didn't even tie the damn thing down. Fortunately, "Devil" Muller is a hell of a pilot and nobody got hurt!

A contract dispute occurred after "my watch" and the Cessna 404s were replaced with the MU-2. The contract dispute and the awarding of the flight support contract to the operators of the MU-2 led to a lawsuit that required Tom Gibbs and "Admiral" John Nelson to show up at the Pentagon for a "pow-wow." According to Nelson the dispute was eventually settled for a price well above Gibbs' pay grade, but not before both Tom and the "Admiral" had endured a "character building experience."

CHAPTER 5

THE CHALLENGES WE FACED

At the beginning of the Red Eagles program we had no idea how long the engines in the MiGs would last. One of the first new recruits I made to our maintenance team was a jet engine mechanic by the name of Ike Crawley. During my watch Ike kept the engines running. I'm not really sure how he did it, but there was able assistance from the General Electric engine magicians at Edwards AFB and at Wright-Patterson AFB.

Spare parts were always hard to come by. On one special trip overseas the hottest items on our "wants" list were igniter plugs for the MiG-21 engines. These are similar in appearance and function to spark plugs in the reciprocating engine of an automobile. The parts searches were never-ending as there was always some component in short supply. Occasionally we had to let our contacts within the contracting authority bid out the fabrication of parts to an external source. In other cases, workshops in special USAF facilities actually made parts for us, such as canopies.

Another major challenge was ongoing security. Security is like mowing the grass on a golf course. You just have to keep working at it. And we did, and so did those that followed us. It always pleased me to note that we were a cover for the stealth fighter operation, even in the classified world. The F-117 was declassified and moved from Tonopah to Holloman AFB and yet the security of CONSTANT PEG survived that transition and stood firmly in place until decisions were made to declassify the MiG project.

Time away from home was always a problem for the men and their families, especially when the latter didn't have any idea what the men's jobs were, or even where they had disappeared to. I'm sure some marriages suffered, and I know many dads missed soccer games, recitals, and other kid-related functions that they truly wanted to attend. Nobody whined, and we had no major marital disasters on my watch although some followed later. So, there certainly were some troubled waters from time to time throughout the program, but that is not surprising given the nature and durations of the absences.

I was thrilled to be asked to tell the CONSTANT PEG story at the first Aggressor reunion following the declassification of the program. This was the first time many of the wives had been told details about the MiG operation at Tonopah. After I had finished the talk and had retired to the hospitality suite for a cool one, Bonnie Scott tracked me down, stating that she just had to tell me a story. Bonnie and Mike were with us at the beginning and then came back for a second tour. Mike Scott was the commander when the program was shut down. I was amused at Bonnie's report of the effect of CONSTANT PEG on her life in the early days.

When the Scotts arrived at Nellis from an Aggressor assignment in the Philippines at Clark AB, the CONSTANT PEG program, with all of its secrecy, was already in place and Bonnie was frequently confounded with the answer, "I can't tell you!" to her many questions. She became increasingly frustrated by the circumstances. One Friday evening Mike came home from work all sweaty and wearing a smelly flightsuit after several unexplained nights away. Soon after getting home Mike noticed Bonnie starting to get all dressed up. He asked, "What's up?" Her reply, "Can't tell you!" He persisted with, "Where are we going?" As she headed for the door, he asked one last time. "Where are you going? Her smug reply was, "Can't tell you."

She had repeatedly reminded Mike that she was his wife and could be trusted with any information. Her lips would be sealed. She begged, "Just tell me what's going on!" He replied, "Bonnie, I know you too well! I can't tell you!" And so she left with Mike standing at the door wondering what was going on. Well, Bonnie met up with a girlfriend on a prearranged "girls night out," had dinner, and may have pulled a few slots. Then she went home. She laughed as she told the story and concluded with, "That stunt got it out of my system!"

At the beginning of the program the enlisted force was exempt from USAF grooming and appearance standards so that they blended into the remote communities where we operated. Added to that the unit was run on a first name or nickname basis between officers and enlisted personnel. These people were so professional with this privilege that it was never a problem. If my seniors were around they reverted to proper courtesies, and sometimes we "disappeared" a man that really needed a haircut or moustache trim when we were expecting visitors. We simply operated in that fashion and never had a problem. But, these special rules were doomed as the project grew in size and numbers, and George Gennin was directed to put the men back in uniform and in compliance with AFR 35-10 grooming standards. That could not have been fun.

Finally, financial maturity happened after my watch. When I left the program we still operated from a fire hose of money sent straight from the Pentagon to Mary Jane Smith at Nellis.

Every Day Was Not a Good Day

While CONSTANT PEG experienced problems and heartache with the loss of some of our people, overall the success of the program was stunning.

There were five major Class A aircraft mishaps and one on the job ground fatality during the program. One of the Class A mishaps happened on my watch and cost me my job as the commander.

Specifically, two pilots were killed in MiG accidents during the program and a maintenance technician died during a fuel cell maintenance operation. In two other events we lost MiGs, but not people.

As previously mentioned, the first loss suffered by the Red Eagles was US Navy pilot Lt Hugh Brown, who died when his MiG-17 crashed on August 23, 1979, following its departure from controlled flight and subsequent unrecoverable spin. Nearly three years later Capt Mark Postai crash-landed a MiG-17 in the desert after an engine failure on April 8, 1982. He was shaken by the violence of the experience but emerged from the jet unhurt.

I have been told that our people rushed to the Postai MiG-17 crash site in an effort to rescue him and upon arriving at the aircraft found the cockpit empty. The rescuers subsequently noticed Mark waving to them from a nearby knoll. He had freed himself, egressed from the airplane, and scampered well clear in case the wreckage caught fire or exploded. The jet didn't do either, but the accident triggered the end of MiG-17 operations at Tonopah.

Sadly, a short time later on October 21, 1982, Mark lost his life in the crash of a MiG-23 – our second, and last, aircraft fatality. I haven't seen the accident report but have been led to believe that Postai was faced with an in-flight fire and died during ejection on final approach when it became apparent that the aircraft would crash short of the runway.

MiG-21 crew chief Jim Dresher and Bob Breault, the Fabrication Branch Chief at the time, reported the loss of NCO Rey Hernandez, a fuel specialist, on February 15, 1984, as follows:

Jim Dresher and Rey Hernandez were repairing a leak in a T-38 fuel cell in Hangar 1 when the fuel cell incident happened. Breault called the ambulance. Dresher and Hernandez knew approximately where the fuel cell leak was located from drips observed in the main landing gear wheel well. Jim, a much larger man, was under the aircraft in the wheel well at the leak location tapping with a tool so that Rey, who was topside and small enough to actually get into the fuel cell, could find the source of the leak.

Rey had purged the fuel cell with nitrogen gas to reduce the jet fuel fumes. Jim tapped and Rey tapped back, and this happened a few times as they zeroed in on the location of the leak. Then Jim tapped and got no response. He tapped again but there was still no response. Dresher sensed that something was wrong and withdrew from the main landing gear wheel well to check on Rey. Jim observed Rey limp and, roughly from his waist up, headfirst in the fuel cell. Dresher jumped up on the wing of the aircraft and attempted to pull Rey out of the fuel tank. He was initially unable to do this, so he adjusted his grip and locked his arms around Rey and pulled hard. Suddenly Rey was freed and both men catapulted off the spine of the aircraft, landing mostly on the wing. Dresher actually fell to the floor of the hangar. He was unable to get Rey off the wing and onto the floor.

Bob Breault rushed over and helped get Rey onto the hangar floor and then responded to Jim's direction to call the medical response team and an ambulance. Dresher then began giving Rey CPR. A short time later the medical team arrived and took over. At this point Dresher had inhaled so much jet fuel that he was reeking of JP4 and was unable to continue with the CPR. Both men were transported to the clinic by the medical response team. Dresher was in one treatment room and Hernandez was in another, receiving a lot of attention. Dresher was soon released and informed that Hernandez was being airlifted to Nellis in one of the MU-2s.

Jim made a comment that he hoped Rey had made it okay, and the medic credited Dresher with keeping him alive. A few beers followed and then came the news that Rey hadn't survived.

Breault recalled that Jim's breath smelled of JP4 so bad that he thought Dresher was going to have some health issues too. Fortunately, he did not.

There is a funny thing about adrenaline and its sudden effect. According to Breault, Jim jumped up on the aircraft and pulled Rey out of the fuel cell in one smooth motion and then did the CPR. But the bottom line is that Rey died. Jim Dresher really felt bad about his loss. And still, in 2011 when we discussed the incident, he had very vivid memories of the entire episode. He had tried so hard to save Rey.

Services were held at the Nellis AFB chapel for Rey Hernandez. Dresher had hoped to escort Rey home but SMS Roger Cartier was selected to accompany his body back to his home in Puerto Rico.

The details of the death of the two officers in the MiG accidents were only shared with their widows after the program was declassified in 2006. Mark Postai's wife, who had remarried, was notified before the public announcement, and she and key family members attended the announcement of the declassification at the National Museum of the Air Force in November 2006.

It took a while to find Linda Brown, who had also remarried. As a result she was not notified until after the public release. Fortunately the US Navy located her and arranged for Vice Adm James M. Zortman, Commander, Naval Air Forces, Pacific Fleet, and former Red Eagle, and naval aviator, Capt (ret) Chuck "Heater" Heatley to meet with Linda and her sons. At that time the family members were told the previously classified details of Hugh Brown's accident. "Heater's" report on that visit reads as follows:

Vice Adm Zortman and I had a very successful meeting with Linda, her sons Brian and Brady, Linda's husband Peter and his brother on Saturday afternoon, December 16, 2006, from 1400hrs until 1535hrs at her home in Del Mar, California.

The family seemed to greatly appreciate every word that was uttered and all of the answers that they received. Though intense and emotional, especially for Linda, I feel that Hugh would have been proud of the way we handled the meeting. They knew practically nothing of the technical details – not the squadron name or designation, mission, location, aircraft type, Hugh's job (Safety Officer) etc. Basically, they thought he was with the 64th AS flying F-5s out of Nellis AFB. They did not know where or how the accident occurred, or even what a MiG-17 looked like. The admiral brought some photographs that they studied carefully.

Linda and the boys wanted to know if the crash site was now available to visit and I told them it was still on classified Ranges. I showed them the crash site on Google Earth, as well as the Tonopah Test Range Airfield and places where Hugh and I walked, worked, flew, etc. They had many questions about the aircraft, and it was obvious to me that they believed it might have been "experimental" or less than air-worthy, and with no ejection seat, so I went into great detail about our maintenance history, procedures and practices, as well as Hugh's last mission. They all seemed relieved and satisfied, and then the boys had several personal questions about their Dad – his personality, characteristics, traits, job, etc. You'll have to ask Vice Adm Zortman how I did with those questions as that part is a blur for me. Luckily, Hugh was a terrific squadron mate and a wonderful human being, so only nice things can ever be said about him.

Thank you all, and especially Vice Adm Zortman, for this opportunity. It brought a great deal of closure to the family and opened up future dialog as they think of more questions. Unexpectedly, it provided a great deal of closure for me as well.

I have been unable to determine if Rey Hernandez's family has been told the details relating to his death.

There are many hearsay reports about different pilots experiencing engine failures and dead sticking – flying the jets without power – back to the TTR without incident. Two pilots ejected from MiGs during the program and I know of at least one who "deadsticked" a MiG-21 into Tonopah after an engine failure. Rick Cazessus ("Bandit 63") had an engine failure in a MiG-21 shortly after take-off on June 25, 1987, and ejected without significant injury. As previously reported, "Hawk" Carlisle – now a three-star general – ejected from a MiG-23.

It was hard to know all the important things about these aircraft. Initially, there were no real documents or flight manuals. We learned from other pilots that had flown the jets and by asking questions like, "What should I do in terms of an emergency procedure if *this* or *that* happens." I am told that eventually flight manuals were written, but I have never seen them. Hopefully they will turn up and be put on display at the National Museum of the Air Force alongside other memorabilia from CONSTANT PEG.

CONSTANT PEG SUMMARY

Fiscal Year	1979	1980	1981	1982	1983	1984	1985	1986	1987	1988
MiG-17	2	2	3	0	0	0	0	0	0	0
MiG-21	6	6	6	8	9	15	17	14	14	14
MiG-23	0	0	1	3	6	9	10	10	10	9
Total Aircraft	8	8	10	11	15	24	27	24	24	23
Sorties	87	1,015	1,340	1,055	1,198	2,099	1,779	2,792	2,793	1,342
Exposures	68	372	462	575	666	800	688	982	905	412
Total Sorties	15,500									
Total Exposures	5,930									

In the chart titled CONSTANT PEG Summary notice that we started operations in 1979 with two MiG-17s and six MiG-21s. We acquired two additional "Frescos" between 1979 and 1981 to replace the two aircraft we had lost. Also in 1981 we began to acquire MiG-23s. The MiG-17s were retired the following year, and we began acquiring additional MiG-21s and MiG-23s in 1982. The inventory had grown to 27 flyable aircraft by 1985 – 17 MiG-21s and 10 MiG-23s – but not all of these jets were flyable at the same time. It was common practice with the MiGs, as it is with USAF and US Navy aircraft, to cannibalize or "can" good parts from otherwise disabled aircraft and install them on another aircraft in order to make it flyable.

During the ten-year interval of CONSTANT PEG operations 15,500 sorties were flown and nearly 6,000 aircrews were exposed to the MiGs in a training environment as detailed in this chart:

AIRCREW EXPOSURES

	US Air Force	US Navy / Marine Corps	Unknown	Total
FY79	68	0		68
FY80	203	169		372
FY81	uncertain	uncertain	462	462
FY82	389	186	·	575
FY83	477	189		666
FY84	566	234		800
FY85	421	267		688
FY86	679	303		982
FY87	552	353		905
FY88	283	129		412
Total	3,638	1,830	462	5,930

Nearly twice as many USAF aircrew were exposed to the MiGs compared to US Navy and US Marine Corps pilots and radar intercept officers. This is not surprising when you consider the comparative sizes of the force structures of the respective services. When the numbers were tallied we were unable to positively account for 462 of the 5,930 exposures, and therefore the military services of the officers participating in those sorties remains unknown.

CHAPTER 6

RED EAGLES' STORIES

In this chapter, individuals assigned to the CONSTANT PEG program provide an up-close and in some cases personal look at what it was like to be a Red Eagle. What follows is a press release followed by a series of leadership reflections, e-mails, working notes, and specific tales contributed by the MiG pilots and maintainers that lived the story.

The lead item is the press release declassifying CONSTANT PEG. It is followed by inputs prepared by the commanders and other Red Eagle leaders. These were originally produced in the *Red Eagle Newsletter*, which was first published on Memorial Day 2009 by Red Eagles Ben Galloway and Bob Breault. There has not been any real attempt to organize the stories that follow the leadership section. Instead, this part flows as though the gang was sitting around the bar, drinking beer or other adult beverages while reflecting on events and telling stories.

PRESS RELEASE

Secretary of the Air Force, Office of Public Affairs

Release No. 071106
November 13, 2006

Air Force Declassifies Elite Aggressor Program
WASHINGTON – After decades of secrecy, the Air Force today acknowledged that it flew Communist-built fighters at the Tonopah Test Range northwest of Las Vegas, Nevada.

From 1979 through to 1988, the program, known as CONSTANT PEG, saw US Air Force, Navy, and Marine aircrews flying against Soviet-designed MiG fighters as part of a training program where American pilots could better learn how to defeat or evade the Communist bloc's fighters of the day.

Brig Gen "Hawk" Carlisle, 3rd Wing commander at Elmendorf AFB, Alaska, is a former member of the 4477th Test and Evaluation Squadron who remembers the valuable training the unit provided. "CONSTANT PEG afforded pilots an opportunity to learn how to fight enemy aircraft in a controlled, safe environment, without having to endure the risks of actual air combat," said Brig Gen Carlisle. "Typically a pilot would start with a basic familiarization flight to observe the enemy airplane and study its characteristics, practicing 'one-on-one' defensive and offensive maneuvers against it and, finally, experience multi-bogey engagements high over the desert scrubland of the Nellis AFB ranges."

As a result of the sometimes marginal performance of the American fighter forces in the skies over North Vietnam due to the tactics they employed, CONSTANT PEG complemented other revolutionary training programs such as Red Flag, Topgun, and the Air Force and Navy-Marine Aggressor squadrons. The program was also intended to eliminate the "buck fever" or nervous excitement many pilots experience on their first few combat missions. Red Flag drew on historical experience that indicated pilots who survived their first ten missions were much more likely to survive a complete combat tour, and CONSTANT PEG was intended to teach them the right "moves" to enable them to come out on top of any engagement.

The end of CONSTANT PEG nearly coincided with the end of the Cold War, by which time some of its "graduates" had already proven themselves in actual air combat.

Threat aircraft flown by the Red Eagles spanned several decades and technical generations of capability. There was the MiG-17 "Fresco," a small, agile single-seat transonic fighter placed in service just after the Korean War and used extensively over Vietnam and the Middle East; the MiG-21 "Fishbed," a supersonic fighter used worldwide in large numbers; and the swing-wing MiG-23 "Flogger," likewise in global service. This aircraft was an attempt by the Soviets to match the sophisticated capabilities of the F-4 Phantom II.

"Although it came too late to influence Vietnam, CONSTANT PEG training greatly influenced the success of American airmen in DESERT STORM, who shot down 40 Iraqi fighters, many of which were 'Fishbeds' and 'Floggers,'" said Brig Gen Carlisle.

COMMANDERS' AND OTHER KEY LEADERSHIP REFLECTIONS

As previously mentioned, on Memorial Day 2009 Red Eagles Ben Galloway and Bob "Bro" Breault published the first *Red Eagle Newsletter*. It could not have been done without the technical assistance of Ben's lovely wife Melody. Since Memorial Day 2009 Ben and "Bro" have published newsletters that correspond to the major holidays through to September 2011. On July 4, 2009, Ben published the second newsletter, and the first in an unbroken series that, with the exception of Glenn Frick, has included a column written by each of the commanders of the Red Eagles. I wrote the July 4 column, and the inputs from the other commanders follow in the order in which they served. Mike Scott was the final commander, and his column appeared in the Christmas 2011 newsletter. The first maintenance officer, Dave Stringer, wrote the next column, and the first GCI controller, Jim Keys, prepared the column for the July 4, 2011, edition. Finally, Bud "Chops" Horan, the second Red Eagles GCI controller, prepared the column that was run in the September 2011 newsletter. This was written in advance of the Red Eagles' October 2011 reunion in Las Vegas.

GLENN FRICK – FIRST RED EAGLES COMMANDER

Glenn passed away prior to the declassification of the CONSTANT PEG program, and hence there is no known written record of his reflections about the project. Nevertheless, those of us that worked with Glenn found him to be an incredibly energetic and sincere advocate of the MiG project. From the very beginning Glenn was a key planner and participant. He arranged for the maintenance force to be assigned to TAC under his supervision even before the unit was formally established. Thus, the restoration of the aircraft was already underway even though the concept of operations and the final decisions regarding the construction of the airfield were still being made at the Pentagon.

GAIL PECK – SECOND RED EAGLES COMMANDER

Thirty years ago (July 1979) the Red Eagles started flight operations at the TTR when eight jets showed up on initial to land. The 4477th TEF was equipped with two MiG-17s and six MiG-21s. We also had three Cessna 404s and a Kenworth tractor.

The initial cadre of people, the jets, the facilities, and the equipment were assembled by 29 men under the leadership of Glenn Frick, the first commander. Glenn got the ball rolling, got promoted, and then was reassigned to the US mission in Egypt to help the Egyptians crank up an F-4 program which replaced their MiG-23s. I have often wondered what happened to those Egyptian MiG-23s, and about the role Glenn might have had in their disposition. It is easy to let your imagination run wild with that one!

The team of people that Glenn assembled was not only without equal in terms of mechanical talent, it was also without equal in the ability to work together and to select others to join the Red Eagles. Men were carefully selected that possessed the same qualities. In my 26 years of active commissioned service nowhere else did I see the equal of the team of men in the 4477th. Every minute spent working with the Red Eagles was truly a joy.

In April 2009 I asked Tommy Karnes to his face, "How do you take a wrecked MiG-21 and build it into a safe flying machine?" Tommy replied, "It's easy Boss. You just take it apart, figure out what doesn't work right, fix what's broken, and put it back together again." It's hard to believe I had missed something that simple!

By the time Phil White relinquished command to Jack Manclark, by Phil's count he had more than 400 assigned personnel, including a Chief [chief master sergeant] who was the "First Shirt." At the peak in 1985 Jack had 27 MiGs, although not all were flyable at the same time.

This unit played an important role in the USA's victory over the USSR in the Cold War. Further, the unit provided the training to our USAF, US Navy, and US Marine Corps air combat fighter forces that led to the air war successes during the Gulf of Sidra shoot downs in 1981 and 1989, DESERT STORM in 1991, and the follow-on Iraqi operations. The Red Eagles also had measurable influence indirectly during the war over Kosovo in 1999.

It is my hope that the veterans of the 4477th TES will band back together and participate in a Red Eagle Alumni Association that publishes a newsletter of important info to us all, keeps a personnel roster up to date, and also sponsors periodic reunions and smaller but more frequent local social gatherings. Perhaps we need "Line Chiefs" around this great country to volunteer to take charge in their own backyards, figure out who lives close by and lead the way locally.

Paul Cox has worked long and hard here in Las Vegas, largely by himself, to collect and organize squadron roster information. I think we have now folded all of the known data into a single roster and have pretty much purged the obsolete e-mails and addresses. Ben Galloway and Bob Breault have picked up the responsibility for the squadron roster and are off to a great start, but there is still a long way to go to make the Red Eagle roster complete. And, in addition to new input information on people, we need updates when things change. I suggest that every Red Eagle put Galloway and Breault in their cellular equivalent of the "T Mobile" Fav Five, even if it is necessary to erase the mother-in-law. Then, when things change or you find someone that has been "lost" you can easily send Ben or Bob updated information.

Just prior to Memorial Day we received the first squadron newsletter. It was designed and published by Ben Galloway. WAY TO GO BEN! The newsletter was forwarded to those with valid e-mail addresses in the Red Eagle roster. This July 2009 edition is the next newsletter, and I challenge the other commanders to follow in sequence with a quarterly commander's column for the newsletter. "Obi Wan" Henderson, "batter up" for the next Commander's Column and Tom Gibbs, you're on deck. Ben, hold their feet to the fire. We need to keep track of each other. That's all for now Gang. Bandit Leader on Initial with a flight of eight, New Day, New Town – it'll be a full stop landing! Hello Tonopah!

Update January 2012: the Red Eagles had a great reunion in October 2011, the newsletter is a great success and the alumni association is up and running with Mike Scott serving as the first president. Not a bad couple of years!

EARL HENDERSON – THIRD RED EAGLES COMMANDER

My short eight months as the commander of the 4477th are filled with so many memories of people and events that it is hard to pin down any favorites, but I will try. Indulge me as I recall some mainstream and some less than mainstream people and events.

I had never met Robert O. Ellis until after I assumed command of the 4477th in September 1979. The day before I took command I was on an airline flight to Langley AFB to attend the accident briefing of the first 4477th accident that killed Hugh Brown. Plus I was told that I would meet Gen Creech and get his "approval" to take over the unit. On board the airliner were Maj Gen Robert Kelley, the TFWC/CC, and my old friend "Jose" Oberle, who was the Operations Officer of the 4477th at the time. Until "Jose" saw me at McCarran airport that morning he had no idea that Gail was about to be replaced. "Jose" and I spent the entire flight to and from Langley talking about the tasks ahead of me in assuming command after Gail Peck. The very first subject he covered was Bobby Ellis, and how important he was to the maintenance of the aircraft and the success of the 4477th.

When I returned to Nellis and walked into the squadron at the TTR I called a meeting of everyone and explained how the events of the past 48 hours had unfolded, and what guidance I had received from generals Creech and Kelley. I then asked for a private meeting with Bobby Ellis, where I requested that he work with me to get past the turbulence of a sudden change of command. He was wary of me and appeared to be apprehensive of what impact I might have upon "his world," but he promised to cooperate. Over the next eight months he delivered on that promise, and we developed a harmonious working relationship and the job got done.

Bobby Ellis was a very complex man. He had a brilliant mind, which he used to retain an incredible volume of information. He was a walking encyclopedia of Soviet aircraft. He was the equivalent of having ten Mikoyan technical representatives on site to provide support. He could tell you that a hydraulic accumulator fitting on a Su-7 would fit a MiG-17 engine fuel supply line, but not a MiG-21 engine. He knew all MiG-17 and MiG-21 engine variants, and the differences in sight and sound. He knew every single MiG spare part we had on hand at Tonopah on a first name basis. He knew everyone in the USA who could reverse engineer everything from fuel bladders to disk brakes. All this information, without referring to a single written word, was kept in his head.

Bobby was revered and idolized by every single maintenance man. He was called "Daddy," and they had all been personally taught their MiG maintenance craft by him. If they faced a problem on any given day and they did not have a solution, they would always turn to "Daddy" and he always seemed to have an answer – and it was invariably a correct one.

Bobby had boundless energy and always seemed to be working ten issues simultaneously. He was everywhere throughout the flying day – on the line watching and correcting crew chiefs if necessary, in the supply hangar helping design a parts stocking inventory system, in the fuel pit trying to figure out why our brand new POL tank was leaking, or looking at blueprints for new MiG-23 hangars to ensure that the correct three phase power supply was in the right location. It was mind-boggling the depth of knowledge he had on so many subjects.

At the same time Bobby was single-minded and nearly impossible to steer in any direction. His independence frustrated me more often and in more ways than any other squadron member. Even when he would appear to be compliant with a plan or proposal, I was often left with doubts about whether he truly implemented what I wanted. He was crafty and elusive enough to work the system and leave no visible trace.

Bobby was a world-class pack rat and hoarder. In the early days of the 4477th operation the budget never quite caught up with the unit's exploding growth (particularly the addition of MiG-23s), and we were always scrounging for makeshift solutions to storage, housing, supply, etc. As a result, Bobby sent his guys out on DRMO raids throughout the southwestern US. They brought back a conglomeration of house trailers, supply racks, temporary shelters, Jacuzzis, pumps, and valves and … you name it. Only Bobby knew the "Grand Plan," and I was constantly being surprised by a new structure or vehicle at the Tonopah complex. It looked like a shanty town, and it was called "Indian Village" for very obvious reasons. More than once I was left trying to explain to my director of operations or the Wing/TFWC commander why I needed a vehicle that had only an engine, a chassis, a steering wheel, and a seat – and "Who was that tiny man driving the vehicle who looked like Yosemite Sam, full beard, unkempt hair, and all?" His name was Billy Lightfoot and he was my (Bobby's) vehicle maintenance specialist.

I could almost never get Bobby to write anything down, and there was a scary amount of information in his cranium – procedures, background data, points of contact, future plans, etc. I worried all the time about his "only man" control. If something ever happened to him we would have been left floundering in the dark for a considerable amount of time.

What a profound loss that he is no longer with us to confirm and astound me with his "remembrances" of our time together in the Red Eagles.

After Bobby left the 4477th and went to work for IMI I saw and heard of his activities on a frequent basis, sometimes from him, sometimes from Bob Faye or Gerry Huff. My impression was that he was constantly on the road, all over the world, flying business or first class, arranging international arms sales (mainly in Soviet equipment), and loving life. His wife Mariel was not that happy with all the traveling but she was very much enjoying the new found wealth. Her mood changed dramatically, however, when she found out Bobby had an Israeli girlfriend who was younger than their oldest daughter.

Long after I surrendered command, Mariel called me in San Antonio, where I had gone for some medical tests, and vented her anger to me about Bobby's girlfriend. Plus she claimed Bobby was bringing Israeli "spies" onto Nellis AFB. I told Mariel that I was now obligated to tell the OSI (Office of Special Investigations) about her accusations, and she seemed to be pleased that would occur. I did call the OSI as soon as I returned to Nellis. The OSI response was lukewarm at best, but they indicated that they would take my report under advisement.

Within the week Mariel had shot and killed Bobby just as he was unloading his Israeli girlfriend's luggage at their new condo in Henderson, Nevada. Mariel was convicted of murder and sentenced to eight years in prison. She served three years and got out on good behavior. My wife last saw Mariel in the late 1980s working as a waitress in Las Vegas.

George Gennin told a story about Mariel coming into his office and complaining about him messing up the squadron with the changes that put the men back in uniform and curtailing the close personal relationship in the unit. Knowing Mariel, that story is totally believable.

With his sudden departure in August 1979, not surprisingly Gail Peck left me with many incomplete tasks and issues. These included the hiring of a new secretary to replace one who had just quit. The maintenance guys (and pilots) referred to the outgoing secretary as "Brunhilda." Needless to say, she was not of their blood, and she could not wait to get away from that weird group of individuals with the super secret mission. The squadron guys were equally happy to see her go.

Secretaries are GS (government civil service) employees, and at Nellis squadron secretaries start as a GS-4 or GS-5. The secretary for the TFWC commander was generally a GS-9 (although more recently a GS-8 position). When there is a GS opening, the position is posted and anyone with the qualifications submits their name. As squadron commander you look at the list of applicants and tell the civilian personnel office which ones you would like to interview. Gail was in the middle of that process when I took over.

The Red Eagle operations at Nellis were conducted out of a white doublewide trailer in the parking lot south of the FWS. There was no privacy. The commander's office was a 10ft x 10ft room with an accordion door that would not even latch. As I interviewed new secretary candidates, everyone in the squadron could, and did, walk by to "check them out!" They would individually give me a secret ballot vote with a thumb up or thumb down. I always had to make sure the new candidate was sitting in a chair where she could not see the men walking by in the hallway. I also had to work very hard to keep a sober game face on during the interview.

After about ten candidate interviews in walks Eunice Warren. Eunice had just recently married Sgt David Warren, a maintenance technician on the Thunderbirds. They had met when the team visited Wright-Patterson AFB, Eunice being employed on base as a GS-11 executive secretary for one of the Directorates in AFSC. She moved to Nellis after marrying David and was looking for work as a secretary. Eunice quickly found out that a GS-11 position was out of the question, and the best she could do was a GS-4. When she showed up at our trailers she was dressed very smartly and business-like. She was both very beautiful and very shapely. The commotion outside my office during the interview was exceedingly distracting. At least 50 men passed my door, and there were only 30 men in total in the squadron! There were a lot of second and third looks and a unanimous thumbs up. She was overqualified, but I hired her despite that shortcoming.

Our daily routine was to gather at the trailers early in the morning, generally before dawn, sort out the day's schedule and figure out the transportation to Tonopah. Then we were off to TTR for a long day. Only one or two people were left behind – the secretary, an admin troop, and perhaps a supply guy. For the first six weeks Eunice came to work dressed just as she had for the interview – a nice business suit. But she soon found out she was "all dressed up with nowhere to go." In her previous job at Wright-Patterson she got a lot of coffee for visiting generals, flashed a pretty smile and did a little typing. In the trailers she did a lot of typing and answering the phone, no coffee, and no visiting generals.

There was a marked difference between working for a three-star general and dealing with a bunch of crusty old sergeants and bone-tired fighter pilots at the end of a long day. Soon Eunice was wearing blue jeans and a bulky sweater. The bulky sweater at least diverted the more obvious stares. She had a sweet personality, and we almost ruined her with coarse treatment. She somehow kept her sense of humor and figured out a way to dish out as much as she got. The result was that it endeared her to all squadron members.

Eunice was one of the first people to know that I was having pain down my left arm, especially at altitude (Tonopah). Like a mother hen, she was genuinely concerned, and she pointed out that her father had similar symptoms and it turned out to be heart related. I was only 38, so she couldn't be right! Turned out, she was.

If she is out there, and receiving these newsletters, "Eunice, please forgive the men of the 4477th for all of their lecherous stares and comments. You were a great trooper!"

One of the more unique groups of individuals in the Red Eagles throughout their history were the firefighters. During my tenure it was Ralph Payne, Kermit Deitz, and Robby Robinson.

Within all USAF installations, firefighters have always been loners, not by choice, but by vocation. Even before 9/11 they were the ones you never saw, the ones you never knew by name, but you always counted on them to be there when the catastrophic event happened. They were the super heroes quietly waiting to be called upon by claxon, by warning horn, or by the sound of an explosion, near or far. Throughout my career they were simply the men in the big red trucks and asbestos suits you saw responding to the emergency landing. Or, they were the men behind the large fire hose spraying you down at the end of 100 missions over North Vietnam, end of tour at a base or final flight in an air force flying career. But almost always they were nameless faces. They did their deed and then disappeared back into the shadows to wait for the claxon.

Ralph, Kermit, and Robby were selected by Ellis, hired by Peck, and gratefully appreciated by me. They belonged to neither the pilots nor the maintenance crowd – they had their own organizational niche and truly reveled in it. At every going away party there was always a presentation by the officers, by maintenance, and by the firefighters. Until the Red Eagles came along, firefighters, as a group within the USAF, had never enjoyed a close association with any single organization, anywhere. When these three men arrived at Tonopah they immediately knew they were a part of a unique group of people, and they quickly made their own mission within that group. Under the leadership of Ralph Payne, they completely reinvented the concept of emergency response at a remote fighter base. Ralph recognized that the strict rules on fire safety and safe separation between combustibles had to be "flexible." He was in my office almost daily discussing the issues, and fire response rules, but always trying to accommodate the mission. He was a master at compromise and a cherished advisor.

A typical base the size of Tonopah would have had at least 12 firefighters – we had three. With significant fire response forces more than 50 miles away, these men knew that if "it" ever happened, it was up to them to do the right thing, whether it be put out a hangar fire to save a "national asset" (a MiG fighter) or pull a pilot out of the cockpit of a burning fighter aircraft in the overrun. They were zealous, ever-ready rescuers always on guard. More than once at a squadron party, Kermit, slightly tipsy, came up to me and my wife, Andy, and told us both that if ever there was a time when I was in a cockpit and on fire, he would physically pull me free and rescue me. Never did I doubt that he would, or could, do exactly as he said. He was like a pro football offensive lineman telling his quarterback "Don't worry, I will always be there to protect you," followed by "I love you man!" As a group, they loved the persona they had become, and I loved them for it.

One of my most treasured memories of my days as a Red Eagle commander was working with the firefighters. The plaque they presented to me upon my departure has a special place of honor in my home on my "I Love Me" wall in my home office.

TOM GIBBS – FOURTH RED EAGLES COMMANDER

Sadly, Tom Gibbs passed away in the spring of 2011 before he had the chance to write a comprehensive column detailing his memories of his time leading the Red Eagles. He did write the following for the December 2009 Red Eagles newsletter:

Hi Red Eagles, from Bandit 21, Tom Gibbs 4th Commander of the squadron. You are a special few whose dedication was instrumental to the special inputs you provided that allowed our fighter crews to excel. That dedication is a true testimonial to who and what you are. Abso-lutely Sierra Hotel!

GEORGE GENNIN – FIFTH RED EAGLES COMMANDER

The positive impact the 4477th TES had on US Navy, US Marine Corps, and USAF aircrew readiness has been verified in several conflicts in recent years. Without question, the mission of the Red Eagles was successfully executed over the years the 4477th TES was operational, and the effectiveness of the training provided to those aircrews fortunate enough to be selected for exposures is underscored by the improved enemy kill ratio enjoyed by our services in recent wars. As an extension of the USAF Aggressors, the Red Eagles provided selected aircrews with the next level of training – exposure to the real "McCoy."

The activation of the Red Eagles and its eventual transformation into an organization that could generate sufficient sorties to expose more of the service's combat aircrews was a monumental task. The security aspects of the program were always an issue that often controlled the schedule and availability of sorties – and this was an issue dealt with by all the commanders throughout the life of the Red Eagles. Another monumental factor – one that had the largest impact on sortie generation – was the ability to obtain an adequate supply of parts needed to keep the MiGs in an operational status and safe to fly.

The commanders who preceded me in the 4477th TES all had different tasks and different challenges. From the very first day, they were faced with generating sorties with a limited number of MiG-17 and MiG-21 aircraft, a very limited and "ad hoc" supply inventory/system, and only a handful of qualified MiG pilots who barely remained current on the types due to limited sorties. Further, some were also involved with building facilities at Tonopah to ensure that future operations could be conducted safely and securely, and to accommodate force modernization plans – for instance, the addition of the MiG-23. All the Red Eagle commanders who preceded me – and all of their personnel – accomplished a tremendous feat in establishing an organization that survived the early years and set the framework for future operations.

However, it was time for change, a transformation to the "real" air force – the USAF leadership was losing faith in the ability of the Red Eagles to accomplish their mission effectively, efficiently, and, most importantly, safely.

My time as commander of the 4477th TES can be defined as the "transformation" era. I was directed from day one to transform the 4477th TES into a professional organization that fitted the mold of other TAC fighter squadrons. While I received a lot of direction and guidance from the TAC senior leadership (including Gen Creech), the TFWC commander (Gen Gregory), and the 57th TFTW commander (Gen Kerby), I also received a lot of support from these same gentlemen. More importantly, while I was given the responsibility for the transformation, I was also provided with the authority to make changes happen.

Changes were implemented on all fronts – personnel (standards, uniforms, code of conduct, professionalism, reinstitution of the military chain of command); operations (standardized and documented training, customary scheduling practices, establishment and compliance with rules of engagement, adherence to regulations, and multiple currency); logistics (establishment of reliable supply/parts sources, audit of existing parts, establishment of a computerized inventory system and establishment of a parts inventory level based on projected utilization); maintenance (establishment of documented/written standardized maintenance processes and procedures that did not rely on the memory of any one individual, a phased maintenance approach that assured aircraft were operationally ready in sufficient numbers to support the flying schedule, accountability within the maintenance organization, introduction of fresh maintenance personnel assuring things were not done just because "that's the way they were always done," professional work ethics based on standards and reinstitution of the military chain of command); and, last but not least, modernization/upgrades to the facilities, infrastructure, and aircraft fleet.

Many of the folks then assigned to the squadron had been around for some time, especially the maintenance folks. As expected, the magnitude of changes were not readily accepted by all, and some even openly opposed any changes. However, the train had departed the station on a determined schedule and agenda, and folks either got on the train or were left behind.

The pilots assigned to the squadron were many of the best available from all the services. However, the "fraternity approach" to the selection process did not necessarily ensure the best-of-the-best were recruited and hired. During my tenure I opened the process beyond the Nellis-based Aggressors to include FWS graduates/instructors and Aggressors from across the combat air forces. The US Navy and US Marine Corps selection process continued to ensure assignment of their brightest and best.

While I was fortunate to have the best fighter pilots and instructors, the approach to flying operations was dismal. To rectify my concerns in this area, I selected Maj Monroe Whatley to be the operations officer and assigned him the responsibility of standardizing flying operations and instituting TAC policies, procedures, and standards. Further, I directed Monroe to fully use the assigned US Navy and US Marine Corps pilots and integrate them into all Red Eagle operations – unlike previously, when they were assigned to a "Navy Flight" and not integrated into the organization. Monroe not only accepted the challenge but also excelled in all areas, and by the end of his tour we were providing the forces more exposure to the MiGs than anytime in previous history. Additionally, he was accomplishing his mission more professionally and in a safer manner.

Obtaining adequate parts to keep the MiGs operational was always a concern. Although the maintenance organization was accomplishing a great job with what it had, if parts were not available to fix a problem, the aircraft could not fly. Cannibalization was a routine practiced on a daily basis, causing maintenance more work than necessary. Due to the limited number of MiGs available to fulfill our operational requirements, aircraft were often put on the flying schedule rather than being scheduled for programmed maintenance. This became a double-edged sword for although the requirements of the flying schedule were initially being met, the maintenance problems eventually mounted, causing the simultaneous grounding of many of the aircraft. As a result of not having a preventative maintenance program, some severe problems surfaced, such as MiG-21 fuel bladder leaks, MiG-21 and MiG-23 ejection seat inoperability, and MiG-23 engine/turbine reliability.

The maintenance organization was the critical element that had to be transformed if the Red Eagles were to meet ever-increasing sortie/exposure requirements. This necessitated changes throughout every facet of the organization, which was met with resistance by the "Old Guard." My approach to transforming maintenance had a simple solution – I hired Maj George Tittle to be the Red Eagle Chief of Maintenance, assigned him the responsibility for the transformation and gave him the authority to make the Red Eagle maintenance organization the star of TAC, and to prepare for growth and expanded sortie generation capability. George took charge, made the tough decisions and implemented changes that made the Red Eagles one of the finest maintenance organizations in the USAF. It became professional, had standardized, documented programmed and routine maintenance procedures, and, eventually, was producing more sorties than ever before in the history of the organization.

Once the groundwork for the transformation was laid and the support of the senior leadership regained, work was initiated to expand the squadron to meet and sustain anticipated future sortie requirements to support the growing exposure requests from the USAF, US Navy, and US Marine Corps. With untiring support from (then) Maj Dave "Marshall" McCloud (the Pentagon manager for classified programs), we were able to obtain support and the funding needed to implement the planned expansion. This included significant funds to refurbish the MiG-23 engines and get them back into operational status, establishment of secure logistics supply channels needed to support both the MiG-21 and the MiG-23, acquisition of additional aircraft for the squadron inventory, and military construction funds for an intelligence facility/SCIF. We also had a modern facility built, as well as additional hangars to support extra aircraft.

Significant changes and improvements had been accomplished by the end of my tour as commander. The Red Eagles had been transformed into a professional USAF unit that was producing more sorties for the warfighters than in the history of the squadron. The combat aircrews were exposed to the professional and capable Red Eagle pilots flying these magnificent MiG aircraft, but behind the scenes never to be seen by the forces were the hard working support personnel that generated the jets that flew the sorties. The maintenance professionals, led by a hard-charging George Tittle, were transformed into the best maintenance department in the USAF. They produced sortie rates equivalent to frontline TAC fighters – but they accomplished their job within a totally unique and limited maintenance capability. They were not afforded the flexibility of calling a sister unit to obtain parts when needed, and could not obtain technical expertise from other TAC units. They were a self-sufficient, self-sustaining professional group that accomplished their job in a professional manner.

While significant improvements occurred during my tenure as commander, and I feel that the Red Eagles were a better organization upon my departure, I was not the reason for these exemplary changes. The folks discussed above, and many others too numerous to name, understood the importance of the Red Eagles to the tactical community, shared the transformation vision, and worked hard and endlessly to make the Red Eagles survivable within the framework of the USAF. Without the support of all these individuals, the Red Eagles could have been deactivated years sooner – but because of their untiring efforts, the tactical fighter pilot community of all the services benefited as proven in recent conflicts. I am pleased to have been a member of the Red Eagles and proud to have served with some of the best from the USAF, US Navy, and US Marine Corps. I salute all Red Eagles.

PHIL WHITE – SIXTH RED EAGLES COMMANDER

Red Eagles! Just to be in the unit was beyond my wildest dreams, and, trust me, my dreams could get plenty wild (operative word here is "could," not can!). But to be the commander was an all time high. Likely, each and every 4477th TES commander had similar feelings.

Although our respective obstacles and tasks may have been different, we all shared a common goal set. Find the best people and take care of them. Build an all-star team, train, equip, and inspire them to catch the vision – then, get out of their way. In short, lead this all-star team to realistically replicate our adversaries' strengths and weaknesses, enabling our tactical fighter services to become the most deadly MiG killers in the free world. All the previous commanders faced innumerable challenges as the unit grew from a fledgling austere operation to one that approached a small wing in size, complexity, and mission import. My time at the helm of this unique unit was certainly no different.

Beginning with my first interviews with Brig Gen Mike Kirby, Maj Gen Gene Fischer, and Gen Creech, my orders were crystal clear. Gen Fischer had been sent to Nellis to "clean it up." Prior to my arrival, an unfortunate accident resulting in the death of an NCO doing fuel cell repairs caused Gen Fischer to have serious concerns about the unit. He was convinced, as was Gen Creech, that our maintenance chief, Maj George Tittle, was at fault. He insisted that "the cancer" within maintenance be isolated and "cut out" before it spread. Gen Creech shared his personal vision for the Red Eagles with me – continue transformation to the "real air force," increase the sortie rate and, last but certainly not least, conduct a major clean up of maintenance. Welcome aboard Lt Col White, and off I go to a condensed Maintenance Officers' course to jazz up my maintenance savvy. On returning to Nellis, to begin my overlap with "G2," one could say I faced my first challenge – Brig Gen Joe Ashy was the new 57th FWW commander (CC), and his reputation preceded him.

My second day on the job saw senators John Glenn and Ted Kennedy visit us at Tonopah. After being shown around the then highly classified F-117s, I hosted them for a briefing on the Red Eagles. Generals Fischer and Ashy also attended. This was a prelude to the level of interest in happenings at Tonopah. The 4450th Tactical Group (TG) with the F-117 stealth fighter was approaching operational status and had become the major unit at Tonopah, which was fast becoming a full-up base, complete with a base commander. We experienced a continuous flow of high-level dignitaries and military leaders visiting the site, including the likes of Secretary of State George P. Schultz and National Security Advisor Robert C. "Bud" McFarlane, to name but two.

Although we maintained our secrecy and funding channels, other normalizing changes were happening. The chain of command for the F-117s changed from reporting directly to TAC HQ to now passing through the TFWC/CC. This put Gen Fischer directly in charge of all activities at the base. He established an office complex and began flying up two days a week to hold staff meetings, which I was required to attend. Our activities were getting a lot more visibility, and I was soon briefing Gen Ashy almost daily to keep him one step ahead of Gen Fischer. Gen Ashy had become my primary supporter during this period of change, but more importantly, he was a strong supporter of the Red Eagles! However, he had also started to get more involved in our "stuff" and had started to put "his touches" on us!

A big concern Gen Ashy had from day one was the multiple aircraft currency of the pilots. One of his first changes was to stop pilots from flying with the FWS – a decision that was unpopular with us, as well as the schools, because of the Intel crosstalk and recruiting. The second currency issue resolved itself shortly after when the air force elected to not renew the MU-2 lease and put a C-12 detachment in place to support Tonopah. Gen Ashy's next move created a whole host of issues too numerous to cover in this article when he changed our reporting chain to go through 57th FWW/AT (Adversary Threat), thus aligning us with the Aggressor mission and blowing our test cover. These changes, and those previously mentioned, clearly put the Red Eagles in a much more visible position, with considerably more levels of supervision and accountability that were not always constructive – not exactly what we wanted or needed at the time!

The good old days of less oversight were a thing of the past. It was time to control collateral damage and protect the mission, and the people. We had a job to do! With Gen Creech's marching orders in mind, I needed to focus on the maintenance issues. My job was made easier by the core of pilots who were in the unit. Upon reporting for duty it was like a reunion. Almost all of them, except the US Navy and US Marine Corps pilots, had worked with or for me previously, and ALL were outstanding pilots and officers. With top-notch pilots, I was able to lay out the ops directions on where we needed to go, and loosen the reigns so they could do what they do best. With a little tweaking now and then, they did not disappoint me!

One of my earliest opportunities to feel the hot seat related to – you guessed it – maintenance. In my first meeting with CMSgt Mickey Masserati (First Sergeant) and Maj Tittle, I learned of a small faction of senior maintenance personnel who wanted to test the mettle of the new "boss" by reverting back to the old way of doing things. Mickey was a big barrel chested 6ft 7in no nonsense, but fair, previous NCO Academy instructor. He was a man I quickly learned to trust and rely on, and he was often my sounding board on many issues.

Given Gen Creech's orders to eliminate "the cancer," and with the help of Mickey, George Tittle, and a number of "on board" NCOs, it did not take long to identify and extricate (reassign) the wannabe rabble-rousers. The others quickly got the message, and fortunately I had no other problems with maintenance personnel. It was following this incident that I also began to recognize the true value of Maj Tittle to the organization, and appreciate him as an outstanding maintenance officer and team member – a view I held throughout my tour, and still do today!

With backing from Gen Ashy, we briefed several Nellis senior NCOs into the program and brought them to Tonopah for several weeks to help us from an "outsiders'" perspective to determine what might need improvement. With their input, and support from generals Fischer and Ashy, we went to Langley to present our recommendations to Gen Creech on what was needed (personnel, facilities, equipment, and organizational changes) to achieve the maintenance program that he had envisioned. He approved all that we asked and the changes were set in motion. However, as we were implementing our plan for changes Gen Creech retired, and shortly after that we were given a "change to the changes!"

As I mentioned earlier, the F-117s were about to go operational. After Creech's retirement, HQ TAC decided it was time for a management evaluation inspection (MEI) for the 4450th, and why not include the 4477th in this too. Wow – talk about change! A month later, HQ TAC Inspector General Brig Gen John Jacquish and a small cadre of senior officers and NCOs visited us for three weeks for the unit's first inspection of any kind. After a thorough look and a few helpful suggestions, we received an outstanding rating in all areas, attesting to the caliber and dedication of the men and women in all sections of the squadron. I could not have been prouder of any group of people than these hard working professionals who sacrificed long hours away from home and family for the good of the air force.

The outstanding rating from the MEI seemed to put a new spark in the squadron. I saw a change in their focus, with the mission becoming even more central and the "I" becoming more of a "we." The transformation started by the previous commanders continued to sweep through the unit at all levels.

But just as all mountains give way to valleys, we experienced a number of setbacks related to the equipment we were using. At the time we had just received new turbine blades for our MiG-23 engines. We thought we were on a roll, but not so fast! The INS (inertial navigation system) units were failing, hence the Air Data Computers would not work – aircraft grounded again! "Admiral" Nelson to the rescue! Through our trusted defense industry, they figured out how the INSs were supposed to work, took a couple of weeks to repair them and once again we were flying.

As our fleet of newer MiG-21s increased we encountered problems with their ejection seats. They required several inputs in respect to pilot weight, height, etc. to dial in the proper setting on the seat for them to work correctly. However, test information was not available, and we had no data. This forced us to ground these newer aircraft for several weeks. Ultimately, we sent a seat to Holloman AFB for sled testing, and to determine pilot seat input settings. After several weeks, we had new data, and each pilot had his personal settings. Problem solved and we were flying again.

A short while later we examined the seats fitted into our older MiG-21s. Now that we had carts to initiate the ejection, we began to wonder just what state the harnesses and canopies were in for these veteran seats? Once again we turned to Holloman, who gave us both good news and bad news. The parachute canopies were in good condition, but most of the harnesses were rotten. We grounded the MiG-21s until new harnesses could be engineered by AFSC. We were fully operational once again three weeks later.

And then there was the time that we were at a full stop for two months for a total rebuild of the Tonopah runway, this halt in flying adversely affecting our sortie production for the year. There were a number of other minor setbacks along the way, but always with a similar result. With the resourcefulness, ingenuity, and make it happen attitude of the entire unit – maintenance, operations, supply, GCI, Intel, life-support, admin, and others – the Red Eagles continued to prosper and sorties increased.

An incident relating to our Kenworth prime mover presented a little humor, and boosted squadron morale. The blue "KW" was due for a major overhaul to include painting at the air force depot in Ogden. Prior to its delivery there, I asked Ogden what color it would be painted. The answer – what color do YOU want it? The new Tonopah base vehicles were all painted a non-descript white, but since we were still operating under an independent budget, our vehicles were not base resources. We were starting to look more and more like that "other" unit at Tonopah, and although things were progressing nicely, I thought a little unit distinction would be good for our troops.

I mentioned that seeing how we were the Red Eagles, red might be an appropriate color for our truck. Imagine the reaction when, upon return from Ogden, the Kenworth drove through the Tonopah gate sporting a bright thunderbird red finish, with large airbrushed bald eagles on both sides of the sleeper box (paid for complements of the NCOs). It was classic – the base commander was furious though I can't imagine why! Our answer to Gen Fischer was that "Ogden made the call on the color," issue closed! "Big Red," as it became known, was a site to behold, and a source of pride for the Red Eagles.

My tour as boss of the 4477th TES was the absolute highlight of my military career. The people were the **best** in their fields, and I can never sing their praises enough to do them justice. While most felt as I did – fortunate to have been a part of such a great unit – there was one notable exception. I believed in and continued to strongly support Maj George Tittle, but the system was not so kind to him – a real injustice to an outstanding individual. Nonetheless, those of us who had the privilege of flying on and under Red Eagle "wings" owe a debt of gratitude to the founding fathers – Moody, "Boots," "Pappy" Frick, especially Gail Peck, and so many others, too many to mention lest I leave someone out. I feel truly blessed and honored to have been a Red Eagle, brothers and sisters all!

Jack Manclark – Seventh Red Eagles Commander

I consider myself blessed to have been a member of the Red Eagles. I have served or worked for the air force for more than 40 years, and I can unequivocally say that the best tour of my career was the time I served in the 4477th TES. The unit personnel were both truly outstanding and professional. The pilots were some of the finest operators in the military, with experience levels unmatched in any unit. But the true heroes of the 4477th TES were the maintainers.

There were many days that I would walk by the MiG-23 hangar and see six or seven of the jets broken in half awaiting engines. I would ask myself how many times can the maintainers put these jets back together without making a mistake?

The answer turned out to be 100 percent of the time, as maintenance never let us down!

I look back on the tour and remember that my most trusted advisors were chiefs Hardy and Thurman. If they said the jet was flyable, we flew it. This trust existed throughout the organization, and it meant that when you went to your jet and your crew chief said it was ready, you didn't need to do a preflight – it was ready.

In the main it was a great time, but there were some turbulent times too. Scotty Rogers ("Bandit 55") lost an engine and had to deadstick a MiG-21 back to the airfield. That was a great aviator accomplishment. I drove out to the runway and picked him up, and for the first several minutes he was unable to talk. I had a half-gallon of Jack Daniels waiting for him when we got back to Nellis that afternoon. His wife said he spent the night on the bathroom floor drunk, being sick. It was not long after that that Ric Cazessus lost an engine in a MiG-21 and had to punch out at the end of the runway.

About a month later, in August 1987, we lost a MiG-23 to a flat spin. When he arrived back at TTR by helicopter I went out and picked up the pilot, Capt "Hawk" Carlisle. The first thing he said to me was "Boss, we have to turn the barometer in the seat up. I was below the mountain before I was kicked out of the seat." The second thing he said was "When I saw the aircraft hit the ground and explode, I thought I am glad the airlines are hiring." Well "Hawk" is now a three-star general with a good shot of becoming a four-star general. Our egress personnel had kept the ejection seats working and saved two pilots!

The leadership was not happy with our accidents, but we always had good support from Brig Gen Ashy and Brig Gen Hall. When we went to brief the accidents to the four-star general at TAC HQ, Gen Kempf had me compute our accident rate the way the rest of the air force reports. The metric was major accidents per 100,000 flying hours. In the air force, if the figure gets to more than four accidents per 100,000 the air force and safety personnel get excited – ours was 100 per 100,000! The four-star general was not happy, but everyone knew it was a high-risk program.

I am currently serving as the Director of Test and Evaluation, with responsibility for our test ranges. I visit TTR frequently, and I can report that the airfield is busy and looks pretty good. Most of the buildings are occupied and the chow hall is open. The F-117s have come home and are in flyable storage in their old hangars. The Mancamp has suffered over the years. We keep about 300 rooms open, but the chow hall is closed and, at best, the bar has about 15 patrons a night, but they do have free popcorn. We are also responsible for the Foreign Material Acquisition (FMA) program, and I can assure you we are very busy.

The USAF budget is being reduced, but we have great leadership and will continue to provide the country with the world's premier air force.

MIKE SCOTT – EIGHTH RED EAGLES COMMANDER

Happy Holidays, Red Eagles. It's my turn in the *Commander's Call* bucket, and I hope I can carry it off as well as my predecessors. Lord knows, they did a much better job in ensuring the continuation of the squadron! To wit, as I write this, it is 23 years after I had the privilege of beginning my short tenure as Red Eagle Commander – a four-month period that culminated with the last flights on March 5, 1988, and squadron closure shortly thereafter.

"Why close the Red Eagles?" was the question of the day during that turbulent period. Although there were many issues that made the decision difficult and complicated, the answer simply boiled down to "affordability." Previous *Commander's Call* articles pretty much sum up the dramatic growth and change of our organization. But maybe a short recap of our ten-year squadron evolution might help you understand why the Red Eagles were viewed as expendable.

Realistically, the Red Eagles consisted of two items – a unit and a mission. The unit consisted of people and stuff. The mission made us a training aid for the Tactical Air Forces (TAF) – USAF, US Navy, and US Marine Corps – of the United States.

Let's address the unit first. The earlier articles described our transformation from a barebones – few people, not much stuff, no luxuries – outfit into a full-up, "MEI-able" organization that paralleled the white world USAF. The "can do" early days, although rough around the edges, provided TAF leaders with a basic confidence that the fundamental core of the CONSTANT PEG concept – US pilots operating MiG aircraft providing the TAF with exposure to potential enemy aircraft before they encountered them in combat – was doable. But leadership was worried about our ability to sustain that early mode of operation. The aircraft were old and, despite the best efforts of the best maintainers in the USAF, their reliability rate generated safety concerns and caused sortie cancellations that sometimes resulted in fruitless TAF deployments to Nellis. Costly reverse engineering efforts, and the siphoning of resources and talented people to support the program are other examples of issues that contributed to our challenge.

In order to survive, we needed to mature. In order to mature, growth in the form of added/new aircraft, facilities, support stuff, supply chains, and people was required. In order to grow, funds were required. In order to get the funds confidence that we could become safer and more efficient was required. And in order to gain/sustain the confidence, leadership mandated we move toward the USAF's tried and true, traditional way of doing things. In summation, if we were to survive change was required, and money was required to affect and support it.

Fortunately, money was available. The basing of stealth fighters at Tonopah, the overall defense oriented Reagan years, and leadership's enlightened attitude towards realistic training (a result of our Vietnam experience) made the 1980s a perfect environment for support of a program like ours. We adapted to the required change, the money was made available and our unit grew – really grew! People, new buildings and hangars, additional "new" aircraft, an integrated supply/parts chain, additional support vehicles, etc. – we got it all! And acquiring "it all" cost money. However, it was also expensive to sustain it all! This eventually became problematic.

Now, let's move on to the mission. Throughout its short life, CONSTANT PEG's core mission – the exposure of American fighter crews to MiG aircraft – remained constant (no pun intended!). However, as the rest of the program matured, so did the exposure concept. Originally, the program simply matched a MiG with a US fighter and various maneuvers were accomplished that provided the pilot of the latter jet with the knowledge of how his aircraft performed vis-à-vis the MiG. However, as the unit grew and matured, the "exposures" gradually evolved to include multiple MiGs versus multiple US fighters, as well as the 4477th's inclusion in Red Flag exercises as the opposing force – our last mission, on March 5, 1988, was a Red Flag operation in which we launched 17 separate MiGs, all within the same flying period!

From day one, TAF aircrews filled out program evaluation/critique paperwork following their participation in missions involving the Red Eagles. Invariably, their comments reflected a "Best Program Ever" theme. Bottom line, the money for growth was money well spent.

So, back to the question of the day, "Why close the Red Eagles?" We changed, we validated our existence, we provided a professional, valuable product, and *we accomplished our mission* – what else was needed from us? Answer, "Nothing." We did our job. However (thankfully), so did a number of other programs, national agencies, and policies. As a result, victory in the Cold War belonged to our nation and our Allies. And, as is typical when a war is won, Congress largess towards defense diminished. The USAF was forced to cut costs. Leadership's challenge became, "How do we reduce overall force structure and maintain both an adequate operational force and a training force?"

Along with other programs such as the Aggressors, we'd done our job extremely well and contributed mightily to the matured air-to-air combat abilities of the fighter communities – to the point where USAF leaders felt that the fighter community could adequately sustain their proficiencies using assets from various TAF operational communities. Furthermore, our potential adversaries were supplanting our MiG types with newer, fourth generation MiGs and Sukhois. So, while we remained valuable as a dissimilar Aggressor/Adversary asset, our value in "exposing" TAF crews to something they could possibly meet in the real world as an adversary was quickly diminishing. Our program required significant funds to operate and, finally, from a safety standpoint, our program continued to be viewed as high risk.

By combining all the factors, the end result became obvious – the cost versus requirement comparisons concluded that the value gained by retaining training assets such as the Red Eagles (and the Aggressors) was less "affordable" than that gained by retaining operational, war fighting assets of comparable cost.

Wow, four months as commander and all I can come up with is 1,100+ words to explain a rather simple concept of affordability! No wonder my legacy is "closure!"

Actually, this period was quite dynamic and reflected the true Red Eagle personality. After the initial shock of the announcement, Red Eagle professionalism was never more apparent. Personnel reassignments, equipment accommodation, facility turnover, and all the other myriad issues associated with closing our one-of-a-kind organization were attacked with the zeal that was the hallmark of the Red Eagles. And, throughout, we continued providing our product right up to that last memorable day when the Red Eagle MiGs gave Red Flag its "best opposing force ever!"

I had the good fortune to be a part of the Red Eagles for most of our existence, being a squadron pilot from 1979 to 1983, a TAC Headquarters CONSTANT PEG manager for most of the next three years and, after a year as a "real world" F-15C guy, Red Eagle Ops Officer, and, then, CO. From each vantage point, it was obvious that, as great as the mission was, and as nice as the stuff became, the people were better! *"I am a Red Eagle"* can only be said by a select few – thanks for allowing me to say it as proudly as I know you do!

DAVE STRINGER – MAINTENANCE

The remote high desert at places like TTR at twilight is beautiful in a way I haven't seen at lower altitudes or among denser populations. As the orange on the horizon fades, you see the blue black of the night swoop westward in a sharp line where soft blue and yellow give way – it's the edge of night. Like the desert itself, it's stark and well defined. You might expect an operation set in such surroundings to mirror these qualities, but anything among humans will always be both less clear and more complicated.

The progress of America can be defined in at least four phases – scouts, pioneers, settlers, and townspeople. Scouts live by themselves, see and do things that others cannot and quickly assess any newcomer as friend or foe. Pioneers share similar traits to scouts, but band together for improved chances of survival. Settlers take fewer risks than pioneers, but begin to specialize their labors in a system of mutual support. Townspeople work within an established system.

The Red Eagles were founded as a flight, with pioneers and a few scouts, most notably Bobby Ellis. As the numbers of airplanes and people grew, the flight became a squadron. Further, growth more than doubled the number of airplanes marking, both in flight line and living areas, the transition from pioneers to settlers. When George Gennin took the squadron, he had his orders – transition the outfit to as normal an air force entity as practical. The 4477th were now townspeople in a much bigger city, with the three-squadron 4450th TG being the dominant user of the airfield and the 4461st Support Group (SG) operating both a commuter airline between Nellis and Tonopah and a base the size of a normal wing.

The transition of scout to townsman usually takes decades, but in the military it can happen much faster. These adjustments are overshadowed in combat because troops focus on staying alive and getting the job done. When the urgency of a shooting war is absent, the setting is stateside and the rules of secrecy make the family involuntary participants. This in turn means that the stresses placed on people are concentrated, in spite of the wonderful opportunity the Red Eagles had – flying bad guy jets to make the good guys instantly lethal on Day One of actual combat.

I got to Nellis in December 1980. Starting as a maintenance officer at Homestead AFB, Florida, before heading to Cope Thunder at Clark AB, I then spent a year as an intern at the Pentagon working in Air Force General Officer Matters, where I was the project officer for two sessions of the Brigadier General Orientation Course, commonly known as "charm school." One of the newly selected brigadier generals was Chuck Cunningham, then the 57th FWW commander, who worked with my boss to divert me to Nellis. Having already been vetted by former Red Eagles Ron Iverson and "Devil" Muller, I was slated for the 4477th, but neither Tom Gibbs nor Bobby Ellis would stand for it. None of us knew each other before I met them in January 1981, but they must have thought I was a spy for those outside the squadron. I was assigned in the interim to "Obi Wan" Henderson, whose typical graciousness helped make my "limbo" period better – I even got to work on a low observable F-16 canopy test.

At the end of January I was told to report to the Red Eagles trailer (just down from the Thunderbird hangar on the Nellis flight line), where Tom Gibbs gave me the deal – I could serve in the squadron as the Maintenance Officer, but the chief of maintenance would remain Bobby Ellis – take it or leave it. I didn't want to squander the significant efforts to get me there *and* I wanted to be part of flying MiGs, so I gladly took it. The key to making this arrangement work was the relationship I would establish with Bobby Ellis.

Bobby Ellis was an exceptionally skilled airman who, like many a leader, made it his business to control his own destiny as best he could. A scout with impressive credentials in acquiring foreign military equipment, Bobby saw the Red Eagles as a way to run his own first-class operation of pioneers without interference. It wasn't that Bobby trusted no one – I saw many instances of his seeking help from engineers, intelligence operatives and analysts, and aircrews, but he had little patience with anyone who didn't add value as he defined it. Maintenance officers led the list, but there were many others.

"Daddy" Ellis also had great faith in those he hired, searching for highly capable self-starters resilient enough to endure both austere living conditions as well as the stress of program secrecy. Frequently, the people he chose had their own Ellis-like unhappy experiences with authority – arbitrary or otherwise – but as long as they did what he said, they were fine. The corollary to this precept was their refusal to take direction from anyone other than "Daddy," which reinforced the mutual support among the "wrench-benders."

And what a team of capable characters it was. I got to learn the rest of the team first, subbing for Capt Leo Bruderer, the squadron facility manager who was at Squadron Officer School for three months. This introduced me to Ralph Payne, Louis Hinostrosa, Kermit Deitz, and Tom Anderson, firemen extraordinary, whose firehouse, just off the runway, had a kitchen and sleeping quarters. Ralph introduced me to Brunswick stew, easy to make with the large number of wild rabbits at hand. The firemen also taught me the ins and outs of fire prevention and response – very difficult given the dodgy level of support their fire trucks enjoyed. Rich Murphy, a New York City native, looked after our fuel tanks and supplies.

I next learned that facility construction and maintenance was as big a job as MiG maintenance. An old fighter pilot turned construction contractor, "Pub" Crouch, taught me that if there is no control over who tells the builder what to do, there is no control over costs and schedules.

A trio of falconers, Link Burdick, Bill Magee, and Mike Wagner, kept hawks in an aerie on the southeast end of the Nellis runway beyond the golf course and deployed the hawks to Tonopah to suppress the migratory birds during flight operations. I had fun using an alternate method – shotguns – around that runway. There was one memorable Cessna 404 sortie where we went to Ely, Nevada, to pick up a hawk that Link had acquired. Once airborne, we got to see the hooded hawk move to stay upright regardless of the aircraft's attitude.

In those days, the unit's housing was in transition. Bobby and a few of the old heads had single-wide trailers that were moved to permit further site expansion. Everyone else had moved out of "Indian Village," a rustic "U" of trailers, in favor of a series of double-wide trailers, sited below and behind the hangars. Entertainment most nights was a movie, gained from the Army and Air Force Exchange movie rotation, shown in "Indian Village" until Bobby got Jack Slusher, the ground communications genius, to site a satellite dish to provide cable to the trailer array. What we were able to get was network satellite feeds, and Monday Night Football was incomparably more enjoyable when you could hear Howard Cosell tell Don Meredith what he really thought using bar stool words, while the commercials ran for everyone else.

The burden of making all this happen fell hard on the enlisted force. The aviators had a natural advantage – they had to come back to Nellis nightly to summarize face-to-face with the aircrews they had trained that day over the ranges, and that's what got the Cessna 404s leased, replaced later by Mitsubishi MU-2s ("Rice Rockets"). Non-pilots could only fly if extra seats were available, unless there was a reason to get back like an illness or a family emergency. Many of the non-pilots didn't like to fly, so they were more than happy to drive one of the vans for four to five hours from Nellis to Tonopah. If "Daddy" really liked you, you'd get checked out in the Kenworth tractor-trailer rig the squadron owned, and you could then drive in style. We had other tractors, but nothing so nice as the "K-W" – no, I was never checked out in it.

Routes used were either US Highway 95 north to Tonopah, then east to the TTR, or north via Pahrump and Ash Springs, then west. The latter route meant at least an hour on some of the most severely rutted roads I've ever experienced. Driving these routes gave you an understanding of the size of America. The new guy would be told which gas station owners could be awakened after hours and which en route establishments were hospitable and which weren't. If you stopped on the side of the road, you would be repeatedly asked by those in vehicles (even school buses), in the neighborly tradition of the West, if you needed help.

All this mattered because until the 4461st SG bought the Wyoming oil shale Mancamp and set it up on the northern end of the Test Range in 1983, all you had to eat was what you brought yourself. Pilots would bring either something to microwave or a sandwich, but if you spent the night, you served yourself breakfast, lunch, and dinner from Monday morning until Thursday afternoon or Friday morning. The logistics of all this meant that ground cargo capacity was essential to the Red Eagles.

People would buddy up to share cooking and cleaning chores, but as any intermountain resident knows, wind and dust begin and end life up range. People would share hospitality, and strays like me who got to stay unexpectedly never had to go hungry. Bill "Big Mac" McHenry was a frequent host, and he, like Jack Davis at the Nellis trailer, insisted over these dinners that "Pappy" Frick's establishment of a flight kept the Red Eagles off everyone's radar at Nellis, and that the squadron's growth would eventually doom it.

Bobby and the pioneers put tires on the corrugated trailer roofs to keep them from acting like airfoils and vibrating all night, and we endured several general officer comments about their unsightliness. I can testify to how much fun it is to try to sleep without them. It eventually fell to me to run one of the double-wide trailers as a dormitory for aircrews when flying schedules, weather, or something else forced them to spend the night. Maj Lenny "Toad-o" Bucko ("Bandit 22") dubbed this trailer "Ma Stringer's," and I kept a supply of toiletries and over-the-counter medication for our folks.

Let's take a tour of the business end of the Red Eagles in 1981. In the original hangars, we kept the older MiGs. The MiG-17s were in the east bay, along with boxed-up collections of parts from various sources. One jet was called "Miss Piggy," and it had a small stuffed doll replica that flew every time the jet went aloft. The MiG-21s were in the west bay. Between the two were a few offices, briefing rooms for aircrews, and a conference room, as well as a snack bar with a television set, coffee machine, and microwave. One of the usual pursuits at lunch among the pilots was stealing each other's food, or engaging in a conversation that was so gross that one would lose his appetite, allowing the winner to chow down – childish, but fun. I won such a match versus the previously undefeated Capt Jim "Wiley" Green ("Bandit 26").

At the end of this hangar was the duty desk, where, on a raised seat, the operations admin tech (or the security guard) manned the phones, the UHF radio to talk to the MiGs, T-38s and other fighters, and a VHF radio to talk to the commuter airplanes. John "Crash" Libner, Tom Sztabnik, and Gary Lewellen shared these duties, and John's nonchalant nasal tone was absolutely distinctive whenever he'd make area-wide intercom announcements – if you remember the loudspeaker guy in the TV series *M*A*S*H*, you get the idea.

Bobby Ellis had maintenance organized (per a 1981 memo I still have) in three branches – Generation (Paul "Goatroper" Long and Chico Noriega shared its leadership), Equipment (John Lorenzen, an NDI tech as well), and Component (Bob "Habu" Hobson, our lead avionics tech). Doug Robinson (an aerospace ground equipment technician) was designated as the quality assurance lead and "Jeb" Baker, helped later by Rick Thompson, ran the MiG-23 side as these aircraft began to arrive.

The team of crew chiefs was a monument to their capability and individuality. Mike Beverlin, Tom Burzynski, and Dave Hollingsworth were three aces on any flight line. Ron Papendick came to us from A-10s, and helped us troubleshoot a Warthog that landed at Tonopah with an in-flight emergency. Tim Enos had helped restore aircraft in his off-duty time at a previous assignment. Also on the team were George Whitaker, Don Walker, and Larry Myers. Billy Maggart was one of the funniest people to be around and "Charlie O" Othold was just as quiet as Billy was funny. Wayne Johnson, Bobbie Jackson, Joe Bohman, and Al Christoff cut their teeth on MiGs, along with Rich Contreras and Russ Osthus. Bill McHenry, Roy "Weird Harold" Miller, and Don Walker rounded out the team. Jim Richardson had the pleasure of being the "do this, do that" guy on the flight line, and teams can't win unless some block so the runners can gain ground.

So, just like the pilots, crew chiefs had to learn an aircraft unfamiliar to any of them. Even less so than the pilots, as maintenance manuals were almost absent and training, necessarily incomplete and informal, gave each individual nowhere near enough clues as to what his jet would do next. Couple this with a randomly available parts stock and you get a small idea of the weight of responsibility on the shoulders of the ones who strapped in our pilots. Imagine the feeling if their pilot didn't come back.

In the first phase of the 4450th construction were several huge hangars, including one built next to our original, which held two bays of MiG-23s as well as many of our workshops. My memory is fuzzy as to which workshop was where, but the people who ran them were memorable. In the personal equipment and life support shop was Charlie Barker, whose South Carolina drawl would greet you as you walked in. Rick Stiles assisted him. "Tennessee" Ernie Ford was the parachute workshop chief, and he told me that his tour length at any base was determined when he had packed his 3,000th drag 'chute. Since the MiG-21 and MiG-23 fleets used them, Ernie sweated steadily. He was joined later on by George "Cupcake" Mayberry. Bill Welcher was our first egress technician, an utterly vital specialty.

Bob "Bubbles" Pascal was an ace hydraulics technician and "Buster" Helms covered the pneumatics side of the house. Bob Hobson (radar), Jerry Bickford (instruments), Randy Horsley (autopilot), and the team of Homer "Squat Switch" Shell and Jim Bartlett (comm) covered the avionics specialties, while Warren Brelsford and Dave Young handled electrical systems. Jeff Barrett worked hard to make the aircrafts' armament flyable, including an early model "Atoll" infrared homing missile. Their workshops would usually carry an array of parts, some from the aircraft we flew and some from wherever – those who received Soviet "stuff" didn't ask questions.

Tech data for parts, as we knew it, was almost absent, so our folks were in a constant cycle of identification, reverse engineering, reconditioning, and substitution. Never was this more urgent than in the engines we flew. Dwight "Ike" or "Dagwood" (as he was sometime known) Crawley was the jet engine mechanic who served as a troubleshooter for the folks who did overhauls somewhere else. The Soviet philosophy of maintenance was to use officer engineers as crew chiefs and enlisted men as helpers, with the best of the latter retained as senior NCOs and warrant officers to manage them. They built aircraft for mass attacks on NATO forces, and expected to lose a lot of them. They built for performance, not for sustainment – their jet engines, for example, were built for 250 to 500 hours of operation, after which they would be consigned to the scrap heap.

The most popular people in the outfit had to be our metal men. Each of them had moustaches (it must have been a hiring trait), and Dave Boudreau and Jim Spader were the sheet metal experts. They were always busy either fixing aircraft or creating parts for other needs. Bob Griese, the machinist, was a genius at making almost any precision part we needed. One of his greatest assets was a lathe with metric on one end and English on the other – vital for dropping in things like pumps and valves from US systems into our Soviet aircraft.

Equally important were our supply folks. Terry Davis and Bob Gibeault knew just how much we could use the air force's "vanilla" system without getting quizzed as to what we were doing with (fill in the blank). Our admin team of Jack Davis, BJ Adams, and Gary Lara also did their best to keep the Red Eagles in touch with the personnel and finance systems.

The job of keeping the vehicles and ground equipment going fell to the team of Billy Lightfoot, whose personal appearance was about as covert as you could get in public, Larry Gruse, and the AGE team of Doug Robinson and Ben Galloway. Their operating area was a canvas-covered arch about 20ft high filled with Soviet stuff, as well as a corrugated metal building behind the hangar. This was surrounded, both inside and out, by a remarkably diverse set of "found for free" vehicles from salvage yards across the country.

One of the AGE projects was to recondition "Ivan" and "Natasha" – two Soviet trucks (mobile power and starter units that could start two MiGs at the same time). This posed fiendish challenges as they had to clean up, assess, and rebuild/substitute any number of systems and subsystems whose constraints were unknown to them. Thanks to the talents of Bob Griese, Ben Galloway was able to drop a US V8 engine and transmission into "Natasha" and get her going.

The array of vehicles we had was impressive – and there was more than just one bare bones buggy with a driver's seat and a slab bed behind. Two were M274 Mechanical Mules, built for the Army as sort of a light jeep for airborne forces. They were fun to drive (I had driven one in my Army ROTC summer camp at Fort Bragg) but easy to flip just like Jeeps, which we also had, and more of a toy than a tool. In the pioneer days, however, the two we had got a lot of use. Bobby Ellis' knowledge of administration taught him that property in a covert military system should disappear from the books as much as possible to avoid the audit trail that the normal system demanded. Getting stuff from salvage yards meant the property was already off the regular records and you could do whatever you wanted with it. If you had enough time and money anything was possible.

Money we had, but time we had not. Construction for the F-117 stealth fighter program dwarfed CONSTANT PEG. Gail Peck had chosen Tonopah to leverage that new investment, but the Red Eagles were soon viewed as the extra mission at TTR, being less important than the newer, sexier one. The 4477th TES, formed and operating under deep secrecy, could remain pioneers or settlers only as long it stayed by itself. As the townspeople came in to supersede the settlement, so did questions about the degree of freedom enjoyed by the Red Eagles. Why permit long hair and blue jeans when the townspeople – the 4450th and 4461st folks – didn't have that freedom?

That transition went down hard among the people who felt they had built an important national capability in extremely difficult circumstances. To many of the old hands, the changes – cut your hair, wear uniforms, comply with "vanilla" maintenance rules (with little prospect of more tech data and parts) – were imposed because the new leadership suspected them of shoddiness or even disloyalty when the troops had simply been following the old set of rules. It's a shame some on both sides still feel that way almost 30 years later.

The Red Eagles are, among many things, a testament to how good our already impressive enlisted force could be. Let me end with part of a recent e-mail from the board president of Mark Postai's MiG-17 accident, retired Chief of Staff of the USAF Gen Ron Fogleman:

"I got some visibility into their operations as a result of conducting an accident investigation when they lost one of their aircraft and as an F-15 pilot given the opportunity to fly against their assets. As I think about the 4477th I am struck by the sacrifices that were made by the officers and enlisted troops who traveled up range every week to do their jobs, but I am also struck by their professionalism and sense of duty that allowed such an operation to be conducted under cover for such a long period of time without leaks or disclosures that would have clearly hurt our national interest.

My other observation is that what the Red Eagles were doing was important, even vital work, at a time when the fall of the Soviet Union was not on anyone's radar scope. In so many parts of the world, and in so many of our war plans, our tactical aviation assets were the tactical and strategic centers of gravity. The things learned by the Red Eagles and shared with the operational forces of the USAF, US Navy, US Marine Corps, and our Allies gave us the confidence that we could fight and win against an adversary that some painted as being ten feet tall."

JIM "BLUTO" KEYS – GCI

In 1978 I was looking to get an assignment in the southwest as my wife and I are from that area. A friend told me about a new unit that needed a 17XX (AFSC for a GCI officer) at Nellis AFB. I called out there and got an interview, flew to Nellis and met with Glenn Frick. I also met with "Jose" Oberle, Ron Iverson, and Gerry Huff. Before I left the base and headed back to Fort Walton Beach, Florida, I was told I was selected for the job. I had no idea what the 4477th did at the time but I soon figured out they had some juice.

When I got back to my office I had a note from officer assignments that I was being transferred to Nellis – that happened in one day. When I arrived at Nellis I was told to go down to the 64th AS and get checked out. I still hadn't been briefed on the mission of the 4477th, but I did get a security briefing and signed the necessary paperwork. After completing the Aggressor course I joined up with the unit. Our Nellis operation was conducted in two single-wide trailers with no name on them. They were located next to the 57th FWW headquarters on the flight line. When I got briefed I looked at Gary Lewallen and Bob Drabant ("Darth") and said "YGBSM" – MiGs!

It was an interesting set-up, as we worked directly for the Air Staff but were supported by the Nellis community. The TFWC and the 57th FWW commanders had been briefed and were very supportive of our mission, but I think there may have been a few people who had not been totally briefed on what we did but were told if they ask for something, give it to them. Sometimes these people were not happy with us. I can't count the number of times I interrupted the TFWC/CC and the 57th FWW/CC with items for them to sign. We were always getting things signed at the last minute and at the end of the day. On one occasion I remember I needed the Wing/CC signature and he had stepped out to fly, so I went out to the flight line and waved to him. He motioned me over to the aircraft and I went up the ladder and had him sign the paperwork. He was shaking his head, but with a smile on his face. Yes, there was a time when you could just walk out on the flight line.

At the beginning we did not have a hangar or jet-capable landing strip at Tonopah, but everyone was busy working towards that end. I would on occasion see Bobby Ellis and his guys come in and out of the trailers, always in civilian clothes. Everyone was given tasks to complete, with little guidance; it was more like, "just get it done, that's why we hired you." Most of the tasks were unrelated to our AFSCs. For example, I ended up on one occasion downtown Las Vegas at Graybar Electric buying a cable trough for the hangar and ops offices in Tonopah. I also had to figure out a way to get it to TTR that same day. There were hundreds of these types of tasks and everyone shared in them. It was challenging, exciting, and, sometimes, even fun. I was also tasked with getting the communications set up for the base in Tonopah. That's how I learned there was a large Motorola office in Las Vegas. I would get to visit it on numerous occasions. I also learned about radio crystals and the Southwest Frequency Coordinator.

All of the tasks were the type that could normally be done quite easily, except you could not tell anyone why or what you were up to – everything was classified. Most of the time you could not even mention the word Tonopah. Telephones were another nightmare. Remember we were out in the middle of the desert. We called it Tonopah, but the town itself was 45 minutes to an hour away, via mostly an unimproved road.

We all also had the normal additional duties found in every squadron. One of mine that posed a challenge was the awards and decorations officer. Whenever someone would leave the squadron, or if someone did something way above and beyond what was required, we would submit them for an award or decoration. This sounds like a normal administrative function, and an easy task to complete. However, try writing a full page narrative on a Red Eagle without saying MiG, Tonopah, Soviet aircraft, or any of the other classified terms and locations that we dealt with. I learned to write like a politician talks, all around the subject without saying what the subject is, but it worked.

In addition to getting TTR up and running, everyone also had to stay current in their specialty. Both the 64th and 65th AS were lifesavers in this endeavor. We were all attached to the Aggressors, and even deployed with them on occasion. Their support was outstanding, and we were treated extremely well and were appreciative of their support. We could not have maintained currency without them. Speaking of staying current, I recall one pilot telling me "where else in the air force can you be current in five different aircraft at the same time?" Here's how – T-38, F-5, two kinds of MiG (MiG-17 and MiG-21) and the Cessna 404.

We often had to go to various places to get whatever was required that day. We usually took the Cessna but on occasion we took a T-38 or F-5. I recall trips to San Diego, Norton AFB, NAS Miramar, Colorado Springs, Randolph AFB, and numerous other places. I was picked to go with Dave McCloud and 20 of Bobby Ellis' guys for an extraction trip. We flew to Hong Kong and stayed overnight and then the next morning continued on to our classified destination. It was not a fun trip at all – hot, humid, and sleeping on a cot with a mosquito net over you for 30 days. I think we ended up getting seven or eight MiGs, a couple of MiG engines and a few boxes of spare parts.

This was where I learned about the speed wrench, and how tired your arms can get from using one all day. We had to take the wings off the MiGs and prepare the aircraft for a long flight back to Nellis. This takes a lot more work than it sounds. It took us 30 days, and we worked every day from 0630hrs till 2100hrs. I never saw an air conditioner the whole time we were at that base. We loaded the aircraft onto a C-5 and had it land at Nellis at night with everything covered in black plastic. Bobby Ellis' guys met the C-5 with flat bed tractor trailers, loaded the MiGs on them and headed north.

What a trip, I remember having to get shots before we left and taking quinine tablets every day as a hedge against malaria. The trip turned out to be super for Bobby and his wrench benders – we got all kinds of items for MiGs, including some dedicated maintenance tools.

Slowly but surely the runway and hangars were getting completed at Tonopah. One guy, Del Gaulker, who worked his rear end off for us, was from the Nevada Test Site (he was a REECo contractor). This guy could make things happen. He was responsible for the runway and hangars, and making sure that they were completed on time and to the required specification. This was about the time I figured I would need some more guys from the GCI AFSC, so we brought Bud "Chops" Horan from the 65th AS on board. Immediately upon arriving at the 4477th, he was given the Security Officer's job. Once he started I think he had second thoughts about leaving the 65th! The security job was huge – no one could fly against us, visit Tonopah, join the unit or have anything at all to do with supporting us in any way, shape, or form without getting briefed and signing security papers with "Chops." Also, anyone that inadvertently got exposed to the program had to debrief and sign security statements with him. He must have done a heck of a job, as no one could believe how well the secret MiG squadron was kept under wraps.

Once we got up and running at Tonopah, a whole new world developed. Usually, we would pre-brief the pilots we were going to fly against early in the morning and then the MiG pilots would get in the Cessna and head to TTR so as to get ready to execute the flying schedule for the day. After the last mission of the day the guys would then get in the Cessna and head to Nellis for a debriefing with all the pilots they had flown against that day. Consequently, we were often pre-briefing at 0530–0600hrs and debriefing between 1800–2000hrs.

This made for some long days and nights, and it was difficult to interact with your squadron mates. It seemed like you were either getting on the Cessna or getting off the Cessna, or having a mission with the Aggressors that day. It was important that we exposed as many US Navy, US Marine Corps, and USAF aircrews to the MiGs' characteristics, performance capabilities, and air-to-air combat capabilities as possible. We like to think that the long days were worth it, and added immensely to the combat readiness of aircrews.

Initially, the GCI function was conducted from a building up near the Communications Squadron at Nellis. As an upgrade to Red Flag, they built a new facility beside the Red Flag building called Black Jack Control. There was a two-month period when they shut down the old GCI facility and moved everything to the new building near Red Flag. During this period we still had to run the missions out of Tonopah, and also provide security surveillance anytime a MiG was outside the hangars. To do this we set up an arrangement with Oakland Center via the FAA. They provided us with two radar scopes and four radios to conduct the Tonopah mission. It required one or two of us to be TDY to Oakland Center Monday through Friday for a couple of months. But it did work quite well as we had good radar and radio coverage. We split up the TDYs between our enlisted (AFSC 276) controllers Pitcher and Emfinger and the officers (AFSC 17XX), depending on the type of missions scheduled. This was about the time we brought over another 17XX from the 64th AS, Capt Dan "Truck" Futryk, who was one of the top 17XX officers around.

Speaking of security surveillance, anytime a private aircraft inadvertently flew near our airfield when the MiGs were out of the hangars we had to get the aircraft number and have the FAA give us the name and address of the owner. We then had to meet with the pilot and do a security debriefing, and have him sign the security paperwork. Sometimes this required us to go TDY – I recall that one time I had to go to Oregon to complete this task. "Chops" was hot on this, and I don't think he ever let one slip through the crack.

Everyone assigned to the 4477th was handpicked. The US Navy, US Marine Corps, and USAF pilots were the cream of the crop, being superb aviators, yet humble with it. But even more importantly they were down to earth good people, and they treated everyone with respect. We all got along and worked hard to get the mission accomplished – whatever it took we did it.

I always thought of Bobby Ellis and his guys as the miracle people. They took old MiGs and turned them into airworthy aircraft. Everything in the cockpit was in Russian, the few manuals we had were in Russian and many parts were not available and had to be made from scratch. What they did was miraculous. I stand in awe of them.

The four commanders I worked for – Frick, Peck, Henderson, and Gibbs – were all outstanding. They put in long, hard, difficult hours, and lost a lot of sleep worrying about the 4477th. Because of the security, there was hardly anyone they could talk to about their problems, or even what they were doing at Nellis. When they got home at night and their wives said "how did it go today?" all they could say was "I wish I could tell you."

Just a word on the Navy and Marine pilots assigned to the Red Eagles. Naturally, they were all superb aviators – they sent us their best. They blended right in with us and became Red Eagles overnight. In fact if I remember right "Heater" Heatley was the one that designed the unit patch and had several items made with the patch on them. They brought with them their skills as aviators as well as their vast knowledge of air-to-air tactics and combat fighter performance. They were few in number, but contributed immensely to the Red Eagle mission. They also got us into the annual Tailhook Convention at the Hilton in Las Vegas. What a great tradition and get together for Naval Aviators.

Three things come to mind when I think back to Tailhook. One – heck of a reunion. Two – Gerry Huff could not find his car for three days after he left Tailhook. Three – after one beer, Lt Cdr Keith Shean ("Bandit 17") could fold his ear inside itself and make it almost disappear, and after two beers he could do both ears.

The 4477th was a great assignment, and we all like to think that we contributed to its success. Were there bumps along the way? There sure were, almost on a daily basis, but you learned how to overcome, adapt, and be flexible. When we lost Hugh Brown – a sad day for all of us and the low point of our early history – they almost closed us down. Somehow Gail Peck convinced the right people that we needed to continue on, and we did so with great results.

There is much more to tell, but I will let "Chops" take it from here, and then the rest of the Red Eagle GCI community can follow up. There is so much more to tell about Bandit Control.

BUD "CHOPS" HORAN – GCI

I started Aggressor training as a GCI controller in May 1977.

The FAA radar at Angel's Peak is located on a mountain top near Mt Charleston. It is about 22 nautical air miles from Nellis, but a whole lot further by road. In order to reach it you first have to drive from Nellis to Highway 95. In those days this was done via Craig Road, assuming a flash flood hadn't closed it. A few miles up Highway 95, the turnoff to Kyle Canyon marks the start of an 18-mile uphill drive through a range of ecological zones from the desert floor at about 2,000ft MSL elevation through the yucca and Joshua tree regions and into an area where scrub trees, probably oaks, thrive. And, eventually, the ponderosa pine zone is reached at about 7,000ft MSL. There, the road forks and the path to Angel's Peak continues along the cut-off road around Mt Charleston from Kyle Canyon to Lee Canyon. The cut-off road is literally carved into the face of the mountain for the first few miles. On pretty summer days it is a delightful drive. In winter, when the snow level can be below 5,000ft MSL, it can be a terrifying trip.

Such was the historic daily drive for the Nellis Aggressor GCI controllers as they trudged their way to their duty station like postal workers, come rain, snow, or shine.

The week I started Aggressor GCI training was the same week the USAF activated the remote feed from the FAA radar at Angel's Peak to Range Control in Building 589 at Nellis, aka "Blackjack." So I never made the trip to Angel's Peak, and I don't think Jim "Bluto" Keys – our lead GCI controller – ever had a reason to make the trip either. Actually, we may have driven up Lee Canyon to ski during the winter ski season, but that was it.

We did hear lots of stories from the GCI controller instructors, calls signs "Jet," "Moose," "Worm" et al, on their harrowing treks up and down the mountain in the days before the microwave radar feed to Nellis.

But "Skipper" Peck can safely remove any notion that either "Bluto" or I controlled him or any of our MiG pilots from anywhere other than Nellis.

When Peck and "Huffer" hired me as the second GCI controller, TAC was receptive to a request by the Red Eagles to get us a Soviet-built radar for Tolichi Peak, or somewhere suitable in the restricted area known as R4807/4809 in the Nellis Range complex. Any radar located near the operational location at Tonopah could have done a much better job than Angel's Peak because radar coverage from the latter site below 10,000–12,000ft MSL was cut off due to terrain masking caused by the mountain ranges. A Soviet radar set didn't materialize in our era, however, so "Bluto" and I alternated in controlling the flights from Nellis. The guy that wasn't controlling would go up-range to Tonopah to take care of additional duties there. I eventually replaced "Devil" Muller as the Red Eagles' Security Manager, so I had a lot to do at TTR.

Anyway, I'm thinking maybe, just maybe, "Bluto" and I were trying to cultivate the Angel's Peak route saga to make the acquisition of a dedicated radar more palatable. Hence the rumor that we drove to Angel's Peak every day, sun, rain, or snow! I wouldn't put it past us!

BEN GALLOWAY – AGE

In the high plains desert somewhere in the middle of Nevada lays the TTR. This is the stuff of myths and legends to be sure.

I walked among giants in the 4477th. The names of some of the most skilled and gifted maintenance men I have ever known and worked with are all but forgotten except to those of us remaining Red Eagles. Names like Bobby Ellis, Don Lyon, Steve Hovermale, Jerry Baker, Tommy Karnes, Chico Noriega, Dave Hollingsworth, Mike Beverlin, Ike Crawley, Jim Richardson, Doug Robinson, and Billy Lightfoot. These men, and others too many to mention, were the heart and soul of the Red Eagles. They made it happen, they made it work. We did the impossible every day. We had the best maintenance men and pilots of any MiG squadron in the world. Our pilots never worried about climbing into an unsafe aircraft. One man had the vision and drive to orchestrate the maintenance side of the house, Bobby Ellis.

In the early years we were what the senior command wanted us to be – civilians in appearance so as to not attract attention to us, or our mission. We wore civilian clothes, had haircuts every two months or so, and grew some really great moustaches. But deep inside we were still military men adapting to the mission requirements. Did we enjoy this disguise? Hell, yes we did. We were on a first name basis with the pilots and co-workers. The commander was called "Boss" and Bobby Ellis was referred to as "Daddy," but not to his face. It was a term of respect when referring to Bobby. He was the head of the maintenance family and capable of more than sending you to your room.

Some may think we became lax and sloppy because of this, but that is far from the truth. It brought us closer together in a way like no other military organization. The closest comparison would be to the famed "Flying Tigers," the American Volunteer Group, in China at the start of World War II. Later, we too would have to transition from civilian to military standards when the F-117s appeared on the ramp. An unpopular move to be sure, and we were told to adapt or move on. "You will be assimilated, resistance is futile."

When I arrived in December 1979 we flew to the site every morning and returned to Nellis late in the afternoon, four days a week. Later on, REECo set up the trailers for the "Indian Village" and we spent the four days and three nights at the site. The pilots flew home every night while we stayed there and put in ten-hour days. We worked hard and played hard. The upside was that we had a three-day weekend every week. Meanwhile, our wives had to be on their own taking care of the kids and running the house while we were away. Once in a while a pilot might spend the night at the site with us. I guess it was like camping out for them. To us, it was a way of life. There were no dining facilities, so we had to bring our own food and drinks to the site. There was the option of getting in the van with some of the guys and driving to Tonopah for dinner and a few drinks. However, you best be at work on time the next day or "Daddy" would find something special for you to do.

Bobby Ellis was the man we all aspired to be. He was the Chief, a mentor and a friend. He expected perfection in everything we did. If it wasn't safe then it wasn't flying. It was just that simple. The most important thing Bobby taught me was "I can only fail if I fail to try." Sometimes I wondered where he got all his unfounded faith in my abilities. Somehow, someway, he found skills in me that I never knew existed. He was simply brilliant. I spoke with his daughter Patti some time ago and she confirmed what I had always suspected about Bob Ellis – he had a photographic memory. You can ask any of the older Red Eagles about Bob Ellis and they will tell you that he was the best damn line chief there ever was. Bob was in the trenches with us, working beside us and directing the job at hand. No words could ever express the amount of respect I had for this man. He was a true leader.

The MiGs we flew came from another land. They were junk, scrap, wrecks, and derelicts when we got them, having been sat in a swamp or a desert and left to rot. We brought them back, and without any tech manuals they were fully restored after many months of hard work by the crew chiefs with the guidance of Bobby Ellis. The crew chiefs were married to their MiGs, and they would not leave her side until the last bolt had been tightened before they put her to bed for the night. No one will ever know the exact number of hours they would spend getting their aircraft ready for the next day's missions, even if it meant working through the night. It was that important, and they would never let our pilots strap on a jet if it wasn't 100 percent airworthy.

The support techs such as avionics, hydraulics, electricians, fabrication branch, and jet engines mechanics worked hand in hand with the crew chiefs to keep our aircraft flying. These men gave everything without expecting praise or medals. It was that important to them and the rest of us. Sometimes, while walking through the hangars, I would be asked to help them push a jet engine into place or the tail section back on. On another occasion I might have been on the ramp when I volunteered to climb into the cockpit to ride the brakes while they towed the aircraft into the hangar. It was just that way. We all helped out when and where we were needed. You men are to be commended for your dedication and skill. Well done.

Everyone made a contribution to the mission. Men like Jack Slusher, our telephone/comms guy. Without him crawling under the trailers – home to the scorpions, rattlers, and spiders – to run the telephone lines we would never have been able to call home at night. He was one hell of a nice guy. And Jack, if you're out there, I'm really sorry about that snake in the toolbox thing. I know it was wrong. Sorry.

An operation like ours couldn't exist without a dedicated fire department. They were the best and they kept us safe. My hats off to you guys too. Some of the best friends I had were in the fire department. Ralph, Lou, Kermit, and "R-2," I miss you guys.

Our supply folks were the greatest. Lord knows how they managed to come up with everything we needed but they did. On second thoughts, I don't want to know. No squadron can expect to function without a great supply section. Terry, Mike, "Gibbo," and Bill were masters of the supply craft. We could never have done it without you. I can still see Mike Cleveland's face when I told him what I wanted.

He scrunched his eyebrows up, shook his head, and rolled his eyes. He then said "and when would you like that?" These guys had tricks that would marvel David Copperfield. Our Admin and Ops guys took care of the home front so we didn't have to deal with Consolidated Base Personnel Office and wear a uniform. Thanks for all the hard work Gary, "BJ," and the others.

There were some egos to deal with, but this was minor for the most part. If the guys weren't ragging on you about something then you wondered if they were pissed at you about something.

As AGE men, Doug Robinson and I worked as much on vehicles as we did on AGE equipment. Working with Billy Lightfoot and Larry Gruse was always a learning experience. We spent many hours turning junk we had brought back from the DRMO yards into sound, running vehicles and equipment. The four of us also spent a lot of time on the road. I never knew what to expect when I showed up for the early morning flight from Nellis. I might actually get on the airplane, or Bob Ellis might tell me to drive one of the trucks to the site or to Edwards to deliver/pick up a jet engine.

If I did make it to the site by airplane or truck, Bob Ellis might tell me to drive a truck anywhere in the southwest, take a truck and head back to Nellis, actually stay at the site to work on equipment, or get ready for "yard work." And if you don't know what "yard work" is (and I'm using the politically correct phrase – those of us that were there know what the real phrase was), then you haven't lived. If you've never moved an avionic connex 10x40 with four forklifts, one on each corner, well my friend you've missed an exciting moment. The Russian Ballet had nothing on us. By the end of the day, if you weren't dirty, greasy, and tired, then you must have been a spectator.

In closing, let me say to each Red Eagle, you were the best! Don't let anybody tell you different. You did the hard part and made it easier for those that came after us. I am proud to have been one of you, and thank you for allowing me to serve with you. As I get older, some memories fade but others stay as sharp and clear in my mind as the day they happened. We worked together, played together, and, at times, cried together. You maintainers were part of my life and I will never forget you. "We few, we happy few, we band of brothers."

In the land southeast of Tonopah, in the barren desert where the silence is broken only by the jets flying overhead, I walked among giants. I walked among the Red Eagles.

"OBI WAN" HENDERSON – RED EAGLES COMMANDER

In the early 1980s the Red Eagles dealt with an office in the CIA that supplied us with technical manuals. Our CIA contacts were more on the operational side of the agency rather than the analytical side. Most of the CIA people in the office would spend a period of time "in the field" and then come in "from the cold" and recover a normal life in the office.

One woman from that office (forever called the "woman in red") was a feisty, gutsy little package (under five feet tall) with a very nice figure, great looks, and she loved going toe-to-toe with fighter pilots in discussions of the issues. She did great work for us in that office and finally we invited her to come and visit us at Tonopah. She arrived in a Cessna 404 and we picked her up in a six-pack crew pickup truck. She wore a very short red leather tight skirt, with matching red leather jacket. It was a real challenge for her to step up into the van for the short drive to the hangars.

When she arrived, several of us were waiting to greet her. When she opened the door and saw the task ahead of her getting down out of the van, she didn't miss a beat and said "If you stay there while I get out of this vehicle, I'm going to have to kill you!" We turned our backs and she got out of the van.

GAIL PECK ON HIRING – FOCUS ON BRIAN "LAZMO" McCOY ("BANDIT 53")

Potential Red Eagles weren't just assigned to the unit – they were selected. The methodology for selection was generally the same for the pilots and the enlisted personnel.

During the time before Lt Col Gennin's period of command, Bob Ellis would put the word out to the Red Eagle enlisted force and to other key friends of his in the air force that he needed one specialty or another. Thus, people were nominated and Ellis made the final interview decision before recommending a hire to the commander. On my watch I initially interviewed a few of the men, but over time my confidence in Ellis became such that I generally hired the enlisted personnel Ellis recommended without further interview.

As the unit grew and more aviators were needed, the assigned cadre of MiG pilots discussed fighter pilots known to them that possessed the professional flying skills as well as the overall personality and support system at home to make a good fit with the Red Eagles. Eventually, the list was cut to match the vacancies and pilots were hired.

Capt Brian E. McCoy remembered and reported to me about his interview process with the chain of command. Some interviews were very serious and others had a light or even humorous element.

When it was time for Operations Officer Maj "Paco" Geisler ("Bandit 35") to interview Brian it was more of a chat. "Paco" felt him out, assessed his tolerance for risk, family support, and other key criteria that he had developed over time. Brian was gung ho to be a part of the unit in spite of the forbidding tone of the questions. Finally, "Paco" said essentially "I'll tell you what Brian, here's the scenario – you're flying one of our airplanes and everything goes wrong! You are out of ideas and have only one option – eject. You pull the handles on the ejection seat expecting it to hurl you to safety and all that happens is the seat sets your boots on fire. Now you think about that overnight and come back tomorrow and we'll continue this chat."

Brian showed up the next day and "Paco" essentially hired him by forwarding the assignment package up the chain of command.

TOM GIBBS – RED EAGLES COMMANDER

Tom Gibbs replaced "Obi Wan" Henderson when the latter started having health problems.

Tom had gone to the F-105 right out of pilot training and then straight to Thailand for a combat tour of 100 missions over North Vietnam. He later had a variety of fighter assignments, including two years as the slot or No 4 pilot with the Thunderbirds. Gibbs also attended FWS in the F-4 and returned as an instructor.

Tom married a stunning young woman named Christine who had worked as a Pan American flight stewardess (as they proudly proclaimed in those days, but now profess to be flight attendants). In 2009, several years after CONSTANT PEG was declassified, I asked Christine about her experiences during Tom's assignment to the 4477th. She responded that she was terrified because she didn't know what was going on since it was all classified. She also had the perception that it was extremely dangerous.

Christine had an emergency phone number, and every time she heard on the news of another Nellis Red Flag crash she went into near panic mode as she frantically dialed the number and waited for it to answer. Sometimes it rang and rang, and fear swelled in her heart that something really bad had happened to Tom. Eventually, she would get through to him, and then when he answered and she recognized his voice she would say, "Okay, thanks. Bye!" and she would hang up.

One of Tom's most treasured officers was John "Admiral" Nelson. As previously mentioned, the "Admiral" wasn't a flyer, but he was one remarkable money manager and procurement officer. As Mary Jane Smith had held things together for me from her desk in the TFWC, the "Admiral" operated right out of the 4477th trailer at Nellis on Tyndall Avenue behind the fire station.

When the contract for the Cessna 404 transportation aircraft ended, the "Admiral" was key to replacing the Cessnas with the Mitsubishi MU-2s.

As the 4477th looked to add airframes, the need for maintenance people soared. Tom Gibbs and MSgt Tommy Karnes embarked on a headhunting trip to Europe to hire crew chiefs. Tony McPeak, who was later the Air Force Chief of Staff and had also been a Thunderbird solo pilot, was the wing commander at Lakenheath AB, England, and he was extremely helpful with Gibbs' people hunt. All in all Gibbs and Karnes hired more than 20 crew chiefs during their European "Tour."

While Tom and "Tonopah Tommy" Karnes were in Europe, Christine was approached and agreed to permit the use of her home as a movie prop for a Hollywood producer making some sort of film about middle-class America. As a result people, including handsome young actors, were coming and going in a stark departure from the Gibbs household pattern of the past. When Tom got home a well-meaning neighbor suggested to him that Christine might be having an affair. It didn't take Tom very long to get the neighborhood straightened out on the rest of the story.

It was also during Tom's watch that Dave Stringer was added to the maintenance team. He was the unit's first Maintenance Officer, and things were not always rosy between Dave and the NCOs that were in the habit of running the logistics operation without direct officer involvement below the commander level. Dave survived that challenge and retired from the USAF as a general officer.

During Tom Gibbs' command the squadron accelerated in accomplishing its mission. When scheduled, the 4477th would launch full-scale adversary reactions to the Red Flag scenarios and fill the sky with MiGs opposing the "good guys." During these events the 4477th pilots would often strap into the MiGs while still in the hangars at Tonopah and wait for the prying eyes of satellites to disappear over the horizon. Once this had happened the fleet was hastily towed out of the hangars, engines started up, and a mass launch would occur, the MiGs rising to face the inbound Red Flag participants.

While this was a great time in history for the 4477th, it wasn't without its trials and tribulations due to aircraft parts and supply problems and the airfield construction that had commenced to support the impending arrival of the first F-117 stealth fighters. Winding down MiG-17 operations helped, but this was offset by the arrival of the MiG-23s.

KERMIT DEITZ (FIREMAN)

I'm not sure how I got into the screening process to be assigned to the 4477th. I was a fireman working on the flight line at Andrews AFB when I first became aware I was about to interviewed for a special assignment. That's when I first met the commander,

AGE mechanic Ben Galloway thanks pilot Capt Dave 'Marshall" McCloud after an incentive flight in a T-38. Ben Galloway via Gail Peck)

Ben Galloway and his wife Melody during the days of the CONSTANT PEG operations. (Ben Galloway via Gail Peck)

icial photo: F-15C pilot Lt Col Rick "Kluso" Tollini, th TFS of the 33rd TFW Eglin AFB) who is credited an aerial victory after destroying an Iraqi MiG-25 19 Jan 1991 during DESERT STORM. (Gail Peck)

At one point in the latter stages of CONSTANT PEG there were only four captain pilots in the Red Eagles, namely (from left to right), Brian "Lazmo" McCoy ("Bandit 53"), "Hawk" Carlisle ("Bandit 54"), Mick Simmons ("Bandit 57"), and Nickie Fuerst ("Bandit 65"). (Nick Fuerst via Gail Peck)

Red Eagle runners and their ladies after a sporting event. In the front row are, from left to right, Lt Cdr Keith Shean (US Navy, "Bandit 17"), Maj Lenny Bucko (US Marine Corps, "Bandit 22"), and Capt Mike Scott ("Bandit 14"). In the back row, from left to right, are Lt Cdr "Sel" Laughter (US Navy, "Bandit 18"), a female friend of Lenny Bucko, Chip Corder (son of Chuck and Margy Corder), Maj Chuck Corder ("Bandit 15") and Margy Corder. (Earl Henderson via Gail Peck)

The Red Eagles softball team at Nellis AFB. (Earl Henderson via Gail Peck)

June 1985
4477 TES / 57 FWW
"SUMMER FUN"

Ron Hill	Eddie Chitwood	John DeVaney	Jack Dain	Ferris (John) Hunt		Walt Triche	Jeff Davis
Fab	C/C	C/C	Eng	Rdr		Avi	Fuel

Jim Marney	Brian Lentz	Ronnie Robinson	Dyke Bennett	Bob Ferrari	Dennis Vandersyde	Jim Bell	Roger Cartier
Hyd	C/C	C/C	C/C	C/C	C/C	C/C	Chief

A Red Eagles maintenance team deployed to an unnamed TDY location. (Anonymous donor via Gail Peck)

A CONSTANT PEG T-38A Talon on the ramp at TTR. Note the Red Eagles decal on the engine intake. (Rich Samanich via Gail Peck)

The CONSTANT PEG T-38s on the ramp with the MiG-23 hangars in the background. (Rich Samanich via Gail Peck)

Eagle maintainer Rich Samanich after an incentive flight with Capt Mick Simmons. (Rich Samanich via Gail Peck)

Rich Samanich at work in the maintenance workshop. (Rich Samanich via Gail Peck)

Derek "Bo" Kemper operates one of the metal shaping jigs in the Red Eagles' sheet metal workshop at TTR. (Rich Samanich via Gail Peck)

MiG-21F-13 "Bort 77" on the ramp at TTR. Note the addition of "th" after the Bort number. (Rich Samanich via Gail Peck)

T-38 with assigned crew chief Jim Vinson. (Rich Samanich via Gail Peck)

T-38 with assigned crew chief Dennis Curran. (Rich Samanich via Gail Peck)

Gail Peck and "Chuck" Heatley ("Bandit 8") aboard USS *Kitty Hawk* (CV-63) in the South China Sea in 1980s. ("Chuck" Heatley via Gail Peck)

This 4477th TES officer cadre photo was taken during Lt Col Mike Scott's brief time as the unit's final CO, which lasted from November 1987 through to the unit's disbandment in March 1988. (Mike Scott via Gail Peck)

Peck next to the MiG-21 originally known as 14 at Tonopah. The aircraft is on static display at the Air Force Armament museum outside the main gate at Eglin AFB, FL. (Gail Peck)

Gail Peck and "OP" Denney, who claimed two MiG-23 kills during DESERT STORM, in Florida. (Gail Peck)

Red Eagle Lenny Bucko (US Marine Corps) gives a lecture on amphibious warfare from the swimming pool of Earl and Andy Henderson during a reunion party. (Gail Peck)

Glenn Frick (first CO of the Red Eagles) and Chico Noriego (initial cadre crew chief) at an early Red Eagles reunion. Capt "Shy" Shervanick ("Bandit 28") and Lt Col George "G2" Gennin ("Bandit 31") can be seen in the background. (Gail Peck)

Gracie Frick, Earl Henderson, Neil Henderson, Andy Henderson, and Rita Ober during a Red Eagles reunion party. (Gail Peck)

Rita Oberle, Joe "Jose" Oberle ("Bandit 5"), and John "Flash" Mann ("Bandit 56") during a reunion party at the Henderson's home. (Gail Peck)

Red Eagles fireman Kermit Deitz and maintainers Ike Crawley, Paul Cox, Dave Boudreau, and Richie Murphy at the Henderson's home during a reunion. (Gail Peck)

[...]G pilots Mike Scott, Gail Peck, Fred Clifton, [...]bi Wan" Henderson, Dave Carr, and Tony Mahoney. [...]ail Peck)

Gail Peck and Don Lyon in the 65th AS "Red Eagle" bar at Nellis AFB. (Gail Peck)

Gail Peck and Steve
Hovermale in Oklahoma.
(Gail Peck)

Gail Peck and Tommy Karnes
in Missouri. (Gail Peck)

Gail Peck, Bob Drabant, and
Tom Morgenfeld. (Gail Peck)

Gail Peck and Don Muller
("Bandit 3") in Florida.
(Gail Peck)

Gail Peck and Phil White,
"Bandit 46", in Florida.
(Gail Peck)

S Navy Red Eagle pilot Tom
orgenfeld ("Bandit 7") and
ail Peck at the Camarillo, CA
port. (Gail Peck)

Believed to have been the original HAVE DRILL MiG-17F evaluated by the USAF in the late 1960s, this "Fresco C" has been on static display at the Threat Training Facility (dubbed the "Petting Zoo") at Nellis AFB for a number of years. It is adorned with the name of Lt Gen David McCloud ("Bandit 10"), who was killed flying his aerobatic Yak over Alaska in July 1998. (Earl Henderson via Gail Peck)

Displayed in front of the 64th AS facility at Nellis AFB, this MiG-21F-13 was formerly CONSTANT PEG jet "Bort 04" at TTR. It was restored and crewed by Tommy Karnes. (Gail Peck)

This MiG-29C was one of 14 single-seat and seven two-seat "Fulcrums" purchased by the USA from the Moldovan Air Force in October 1997. Restored in a spurious color scheme, it resides in front of the 65th AS building at Nellis AFB. (Gail Peck)

A MiG-23 "Flogger" in the Threat Training Facility at Nellis AFB. (Gail Peck)

This MiG-21F-13 is on static display at the USAF Armament Museum at Eglin AFB. The jet was formerly the CONSTANT PEG aircraft initially known as "Bort 14" at TTR. It later carried the Bort number "85" on the nose, and it has been marked this way ever since its arrival in Florida, even though the aircraft's current camouflage scheme is different. The aircraft simply "arrived at the museum overnight," the curator being told not to ask any questions as to its origin. (Gail Peck)

Red Eagles and host nation personnel gather around a Sabre during an extraction trip. (Don Lyon via Gail Peck)

A USAF C-5A Galaxy is loaded with disassembled MiGs and spare parts during an extraction airlift. (Don Lyon via Gail Peck)

Red Eagle crew chief Jerry Baker (left) and vehicle mechanic Billy Lightfoot relaxing during an extraction trip. (Don Lyon via Gail Peck)

Don Lyon (left) and Jerry Baker next to a Sabre while overseas during an extraction trip. (Don Lyon via Gail Peck)

Red Eagles gathered on August 15, 2009, at the Evergreen Air Museum to honor the dedication of a MiG-21MF to the unit. In the top photo, from left to right, are Brian McCoy ("Bandit 53"), Dudley Larson ("Bandit 60"), "Smokey" Sundell ("Bandit 58"), Mick Simmons ("Bandit 57"), Gail Peck ("Bandit 9"), Ike Crawley (jet engine mechanic), John "DJ" Dvorachek (crew chief on "Bort 84"), and Ben Galloway (AGE). In the bottom left photo are Maj Charles "Smokey" Sundell and his crew chief MSgt "DJ" Dvorachek at TTR in the 1980s (left), and at bottom (right) the two men pose in front of the MiG-21MF, which bears their names beneath the cockpit canopy. "DJ" Dvorachek is holding a copy of the photo seen on the left. (Ben Galloway via Gail Peck)

Red Eagle MiG-21F-13 in formation with a US Navy -14A Tomcat. (USAF via Gail Peck)

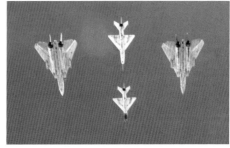

A diamond formation of Red Eagle MiG-21s and US Navy F-14A Tomcats. (USAF via Steve Davies)

A flight of two CONSTANT PEG MiG-21F-13s in contrasting camouflage schemes head back to TTR. (USAF via Gail Peck)

A Red Eagle MiG-21 taxis past the TTR control tower sometime in 1986. With "Bort 84" on the nose, this aircraft is believed to be the MiG previously known to the early Red Eagles as "Bort 11." (USAF via Steve Davies)

The Red Eagle officers under the command of Lt Col Jack Manclark assembled in the VIP hangar, with "Bort 85," bearing the commander's name on the canopy rail, serving as a fitting backdrop. (USAF via Steve Davies)

"Ivan" or "Natasha" is parked in between two MiG-21s. The vehicle is one of the two Soviet self-propelled aircraft starting trucks extracted by the Red Eagles from foreign climes. The trucks were restored to operability by Ben Galloway and Doug Robinson, with a lot of help from the other Red Eagles, including vehicle mechanics Billy Lightfoot and Larry Gruse and master machinist Bob Griese. At different times the trucks had various other nicknames in addition to "Ivan" and "Natasha." (USAF via Gail Peck)

Mission over, a "Fishbed" lands at TTR sometime between 1987 and early 1988. (USAF via Steve Davies)

d Eagle commander Jack Manclark at the speaker's podium during the declassification "coming out" press nference held at the National Museum of the Air Force in November 2006. (USAF via Gail Peck)

The "Gang of Three" (Peck, Smith, and Frick) got things going. Smith was replaced at TAC HQ by Joseph "CT" Wang and Peck was replaced at the Pentagon by Bill "Saki" Sakahara. Peck replaced Frick at Nellis. Shown here are Sakahara, Peck, and Wang at a Red Eagle Reunion in Las Vegas in November 2011.

A flight of two MiG-21s on the flight line at Tonopah. (USAF via Gail Peck)

Six MiG-21s on the flight line at Tonopah in the mid-1980s. (USAF via Gail Peck)

Wall of DESERT STORM heroes in the 58th TFS bar at Eglin AFB. The plaque and other memorabilia commemorate the aerial victories scored by the squadron's F-15C pilots during DESERT STORM. (Gail Peck)

Lt Col Gail Peck. He showed up, and after some pleasant small talk we boarded one of our big trucks and took a cruise around the backside of Andrews, where we trained routinely. Lt Col Peck and I really got along well from the very beginning, and I think I sealed the deal when I let him drive the fire truck and operate the foam turrets. The next thing I knew I was hired and was soon on my way to Nellis, where I served with Ralph Payne and others hired to provide the fire services for the MiG aircraft operation at the new TTR.

Lt Col Peck told me that one of the oversights in the initial planning for the unit was their failure to include fire services. Ralph and I, along with Louis Hinostrosa and Evan Robinson ("R-2"), were assigned to fix that problem. Our fire station also came along later. We initially acquired an 0-11A crash truck, along with P-4 and P-6 ramp trucks. We basically sat strip alert in the trucks during flight operations because we initially had no fire station.

When the second stage of construction was completed at Tonopah to facilitate the F-117 operations we moved into a fancy new firehouse adjacent to our ramp. Eventually we shared firefighting responsibility with the stealth fighter people.

Mark Postai was taking off in a MiG-17 on a routine training flight one day when his jet caught fire down the right side of the fuselage. Our controller (I don't remember who it was) told Mark to abort and get out of the burning MiG. But not Mark! He continued with his take-off and tried to bring it back to the base. I was notified by the controller while in my standby position (as we manned on every flight) that we had an emergency. I watched Mark bank to the left, trying to return and land, but he was losing altitude fast and he decided to put it down in the desert in a spot where we could get to him quickly.

I took off across the desert to find him, all the while hoping for the best. I found the downed aircraft, and my first priority was to see if the pilot had made it out safely. To my amazement, I spotted Mark standing on a hill well away from the jet and waving for me to come and get him. What a sight it was to see that he had survived and was unhurt. Bobby Ellis was also quickly on the scene. After making sure that Mark was safe and out of harm's way, I turned my attention to securing the aircraft wreckage. The fire equipment had followed the path that Bob Ellis and I had cut through the desert in our initial response.

We had several barrier engagements, but the one that sticks out in my mind was an engagement by a US Navy A-4 that had hit the barrier so hard that the airplane jumped off the ground and went sideways, causing all of the webbing to get wrapped around the nose. This in turn prevented the pilot from exiting the jet. It took us a long time to cut all of the nylon straps away from the canopy, and I don't think that the pilot ever got those stains out of his flightsuit. He was a bit shaken up.

One day Mike Beverlin, Ike Crawley, and Paul Long were on the engine run-up pad in front of the fire station when I noticed that the MiG-17 they were working on had flames coming from the aft section. I blew my siren to get the attention of the crew and to point out the problem. They quickly shut the aircraft down and got the hell out of the area. I notified the other truck that was on his standby position that we had a fire on the pad. Evan Robinson and I started attacking the fuselage fire and quickly put it out. Our Fire Chief, Ralph Payne, informed us later that if we had not noticed the fire and acted as quickly as we did, the airplane could have exploded on the pad, resulting in people being killed or severely injured.

TOM MORGENFELD AND RON IVERSON

On one occasion we sent MiG pilots Lt Cdr Tom Morgenfeld and Maj Ron Iverson on TDY trips to two different locations at the same time. Unknown to either, they both arrived at the Dallas Fort Worth airport to catch the same flight back to Las Vegas. Morgenfeld entered the men's room near the departure gate and was surprised to see Iverson busy at a urinal midway down a pretty crowded row of fixtures. The spot next to Iverson was vacant and Morgenfeld took up that position, carefully honoring the unwritten men's room rule of avoiding eye contact with the adjacent male.

After a moment, Morgenfeld elbowed Iverson in the ribs and bellowed out in a loud voice, "My God, a miniature penis!" What little buzz of soft conversation there had been in the men's room instantly fell silent. The stunned silence was followed by Iverson's instant realization that he had been "had." Iverson fired back with an expletive likely to have been "You son of a bitch!" and they both roared with laughter as they left the room, while the remaining group gawked at them, wondering what the hell had just happened.

Such are the pranks that occur among American fighter pilots, even if the aircraft they fly are MiGs.

STEVE HOVERMALE (CREW CHIEF) AND DON LYON (ASSISTANT NCOIC)

This caper happened on February 26, 1981. Steve Hovermale and I had decided to hang it up and retire (the thrill was gone), and one day Lt Cdr "Heater" Heatley asked me if I had planned any sort of "last day at work" stunt. I hadn't. One thing led to another and I got to talking to Steve, and we reflected that we had always thought of ourselves as decent "flyers" – at least we never ran an airplane into anything expensive.

We talked about alternative stunts, and I told Steve I had enough F-4 back seat time and didn't need or want any more of that. And we got to fly in the T-38 all the time, so that was old stuff too. We decided maybe a Navy or even a Marine aircraft would be something different to fly in for an end of career event. "Heater" jumped on the idea and one day soon thereafter a pair of two-seated TA-4 Skyhawks arrived at Tonopah under the guise of delivering some Air Combat Maneuvering Instrumentation pods to us for use during flight operations from TTR. These pods are carried on the aircraft like a missile and talk to computers on the ground, presenting a three-dimensional view of the fighter's air track. The tracks are recorded and are extremely important to the pilots during debriefing. When the jets are carrying the pods there can be no more lying about who did what and when. The pod tells the exact truth.

I think the TA-4s were adversaries from VA-127, based at NAS Lemoore, California. One of the pilots was Tom Hogue, and I flew with him. Steve was aboard the other jet. Now the back seat in a TA-4 Skyhawk is tiny. We had to twist sideways with our arms in front of us in order to get the canopies down. Then, the little jet fits like a glove. The two-ship of TA-4s were flown initially by the Navy pilots, with Tom and me along for the ride. But before long it was our turn. The pilots gave the controls to Tom and me and we had at it in a one-versus-one dogfight. I don't recall that either of us got a decent shot at the other, but we had a good time.

We came back all hot and sweaty and happy, and when we got out of the jets the firemen got into the act by hosing us down with water from the fire truck. It was great EXCEPT no one had told Tom Gibbs, our commander, what was going on. Suddenly, he saw us taxiing out to take off and asked why the Navy was leaving early. He was more than a little annoyed with us and, yeah, looking back, we should have briefed him on the plan. We hadn't bothered to brief Ellis either. So now instead of basking in the glory of our last military flight, we were engaged in a two-versus-two with the commander and one mad Bobby Ellis.

They got over it.

PRANKS

There were always pranks going on at Tonopah. While not totally limited to the enlisted men, usually the pranks were aimed at the new guys in the enlisted force, pulled on them by their "old head" NCO colleagues almost like a fraternity house rite of passage. One prank that backfired on the perpetrators was pulled on Ben Galloway. His buddies caught him one day solo in the bathroom, and noticing a piece of chain and an open pad lock nearby, they locked Ben in the "facility." Ben attempted to exit, opened the door a scant inch, saw the chain holding the door shut and knew instantly that he had been "had."

He took on a *McGyver* like mindset, realizing he had a few tools in his pocket, and proceeded to quickly dismount the door of the facility from its hinges by driving the pins up and out. Ben said nothing and returned to work without making a fuss. However, inside his brain a plan was developing to get even. He knew who had locked him in because only a few people had been on the site at the time, and he could account for all of them except a small group. The bad guys, as it turned out, were from the NDI and tire workshop next door. Their facility shared a heating system with Ben's workshop. A plan emerged.

The heating system was a typical Red Eagles solution to a problem. It was cold in both workshops, and there was only one heater to solve the problem – a device known as a H-1/Herman-Nelson. The heater output was connected to a Vee duct, with one duct going to Ben's facility and the other duct going to the NDI workshop of the target crowd.

Bobby Ellis had previously brought a kitten named Sylvia to the site, and she was litter box trained, living in the trailers with the men that stayed overnight. When the F-117 construction was complete our men were forced to move from their trailers to the Mancamp facility, which was designed to support the entire TTR operation. Mancamp rules prevented Sylvia from making the move, and thus she and her litter box moved to Ben Galloway's AGE workshop, where she played the role of "mouser."

To get even with the NDI/tire workshop guys for locking him in the bathroom on that particularly cold winter's day at Tonopah, Ben cleaned the cat's litter box, placing the fecal material in an empty cat food can which he filled with hot water. The next step was to disconnect the Herman-Nelson output duct to the adjacent workshop and push the can full of hot water and cat poop as far up the duct as he could in the direction of the outlets to his pals' facility. With the duct reconnected and the Herman-Nelson heater cranked up high, it didn't take long for the water in the bucket to boil and for the kitty poop to give off a terrible aroma straight through the duct into the adjacent NDI/tire workshop. The men next door came over to Ben complaining about the odor, and they asked him if he was bothered by it. Of course he wasn't, and Ben played ignorant.

This went on for about an hour, and by that time both doors to the NDI workshop were wide open, in spite of the 32° F outside air temperature. After a little while they came back to his workshop admitting the bathroom caper and begging forgiveness if he would just fix the heat and stink problem and back off from getting even with them. Not to be outdone, he accepted their apologies, had a good laugh with them, and then left them to fix their problem.

Ben wasn't done with them yet though. He later took a forklift and hoisted the rear end of their truck up so the rear wheels were just off the ground. He built a wooden jack under the rear end and departed with the forklift. The next time the NDI boys headed out in their vehicle all that happened when it was put into gear was the spinning of the rear wheels.

Another favorite prank was to deflate the tires in a new guy's vehicle of choice, add some water to the tube, and then inflate the tires again. The water would flow to the bottom of the stationary vehicle's tires and then during the cold Tonopah nights it would freeze solid. The next morning it would seem to the unsuspecting driver that the tires badly needed balancing as he drove off, "clumpidy, clumpidy, clump."

It's amazing we got any work done, but the men always had the jets ready to fly in spite of the never-ending series of gags they played on one another.

JOHN SANDERS REPORTS ON AN NDI PRANK

Non-Destructive Inspection is a very important element in the maintenance of high performance aircraft. Various techniques are used to make the inspections, and one of them is the X-ray.

One day the men that worked in the NDI lab at Tonopah had had as much as they could stand of the pranks being pulled on them by one of the crew chiefs. They concocted a plan to get even. They found a dead mouse and put X-ray film under and over it, then took an X-ray of the wing on the MiG-21 that belonged to the target crew chief. They showed the developed film to the crew chief, informing him that there was a mouse inside the wing of his aircraft. The crew chief immediately started taking the panels off the wing in search of the non-existent mouse. At one point they nearly cracked up laughing when they overheard him say that he was close because he could smell the critter.

Lt Col Manclark, who was the commander at the time, came into the hangar and immediately became interested in what was going on with the wing on the aircraft. The NDI boys confided their prank and Manclark laughed out loud too. A good time was had by all. Later, the dead mouse was placed in a desk drawer in one of the offices, and the drawer was then locked. It was only after the smell became readily apparent that it was realized that the owner of the desk was on vacation for a week! Another day at Tonopah.

"ELEPHANTIZE"

The following is an attempt to describe a word that was part of the Red Eagle language so many years ago. That word is "Elephantize," and it was a verb.

Bob Breault reports:

I was first introduced to the term "Elephantize," or "Elephantizing" in 1983 at the old "25 Club" near the main gate at Nellis AFB. "Elephantizing" was a welcoming of sorts primarily to the spouse of a Red Eagle. This normally would take place after several adult beverages had been consumed by the "elephanteers." Usually four or five of these select Red Eagles would rise up, using their arms as a simulated Elephant trunk, and loudly make their awful imitations of a trumpeting elephant. They would circle the frightened spouse and thoroughly mess up her hair with their simulated trunks. I do not know the origin of this activity, but I'm fairly sure of its ending. "Elephantizing" was meant to make the spouse feel like she was part of the crowd, and for the most part it was all in fun, and not intended to hurt anyone.

After the "25 Club" was destroyed by a fire, "Elephantizing" took up shop at the nearby "Hitching Post Saloon." One day in 1987 MSgt Ron Hill and his wife (who had never been "elephantized") showed up, and me being the good-natured soul that I am, wanted to make her feel welcome. I did not take into consideration that she may not approve of "elephantizing," nor did I know she had a black belt in Kung Foo Kwan Do Joo Jit Sue something or other. I found myself on my back, on the floor, wondering "fut the wuck" just happened? To my knowledge this was the last Red Eagle "elephantizing" to *almost* take place.

DON LYON AND BILL McHENRY CAPTURE A JAGUAR

It was windy as hell, and Bill McHenry and Don Lyon were the only maintenance guys still on duty for some reason. Red Eagles CO "Obi Wan" Henderson was the last officer to leave, and he was cleaning up some paperwork prior to taking the maintainers home in one of the Cessna 404s. Don Lyon takes up the story:

When the Royal Air Force Jaguar fighter aircraft landed without notice or clearance at Tonopah, the pilot deployed his drag 'chute to slow the jet. As he attempted to turn off the runway, the crosswind changed direction into a quartering tail wind and the 'chute blew through 90 degrees and wrapped itself around the left main landing gear. The pilot didn't know this had happened, however. We quickly drove out to the Jaguar, frantically waving at him to stop. Bill and I quickly cut the drag 'chute into several pieces to extract it from the wheels, tires, and brakes. We then guided the pilot to a parking spot outside the MiG compound and he shut the Jaguar down. When the pilot de-planed, I sliced the Jaguar patch off his flightsuit!

Security showed up immediately and essentially took the pilot into custody. He wasn't the least bit upset and only wanted to get to a phone so he could talk to his unit at Nellis and tell them what had happened, and that he and the aircraft were secure. I believe George Thomas was the security guy that "bagged the Brit." Security then came into the compound and found "Obi Wan" Henderson in his office and reported that some guy had landed a funny looking airplane on their air base and was talking some kind of funny English!

"Obi Wan" dealt with the issue, and the next day a couple of maintenance guys and a pilot showed up, fixed the aircraft and the jet was flown out. Neither the Brit pilot nor the maintainers saw anything unusual because all our "toys" were out of sight.

This episode started my "patch cutting" quest that targeted unannounced visitors. I continued to do this and built up my patch collection until I left Tonopah.

DON LYON'S STORIES ABOUT VISITORS

The first visiting A-10 that landed at Tonopah after we started MiG operations was camouflaged, as I recall, and it came in with an engine problem. The pilot taxied right up to our gate and stopped. When we tried to marshal the jet into the compound we found that it wouldn't fit through the gate because the gateposts were too high and the wingspan of the aircraft was wider than the gate opening.

While the pilot sat there watching and wondering what was going to happen next, his eyes grew as big as saucers as two of our men sporting beards and wearing blue jeans approached with welding equipment. They used the welding torch to "shorten" the gateposts, thus quickly solving the problem. However, from his expression, I think the pilot at first thought that they were going to attack his aircraft with the welding torch. And in that brief moment he realized he had no reverse gear in his A-10 and no way to turn around and escape!

On another occasion a US Navy F-14 was photographed while parked on the CONSTANT PEG refueling pit in front of the original hangars. Taxiing the jet onto the fuel pits wasn't a good idea because the Tomcat generated too much jet blast. As a result of that experience our policy evolved, and from then on we would shut the aircraft down outside the compound by the fire station and then tow it in for fuel.

DON LYON DISCUSSES THE OFFICERS ASSIGNED TO THE RED EAGLES

I want to comment on the high quality of our officers. Neither before nor after I served in the Red Eagles did I have the good fortune to deal with guys of the caliber of these individuals, including the GCI officers and John "Admiral" Nelson. We were trusted with blanket travel orders and the "Admiral" took care of all our pay/per diem/travel processing, which in turn meant that we didn't have to waste time traveling to Nellis to submit paperwork at base finance and then wait for reimbursements. That was a great help to us.

I knew that anytime I needed flight support it would happen. If I needed a pilot to fly a test flight or take someone somewhere in the Cessna or go somewhere and get a replacement for a broken part, it would happen. I was never told no, or given an excuse. It just got done, and that reflects strongly on the quality of our team.

On the other hand, I didn't do well when the air force started assigning officers to run the maintenance department. After all, we set it up and built the aircraft into safe flying machines, and we did it without nitpicking supervision.

Tommy Karnes reminded me of the day I threw a new maintenance officer off the ramp. That caused a stir. This actually happened twice! Those of us in maintenance had ABSOLUTELY no idea we were getting a maintenance officer assigned to the Red Eagles. The first one just showed up one day and pissed off the wrong guy. The same thing happened the second time around too. The second one had a reason to be on site, but not on my flight line giving instructions regarding practices and procedures that were in place – that he knew nothing about – to people that didn't know him.

I was not "anti-officer" as Bobby Ellis sometimes tended to be, and I had a good rapport (at least I thought I did) with all of our officers, including the pilots and the GCI guys.

In my career I had worked for and helped train a fair number of maintenance officers, at least two of whom became general officers. Some were outstanding, some were average, and a few were not trainable. I refused to submit to two of these new guy maintenance officers and never made it a secret, but I never talked about them behind their backs. Our communications was always straight up, face-to-face. All the men in the unit knew my feelings, and at least once I was called to Tom Gibbs' office for a special session. Enough said.

One very fond memory I have was getting my ass chewed by Chuck Corder in front of EVERYONE. I had sliced off a patch from the jacket of a visiting Navy pilot, and he was so upset that he cried to anyone who would listen. To appease him I went to our supply store and gave him a BRAND NEW Nomex jacket, but I kept the patch. Chuck got the job of chewing me out. He must have been the ranking officer on duty that day. It was a little hard for either of us to keep a straight face, but we made it.

Off base, when we first went to Tonopah it had two motels – one at each end of town. We sometimes stayed at one or the other. The "Silver Queen," which was at the western end of town, had a restaurant. Some of the guys occasionally went there for dinner. Dave Hollingsworth and Jerry Baker dined there one night I know of for sure. As they were leaving some dude started shooting in the parking lot and Jerry spent the rest of the evening under one of our pick-ups waiting for things to settle down.

The motel at the eastern end of town was a two-storey affair. One evening, Billy Lightfoot was skinning a snake outside on the balcony while several of us watched – alcohol was present. Billy only wanted the skin, so when he finished he threw the carcass over the railing, which overlooked an alleyway. The latter was being used by an older couple for their evening stroll. I thought we had a double heart attack scenario on our hands for a few minutes when the sky started raining dead snakes on them. Once we explained what was going on they were okay, and they actually showed an interest in Billy's "craft" of making things of value with snakeskins.

The saloon of choice was "ACES," owned by Jim Wilmoth. He also owned a trailer that we rented for a while to use as an overnight crash pad. He treated us well, and would do anything in the world for us. It wasn't the favorite hangout of the locals, and that worked out good for us. We hosted Gail Peck there one night when he stayed over with us. The boys had crock-pots filled with chili, and it was like a feast in a firehouse kitchen, all at the very back of the bar. A good time was had by all. I think Gerry Huff even made a courtesy stop with the only woman in Tonopah, his girlfriend. There were other women in town, but we DIDN'T go to that place!

Jim Richardson showed a couple of slightly intoxicated cowboys the finer points of playing a game of screws one evening. This was something he thought up on the spot, and he had these two convinced it was as real as any game of chance, and when I called it a night those guys were still at the bar with a cup of screws, shaking and rolling and arguing who had the best hand. Jim was a very devout, non-drinker, non-smoker who still always seemed to have as good a time as the rest of us idiots, and he NEVER came down on us for what we did.

Richardson made up our unit stencil for "zapping" other people's airplanes. If they came to TTR they left with our mark on their jet. The stencil was far more sophisticated than the average run-of-the-mill one. Even though it was above and beyond a plain old stencil, nobody remembers what it looked like! It just looked good and distinctive.

I believe Jim took on the job of First Sergeant and maintained all our training records too. He had been my neighbor at our previous assignment (we both lived on base), and he had inherited a 1933/34 Dodge coupe with a rumble seat. Most weekend afternoons you could find Jim Richardson hauling kids around the neighborhood in that old Dodge.

Don Lyon Discusses Bob Hobson, Jack Slusher, and Television

Somehow Bobby Ellis uncovered an electronic cache similar to "Santa's Sleigh" in terms of the quality and quantity of electronic equipment that was available for the asking. The cache was located at the White Sands Missile Test Range in New Mexico, and the inventory of equipment was aimed at supporting various test endeavors. When a test was completed the spare parts and unused supplies were of no further use to the test team, and were therefore labeled as surplus equipment and "stored" at White Sands. What "stored" really meant was that after a test wound down at White Sands no one knew how to dispose of the unused equipment other than to send it to the DRMO, otherwise known as the salvage yard.

Thus, the surplus became easy prey to hoarding predators like Bobby Ellis and his gang of road warriors. White Sands was glad to get rid of "stuff" and Ellis was glad to get it.

Early in the selection of the maintenance team Ellis convinced a brilliant avionics technician named Bob Hobson to join the team, which at that time was simply called the "TAC Red Hats." The Red Eagles squadron name came later. The early MiGs were very simple with almost no avionics, and this left Hobson somewhat underemployed. But Bobby Ellis kept a close eye on his "spark chaser," as he called Hobson, and challenged him in ways even Hobson probably never envisioned.

I don't have all the details, but it has been reported to me that Hobson teamed up with the communications expert Jack Slusher and they built a television downlink and distribution system with parts that Ellis had liberated from White Sands. Long before the advent of Direct TV, our men had commercial-free tunable television at the remote TTR, including the Playboy Channel, all thanks to Bob Hobson and Jack Slusher.

Don Lyon Discusses Ike Crawley and the F-111

One day Ike and Mike Beverlin were working outside when they saw an F-111 on fire and approaching TTR in preparation for an emergency landing. The pilot got the airplane on the ground and turned off the runway onto a taxiway with a downhill grade. The jet obviously had no brakes and was rolling dangerously toward the compound hangar area. The hangars were full of our MiGs. Ike and Mike grabbed MiG wheel chocks and raced to intercept the lumbering F-111, which was now moving relentlessly forward downhill at the pace of a fast walk. The burning jet was totally out of control.

The two Red Eagles coordinated their efforts and ran alongside the big jet, putting the MiG wheel chocks in front of the main landing gear tires of the F-111.

The latter, which was very big and very heavy in comparison with a MiG, simply hit the chocks and jumped right over. But the jet had slowed slightly. The men grabbed the chocks and tried again, despite the flames, with the same result. Each time the F-111 slowed slightly and they finally managed to get it stopped.

Next came the task of extracting the aircrew from the jet. They considered jettisoning the canopy, but not being 100 percent sure about how the system worked they were afraid they might inadvertently eject the crew. As our Red Eagles went up the side of the jet, the canopy opened and the aircrew went forward over the windscreen and slid down the nose of the aircraft to safety while the fire department was extinguishing the flames at the other end of the F-111. A few weeks later our guys read a story in *The Air Force Times* about the crew receiving an award for saving the aircraft. Wheels were put in motion to recognize the groundcrew as well, and Ike received an Airman's Medal for his efforts that day.

Without the good fortune of TTR's location and the heroic efforts of all involved, especially the Red Eagles, the air force would have lost an airplane that day and perhaps the crew as well.

A MEMORABLE TRIP ABOARD THE CONVAIR COMMUTER

Originally, the Red Eagles commuted to the TTR either in private vehicles, in one of the squadron trucks, or via one of the Cessna 404s. The latter were eventually replaced by MU-2s, which provided a similar airlift capability to the Cessnas.

As the F-117 project matured at the northern end of the airfield, decisions were made to drop the MU-2 contract and move the Red Eagle personnel back and forth via a Convair type aircraft under a contract with Key Airlines. Eventually, the twin piston-engined Convairs were replaced by Boeing 727 and then Boeing 737 aircraft as promised to Sam Moore in Gail Peck's original conversation with the Department of Energy site manager at TTR.

One day while airborne in the Convair for a long trip home Ben Galloway, who was seated over the wing of the aircraft in a window seat, felt a sharp jolt followed by a vibration. He then noticed the engine on his side was producing a slight wisp of smoke. A few moments later another jolt was accompanied by a significant increase in the vibration and more smoke. As he was peering out the window at the engine speculating on exactly what had failed, Ben noticed the captain of the aircraft striding down the aisle from the cockpit toward Ben's seat attempting to casually look out the windows of the transport.

The captain stopped adjacent to Ben's seat and peered out the window. Ben speculated, "I think you blew a jug on that engine." The captain responded,

"That's what I was afraid had happened." Ben further speculated, "I guess this means we will be turning around and going back to Tonopah." The captain replied, "Yep." Thus, the stage was set for another unexpected overnight in the "Indian Village" at the TTR.

GALLOWAY, ROBINSON, AND ELLIS AS ROOMMATES AT TONOPAH

Bobby Ellis, Ben Galloway, and Doug Robinson shared one of the trailers in the "Indian Village" as their home away from home for about two years. During that timeframe they shared cooking duties and hung out, often consuming generous quantities of adult beverages.

Galloway had brought a pregnant wife with him when he reported to Nellis for duty with the Red Eagles at Tonopah. Ben's wife Melody was assured by the secretary, Eunice, that there would be no problem getting hold of Ben when Melody went into labor. One day Eunice called Melody and asked her if she was really in labor. Melody said, "No, but why did you think I was?" Eunice replied that she had thought she had received a call in the middle of the night from Melody announcing the onset of labor. But for some reason she had fallen asleep and wasn't sure whether the call had been real or a dream.

Melody is not a person to fool around with, and her reaction was to ensure she could reliably contact Ben. She created enough of a fuss that she was eventually able to obtain a telephone number that might connect her with her husband in an emergency. Unbeknownst to her, the other end of the telephone number she was now permitted to call was in the trailer that Ben, Bobby, and Doug shared during overnights at Tonopah. Melody's first attempt to call happened on the same night that Ellis and the boys had finished an early dinner in the trailer and then settled into a long evening of drinking. When the phone rang it startled the men, and Ellis, who was well into his "cups," answered the phone "Home of the fucking brave! One of the fucking heroes speaking." Then hung up. No one knew who had called.

Ben heard all about that later.

"WEIRD HAROLD"

It seems like every fighter squadron has at least one person that can be called a true character. Long after my watch the 4477th inherited a gent who became known in the squadron as "Weird Harold." He was a prior Thunderbird, and it was reported to me that he was fired because he got on the backbone of a T-38 and mooned 20,000 people at a Cleveland, Ohio, airshow!

"Weird Harold" was a terrific airplane mechanic and MiG crew chief. As a master sergeant, he was also a shift leader. There is no question that he knew just about everything there was to know about our jets.

"Weird Harold" was strange to say the least. He liked to dress up in women's clothes just for the shock factor, even though he wasn't a transvestite. He did the whole bit with high heel shoes and wigs. This guy behaved like the "Klinger" character in the hit TV show *M*A*S*H*. The more booze he drank, the more his antics picked up. In spite of his crazy behavior "Weird Harold" was married. One of his favorite stunts was to kiss every new guy in the squadron, and it wasn't just a little peck on the cheek.

One of "Weird Harold's" most memorable escapades happened after someone dared him to pull his "naked crew chief stunt" when he marshaled and parked a visiting aircraft. The aircraft belonged to a general that was a visitor to the TTR. "Weird Harold" did the deed, parking the general's aircraft wearing only boots and a radio belt hanging over his private part. Then, while "Weird Harold" was doing the marshaling job, one of the other maintainers stole his clothes. "Weird Harold" got even by taking a dump in the thief's tool bag. A few days after that it was reported that the guy with the stinky tool bag got caught trying to take a dump in "Weird Harold's" desk drawer. Such were the antics that happened just out of sight of most of the officers, but well known and heralded among the men that were the heart and soul of the squadron. It never ended.

There was also the "baby chicken" trick. "Weird Harold" had cut a hole in a box, and he would walk up to a new guy holding it, with his "pecker" inserted in the hole. He would then ask the new guy if he wanted to see his baby chicken, neatly nested in Easter straw. It didn't take but a second or two for the new guy to realize he had been had as he poked around in the box with his finger looking for the baby chicken.

On one occasion two painters from Nellis came up to TTR to paint a couple of our airplanes. By the time they got there they were scared to death just from the security briefing. The Red Eagle escort did his best to calm them down and get them a place to stay overnight in one of the "Indian Village" trailers in the TTR compound. The escort also worked hard to get the painters the supplies they needed, and generally make their stay as pleasant as possible. After a long hard work day, the painters cleaned up and the Red Eagle escort took them to the compound bar that was called the "Eagles Nest" for a well-deserved beer or two. The on duty bartender just happened to be "Weird Harold," who announced that "new meat" was present and then disappeared. A few minutes later he returned wearing a full dress, announcing "I don't have nothing on underneath this dress."

Before anyone could say or do anything, "Weird Harold" pulled the dress off over his head and plopped it down on the table, standing there buck naked with all of his parts hanging out. He then grabbed one of the painters and put a full lip lock kiss on him. The other guy's eyes nearly popped out and he headed for the door. Another Red Eagle grabbed him and tried to calm down the rising panic. By then "Weird Harold" had disappeared as fast as he had arrived. The painters got the job done the next day and were then anxious to get the hell out of there as soon as possible.

CHIP CORBETT FLIES AGAINST THE RED EAGLES

Chip Corbett is one of "Obi Wan" Henderson's partners in their defense contractor company AVTEC. Chip also had a long and memorable career in jet fighters. Whilst he was stationed at Eglin AFB flying F-4Es with the 4485th Test and Evaluation Squadron the squadron was deployed to Nellis in December 1987 to accomplish some live drop testing and to be available to fly against some "special" aircraft.

One day Chip was not scheduled to fly but was told to come in anyway for an "O-Dark-30" (early morning) show time. After arriving, he was instructed to go to an old World War II type building at the other end of the flight line where the current government automobile gasoline station sits on Nellis AFB. Upon arriving at the structure, Chip and his squadron mates were threatened with personal death and bodily harm to their families if they ever spoke of the experience they were about to have. Then, he and others from his squadron were briefed on the MiGs, after which they set about preparing for their first encounter with Soviet jets over the high desert in the northernmost portion of the Nellis range complex.

Chip was totally surprised because his adversary in the MiG-21 was to be his former aircraft commander Maj Nick Fuerst ("Bandit 65"). Chip and Nick had been crewed together in an F-4E with the 4th TFW at Seymour-Johnson AFB, North Carolina. When Nick left Seymour the word was that he was going to Nellis to fly A-7s. Nobody thought that there was anything abnormal about that. It is interesting that the A-7 was also the cover jet for the F-117 program – indeed, there were actually A-7s at Nellis belonging to the F-117 group, and their only tactical application was to serve as a cover. The assigned pilots flew them regularly. The cover stories for the MiG operation and the F-117 operation had intertwined. Chip's old F-4 aircraft commander was now actually a Red Eagle MiG pilot. Who would have thought it? Chip's mission report read as follows:

Take-off and en route to range 71-North were uneventful, and as we entered the range complex from the West, little did we know we were already being joined upon by Nickie Fuerst in his MiG-21. The one-on-one mission proceeded, with the F-4 performing a clean and dry check on the MiG-21. Following the clean and dry check, the performance comparison profile was accomplished, and sure enough there was Nickie in the MiG profoundly enjoying the moment while my eyes were popping out. Close formation with a MiG-21. I was dazzled.

At 20,000ft MSL, with both the F-4 and the MiG lineabreast, some 200ft apart at 350 KIAS, we simultaneously selected full afterburner. There was no comparison as the MiG quickly accelerated and pulled away from the F-4. Next came the turn performance comparison, and when the spacing was set each aircraft performed a maximum g turn. Once again I was awed by the turn performance of my opponent. If ever engaged in combat with a MiG-21, one would have to think twice about "crawling into the phone booth" (in a slow-speed dogfight pilots often use this expression, which relates to the disadvantage a giant would face if he encountered a midget with a big knife in a telephone booth) with such a superior-turning aircraft.

The one disadvantage of the MiG-21 is its extremely short legs, and after the turn performance exercise Nickie made one last radio call ("BINGO") and departed for home. Of my 2,200+ hours in the Phantom II, I can honestly say that that was the most remarkable 18 minutes airborne during my active flying career. And, as happens on most special flying days, it all ended up at the local watering hole following the mission debriefing in the vintage World War II structure at Nellis.

It was at the Nellis Officers' Club bar that Chip had the opportunity to buy his former F-4 aircraft commander a cold beer. Not a word was said that would compromise security, but the experiences of the day made it truly one for Chip to remember.

BEN GALLOWAY LEARNED TO PACK DRAG-CHUTES

We had a heavy flying schedule this one day. Everything we had was operational and going to fly. Bob Ellis asked if I could help out and learn from crew chief Mike Beverlin how to pack drag-chutes for the MiG-21s. Mike took about 45 minutes to train me and then make sure that I had the process figured out. Then I was left on my own as he went off to preflight his airplane. For the next three hours or so that was all I did. It seemed the crew chiefs were dropping off drag-chutes still hot from the jet exhaust and picking up fresh ones as fast as I could pack them.

The night before, I had built up my flight helmet and checked out the oxygen mask. As a reward for a full day packing drag-chutes, Bobby Ellis asked me if I would like to fly chase in a T-38 that afternoon. I jumped at the chance. I was in the back seat of a T-38 in flight chasing a MiG-21 all the way through the fighter's landing. I watched the pilot pop the drag-chute and thought "How cool is this? I packed that drag-chute and I'm wearing the flight helmet I built up just last night."

JOE MIKE PYLE

During George Gennin's watch the "crush of business" included the seemingly continuous and never-ending need for information. The media for communicating the information was typically through high quality briefing slides. George searched out and hired a magnificently talented artist named Joe Mike Pyle. The only problem was that Joe Mike was assigned to the Thunderbirds, the USAF's official aerial demonstration team, and they were not about to release one of their prize people before they absolutely had to. This meant that Joe Mike didn't actually start work with the Red Eagles on Gennin's watch. Instead, by the time he was finally able to join the unit, Phil White was the commander of the 4477th TES.

Joe Mike performed a variety of extremely valuable tasks during his assignment to the Red Eagles. In addition to the never-ending demand for overhead projector slides for one briefing after another, Joe Mike also made cockpit and other MiG-unique illustrations for use in the unit's ever expanding technical library. The latter contained the information that the pilots and maintenance personnel relied upon for the safe and effective operation of the MiGs.

Cameras weren't allowed at the site at the time for this kind of work, so hand-drawn illustrations were the order of the day. The overhead projector slides that Joe Mike created were needed to explain operations at TAC HQ level and above as successive commanders fought for the funding necessary to keep the program alive. The cockpit illustrations drawn by Joe Mike Pyle evolved into checklists and procedure documentation for use, especially by the pilots.

Joe Mike became such a valued part of the Red Eagles team that he remained assigned as a civil service employee until the program was finally shut down in March 1988. At that time Joe Mike was initially assigned to Col Doug Melson, the adversary tactics group commander at Nellis. After a short time Joe Mike moved to the FWS, where he was teamed with noted artist and former fighter pilot Blake Morrison. Brig Gen John Jumper was the commander of the 57th FWW at the time, and the FWS was essentially another group under his control.

Joe Mike worked with Blake on the official document published by the FWS known then as the *Fighter Weapons Review*. During the period of his assignment at the FWS, Joe Mike contributed much of the artwork published in the review.

The publication was later renamed the *Weapons Review* when the FWS became the USAF Weapons School.

At one point it was decided to feature an F-4 on the cover of the *Weapons Review*, and Joe Mike used my F-4 model for artistic reference in the preparation of the painting. My jet at Ubon RTAFB, upon which the model was based, was named *Kayte Baby*, and the name is clearly visible on the nose of the aircraft in Joe Mike's painting. It was an honor to have Joe Mike's painting of my F-4D "750" on the cover of the *Weapons Review*, complete with the 8th TFW "FG" tail code markings signifying its assignment to the 433rd TFS.

When Blake retired Joe Mike took over the job as the chief illustrator and editor at the Weapons School – a job he cherished until retirement in 2005.

JOE MIKE PYLE REMEMBERS A PRANK AT TONOPAH

One day the boys pranked "Paco" Geisler, the operations officer, and called me over to watch the drama.

The maintenance guys had scrounged vehicle parts from all of the salvage yards on the west coast and had actually built functioning jeeps and at least one weapons carrier from the scrounged pieces. We used these vehicles for transportation at Tonopah. By now the F-117s had arrived at Tonopah, along with adult supervision in the form of full colonels who were in charge at that end of the airfield. Over time they thought they were in charge of the entire airfield.

I had painted a couple of little alligators as if they were dancing. Well, the boys took the painting, which was on metal, and welded it to the back of the jeep that "Paco" typically drove around the base. They added the slogan, "Paco's Little Gator Club!" That day one of the colonels from the F-117 operation ended up behind "Paco" and noticed the sign on the "government vehicle." He thought it highly inappropriate and stopped "Paco."

So, there we were watching the scene through a telescope as "Paco" got dressed down "seven ways from Sunday" by the colonel who was destined to become a general officer. "Paco" thought he could just remove the sign, and was totally stymied by the fact that it was welded to the jeep. Such was a day in the life of a Red Eagle at Tonopah.

Anytime you chat with "Paco" ask him about his dancing alligators and "Paco's Little Gator Club."

EXTRACTIONS

Many of the parts that were needed to maintain the fleet of MiGs came from friendly nations that were previous client states of the USSR. We traveled to these countries and were invited to pick and choose what we needed from their aging inventories. We called these events extractions.

One of the biggest problems experienced by some of the senior NCOs in the Red Eagles that remained with the unit from its very beginnings to the mid 1980s was the simple fact that it took about four years minimum to get a new guy trained up on all the aspects of "going in" on an extraction – some used to call it "The Dental Team." The extractions followed a "shopping trip" to a foreign country that possessed an inventory of MiG parts that the Red Eagles were interested in acquiring.

The first such trip came soon after flight operations started at Tonopah in July 1979. I led a team of three to search warehouses in a country far offshore from the United States. Bobby Ellis was the real engineer of the trip. Our third man was a jet engine mechanic named Ron Perry. Ike Crawley had been hired as our jet engine mechanic, but Perry, who was stationed at Edwards AFB, was far more experienced in respect to the specific components we needed very badly. One such item was igniter plugs for MiG-21 engines.

The three of us met with the Embassy Country Team and then traveled to a major air base in search of MiG treasures. At the time I didn't truly realize how rich the harvest would be from this trip. We explored damp and dark warehouses, were surprised by huge spiders and other insects, some of which we killed and others we simply dodged. They seemed to resent us poking around in their domain. After several days of this we judged our inventory action complete and journeyed back to the capital for our out briefing at the Embassy. The Country Team informed us that they had arranged for us to visit another location some distance from the first, but that there would be a delay of several days before we could go while arrangements were finalized.

The cost of spending several days in the capital doing nothing was staggering, so the Embassy staff arranged for us to journey to a distant location to wait out the permissions from the host nation. We had no idea where we were going, but it seemed like an okay idea to us. When we realized we were being sent to a destination resort area we were stunned. Years later one of the hotels in the area was targeted by fanatics and a significant loss of life occurred during that terrorist attack. But all was quiet during our visit.

The first night the three of us were seated at a large table for dinner with two couples, and they were obviously European. The women were young, blonde, and very pretty. Both couples were on their honeymoons in a curious set of circumstances. They were all Dutch and the women had been childhood friends raised in the host country. Following their marriages in Holland the women had decided to bring their new spouses to see the land where they had grown up. The three of us enjoyed the evening very much and even danced with the ladies. It was a stunning atmosphere with the heavy thatch roofed buildings all with open walls that allowed the sea breeze to flow through. The ocean roared in the background and the air smelled of salt spray. Torches around the adjacent swimming pool further accented the situation.

Soon the couples responded to the romantic atmosphere and excused themselves for the evening. In parting they made us promise to meet them the next morning at the swimming pool for a poolside breakfast. We agreed and retired to the bar to contemplate the situation. The next morning we showed up as promised and were startled to find the women topless at the pool. It was really difficult not to be distracted. At first it seemed we had been deposited in Heaven, but it dawned on us that it could really be Hell as there was abundant temptation. We behaved ourselves for the most part, explored the island, and generally enjoyed the time. We were ready to go back to work when the call came that all was set for the second part of our shopping trip.

The second visit was to a different air base, but the situation was basically the same. We looked, we inventoried, and then we came home. Everyone was pleased and we were glad to be heading back to Tonopah. My command was to last only a few more weeks, but I didn't know that at the time. And when I was relieved I didn't know that an extraction plan was already developing. By the time the actual extraction, based this earlier shopping trip, had been fully coordinated by Bill Sakahara at the Air Staff and "CT" Wang at TAC HQ, I was long gone and "Obi Wan" Henderson had taken command of the 4477th.

An extraction is not a simple task. First, you must relocate the items of interest found on the shopping trip. Things can change during the time in between the shopping trip and the extraction. Once found, the acquired goods must be packed up according to strict procedures for airlift aboard a US military aircraft. The new enlisted Red Eagle was not a trained loadmaster, hence the old guys led the way. Plus, for security reasons, the packing and loading was often done at night. The pallet load math had to be precisely accurate to ensure the weight and balance was properly calculated for the overall airlift plan. So, every pallet had to be individually configured, and a part of the learning was figuring out the "maximums" for each one – width, height, and weight.

Sometimes, it can be hard to find batteries in remote locations in far away lands, and the solar powered hand calculator seemed like an easy solution. But the new men with "all the answers" quickly learned that solar powered hand held calculators do NOT work well at night!

The Red Eagles were continuously training the new people on how to complete an extraction. Air Force Military Personnel Center, to this day, does not like a guy to be assigned to one place for very long, so all the talent developed would sometimes be transferred to a new assignment with less than five years on station. In some cases the Red Eagle commander was pushing for a flow of people to counter the lethargy that comes with homesteading.

There were times when the men slept atop empty pallets on the "way in" for a pickup, knowing it might be 25 to 30 hours or so before they would again have the chance to sleep. Such is the situation with covert activities. The assets to be extracted usually had to be disassembled, pieces wrapped, packed according to the airlift plan, and then secured to pallets. It was also common to load up a stack of empty pallets for an extraction and on top of them would be cases of standard issue toilet paper rolls, boxes of 2in duct tape rolls, and many rolls of the widest black plastic sheeting available. These were extraction supplies. The toilet paper rolls were taped to aircraft probes or any "pointy objects" to prevent tearing the black plastic sheeting. The sheeting denied prying eyes from determining the nature of the cargo, and it was secured with more duct tape. We never knew for sure where we might land for fuel or in an emergency, and so each item was wrapped up to "go home" as securely as possible.

A guy had to be smart on how to "marry up" or join two pallets to ship along items like a wing. There is a wrong way to do it. When the load is hanging on a forklift on the way into the cargo jet's cavernous belly is NOT the time to learn that the pallets were assembled the wrong way. The men also had to be smart on all C-5, C-130, and C-141 floor plans, including maximum load, height, and width, etc.

Bobby Ellis led this actual extraction. Since there were multiple locations the teams were split. Earl Henderson eventually joined the group, suffering through a very long ride on a C-130. Don Lyon captured the specifics of the extraction:

> There were two crews for the extraction. Bob Ellis took a crew to one base and I had a group that actually hit two bases. The first stop was to prep the MiG-19. As it was being torn down I was told to go to our next base. Billy Lightfoot was already there, and had procured a large forklift. When the MiG-19 was prepped, the maintenance guys came to our location via C-130. We pushed the MiG-19 pieces out of the way and got busy with our primary job, which was prepping the MiG-21s for shipment. We brought out three "Fishbed" airframes, one of which had a large cavity in the forward right wing. We thought that maybe it had been a recce conversion, or had had a large floodlight fitted for some special project. The locals had no clue, and I'm not sure we ever figured it out.

We were on the opposite end of the airfield from the resident fighter squadron, and were hosted by the nation's aerial demonstration team. The hosts were great folks, believe me.

At this point we actually weighed and determined the exact center of gravity for the three MiG-21s and the MiG-19. I don't know how many maintenance guys there were out there at that time who were current on weight and balance, but it's quite interesting. Mind you, these were TAC fighter aircraft wrench benders who had been trained by the VERY BEST load specialists in the USAF. The airframes were palletized and then loaded onto a C-5 SIDEWAYS, thus creating more room for wings and other gear.

Ellis and the other team brought out parts and support equipment, but no airframes. Only once did our two crews get together during the extraction. That was when Bobby asked us to come to his location to help pack up crates of parts. We went to help, but only stayed one night. That was all it took to determine we had the best end of the deal.

A guy also had to be smart on how to manipulate the locals to "legally" dump drained fuel, oil, and hydraulic fluid. Most of it was flammable and "could" be used as fuel, but we always stressed to them not to use it for cooking. Then, we hoped for the best.

Once or twice we "wandered" to the other end of the field, but there was a foreign representative there assisting with the host nation's transition from MiGs to another type of western fighter aircraft. The rep was kind of curious so we tried to avoid him. Baker and I saw a couple of T-33s taking off and said "Shit, they're carrying 500lb bombs." We then talked to two of the Demo Team pilots and they told us there was a local skirmish going on nearby, and someone had called for close air support. The host nation pilot said that it was a good training opportunity because "they didn't have a bombing or gunnery range!"

Ben Galloway added:

I arrived at the 4477th on December 1, 1979, so the teams were already gone, and I didn't get to go with them. But I took part in unloading the equipment/assets when they arrived at the TTR site. The others were gone for some time, off and on, from July 12 (shopping trip) to December 22, 1979, getting the stuff ready to ship and load. Compared to the other squadron members, I played a smaller part. I remember offloading and seeing the following:

1 MiG-19

Several MiG-21s

25 to 30 crates, 3ft x 3ft x 3ft, with assorted replacement parts for the MiG-17s and
    MiG-21s

2 jet starter/generator trucks

2 hydraulic units

2 large air compressors

4 to 5 MiG-17 drop tanks

5 to 6 MiG-21 drop tanks

3 to 4 rocket pods

Miscellaneous airframe dollies, jacks, stands, tow bars, and tools

We hauled all this stuff into Hangar 3, and sometime later we took all the boxes and equipment to a warehouse close to the supply building. I remember it was odd because that warehouse had a dirt floor. The airframes stayed in the hangar. Many of the new parts were in the original cosmolene and wrapping paper. There were boxes of gauges, avionic stuff, engine parts, wheel bearings, and miscellaneous parts.

It was like Christmas had come early for the Red Eagles on December 22, 1979.

Don Lyon recalls a MiG-19 extraction:

The MiG-19 was on a concrete pedestal on the closed military side of the international airport, and apparently had been there for some time. Jerry Baker and I started "soaking" the key nuts and bolts on the jet with penetrating oil as soon as we arrived. After some "negotiations" we were told it was ours. We borrowed a farm tractor from some local guy, and "Marshall" McCloud, Baker, and I used some lumber and rocks to free her from the pedestal, before eventually towing her off on flat tires.

It was a COMPLETELY INTACT aircraft. The Plexiglas canopy was brown from exposure, having had no protection from the elements. When we opened the canopy, it was obvious the egress system had NOT been de-armed. And, protruding from the seat catapult, was a yellowish colored football-sized hunk of what appeared to be jello. Capt McCloud and I were concerned about loading her onto a transport aircraft with this goo all over the place. Long story short, we removed the crap and safety wired the seat and canopy.

Then, Baker and I were ordered to go to the site where the MiG-21s were, so we left Burzynski, Hollingsworth, and Beverlin to finish the disassembly and loading of the MiG-19 onto a C-130 for transport to the other staging base. There, the plan was consolidation into a single package for airlift back to the US. After Baker and I left, the men remaining behind to work on the MiG-19 extraction were literally threatened (by the previous owners) with their lives if the job of removing the jet wasn't finished within a day or two. "Ski" (Burzynski) called me and told me what was up. I gave them a "Zero Hour" and told him to subtract a couple of hours from that for a cushion. If they couldn't get the job done they were instructed to abandon the project and haul ass. We never told Ellis until later.

The MiG-19 was initially moved by C-130 to the base where Baker and I were working with the rest of the team on the MiG-21 extraction. When we prepped the MiG-21s, we also crated up the MiG-19 for a C-5 ride home.

Later, while wandering through a cow pasture to look for some missiles rumored to have been dumped there, we stumbled upon the cans that were supposed to contain missile warheads. They were oozing yellow jello too. A lieutenant colonel who was with us on the trip as a higher headquarters supervisor wanted to bring the warheads home and I said no.

The MiG-19 was complete, engines and all, including its big 30mm guns. Those guns looked like they belonged in a tank (they were the same type of weapons that shot Bob Lodge out of the sky over North Vietnam on May 10, 1972). The previous owners said that if we were going to fly it to make sure everything was "very tight!" I don't recall ever seeing the MiG-19 at TTR when we returned home, and never heard any reports about the ultimate disposition of the aircraft.

SOVIET JET-STARTER GENERATOR TRUCKS

As Ben Galloway explained earlier in this chapter, he didn't get to go on the extraction trip that delivered the grand inventory described in the story about extractions. However, he sure was involved in what happened next.

Looking at the two jet-starter generator trucks that had been brought back, Ben and Doug Robinson were immediately able to see potential in the vehicles if they could somehow be restored. This initially looked to be a hopeless task, as their tires had either rotted out or were flat and threadbare. The units themselves had the overall appearance of vehicles left outside through numerous hurricanes or typhoons with little or no follow-on maintenance or effort to prevent corrosion and rust. Simply put, the vehicles were a mess. But if they could make the generators work the restoration would be worth the effort.

The operational configuration and utility of the vehicles is beyond my ability to paint a picture beyond verbalizing the schematics. Let it be said that they were self-propelled by a diesel engine and the entire apparatus included a generator and sets of electrical cables which, when connected to the aircraft starting systems, provided the electrical startup power for the MiG engine. When the vehicle was completely operational, it could be driven from one aircraft to another, the unit providing starting power for two jet fighters at a time.

Upon closer inspection of the trucks, Ben realized the engines were clones of Detroit diesels, and he was right when he speculated that spare parts readily available in the US could be used as suitable replacements. The Russians had been at it again, copying our equipment. It was time to get to work. The Red Eagle vehicle maintenance experts Billy Lightfoot and Larry Gruse joined the team and set Ben up with the necessary diagnostic gauges.

Ben pulled the fuel injectors and cleaned them up, and he also got a new battery. After a good amount of work they were ready to attempt to operate the generator and see if it would output electrical power. Lightfoot made the first attempt to fire up the generator, grinding the starter for 20 or 30 seconds. On the third try, the fuel finally got to the engine and it cranked up with a roar. The system ran fine and the electrical power output stabilized after a few rheostat switches were adjusted. The men soon discovered that the Soviet generators could put out whatever power was needed simply by adjusting the rheostats.

The mechanical skill possessed by all of the men involved in this restoration was stunning. No tech orders or instruction book had come with the equipment, but this did not prevent them from figuring things out and making the generator work.

While Lightfoot, Gruse, Ben, and Robbie were overhauling the vehicle's engine, which permitted the unit to be driven around like a truck, Red Eagle electrician Dave Young began fabrication of the cables that would eventually connect the starting unit to the jets. The Red Eagles had previously needed two US MD-3M starting units for each jet. With the Soviet system they could start two jets simultaneously from a single starting system.

New tires followed prior to engine work. Ben figured they could at least tow the generator into position even if the vehicle engine would not work. The vehicle engine initially appeared to be in pretty good shape and there was hope that it could be restored. Then Lightfoot found a hole in the engine block and all bets were off for using that particular powerplant. Knowing the Russian propensity for commonality, the men went back to the spare parts pile and upon closely looking at the engine on a compressor assembly realized it was the same flat head six cylinder motor as the one with the hole in the block that had, in a previous life, propelled the jet-starter truck. The junk pile engine was removed from the compressor and installed in the jet-starter truck, and following a few new parts and a lot of elbow grease it ran like a champ.

The now fully functional jet-starter truck was named "Ivan" and was outfitted with a paint job that included a big red star with yellow trim. It was time for "Ivan" to go to work, and "he" duly aided the engine starts for the MiGs for the duration of the program.

It took three to four months to restore "Ivan." The second jet-starter truck had no engine or transmission. Therefore, after getting the generator running, the task was to find a suitable engine for the vehicle. This time they had no luck with the Soviet junk pile. As it turned out Lightfoot had semi-restored a wrecked vehicle that had been rolled. Billy then cut the cab and the remaining superstructure off the chassis. It was like a comedy routine watching the little man with the red handlebar moustache and the cowboy hat driving around in the remains of the vehicle. The side-view profile was the radiator, engine, and then the steering column and seat. Nothing else. The "powers that be" instructed Lightfoot to get rid of it, and that's where the engine and transmission for the second jet-starter power generator truck came from.

It wasn't an easy installation, as the Dodge 318 engine mounts had to be fabricated onto the Russian truck chassis, along with an aligned coupling of the transmission output shaft to the truck's driveshaft. The talents of Red Eagle master machinist Bob Griese were called upon, and when he was done there were two drivable jet-starter generator trucks. Griese, like a magician, used his machine and welding skills to align perfectly and complete the interface of the American engine and transmission with the Russian truck.

But the latter still required a compressor, which was missing, to operate its brakes. Galloway and his team took the compressor off an International Harvester truck that was headed to the salvage yard and installed it in the jet-starter truck. With that fix the braking problem was solved, and after some cosmetic clean-up the second vehicle was declared functional. It had also taken about three to four months to completely restore the truck. When up and running, and painted, the second vehicle was named "Natasha." On a daily basis she joined "Ivan" in cranking up the engines of the growing fleet of Red Eagle MiGs.

AN ANONYMOUS MAINTAINER RECOUNTS CHALLENGES FACING THE RED EAGLES

There were several other areas a MiG maintenance man had to be smart about. There were never publications or technical orders available to provide guidance on how to "break down" any part or component. Instead, you had to figure it out by taking a hard look at the item (often after dark with a torch during an extraction). The situation at home wasn't much better. At home we had better tools, more time, and the advice of a colleague to ease the pain. Either way, if a part didn't work you had to take it apart, fix it, and put it back together again.

Certain items were critical to have for an extraction. Juice, H_2O, fruit, MREs (Meal Ready to Eat), and coveralls were all simple things that had to be considered as basic staples for going in – they were MUST haves! Also, we didn't have credit cards back in those days, so the "wizards" at our remote finance shop had to figure out a way to provide each guy with at least $5,000. We didn't have money belts, and you don't walk quite the same when there are 25 $100 bills in the bottom of each boot. Some of the local guards in the host countries would literally fist fight for the rights to any juice cans, water, coveralls, or MRE extras that we had to leave behind.

Currently, maintenance technicians want the most up to date tools like the latest and greatest digital multi-meter, etc. In the old days – and this remains applicable in the minds of the "old guys" today – anything was better than nothing. An old "beat-to-hell" oscilloscope would provide a signal, to show if a part was good or bad, and it could perform that role by helping with the go/no-go decision when we were deciding which parts to take and which parts to leave behind.

Maintainers now need more tools and equipment to do the same job that took far fewer tools and test equipment a few decades ago. It is clearly a different concept for the same job. And the renewed concern over safety in the workplace has gone too far! The following paragraphs from an anonymous Red Eagle mechanic and supervisor are included unedited to clearly illustrate the mindset about safety, and the way procedures have evolved in an effort to ensure maximum safety levels whenever possible:

There is obvious common sense if you are a professional, but the fact that you have to put on goggles, an apron and rubber gloves to do a simple job takes longer and causes the aircrew to wait for someone on the groundcrew to do all the prep (dress up) just to hold a special non sparking bucket under a running engine vent/drain, prior to shutting down an engine.

Next, they will have certified nose plugs because of objectionable smells or offensive fumes.

Back in the day, you dipped a rag in a bucket of drained fuel to wipe down the top/bottom of your jet to keep it clean. Nowadays, you cannot have fuel in a bucket, rags are counted and cannot be fuel soaked, and only approved cleaners can be used for the jet surface or canopy, etc.

The things we have done to ourselves and "the system" is VERY SAD.

It is understandable that as we identify a potentially problematic maintenance trend, we try to solve it with corrective actions, but the preflight cards on an old jet were less than an inch thick. Now, the five prep books to get ready for the same preflight stack are each at least 1.5in thick. Then, finally, you get to the two-inch stack of preflight checklist inspection cards.

It used to be "ingrained knowledge" (like TO 1-1A-8) that little Johnny knew to ensure the ground wire was connected, the fire bottle extinguisher was nearby, the chocks were in and the canopy strut(s) was installed before you walked around the jet to preflight it. You always checked EVERYTHING yourself before an engine run, you knew every inch of the jet and had minimal additional duties to distract you from the job you were doing.

Another thing was the way we did chow breaks. Sometimes you had a double brake change and could not go to eat. If you were lucky, someone would bring you a raunchy sandwich that you would eat without washing your hands, instead wiping them with the cleanest rag you could find. Usually, there was no latrine and no sink with soap and water handy, and you did what you had to do.

When you worked four days for ten hours, you were always glad to see Friday arrive so that you could go home to take care of the things everyone now considers normal. Those were tasks like trips to finance, CBPO, military ID cards for yourself and your dependents, vehicle tags, hospital and dental appointments, and prescription refills. Most of that is all automated now, and active duty personnel always have priority in ANY line. It does not matter who you are or what you do for a living. So, some of the changes have been good.

Travel to and from work was always "fun" and often an experience, especially if you were driving one of our long haul trucks or hunkered down in the back of one of the Cessnas with a puke sack while a new pilot was getting used to flying the aircraft.

When you worked hard, you played hard. Indeed, people spent considerable time playing practical jokes. I remember seeing a guy's room at our operating location jammed packed full of tumbleweeds. On another occasion several guys had a hard time getting their room door open because a 12ft diameter weather balloon had been inflated inside, perfectly filling the room.

There were special surgical tubing launchers (Tom Sawyer would call them a sling shot, or worse) fitted with a padded pouch that could easily fire a raw egg more than 100 yards. The best part of the "Raw Egg Toss" was that by the time it got to the target, the three guys in the launch crew had had time to huddle around a jeep tire and pretend they were fixing a flat. It was always humorous to see a guy's reaction when the egg whizzed by him, and when he looked around to see who had thrown it there was no one there.

The craftiest trick I ever saw was a wiring set-up that would mechanically lift the ceiling tile directly above a room door so that when the door was opened, it would dump a load of foam peanuts onto the entrant. Once triggered the ceiling tile door would "latch" up, so the load would not stop pouring until the entire cache had been expended.

Other award winning pranks included outdated "sea dye" from survival kits being sprinkled onto a bath towel. It would usually leave the victim's face bright orange for three or four days. Any number of things could be placed into someone's tube of toothpaste – you only knew you had been "had" when you tasted it, and by then it was too late. Another favorite was the installation of a new shut off valve in the fuel line of your vehicle, which would let you get about halfway to where you were going and then stop the flow of fuel to the engine. You knew the fuel tank was full, so the puzzle to solve was "why the damned thing would not run?"

A common new guy trick was to put out bar snacks in bowls for folks to nibble on while enjoying a brew at the end of a long day. But the new guys' bowl would have "Kibbles & Bits" (dog food) in it, thus providing entertainment for all the other folks in attendance. You always looked forward to the next new guy arriving at TTR so that you could be in the peanut gallery observing the antics and laughing at the reactions.

Black grease was also a favorite tool of the Red Eagle prankster. It never failed to bring a smile on the ramp when your saw the face of an unwitting victim covered in it after they he had handled an intercom mouthpiece or telephone earpiece that had been smeared with grease. Often, you were only aware that you had been targeted at day's end when you saw the black grease on your ear or around your mouth. This cleared up the mystery as to why everyone had been smiling at you all day long!

Food was often a relief – something you looked forward to. As a result BBQs were common. We got to the point of buying the full sized pigs (one at a time), along with chicken, brisket, ribs, etc. Chili was always good, and you couldn't make it too hot – someone would always eat it. "Dave's Insanity Sauce" was popular, but it could ruin anyone's day!

It wasn't always easy to keep a stocked bar until the later years. You quickly learned NEVER to say things like "No one here is man enough to throw me in the pool," or "I don't drink."

During our time on the Red Eagle flight line your toolbox was yours exclusively. You knew exactly what you had, where it was and who borrowed what. Hardly anything in it ever broke either. It was extremely rare when a tool or rag fell out of a door on an airplane – our quality control people made sure of that. It seemed like we had a lot of pride in our equipment back then, and we constantly told ourselves that the equipment was the same as taxpayer dollars. We respected our tools and never mistreated them because we didn't know if they could ever be replaced!

Ben Galloway on Flying Airplanes

In the early days we were all issued flight gear. So, when I arrived at Nellis I received flight gear, including a flight helmet. The equipment was issued so that we could hop in the back seat of one of the T-38s without having to use any assigned pilot's gear and either fly with the chase pilot during a MiG functional check flight or, if need be, we could operate a camera on a photo-shoot. This worked well because the pilots could get fussy about someone else using their helmet, oxygen mask, or g-suit – especially the mask, as they expected any loaner would be returned to them half full of puke!

On my first ride in a T-38, Dave "Marshall" McCloud let me take the stick for a short time and talked me through an aileron roll. What a blast. Several of the enlisted personnel had received some previous flight instructional experience, and we relished the opportunities to fly in the T-38 or sit in the right seat of the Cessna or Mitsubishi on our trips back and forth between Nellis and Tonopah.

The pilots knew who wanted to fly and who didn't, and Doug Robinson and I were two of maybe three guys that got to ride up front a lot. Anytime we were allowed to take control of the aircraft it was closely supervised and very professional. It was only when the Cessna or Mitsubishi was on a heading for the site and climbing to altitude that we got the chance to take the yoke and get a little stick time. It was all straight and level, with the pilot nibbling at us to stay on course. And we never did get to make take-offs or landings.

I particularly remember one T-38 sortie when we were chasing a MiG-21 that was on a test hop. We were high – maybe 35,000ft – and as the MiG pilot began his high speed run he lit the afterburner and just walked away from us leaving a beautiful white contrail in his wake.

Sometimes, when the pilots were flying a Cessna or Mitsubishi, things flowed a little differently. "Huffer" was flying one day, and he had given me the stick for a few minutes when he yelled "Wow, look at that! I've got the airplane!" He had spotted a herd of mustangs roaming the desert below us and decided it was time to chase them. The guys in the back were caught by surprise with the sudden descent and the maneuvers that followed as Huff gleefully scattered the herd. Nobody got hurt and there was no damage to the aircraft, the people on board or the environment, including the horses, but you might have thought otherwise listening to the outrage coming from the back of the airplane.

FLY-BYS, JET NOISE, AND "FINI" FLIGHTS

There were temptations that the pilots sometimes yielded to, and the remote nature of the location, as well as the camaraderie of the group, added fuel to the problem. This was especially an issue if the "boss" was off station. The ultimate temptation was to beat up the airfield! That meant arriving in a MiG or a T-38 right over the top of the hangars unannounced (to the rank and file) at minimum altitude and high speed with full afterburner selected. The noise was so loud that startled ground crews usually dropped tools and reacted with vile and loud profanity. It was a "gotcha event," and in reality the men loved it.

There was never a safety incident as a result of a fly-by, but no commander, including me, would have ever approved such a pass ahead of time. I can report that the perpetrators received a verbal one-on-one with the "boss" over the shenanigans. Then, I must confess, I turned away and smiled. I loved their spirit.

Another separate, but related, issue was the final ("Fini") flight flown by a MiG pilot. With my sudden and unanticipated departure, I was never scheduled for, nor ever flew, a "Fini" flight. Almost everyone else did. Even some of the enlisted personnel managed to schedule a "Fini" flight. As related earlier, Don Lyon and Steve Hovermale worked with one of our US Navy pilots, "Heater" Heatley, to arrange for two TA-4s to show up for their "Fini" flights. There are photos of their post-flight celebration included in the photo gallery.

Rich Samanich, one of our maintenance NCOs and a highly skilled welder, told me about a "Fini" flight that included a pass by a "Flogger" which was perpendicular to the runway and between the control tower and the large Red Eagle MiG-23 hangars. The jet was lower than the roof of the control tower cab throughout the pass. On another occasion a "Fini" flight pilot was photographed exiting his MiG-23 completely naked after he had landed from his last flight. We have an unpublished photo to prove it!

"Obi Wan" Henderson was suddenly grounded due to a heart problem. Nevertheless, he was encouraged by the men to take one final flight in a MiG, which he did without incident, even though he had been officially grounded.

Once the F-117 community arrived at TTR the screws tightened down because there were more senior officers on base on a daily basis who could react to the indiscretion of an overzealous MiG pilot engaged in local airfield antics.

We were men that, in addition to being stunningly professional, also had a propensity to enjoy playing. Fortunately, the pilots were good enough to pull off such antics without a tragic incident or event of any consequence.

HOPE MURPHY'S MEMORIES

The late Hope Murphy recalls how her husband Richie got hired by the Red Eagles:

They were not looking for a master sergeant, but after all the POL candidates had been interviewed, Richie was selected because "Daddy" Ellis said that Richie's hands were the only ones that were calloused, and that meant he would not be afraid of hard work. Later, when reviewing orders assigning airmen, it was noted that Bobby Ellis and Richie Murphy had been in the same basic training class at Lackland AFB, Texas, graduating in September 1959.

Hope's recollection continues with a tidbit about the Kenworth truck:

Richie really loved that truck. Long after he retired, he was leaving Nellis AFB one snowy day and saw the Kenworth. There were a couple of guys standing by it so Richie went over and started asking them questions. He was interested in knowing who was still around, and so his questions focused on "is so-and-so still up there, etc." They completely ignored him. The next day he took his video and still cameras to take photos of the Kenworth.

A week later the OSI called and asked him to stop by their office at Nellis. They wanted to know why he was so curious about the truck and who was working up north. Richie explained that he had driven the truck on numerous occasions during his time with the Red Eagles. Initially, the OSI officer asked for the videotape, but Richie said he would just go over there and take the photos again. Finally, the OSI relented and said, "Okay, you can keep the tape, but we don't want to see any of those pictures on the local news channels." Soon thereafter the Kenworth was moved.

Hope continues:

First, I have to tell you about Richie going out to Nevada to interview for the Red Eagles job. His old boss at Lakenheath had called and asked Richie if he would be interested in a secret job. If so, he needed to come on over to Nellis AFB for an interview. Richie left, and two days later I got a call from him. He said that *they* wanted to know if I (the wife) could put up with him being gone four days out of the week. I said, "Tell them that is the kind of job I've been hoping you would find for 19 years" (we have now been married 48 years).

Richie stayed there TDY for some time, and when he came home he looked horrible with long hair (he always had a crew cut) and a red beard. He had been hired. Along with our teenage daughter, we left for Nevada. When we got to Nellis we went to the trailer that was the Red Eagles' operating location. There was a party going on inside among the enlisted men, while the officers were playing softball outside. While the officers were thinking about the beer cooling in the trailer, the NCOs decided to drink it.

Red Eagle fire chief Ralph Payne had a daughter about our daughter's age, so they said we could leave her there while Richie and I went to the BX. When we returned I opened the door to the trailer, and quickly closed it. Richie asked me what was wrong, I said they are throwing eggs at each other.

On Friday nights, when the men returned, they would go to the "Road Runner Saloon" near "Lamb and Stewart" in Las Vegas. One evening I was sitting at one of those high tables drinking a coke when Lenny Bucko and a fellow Marine Corps pilot sat down and put a gallon jar of jalapeno peppers on the table. I sat there watching them eat the contents of the jar, and it was like being at a tennis match. Finally, when the jar was half gone, they called a truce. I was just about to take a drink of my coke when Bucko grabbed it out of my hand and proceed to chug it.

When Billy Lightfoot retired, his mother asked Richie to escort him home to Venice, Florida. His mother knew that Billy would not make it if he was alone. Billy first married "Bonnie 1," but they divorced, and he then married "Bonnie 2." They divorced too, and he remarried "Bonnie 1." Billy always said that he would never see 50 and, sure enough, at the age of 49 "Bonnie 1" was driving him to a doctor's appointment when he died in the car.

Then there were the parties on Arthur Street. "GBo" and Mike lived there, and "Popeye" did too for a while. The first time "Popeye" was at one of the parties, Mary Helms, then wife of "Buster" Helms, sat on "Popeye's" lap and got very friendly with him, and he was terrified. "Popeye" had been in the US Navy, and he was the only naval hydraulics man in the Red Eagles.

Richie drove the Kenworth truck a lot. Every Monday morning he would go to the Red Eagles' parking spot on Nellis, hook up the trailer and take the rig up to Tonopah. One time when he got to TTR, everyone was waiting for him and he asked what's wrong? Ellis said "look in the trailer." He had hooked up to an empty one. Ellis made Richie turn around and return to Nellis to pick up the correct trailer. This proved to be a very long day.

On another occasion the commander of the Threat Training Facility museum on base at Nellis asked a favor of the Red Eagles. He wanted them to go to Fort Huachuca, Arizona, southeast of Tucson, and pick up some tanks for him. In the process Richie was pulled over by the highway patrol for a weight check. They said he was riding empty, but he said "No, I've got two tanks in the trailer." The highway patrolman didn't believe him, so Richie opened the doors and there sat two "plywood" tanks destined for relocation onto the Nellis bombing range.

One time when Richie was riding back to Nellis with Billy Lightfoot, Billy all of a sudden stepped on the brakes (Richie said they were traveling at about 80mph at the time). Billy ran out into the desert and came back with a snake – guess all that booze didn't hurt his eyesight any. He kept several snakes on his patio, and on Sundays he would have the neighborhood children come to watch him feed mice to them. Billy also liked to wind a snake up by putting it on his head and then covering it with his cowboy hat. He would then knock on someone's door and when they answered he would take off his hat, thus exposing the snake.

These are memories to treasure.

BEN GALLOWAY'S REFLECTIONS ON LIFE AND CAREERS

When we were initially trying to continue Paul Cox's dedicated effort to create a roster of 4477th TES members, a lot of e-mails went back and forth. In an e-mail to me, Ben Galloway wrote:

I know exactly what you mean about life. The journey has taken me to where I am now. I wouldn't change a thing. Ten years of my service was on special assignments. Five with the Presidential detail and Air Force One and five with the 4477th. I would give anything to go back in time and start at day one with the 4477th. To be able to live it all again, that would be something. I can't go back in time, but I can remember the time I had there. To work with you sir is an honor. Our story should be told and I hope we can round up the Red Eagles and make the alumni a reality.

Info on where the guys are living now is trickling in and it's a start. We'll get there and produce a unit roster. I sent out a Memorial Day flyer to everyone with an e-mail address and I hope you got it. I plan to start a quarterly newsletter sometime in the future, and a commanders' section would be a great addition.

As I write this, my wife is looking over my shoulder, smiling, and saying "You love this, admit it." "Yep, I sure do," was my answer.

DON LYON ON FIRE

Okay, here's a true story. In Red Eagle lore a vehicle fire is sometimes mentioned. I WAS the fire.

It happened at McClellan AFB in the salvage yard, and involved two idiots who we will call, "Stevie Stupid" (Hovermale) and "Donald Dumbass" (Lyon), who were sent to pick up an international gas-engined fifth wheel tractor – it was supposed to be drivable. When we arrived, it wasn't drivable, and in trying to resurrect it (with a carburetor FULL of fuel and the air cleaner REMOVED), ignition was achieved. Steve was in the driver's seat and where was I? Under the hood of course, shirtless and with my left arm on fire. As I egressed the scene of the blaze in a hasty fashion, Steve knocked me down and rolled me in the dirt, which extinguished the fire.

Although no damage had been inflicted on the truck that we couldn't handle, I was a sight to behold. Base hospital was out of the question, so we found a shopping center with a drug store. We went in and asked the lady at the counter "What you got for a burn?" Naturally she asks "What kind?" I show her. She gets dizzy and falls to the floor, which immediately catches the attention of the pharmacist. Same thing. I show him what looks like to me like this HUGE water filled thing hanging on my arm, which I'm estimating is holding about 3-5 gallons of water (probably only a ½-cup). He says "Here's some ointment. Clean your knife, break the blister, wash with vinegar and apply ointment. Go to market next door, purchase gauze, vinegar, Budweiser and Smirnoff." We followed the instructions and the procedure went just fine. We hooked up with Burzynski and Hollingsworth later that night for dinner, and I was in NO pain.

I don't know how, but word got home before we did. Jim Richardson duly made up a plaque for me that he called the 1978 Torch Award. It had a small extinguisher on it and came with a certificate. I was lucky, for if Steve hadn't been there I might not be here.

NOTE: The fact that Lyon had no eyebrows was a verifying clue that the event actually happened.

SOME OF GAIL PECK'S MEMORIES

As previously noted, Glenn Frick was the first 4477th TEF commander when the unit was formed at Nellis AFB. Once we got air force approval to proceed with the project, Glenn Frick worked with "DL" Smith at TAC HQ to get the squadron approved and constituted, or "stood up." I was a witness to these details because I was at the Air Staff, and the process was a major air command prerogative and function.

Under Glenn's watchful eye the initial airfield plans grew from my napkin sketch into blueprints, which I was called to Orange to approve one day. Those were the same blueprints used in the construction of the airfield. Additionally, Glenn put together the initial manpower package, recruiting both pilots and enlisted personnel.

Nellis has always been short on available operations workspace. So Glenn arranged for a pair of double-wide trailers to be temporarily positioned in the parking lot behind the fire station on the Nellis flight line road (Tyndall Avenue). This positioning was handy because in those days both the offices of the 57th Wing Commander and the Deputy Commander for Operations (DCO) were located in the FWS, Building 282, right next door. The wing DCO also served as the Commandant of the FWS. Most of our communications occurred though classified message channels. But at times the Autovon was vital, especially for coordinating meeting and travel plans.

As described earlier Glenn got promoted to colonel about 15 months before the airfield was completed, and six months later he left Nellis and headed for Egypt, taking up a USAF military training mission assignment. The Egyptians were in the process of changing over from being a Soviet client state flying MiGs to becoming a US ally. Glenn was being sent to Egypt to help its air force transition from MiGs to the F-4E Phantom II.

Glenn Frick was the most enthusiastic fighter pilot I ever met. He could look at a pile of horse manure and immediately start looking for the pony. One day he called me from Cairo, all excited. I think his family had arrived. He told me that there was an abundance of economic domestic help available in Egypt. The only problem was that they couldn't see dirt.

I took command from Glenn on October 1, 1978, and with the able assistance of the initial cadre got the airfield completed and the airplanes ready to fly. It wasn't a formal change of command as we know them. Instead, we briefed a multi-ship-versus-multi-ship DACT mission. Glenn was the leader on one side and I think either Iverson or Oberle was the leader on the other side. I tagged along as a wingman. Then we all abandoned the plan and sequentially pounded Glenn like he was a seal pup. When it was all over we landed, Glenn and I saluted, shook hands and that was that. No band. No flag other than the American Flag in the background, no troops in review. No one more senior than us was present to give speeches or conduct the change. A simple handshake and salute and that did it!

Operations started from Tonopah in July 1979. It had taken just two years to move from concept approval to operational reality. As previously noted, my tenure in place at Tonopah didn't last very long. On August 23, 1979, Lt Hugh Brown (US Navy) was killed when MiG-17 "Bort 002" spun in and crashed. Hugh and I had been scheduled to sortie together as a flight of two against two Aggressor F-5Es. Hugh flew the MiG-17 and I led our two-ship in a MiG-21.

We briefed that we would take off and rendezvous with the Aggressors and then split up for one-versus-one BFM engagements. The plan was to use half of our fuel fighting the first F-5E and then trade-off so that both Aggressor pilots had the chance to fight the MiG-17 and the MiG-21.

At about the time the swap was planned I heard the call "knock-it-off!" over the radio, which meant all maneuvering was to cease immediately. The following events are a little foggy in my memory, but I think someone transmitted that "Bandit 2" was down. I don't recall seeing a smoke column or other indications of a crash, but when "Bandit 2" did not answer my radio calls I immediately landed at Tonopah. I was met at the aircraft by our people and was informed that the civilian security personnel had made their way to the crash site, and confirmed a fatality. With that news I immediately departed Tonopah in a Cessna 404 and flew back to Nellis to put the notification process into motion. I informed Brig Gen Tom Swalm, and I think the two of us went to the TFWC office of Maj Gen Robert Kelley and gave him the news.

Next, a team was put together to proceed to the Brown home to notify Mrs Linda Brown about the fate of her husband. I am sure that my wife Peggy came along, and there was probably a chaplain and a doctor in attendance too. Neither Brig Gen Swalm nor Maj Gen Kelley participated in the notification. As far as I know neither officer ever had any contact with Linda Brown. In their eyes the problem was exclusively mine to deal with. The team assembled and proceeded to the Brown home. Fortunately, Mrs Brown was at home, along with her two children. She knew immediately that the news was bad when she opened the door and saw both Peggy and me, along with the others. She invited us in.

As I recall I took both of her hands and said, "Linda, we have had an accident and Hugh did not make it!" She burst into tears and the little boys clung to her legs, knowing something bad must have happened but not comprehending the gravity of the event. She inquired as to what had happened and I had to resort to the cover story, leading her to believe that Hugh had died flying an F-5. The chaplain and the doctor did what they do in such circumstances and Peggy sat with Linda for a long time. I think she may have spent the night. After a reasonable time I excused myself and made my way back to Nellis, not knowing really why.

After I left Tonopah on the day of Hugh's crash "Jose" Oberle and Chuck Heatley pretty much took over the leadership and management of the recovery process, the details of which I don't really know except to say that the impact on the men of the human remains recovery task was severe. Nevertheless, we got back to work quickly and I flew a few more times in the MiG-21 all the while we were assessing the situation and attempting to work out any corrective actions that should be taken.

Linda Brown and her children left the area almost immediately and my contact with her was soon lost.

I got a call from a general at Langley on a Saturday morning with words of encouragement. On Monday morning Gen Kelley called me into his office and I was relieved. What I didn't know at the time was that the wheels were already in motion to relieve me in spite of the assurances of the TAC HQ general. I can't be sure of the details, but evidently "Jose" Oberle was suddenly scheduled to go to Langley AFB with Gen Kelley, and upon arrival at the airport and encountering Lt Col Earl Henderson he realized that I was about to be relieved.

Peggy and I borrowed a Bellanca Viking from a friend and flew to Truckee Tahoe, spending a few days at Lake Tahoe with dear friends Mike and Jan Van Wagenen while I licked my wounds and tried to figure out what to do with the rest of my life. After a few days at the Lake, we returned to Las Vegas. Soon after getting home Brig Gen Chuck Cunningham called me and said Gen Kelley wanted me to come and work for him at the TFWC as the chief of plans. At this point I felt as though I had no choice, so I showed up. Soon thereafter Col Jack Thomason took me under his wing and he and Gen Cunningham arranged for me to keep flying the F-5 as an Aggressor pilot – a role I fulfilled for about nine more months.

Col Jack Thomason was the TFWC chief of staff, and he was pretty much universally disliked by the rank and file. But I have always treasured Col Thomason's friendship and loyalty to me. He never said it directly, but he sensed the injustice of the decision to let me go. I wish that I had had the chance to thank him in person before his passing. Alas, it didn't happen. I will always respect Gen Cunningham too. He also was a true friend for many of the years that followed.

As my new job unfolded I was tasked by Gen Kelley, as his Chief of Plans, to design a five-year operational test and evaluation plan to be used as a roadmap for the future. Over several months we accomplished that task, and I even traveled with Gen Kelley to Langley to sell the plan. One day in the middle of the OT&E plan project Gen Kelley said to me, "I never asked you for your side." Well, with that opening, I unloaded on him in a respectful fashion. I told him I thought it curious that Hugh Brown had been out of control in the MiG-17 on several one-versus-one engagements with F-5Es flown by members of the 64th AS. I had learned that the Aggressor squadron leadership elected not to tell either me or the senior Naval officer in my command, Lt Cdr Tom Morgenfeld, about the events with Lt Brown. Instead, they said later that they talked to Hugh and "handled" it. Gen Kelley became irate and threw me out of the office.

A few days later he called me back into his office and said basically, "I checked on what you said and it was correct. It is too late now, so just stick with me." To do that was a real challenge, let me tell you. I have to add that I hold no grudges against any of these officers. They reacted to events and did the best they could under the circumstances.

In addition to Hugh Brown, "Huffer," "Darth," and I were the victims. I say that because Huff abandoned the Air Force – a tragedy in itself – with about 14 or 15 years completed toward a 20-year retirement. Drabant essentially resigned from the 4477th and found other things to do with his life while he completed an Air Force career. For a while I was a man without a job or a future. I will always treasure the loyalty demonstrated by "Huffer" and "Darth," but I jokingly add that I wish I had spent more time developing their judgment.

Looking back now after many years of dormant thought on the subject I can understand the situation much better. I was the leader of the "young Turks" that a previous leadership regime at Nellis had installed. We represented an expensive project that the Nellis leadership had not asked for, nor was prepared to embrace. Some of the generals were skeptical but cooperative until a month into the program when we had the major aircraft accident resulting in a Naval officer fatality. That day we lost a valuable US Navy pilot, human being, and friend, and 12.5 percent of our flyable resources. I understand why they let me go.

I survived professionally because of Gen Chuck Donnelly, who insisted I come and work for him at the US Military Training Mission (USMTM) in Saudi Arabia. I asked him why and he said because he didn't like the way I had been treated at Nellis. I resisted the assignment to Saudi Arabia for a while and we went back and forth. After he sweetened the pie with a number of incentives I yielded. These started with the promise to fly the F-5E in Saudi and included a plan to get me an air-to-ground checkout in the aircraft. He sealed the deal when he ultimately arranged an F-15 checkout for me too. I went to Riyadh and never looked back.

The Iran-Iraq war started almost immediately after my arrival, and after six months of hard work Gen Donnelly arranged for me to have a "bonus lieutenant colonel command" in Dhahran as the Advisory Detachment commander. In that position we facilitated the delivery of the first F-15Cs to the Royal Saudi Air Force (RSAF) and established the groundwork that created ELF 1, which was essentially a command and control system for integrating USAF tankers and AWACS assets with RSAF GCI, interceptor, SAM, and flak battery units. The goal was to prevent the Iran-Iraq war from spilling over into Saudi Arabia or having an adverse impact on the oil transshipment facilities at Ras Tanura and the nearby sea lane into the Indian Ocean.

I made colonel on time and went on to National War College, followed by a posting to the F-15-equipped 18th TFW at Kadena AB, Okinawa. This unit came under the control of Fifth Air Force, whose commander was none other than Gen Donnelly. For the next two years I served as the deputy commander for operations and the vice commander of the 18th TFW. When Gen Donnelly got his fourth star and took command of USAFE, I joined him in Europe after a few months as the wing commander of the 26th TRW at Zweibrücken AB.

I visualized my command and the reconnaissance mission as a career broadening holding pattern until Col "PD" Robinson got promoted to brigadier general at nearby Bitburg AB. Then, I hoped, I would inherit the F-15 wing from my friend and Air Force Academy classmate and return to my area of expertise. However, Gen Donnelly ran into the square corner of a forced retirement at the same time that I was up for transfer, and with his departure so ended my future in the USAF. I joke now about the clear signal that I had received informing me I had been "voted off the island."

It is curious how that all worked. Loyalty DOWN the chain of command from Gen Donnelly worked out nicely for me and things turned out okay. Getting fired at Tonopah definitely derailed me from the fast track I was on and possibly denied me higher rank and responsibility, but it ultimately worked out fine for both my family and me. I will also always value the close friendship I had with Chuck and Carolyn Donnelly. They were thoughtful and considerate people and they treated Peggy and me with great warmth and respect. It was typical of their mode of operation with all of their subordinates. They made a great Air Force couple, and both had unbelievable leadership skills.

So, I have no regrets about the end of my Tonopah experience, except for the loss of Hugh Brown and the end of Gerry Huff's Air Force career. Like me, "Darth" Drabant survived and went on to bigger and better things. He is currently (2011) a senior civil service officer and test plan director at Nellis.

I learned a lot from the leadership during my brief period in command of the 4477th, but it wasn't very often fun. One of the senior officers I worked for was good at mentoring my fellow squadron commanders, and I still pass on some of those lessons to the current crowd of commanders when I have the chance in my job at the USAF Weapons School. Things like where to "plug in" with another unit comes to mind as an example of the mentoring. In other words, commanders don't "plug in" or call operations officers or more junior people, commanders work with other commanders. That is an important lesson that many officers never grasp.

One event that happened in the three months prior to Hugh Brown's death still makes me sad when I think about it. Indeed, I wish I had been tougher minded on the subject.

"Jose" Oberle was the senior MiG-17 pilot and was concerned over the propensity of the little jet to snap out of control and act like it was about to enter a spin. That happened to me on several occasions during the time I flew the aircraft, and I actually learned to use that propensity to my tactical advantage. But "Jose" was worried, and he thought we needed to send the MiG-17 pilots to NAS Miramar for spin refresher training with the US Navy. At the time the base was home to a very highly regarded spin awareness and recovery training program, employing the T-2 Buckeye aircraft. It made sense that we take advantage of the spin training opportunities to be sure that our MiG-17 pilots were proficient given the jet's propensity to act feisty sometimes.

I concurred and supported Oberle's proposal. When I presented the package to the leadership, I was dismissed with a wave of the hand and the words that there would be no approval of another 4477th "boondoggle." The point being made to me was that there was a perception at our leadership level that the Red Eagle organization was some kind of "hot shot" unit manned by officers that were less than 100 percent professional. Nothing could have been further from the truth. I lost the battle for spin training, and less than three months later Hugh Brown was dead after a spin and crash in the MiG-17.

From the very beginning the officers and NCOs of the 4477th knew exactly what we needed to do to operate a safe and effective organization. My failure was in not proving to the leadership at the local level that we were indeed capable and responsible.

GAIL PECK ANSWERS AN E-MAIL

Col Andy "Sparky" Croft e-mailed me a question about Steve Davies' book *Red Eagles – America's Secret MiGs*, which was first published by Osprey in 2008. "Sparky" was an instructor in the F-15 division at the Weapons School and later became its commander when the division was redesignated the 433rd Weapons Squadron. It was my pleasure to serve as an academic instructor with this squadron during "Sparky's" assignments in the first decade of the 21st century. Over the years we developed a warm friendship, and I enjoyed the opportunity to share my life's experience in a mentoring sense with this outstanding officer. "Sparky" wrote:

"Evil," Steve Davies' book had mixed reviews of your MX (maintenance) guys, particularly Bob Ellis. Any comments on that part of the operation?

I replied:

I should review the parts of the book you are referring to specifically to give you an accurate answer. Nevertheless, with that said, I do recall George Gennin's input to the book which was largely negative regarding Ellis. I think there was something of a power struggle based on a lack of mutual respect. Up until George's watch the commanders before him (Frick, Peck, Henderson, and Gibbs) recognized that we could not do the job without excellent maintenance and a lot of innovation to close the gap on a short budget. Bobby's leadership and knowledge brought both to the table. He was especially revered by the younger guys. The more senior NCOs followed Bobby then, but they are quick to say now that they didn't always buy into his style and "BS," as they put it. Nevertheless, he took the incredible challenge of setting up the logistics and molded nothing into something of tremendous value.

So, none of us are perfect and Bobby was no exception, but overall I give him VERY HIGH marks. By the time George Gennin took command, while there were still a lot of loose ends and projects to be completed (engines, seat carts, etc.), MX and the logistics were largely established, even though they weren't based on the USAF maintenance model.

Another part of the puzzle centers on the fact that when we started the program none of us, even in our wildest dreams, expected to have a 27 aircraft flight line. Our initial equipage was two MiG-17s and six MiG-21s. Further, we had no inkling about the MiG-23s that would be added to the squadron. And, we had no billeting facilities or chow hall at TTR until the F-117 program matured and brought more construction money to Tonopah. So, in the early days the men had to blend in when they visited downtown Tonopah. I directed them to do that. And this meant look like a desert rat/miner and pretty much act like one. Draw no attention to the TTR or our highly classified mission. They did this very well.

The growth of the program and the construction of military billeting and eating facilities for the F-117 operation may have subsequently caused our guys to appear to be mavericks who didn't follow strict military dress codes. I'm sure that is true. What I'm not sure of is whether George had orders to put the men back into standards or he took it upon himself to do this. Either way, I think that was what brought George and Bobby nose-to-nose. Plus, by that time Bobby was probably pretty tired and uncompromising. After all, he had been with the Red Eagles for about eight years by then, and had worked with at least four commanders. George had never been directly, or even indirectly, involved before. So, you can see the frustration that Bobby must have felt at the prospect of breaking in a new commander with the unit methodology or ROE and George having none of it. Bobby was also involved in various high pressure activities with AFSC before CONSTANT PEG, and they must surely have added to his tolerance for change – NOT!

By the way, I have known George for nearly 40 years and hold him in VERY HIGH regard. In writing this I am just trying to help you understand by reporting the situation as I reflect on events. George is included in the cc. to this e-mail.

So bottom line – BUM RAP to print anything less than OUTSTANDING words on any of the MX people or their operation.

To summarize this part of the story, recognize that change can be a bitter pill. This has long been understood, as the following passage from chapter six of *The Prince* by Niccolo Machiavelli (1513 AD) proves:

It must be remembered that there is nothing more difficult to plan, more doubtful of success, nor more dangerous to manage than the creation of a new system. For the initiator has the enmity of all who would profit by the preservation of the old institutions and merely lukewarm defenders in those who would gain by the new ones. The hesitation of the latter arises in part from the fear of their adversaries, who have the laws on their side, and in part from the general skepticism of mankind, which does not really believe in an innovation until experience proves its value. So it happens that whenever his enemies have occasion to attack the innovator they do so with the passion of partisans, while the others defend him sluggishly so that the innovator and his party are alike vulnerable.

E-MAIL FROM JOHN POLLET ON AUGUST 25, 2009

The following e-mail helps to clarify the role of the DoE and its sole source contractors, Holmes and Narver and REECo. John wrote to me:

I was the Vice President of the Holmes and Narver (H&N) Orange Division located in Orange, California. The Orange Division performed all the architectural and engineering (A&E) design for the facilities constructed at Tonopah Airfield. We called the project the Tonopah Integrated Air Defense System (TIADS). Our project manager was Lynn LeBaron. Other A&Es may have designed facilities at the base after we completed the TIADS project.

Augie Gurrola was the Vice President of the H&N Energy Support Division (ESD) located in Las Vegas. The ESD was captive to the Department of Energy, Nevada Operations Office (NVOO), also located in Las Vegas. The ESD performed only work authorized by NVOO under a long standing cost plus award fee contract. All construction for TIADS was performed by REECo under a NVOO agreement similar to the H&N contract. Dale Frazier was the Vice President and General Manager of REECo at the time.

A section of the Las Vegas Bombing and Gunnery Range was controlled by NVOO. This section of land was designated as the Tonopah Test Range, and it was managed by the Sandia National Laboratory. Sandia used the range primarily to develop and test bomb cases for nuclear weapons. Since TIADS was to expand from the existing 6,000ft air force runway on NVOO property, the latter became involved in the TIADS project and requested that the USAF utilize their contractors for design and construction of the expansion.

The TIADS project was a major effort, and the H&N ESD did not have the staff or the expertise to design the facilities in the timeframe required by the USAF. The H&N ESD contract with NVOO included a means for subcontracting peak workloads to the H&N Orange Division. We in Orange had a large number of architects and engineers with DoE "Q clearances" that allowed us to provide the design in the necessary timeframe. We were also very familiar with USAF design manuals and standards.

All TIADS design work was performed for TAC under the direction of Bill Duffey. He was assisted by a major who handled the USAF money. The funds for the project were transferred from TAC to NVOO through Nellis AFB. NVOO then modified the ESD and REECo contracts to include the necessary design and construction funds. With the money in place, ESD duly issued a work order to the Orange Division to proceed with the contract. It took about two or three weeks to set this procedure in motion.

The entire project had to be completed in a 22-month period – an extremely short timeframe for such a significant project. I can vividly remember the meeting at NVOO when Dale Frazier and I made a commitment to NVOO and TAC that TIADS would be completed on time and within budget. It was a most challenging assignment. At its peak we had around 100 people assigned to design work on the project. We also accomplished the field inspections as the construction proceeded. Monthly coordination meetings were held with all parties, first in Orange, then in Las Vegas, then in Tonopah town and, finally, at the base to review progress, resolve problems and keep everything on schedule and on budget.

At the start of the design process we in Orange were not told about the F-117. We only were aware of the Red Eagle involvement. Near completion of construction we learned about the still classified stealth fighter/bomber being manufactured by Lockheed.

It was a most interesting and exciting project for us, and led to our selection for a number of other Army, Air Force, and Navy airfield design assignments. I have an enlisted man's shoulder patch (black star) for the 4477th TES as a memento of the project. I very much treasure this patch. We held one follow-on meeting in the 4477th's conference room at the base, and I was most impressed with the various photos on the walls showing the wing and tail insignia and the sheer number of MiGs being flown by various countries around the world.

After retirement Augie Gurrola went on to become a commissioner for the Nevada State Gaming Commission. Dale Frazier and I are both Board of Trustee members for the Nevada Test Historical Foundation and supervise the Atomic Testing Museum (a Smithsonian affiliate) here in Las Vegas.

Two years ago when I passed through Tonopah I noticed a Lockheed company car, and I wondered what was then going on at the base. How many secrets are kept by our government? At one time I could get into any nuclear weapons area or NRO satellite facility. Today, I can't get on any military base.

In spite of the role of NVOO as reported by John Pollet, the DoE operation at Tonopah was under the jurisdiction of its office in Albuquerque, New Mexico, and much of my time was spent there during the early program advocacy days when I was still stationed at the Pentagon. Once DoE Albuquerque agreed to our program, as John reported, DoE control shifted to DoE Las Vegas (NVOO) to get the job done.

CHAPTER 7

WAS THERE A REWARD FOR THE USA?

Looking at CONSTANT PEG in retrospect, it initially seemed that it would be a challenge to determine a return on investment for the overall MiG project. I had many conversations with colleagues and spent a lot of quiet time attempting to remember events, and the sequence in which they happened, so as to answer this question. It soon became clear to me that CONSTANT PEG, along with other important units like the FWS and the Topgun school, as well as the invention of the Aggressors and Red Flag/Cope Thunder all helped American air forces evolve from employing the tactics used in World War II through to the end of the Korean War to the modern tactics essential in the jet and missile environment.

A 15-to-1 kill ratio is often the number used to describe the USAF's aerial successes in the Korean War. The kill ratio means that for every aircraft we lost to an air-to-air shoot down we shot down 15 of their aircraft – this figure has been drastically scaled down over the years. The kill ratio in Vietnam is less certain, with the most optimistic figure being perhaps 7-to-1, but probably less. Uncertainty reigns because of the extremely hostile environment in which the actions took place and the documentation disputes over the causes of the losses suffered by American air forces in that conflict. Were jets shot down by MiGs, SAMs, and AAA, or was a mechanical failure or severe weather the cause? We may never know in absolute terms.

It has been reported that a US Navy F/A-18 from VFA-81 was lost in an air-to-air engagement on the opening night of DESERT STORM, the jet falling victim to an Iraqi MiG-25. I cannot verify or confirm that as fact, and other reports indicate that the Hornet was downed by a SAM. However, if it is true that the F/A-18 was downed by a MiG, it would be the only US/Coalition force loss of the war to an aerial threat.

What is known throughout the aviation community and accepted as truth is the historical **worldwide** kill ratio of the F-15. The kill ratio has been reported both as 101.5 kills to as many as 107 kills without the single combat loss of an F-15. These numbers include Israeli and Saudi kills. The number of kills scored by F-15s is less important than the number of losses of F-15s – ZERO!

Tuck McAtee, my Air Force Academy classmate, has some impressive credentials – F-15 FWS graduate and Director of Operations, USAF Flight Test Pilot School graduate and an F-16 OT&E pilot. Tuck reported to me that the F-16 worldwide kill ratio is 71-to-0. This figure also includes Israeli and Coalition air force kills. So, combat success has spilled over into the Viper community as well.

Each of the pilots from these air forces that scored aerial kills with the F-15 and the F-16 have embraced an advanced training progression that generally uses the same methods described earlier in this volume. The exception to this training regime would be the CONSTANT PEG exposure to the actual threat, which was limited to US pilots from all three of the American services with air combat capable air forces. I have not heard, nor would I speculate on, whether any other air force operated a training program similar to CONSTANT PEG.

During the nearly ten years of CONSTANT PEG operations and the 15,000+ MiG sorties flown in that time, the greatest single value to the nearly 6,000 participants was giving each crewmember a chance to see the MiGs and at least partially overcome what is widely called "buck fever."

"Buck fever" is the euphemism that describes a hunter's first opportunity to bring a deer into the sights of a rifle. The excitement mounts, one's heart races and the pulse pounds so hard that it is difficult to hold the gun steady. In air-to-air combat, putting the bandit in your gunsight will always be a heart pounding event. But those that participated in sorties with US-flown MiGs believed that actually seeing the Soviet fighters up close and having a chance to dogfight with them made a significant difference in their self-confidence and ability to perform in combat. Learning to look over their shoulders and search successfully for a little jet was a major factor in the training process. Canopy glints and dots moving against the sky background became cues that our crewmembers learned to look for to alert them to the presence of a MiG.

Early research has been done that attempts to correlate air-to-air kills in combat with a pilot's training background and exposure to the CONSTANT PEG MiGs. No one would rationally conclude that CONSTANT PEG exposure by itself would have created the kill ratio results achieved by the F-15 and F-16.

Instead, CONSTANT PEG should be seen as the "icing on the cake," the layers of the cake itself consisting of the key training events or building blocks that are now understood to be necessary to ensure success in air-to-air combat.

So, while opinions may vary, the widespread subjective view is that the CONSTANT PEG program was of significant value. History substantiates that opinion. The following study starts with the 1981 Gulf of Sidra incident, continues to the 1989 Gulf of Sidra incident and then details facts about certain kills achieved in DESERT STORM.

FIGHTING THE LIBYANS

In August 1981, while cruising in the Mediterranean Sea with Sixth Fleet, the aircraft carriers USS *Forrestal* (CV-59) and USS *Nimitz* (CVN-68) crossed Libya's so-called "Line of Death" into the Gulf of Sidra. This mass of water is like a very large bay adjacent to the Libyan coastline.

On August 19, two Sukhoi Su-22 fighters were shot down in the first air-to-air combat involving US Navy pilots thought to have trained against the CONSTANT PEG MiGs. The following details pertaining to this shoot-down were taken from a website:

In the 1970s, Libya had claimed a 12-mile extension zone of its territorial waters in the Gulf of Sidra, which had prompted US naval forces to conduct Freedom of Navigation operations in the area that saw them cross the so called "Line of Death." These operations further increased when Ronald Reagan came to office. In August 1981 he authorized a large naval force, led by the aircraft carriers *Forrestal* and *Nimitz* to deploy off the Libyan coast. The Libyan air force responded by deploying a large number of interceptors and fighter-bombers, and early on the morning of August 18, when the US exercise began, at least three MiG-25 "Foxbats" approached the US carrier groups, but were escorted away by *Forrestal*-based F-4J Phantom IIs (of VMFA-115 and VF-74) and *Nimitz*'s F-14As (from VF-41 and VF-84).

The Libyans tried to establish the exact location of the US naval force, sending 35 pairs of MiG-23 "Floggers," MiG-25 "Foxbats," Sukhoi Su-20 "Fitter-Cs," Su-22M "Fitter-Js," and Mirage F1s into the area. These were soon intercepted by seven pairs of F-14s and F-4s. The situation was tense but neither side fired any weapons, despite MiG-25s trying to breach American fighters by flying high and fast on at least two occasions.

On the morning of the 19th, two VF-41 "Black Aces" F-14As – "Fast Eagle 102" BuNo 160404 (pilot Cdr Henry "Hank" Kleeman and RIO Lt David "Inlet" Venlet) and "Fast Eagle 107" BuNo 160390 (pilot Lt Lawrence "Music" Muczynski and Lt (jg) James "Amos" Anderson) – were flying a combat air patrol to cover aircraft engaged in a missile exercise. An E-2C Hawkeye from VAW-124 gained radar contact with two Su-22s that had taken off from Okba Ben Nafi Air Base (formerly the USAF's Wheelus AB) near Tripoli.

The two F-14s from VF-41 were ordered to intercept the Libyan aircraft. Only a few seconds before the two formations merged, at an estimated distance of 300m, one of the Su-22s fired an AA-2 "Atoll" air-to-air missile at one of the F-14s, which missed. Then the two Sukhois flew right past the American jets and tried to escape. The Tomcats evaded and were cleared to return fire by their RoE, which mandated self-defense on the initiation of hostile action. The F-14s turned hard port and came in behind the Libyan jets. The American pilots fired AIM-9L Sidewinder missiles, and the first kill was credited to "Fast Eagle 102" and the second to "Fast Eagle 107." Both Libyan pilots ejected, and although the official US Navy report notes that both men were safely recovered, post-mission analysis of the official audio recording of the incident taken from the cruiser USS *Biddle* (CG-34) reveals that one of the F-14 pilots saw a Libyan pilot eject, but that his parachute failed to open.

Less than an hour later, while the Libyans were conducting a search and rescue operation for their downed pilots, two fully armed MiG-25s entered the airspace over the gulf. They headed for the US carriers at Mach 1.5, conducting a mock attack in the direction of *Nimitz*. Two Tomcats from VF-41 and a single jet from VF-84 headed towards the Libyan fighters, which then turned around. The Tomcats also turned for home but then had to reverse their course again when the Libyan pilots headed for the US carriers once more. After being tracked by the F-14s' radars, the MiGs finally headed home. Another Libyan formation ventured out into the gulf towards US forces later that day.

I made numerous inquiries about Cdr Kleeman and the other naval aviators from VF-41 that scored victories on August 19, 1981, but received no replies. Finally, I emailed US Navy CONSTANT PEG MiG-21 pilot Tom Morgenfeld in April 2009, and he told me that Hank Kleeman was a US Naval Academy classmate of his. He further reported that Kleeman had been killed in an F/A-18 landing accident at NAS Miramar on December 3, 1985, while serving as the commander of VX-4 at NAS Pt Mugu. That is the same squadron that both Tom Morgenfeld and Hugh Brown had left when they were assigned by the US Navy to the CONSTANT PEG project at Nellis.

Tom further stated that Hank Kleeman had not flown against CONSTANT PEG MiGs during the time Tom was assigned to the 4477th. However, Morgenfeld went on to speculate that in all probability Hank Kleeman had indeed had the chance to train against the MiGs over the Nevada desert at some point in his career as a Miramar-based fighter pilot. I have had no luck locating the other officers involved or learning, beyond speculation, of their training history.

On January 4, 1989, this drama was repeated in the Gulf of Sidra, and this time two MiG-23s fell from the sky. Here is the story of the engagement as detailed on the internet:

In 1973 Libya claimed much of the Gulf of Sidra as its territorial waters and subsequently declared a "Line of Death," the crossing of which would invite a military response. Tensions between Libya and the US were high after the American government accused Libya of building a chemical weapons plant near Rabta, causing the US Navy to deploy the aircraft carrier USS *John F. Kennedy* (CV-67) near the Libyan coast. A second carrier group, with USS *Theodore Roosevelt* (CVN-71) as its flagship, also prepared to sail into the Gulf of Sidra.

On the morning of January 4, 1989, the *Kennedy* battle group was operating some 130km north of Libya. A group of A-6 Intruders from the vessel were exercising south of Crete, the bombers being escorted by two pairs of CV-67-based F-14As from VF-14 "Tophatters" and VF-32 "Swordsmen" that were in turn being controlled by an E-2C from VAW-126. Later that morning the southernmost CAP station was taken by two F-14s from VF-32, "Gypsy 207" BuNo 159610 (pilot Cdr Joseph B. Connelly and RIO Cdr Leo F. Enwright) and "Gypsy 202" BuNo 159437 (pilot Lt Hermon C. Cook III and RIO Lt Cdr Steven P. Collins). The officers had been specially briefed for this mission due to the high tensions regarding the carrier group's presence – the naval aviators had been advised to expect hostility from the Libyan air force.

At 1150hrs, after some time on patrol, the E-2 informed the F-14 crews that four Libyan MiG-23s had taken off from Al Bumbaw, near Tobruk. The F-14s turned towards the first two MiG-23s, which were some 27 nautical miles (50km) ahead of the rear pair, and acquired them with their radars. At the time the Floggers were 72 nautical miles (133km) away at 10,000ft (3,000m), and heading directly towards the Tomcats and their carrier.

The F-14s turned away from the MiGs' head-on approach so as to indicate to the Libyans that they didn't want to engage them. The "Floggers" changed course to intercept at a closing speed of about 870 knots (1,000 mph/1,600 km/h). The F-14s descended to 3,000ft (910m) to give them a clear radar picture of the "Floggers" against the sky and leave the Libyan pilots with look-down sea clutter to contend with in return. The F-14 crews repeated their turning away maneuver four more times, although they continued to track the MiGs. At 1159hrs Cdr Leo F. Enwright (RIO of the lead Tomcat) ordered the arming of the section's AIM-9L Sidewinder and AIM-7M Sparrow missiles. The E-2C had given the F-14 crews authority to fire if threatened, thus preventing them from having to wait until after the Libyans had engaged them with missiles.

At 1201hrs Cdr Enwright told the E-2 that the "Bogeys have jinked back at me again for the fifth time. They're on my nose now, inside of 20 miles," followed shortly by "Master arm on" as he ordered arming of the weapons. At a range of 14 nautical miles (26km) Enwright fired the first AIM-7M Sparrow – this surprised his pilot, Cdr Joseph B. Connelly, who did not expect to see a missile accelerate away from his Tomcat. The RIO reported "Fox 1, Fox 1." The Sparrow subsequently failed to track because of an incorrect switch setting. At ten nautical miles (19km), Enwright launched a second Sparrow missile, but it also failed to track its target.

The "Floggers" accelerated and continued to approach. At a range of six nautical miles (11km) the Tomcats split and the MiGs followed the wingman while the lead F-14 circled to get a tail angle on them. The wingman engaged with a Sparrow and downed one of the Libyan aircraft. One of the US pilots broadcast "Good kill! Good kill!" The lead Tomcat closed on the remaining "Flogger" from the rear quadrant and at 1.5 nautical miles (2.8km) Connelly fired a Sidewinder, which hit its target. One crewman broadcast "Good kill!" followed by "Let's get out of here." The Libyan pilots were seen to successfully eject and parachute into the sea, but they were not recovered. The Tomcats then proceeded north to return to the carrier.

No one is sure why the two MiGs operated in this manner and provoked the engagement, and the Libyans did not launch a successful rescue operation to recover the pilots. The following day, the Libyan government accused the US of attacking two unarmed reconnaissance aircraft, but footage from the Tomcats' gun-camera videos showed that the Libyan jets were armed with AA-7 "Apex" air-to-air missiles. Depending on the model, this can be either a semi-active radar-homing weapon or an infrared-homing (heat-seeking) missile.

The clash had repercussions on the NATO base at Lampedusa and NAS Sigonella, Libyan leader Col Muammar Gaddafi reportedly threatening reprisals against the commanders of both bases.

DESERT STORM

By 1990 the fighter squadrons at Bitburg AB and Eglin AFB had a number of pilots experienced in fighting MiGs from their CONSTANT PEG exposure at Nellis, and they also had veteran MiG pilots amongst them in Capt John C. Mann ("Bandit 56") and Maj "Paco" Geisler. The stage was set. Little did they know that Iraqi dictator President Saddam Hussein was preparing the "screenplay" that would thrust them into combat and allow a select few to score aerial victories.

Saddam was preparing to invade Kuwait. This decision would ultimately turn out to be a big mistake for him personally and a tragedy for his air force. On August 2, 1990, Iraqi forces conducted the bold and unwarranted invasion of neighboring Kuwait. The world waited to see what would happen next. President George H. W. Bush assembled a coalition of forces with allies equally outraged by Saddam's actions and began deploying forces to the region. The military build-up was called DESERT SHIELD. By mid January 1991 significant American forces had been deployed to Southwest Asia for some time in support of DESERT SHIELD.

Amongst the first assets sent to the theater were USAF F-15Cs from the 58th TFS of the 33rd TFW at Eglin AFB and the 1st TFW at Langley AFB, these units transferring to bases in Saudi Arabia. Additional F-15Cs were deployed to Turkey from the 36th TFW at Bitburg.

As the planners agonized over the best combat employment strategy, it was speculated that F-15s would be lost during the upcoming battle, if for no other reason than the comparative combat experience of the pilots on both sides. In 1980 Iran and Iraq had gone to war, and in the eight years that followed the Iraqi Air Force (IrAF) gained extensive combat experience. The F-15 community had little to no combat experience. Ultimately, however, the final aerial victory count in the war that was coming would give the F-15 credit for an undisputed knockout blow against the IrAF. The aerial combat training of the American forces especially gave USAF Eagle pilots the edge that enabled them to prevail.

On the night of January 17, 1991, the waiting for whatever was coming next was over for the deployed F-15C pilots. DESERT SHIELD was finished. DESERT STORM had commenced. 58th TFS F-15s launched from King Faisal AB (which is also known as Tabuk) in western Saudi Arabia. The jets aerial refueled and headed north for their CAP orbits west of Baghdad. Their job was to deny any IrAF reaction to the opening aerial attacks of DESERT STORM by Coalition forces.

Capt Rick "Kluso" Tollini was the mission commander of the eight-ship formation. On "Kluso's" wing was Capt Larry "Cherry" Pitts, No 3 was Capt Jon "JB" Kelk, and his wingman was Capt Mark "Willie" Williams. Leading the second four-ship was Capt Rob "Cheese" Graeter, with 1Lt Scott "Papa" Maw on his wing. 58th TFS commander Lt Col "Tonic" Theil was No 3, with 1Lt "LA" Brooks on his wing. Tollini, Kelk, and Graeter were experienced Weapons Officers, having graduated from the FWS at Nellis AFB.

The weather was very poor that night in the refueling track. After topping off his four-ship of Eagles with fuel from the tanker, "Kluso" Tollini headed north. "Cheese" Graeter steered his four-ship on a more southerly route around the bulk of the weather. Both of these officers were typical of the flight leads scheduled to head the early raids of the war. Most were FWS graduates.

The war's first aerial victory was subsequently scored by "JB" Kelk, "Kluso's" No 3 man. "JB" had learned to fly through the USAF Undergraduate Pilot Training (UPT) course, and upon graduation he was assigned to fly the F-15 Eagle. The entire UPT and initial F-15 training took nearly two years to complete, including survival training and fighter lead-in training.

Initial qualification in a combat aircraft is accomplished by completing what is called a B Course in a dedicated organization called a Replacement Training Unit. More recently this terminology has changed to Flying Training Unit. The B Course is a comprehensive syllabus of academic and flight instruction augmented by a significant amount of simulator training. Pilots first must learn all of the details of the operation of the new airplane. After administrative in-processing, the academic flow begins with courses like Airplane – General, where the hydraulics, fuel, electrical, and flight control systems are mastered academically. Courses follow dealing with the avionics, including the radar, communications, and navigation systems, and then on to weapons and the aircraft's supporting weapons system.

Oddly enough, just learning about the systems is not enough. Courses are also taught in switchology. To clarify this point, recognize that learning about a piano by studying the number of keys and the strings and pedals doesn't create a pianist. Similarly, learning to employ a weapons system like the F-15 in combat can be as difficult as learning to play a masterpiece on the piano. Simply knowing what the switches do isn't enough. Switches are located both on the aircraft's throttles and control column. Other switches are located on the instrument panel and the cockpit side panels. Early on, pilots learning to operate the F-15's weapons system called the mastery of the essential switchology "learning to play the piccolo." The number of different switch positions, combinations, and the use of different fingers on different switches prompted this metaphor.

When the B Course pilot has completed the requisite academics, it is off to the simulator to learn how to fly the jet. Tuition is also given at this stage on which switches to activate and when. Simulator or "sim" training quickly advances to dealing with various aircraft system failures, which are characterized as emergency procedures, or EPs. The pilot must demonstrate complete fluency in dealing with all of the aircraft's EPs without reference to a checklist. This demonstration is accomplished during a check ride with an experienced instructor pilot at the sim console, who creates havoc for the new pilot to unravel.

If a pilot fails the simulator EP check ride, the pilot doesn't fly! This isn't recitation from rote memory of the EPs either. Instead, it requires in-the-cockpit observation of something abnormal, the interpretation of the situation, the selection of the proper course of action and the application of the correct switchology, all the while maintaining control of the simulator as if the pilot was flying a real aircraft. The check ride is a true milestone in training, and many pilots have washed out of the program because they could not master the EP challenge in the simulator.

The B Course then advances beyond simulator emergencies into actual simulated flight profiles, and these are matched with actual training sorties in the aircraft. The first flight challenge is transition training, during which the pilot learns how to take-off and land. This typically happens in a two-seat trainer F-15D, with the instructor monitoring progress from the rear cockpit. Very quickly the student is soloed out into the single-seat F-15C, and his or her training advances through the instrument and formation syllabus into the tactical application of the fighter using the radar and the weapons system.

Every aspect of the flight is recorded for debriefing purposes, and once back in the squadron the debriefing room reverts into a classroom. The pilot initially reviews the video recording of the head-up display, which is essentially the view straight ahead out through the aircraft's windscreen. Other recordings preserve the radar display and voice communications history. The instructor then critiques every element of the student's performance aimed at harvesting the maximum amount of learning for the student. During the debriefing, the instructor's critique often progresses one film frame at a time to maximise the student's experience from the sortie.

The tactical building blocks start with basic fighter maneuvers, which can be visualized as a classic one-versus-one dogfight. Very quickly the young pilot learns that there is a significant difference between being offensive and going for a kill and being defensive and denying the adversary the kill. This training is conducted with an instructor in one F-15C and the student in a second aircraft. The mock attacks start from a perch or position of advantage, with one aircraft usually above and behind the other. Then, they switch positions so learning is accomplished from both the offensive and defensive initial set up.

The student learns that because of turning performance there is a difference between a perch attack that starts from only 3,000ft behind the target and a perch attack that commences from 9,000ft back. With 9,000ft of spacing, the defender can turn hard enough to nearly meet the attacker head-on, thereby neutralizing the attack.

The pilots learn that turning aircraft transcribe a portion of a circle in the sky, and they learn to look across a circle at another turning aircraft and judge rates. Am I losing the turn rate or am I closing into a position of advantage where I can launch an air-to-air missile or, better yet, close to gun range? Do I have the energy in the form of airspeed to cut across the circle and expedite the attack? Am I equipped with a functioning helmet-mounted (gun or missile) sight, or not? How does that equipage change things? Should I maneuver below the opposing fighter's turn circle or yo-yo above his turn circle to obtain a position behind him – like tying a knot in a rope, which will shorten the rope as it does the flightpath.

The training continues until each building block is mastered in the one-versus-one arena. Then, pilots learn to fight as pairs of aircraft against another aircraft. This is called air combat maneuvering or ACM, and is a logical advance beyond basic fighter maneuvers. Dogfights don't just happen generally. Instead, they develop starting with a radar vector from a control agency that could be ground based or airborne in an E-3 AWACS. The radar vector sets up the intercept geometry for the aerial engagement and the pilot in the F-15 then uses the on-board radar to take over the intercept. In a perfect world the F-15 pilot finds the target, electronically identifies it as hostile and launches a missile from beyond visual range. If that all works, great, but in the real world there may be more targets than are observed on radar and the bad guys might start shooting back. The fighter pilot must decide whether to continue or retreat to fight another day.

If the decision is made to continue the attack, the ACM and BFM training may be called upon for survival if the beyond visual range attack closes into the visual arena of the classical dogfight. If that happens it is good to have your buddies there to help you fight your way out.

"JB" Kelk completed B Course training and launched his career as a fighter pilot. When a pilot finishes the B Course, he or she is an absolute entry-level fighter pilot, and upon arriving at the operational assignment is entered into Mission Readiness (MR) training. The pilot goes through a syllabus-like sequence of evaluation and advanced training in the operational unit. Upon completion of the training, a successful MR check ride with a senior squadron check pilot finally qualifies the new guy to fly fighters in the squadron as a wingman.

The role of the wingman has changed significantly from the days of "Boots" Blesse and his classic fighter pilot "How to" document called *No Guts, No Glory*. Gen Blesse wrote of the responsibilities of the flight leader and the wingman. This product of the Korean War was a "biblical" document for fighter pilots, and it classified the flight leader as the shooter and the wingman as his cover. The job of the wingman historically was to keep a bad guy from sneaking up behind the flight leader and shooting him down while he was otherwise busy hammering another bad guy with his guns.

Things were rather different during the Vietnam War, and May 10, 1972 is as good a date as any for marking the change in the role of the wingman. Things didn't work out well for Maj Bob Lodge that day. As described earlier, Bob was gunned down by a MiG-19 flown by Pham Hung Son. Bob had briefed his flight that every jet was a shooter, and he had directed his wingman John Markle to engage one of the four MiG-21s that "Oyster" flight (four F-4s) had engaged nearly head-on. Bob Lodge shot down one of the MiGs and John Markle shot down another. Meanwhile, Steve Ritchie had destroyed a third MiG. Bob then turned in pursuit of the fourth, and only, surviving MiG-21.

In the flow of the engagement Markle in an F-4D (without a gun) was not in position to intervene directly and protect his flight leader when MiG-19s popped up into the formation from low altitude. The latter jets initially overshot, and then Pham Hung Son maneuvered his MiG-19 into a guns tracking position behind Bob and unleashed a salvo of 30mm cannon fire that shot "Oyster 1" down. In spite of Markle's frantic calls for Bob to break and defend against the attacking MiG-19s, for reasons that will never be known Lodge continued his attack on the surviving MiG-21, ignoring the threat to himself. He paid the ultimate price.

The mission had not gone the way one would have expected during a renaissance change in the role of the wingman. While the loss of Lodge seemed to vindicate the traditional leader/wingman mantra preached in *No Guts, No Glory* that stated the wingman was to cover his leader at all times, aerial warfare was also changing. The old world of guns-only during close-in dogfights was now being rapidly replaced by the new world of the guided missile that could be fired at beyond visual range or at greater than gun range in a visual dogfight.

As a result of this change, seen during the course of the Vietnam War, it soon became official USAF policy that the primary tactic for F-15 units was to form a "wall" of fighters that met enemy interceptors head-on, with every Eagle pilot being a missile shooter. And that policy has yielded the worldwide kill ratio of more than 100 kills to zero combat losses for the F-15.

As previously noted, Capt "JB" Kelk scored the first of those Eagle kills for the USAF on the night of January 17, 1991. How did he proceed from being a fresh B Course F-15C graduate to a DESERT STORM MiG killer? He started with Mission Readiness training and worked his way up through all of the post-B Course building blocks, attending the FWS at Nellis AFB and then returning to his unit to serve as the squadron weapons and tactics instructor. All this training, and his natural ability as a fighter pilot, combined to make Kelk one of the most skilled flight leaders in the entire 33rd TFW when his squadron was called to combat.

As part of his training evolution, Kelk flew against the USAF's MiGs at the TTR. When I first contacted him and asked about his participation in CONSTANT PEG, "JB's" "semi-coded" e-mail response, written in "fighter pilot speak," was as follows:

> I had a few sorties north on the range. One F-5 mission shortly after MR as a 2Lt – way cool – in Mar/April 1983. Next opportunity came in FWS in 1987. Flew another F-5 BFM mission. Then had 2 ME sorties vs F-4s and F-5s. Bottom line is the experience was priceless, especially to have seen it at so young in my career. Added big time confidence and exposed the inherent weaknesses of those platforms. It puts meat on those Intel briefs – nothing like the real thing baby.

Deciphered, "JB" was saying that soon after finishing the B Course and completing MR training, and while still a second lieutenant, he deployed to Nellis and flew an F-15C on a training mission against a MiG-21. Four years later he was a student at the FWS, and during the early part of its training syllabus he flew one-versus-one against a MiG-21 in a classical dogfight. F-5 terminology was the cover story for the MiG-21. MiG-17 cover was the A-4 and MiG-23 cover was the F-4.

The final syllabus sorties at the Weapons School are called the ME phase. In this graduation exercise all of the different courses at the Weapons School participate in an integrated combat training exercise similar to Red Flag. It is as close to actual combat as the exercise designers can make it, and the intensity is an adrenalin gushing experience for all participants. They definitely feel the heat of battle.

In the ME phase "JB" Kelk had had the opportunity to tactically engage both MiG-21s and MiG-23s from the Red Eagle CONSTANT PEG operation at Tonopah. His emphasis on the early part of his training in his e-mail is especially revealing in that he attributes the CONSTANT PEG exposure to actual MiG fighters to his added self-confidence and understanding of the capabilities and limitations of the enemy's fighters. Finally, the MiG exposure in a training environment added depth and credibility to the intense relationship that existed between combat pilots and the material presented to them by their intelligence officers in both continuation training and during pre-combat mission briefings. Along the way "JB" also had intense exposure to the Aggressors and Red Flag in addition to the CONSTANT PEG assets. His Red Eagles experience was the ultimate building block in his pre-combat training.

That night on January 17, 1991, Capt "JB" Kelk, flying F-15C 85-0125 as "Penzoil 63," launched as the No 3 in a flight of four F-15Cs led by Tollini, aerial refueled, flew to his CAP, was vectored toward the enemy and blasted an Iraqi MiG-29 out of the sky with an AIM-7 missile. He went on to enjoy a distinguished career with the Air National Guard in the state of Missouri and as an airline pilot.

As the leader of the second formation of four Eagles in the eight-ship commanded by Tollini, Maj Robert "Cheese" Graeter lifted off from Tabuk AB. Because of poor weather in the refueling area, "Cheese" took a more southerly route to his CAP in order to find clear air, thus giving his wingmen a chance to relax a bit after the intensity of the aerial refueling.

"Cheese," like "JB," attended UPT and then the B Course in the F-15. His first assignment was with the 12th TFS of the 18th TFW at Kadena AB, Japan (Okinawa). Excellence was bred there, especially during the 1980s. All three fighter squadrons in the wing – 12th, 44th, and 67th TFSs – each won the annually awarded Hughes Trophy during a three-year period. The Hughes Trophy, which is now known as the Raytheon Hughes Achievement Award, is presented to the top squadron in the USAF with an air intercept or air superiority mission. Kadena AB itself also won the award as the best air base in the entire USAF during this period. Blessed with great leadership, Kadena was a training ground for general officers in those days. At least three future four-star generals were captains and majors (Moseley, Chandler, and Martin) at Kadena at the time, along with an extraordinary number of future two- and three-star generals.

The competition among the junior officers on base was intense too, and their performance was never disappointing. "Cheese" was one of those that stood out as a shinning star even at that young age. He deployed to Clark AB numerous times for Cope Thunder, the western Pacific's version of Red Flag, where he routinely fought with the F-5Es assigned to the locally based Aggressor squadron at Clark. Graeter also sat Air Defense alert at Osan AB, in South Korea. Kadena was a busy time for "Cheese," and it sowed the seeds that led to his superior performance as a fighter pilot.

His next assignment was to Nellis as an Aggressor pilot flying F-5Es and then on to the co-located, F-15-equipped, 422nd TES. It was during his assignment as an Aggressor that he was first exposed to the MiGs at Tonopah. While completing the Aggressor conversion course and later flying as an instructor in the Aggressor training program, as well as during his time as an F-15 test pilot, "Cheese" had frequent opportunities to be paired up in mock air combat with MiG-21s. He added this eye-popping experience to his list of building blocks and fully harvested the lessons the MiG adversary pilots offered.

Graeter attended FWS while serving as an F-15 test pilot at Nellis. Later, he returned to the school as an instructor and eventually became the "Barnyard" commander at the FWS – one of the most coveted jobs in USAF fighter aviation. In those days the pool of instructors at the FWS were known as the "Barnyard IPs" due to their livestock oriented nicknames such as "Pigpen," "Pig Farmer," "Buffalo," etc. Collectively, they brought their students to yet another level as they trained them to be weapons officers – the chief instructor in a fighter squadron. The course included flying against actual MiG adversaries of the CONSTANT PEG project as a routine part of their syllabus of instruction.

Throughout this period the entire CONSTANT PEG project continued to be highly classified, officers being exposed only if there was a "must know" stated requirement. Nevertheless, more than 5,000 Air Force, Navy, and Marine Corps air crewmen had the chance to fly against the Red Eagle MiGs. The respect they had for the program was so strong that security was maintained for more than 18 years after the project was terminated.

"Cheese" Graeter was perfectly positioned for DESERT STORM when he reported to his next assignment as an operational F-15 pilot within the 33rd TFW at Eglin. When contacted and asked about CONSTANT PEG, "Cheese" was quick to compliment the program. In almost the same breath he included CONSTANT PEG as one of the significant building blocks in his overall training sequence. He also commented on the quality of his instructors along the way, the complex scenarios he had been exposed to and the large force planning he had accomplished during and after his team spirit experiences in Korea during his time at Kadena. The planning and execution of large force operations was done so frequently that the administrative aspects were almost automatic, allowing the planner and flight leader to focus on the operational and tactical aspects of the mission.

With CONSTANT PEG experience as one of the arrows in his quiver of building blocks, "Cheese" reported to me that when the adrenalin started flowing during combat in the early morning hours of January 17, 1991, it was entirely manageable.

In his account of the action that followed, "Cheese" describes the events that led to his AIM-7 kill of an Iraqi Mirage F 1EQ, and his success in running another F 1EQ into the ground a few minutes later. He was flying F-15C 85-0105 with the 58th TFS as "Citgo 65" at the time, leading a flight of four Eagles:

I had the element in an offset trail and I was searching low at 18 miles. My wingman, 1Lt Maw, was searching high. We got radar contacts and I eventually unleashed an AIM-7. The missile guided and eventually splashed the guy. It turned out to be a Mirage F 1. He was shredded by the AIM-7 warhead and probably had no chance of surviving the missile impact – he probably never knew what hit him. That gave me pause for thought later on, but we quickly realized that he would have done the same to us given the chance. His jet hit the ground, and very soon thereafter another F 1 also hit the ground and tumbled across the desert.

When I talked to "Cheese" about that night and attempted to learn the value, if any, of the CONSTANT PEG training, he left me with the clear impression that CONSTANT PEG was an important building block, and those experiences had helped him manage the rush of adrenalin that comes during actual combat.

That same night captains James Denton (pilot) and Brent Brandon (EWO), flying EF-111A 66-0016 of the 42nd ECS/66th ECW, were also unofficially credited with running a Mirage F 1EQ into the ground. And Capt Steve "Tater" Tate of the 71st TFS/1st TFW, flying F-15C 83-0017 as "Quaker 11," also shot down a Mirage F 1EQ with an AIM-7. The US Navy and US Marine Corps tasted aerial success as well on January 17. F/A-18C pilots Lt Cdr Mark Fox and Lt Nick Mongillo (in BuNo 163459/call sign "Quicksand 64" and BuNo 163502/call sign "Quicksand 62," respectively) each shot down a MiG-21. Fox used an AIM-9L and Mongillo an AIM-7M.

The first daylight mission of the war for the 33rd TFW happened later on January 17, and during the course of the operation the 58th TFS's US Marine Corps exchange pilot, Capt Chuck "Sly" Magill (flying F-15C 85-0107/call sign "Zerex 71") downed a MiG-29 with an AIM-7. "Sly" was leading his flight of four and "Kluso" Tollini – on his second mission of the 17th – headed up the other Eglin flight. An additional eight aircraft from the 1st TFW at Langley gave an overall fighter escort of 16 F-15s for a Coalition strike package of 40 jets. They got the job done.

The plan was to conduct a counterclockwise flow sweep through the assigned area and engage any airborne IrAF assets. AWACS called out bandits and cleared

"Zerex" flight to fire from a distance in excess of 100 miles. Somewhat distracted by this turn of events, "Sly" and his flight were surprised when they over flew Iraqi ground forces that started shooting SAMs at them. The missiles were evaded and the flight regained its combat formation in pursuit of the targets that AWACS had previously declared hostile. The bandits turned away and a fuel-consuming tail chase resulted. Then, the bad guys made a 180-degree turn and faced the four F-15s head-on. Capt Rhory "Hoser" Draeger (in F-15C 85-0119/call sign "Citgo 3") fired first followed by "Sly," who shot off two AIM-7Ms – he thought that his first missile had malfunctioned. Draeger's Sparrow killed the lead MiG-29 and Magill's first AIM-7 hit the second jet. His second missile went through the resulting MiG fireball. "Splash Two!"

In the wake of all this success, January 18 was quiet. On the 19th, however, the action picked up again during a day mission when Capt Rick "Kluso" Tollini from the 58th TFS (flying F-15C 85-0101/call sign "Citgo 21") scored a MiG-25 kill with an AIM-7. His wingman, Capt Larry "Cherry" Pitts (flying F-15C 85-0099/call sign "Citgo 22"), also downed a MiG-25 with an AIM-7 during the high-noon daylight encounter. This engagement brought about the first success of the war for an F-15 wingman while his flight leader was taking care of a different enemy aircraft.

Rick Tollini was another of the gifted pilots that cut his teeth in the F-15 at Kadena, his first operational assignment. "Kluso" jumped through the same hoops that "Cheese" and "JB" had mastered as he advanced from wingman to FWS graduate, combat flight leader and, finally, mission commander. "Kluso's" CONSTANT PEG story is a little bit different, however. It started when, in October 1984, the Kadena WILLIAM TELL gunnery team led by Lt Col Roger Taylor (12th TFS commander), with me as "Top Cover," deployed from Kadena to Eglin AFB and then on to Tyndall AFB for the air-to-air gunnery competition called WILLIAM TELL after the famous Swiss archer.

The deployment and competition was completed mostly without incident, and after WILLIAM TELL was over, the Kadena jets deployed to Nellis AFB as the first stage of their return trip home to Kadena. The purpose of the stop at Nellis was to fly against the MiGs of CONSTANT PEG. This was especially important to me in that it was the first time I had returned to Nellis since Lt Hugh Brown's fatal MiG-17 accident and my relief from command of the Red Eagles.

It was kind of strange coming back to Nellis and preparing to fly against the MiGs. I went to the mandatory briefings and was threatened with my life for any breach of security – I thought of "Devil" Muller, the security architect. These guys had no idea they were giving a new guy briefing to the dude that had been one of the kingpins in building the airfield and starting up the CONSTANT PEG program, nor did they have a clue that I was married to the "Peg" in CONSTANT PEG. I kept my mouth shut and briefed to fly.

I was paired against a MiG-23 in a tactical intercept set-up to a visual engagement. After some launch delays and fuel-consuming loiter time in a CAP, I got a good vector from the GCI and quickly made radar contact with the MiG-23, which was high above me and crossing from right to left. I had plenty of energy and took a lead pursuit cutoff angle and began a climb. When I came into range I hosed off a simulated AIM-7 and continued to press the attack as if the missile had malfunctioned. I made visual contact with the MiG-23 and continued the cutoff so as to close to its "seven o'clock" at about three-quarters-of-a-mile, where I simulated firing an AIM-9. At this point I was sucking into trail and the MiG was hauling ass and leaving me cold.

As I remember, GCI passed words from the MiG pilot that he was BINGO and was returning to his base at Tonopah. The engagement had lasted only a short time before it was over. I landed and conducted an administrative debrief without ever talking to the MiG pilot, and was then debriefed by an Aggressor instructor. That was it. I was on the outside again, and was to remain outside until the USAF began efforts to declassify the program.

Two years later the same sequence of events occurred, with the Kadena WILLIAM TELL team again stopping at Nellis on the way home to fly against the CONSTANT PEG MiGs. This time "Kluso" Tollini was one of the Kadena pilots that flew by commercial air from Okinawa to Las Vegas to participate in CONSTANT PEG while the 18th TFW had its ZZ-tailed jets in place at Nellis. Upon contacting "Kluso," I initially received the following reply:

> Will do my best to recall details, but most of what I remember is some of the specific results/learning from the two sorties I flew, and not much beyond that. I was still a young bug, and I think was overwhelmed with just the thought of flying against MiGs – plus there was a LOT of drinking on that trip as I recall.

My ski buddy Larry "Bubba" New was also on the deployment with "Kluso," and his report of the Nellis trip read as follows:

> I was instructing in the F-15 FWS from 1982 to 1986, which places me in the heart of the time frame that you are writing about. I was also on that 1986 WILLIAM TELL deployment from Kadena, which "Kluso" briefly mentions. Having instructed many guys who then went up to TTR for the first time, I can attest to the "buck

fever" syndrome you talk about. I can also confirm that every guy walked away from that experience a better fighter pilot.

Further details from "Kluso" about the specific results of the CONSTANT PEG sorties, and what he learned from them, unfolded as follows:

> To get right to your question – yes I did fly a couple of PEG sorties. I think I recall it was late 1986, and I was on a CONUS TDY. We met the WILLIAM TELL jets (as you did I assume) as they were coming back from Tyndall and did a two-week PEG/DACT. I did a MiG-21 1-v-1 and a 2-v-2 (MiG-21) – I had a blast and it was a great experience. I can say it was definitely a benefit to see a real MiG in training prior to seeing one in combat ("buck fever" kind of idea), but obviously it was just one event in a long line of great training opportunities I had, so I am not sure how to quantify that other than by saying I was really fortunate to have that experience.

In this report "Kluso" is describing the building block approach used to acquaint our Blue Force pilots and WSOs with the MiGs, starting with one-versus-one to give them a look at the MiG and then advancing into basic fighter maneuvering from the perch in both offensive and defensive set-ups. Then, when adding building blocks to the training sequence, it is a natural progression to advance to the ACM training step in two-versus-two engagements. These typically started with a GCI or AWACS radar vector, followed by an on-board radar contact and the transition to the visual entry into maneuvering dogfights. WONDERFUL training for fighter pilots!

On January 19, 1991, events during DESERT STORM took on real meaning, with "Kluso" and his wingman "Cherry" Pitts both scoring kills. Later that same day squadron mates captains Cesar "Rico" Rodriguez and Craig "Mole" Underhill (flying F-15C 85-0114/call sign "Chevron 25" and 85-0122/call sign "Chevron 26," respectively) downed two more MIG-29s. "Rico" ran his MiG adversary into the ground after "Mole" had destroyed his "Fulcrum" with an AIM-7. A website account of the battle read as follows:

> After Underhill shot the first MiG-29 down, both he and Rodriguez had the remaining IrAF jet bracketed. In an attempt to dive into an escape window that had already closed, the Iraqi MiG-29 pilot tried to execute a split-S from a starting altitude of about 2,000ft. Rodriguez, who was the engaged low man, recognized the problem and took his jet "upstairs." The MiG-29 pilot attempted to follow through with the split-S and hit the desert floor.

The Underhill-Rodriguez engagement occurred as "Chevron" was clearing the tail of "Citgo" flight, which had just downed its pair of MiG-25s and was retreating south to the tanker track. It is said to have been the only turning fight of the war. In post-war interviews, Rodriguez expressed his opinion that they had been extremely lucky in the intercept, since AWACS did not call the pair of MiG-29s approaching from the left beam until they were roughly 13 miles away. Prior to that call, "Chevron" had been unaware of the MiGs' presence.

A conversation with "Rico" revealed that he had never had the opportunity to participate in the CONSTANT PEG program, but he was a product of the "building block approach" to air-to-air combat training. He therefore profited from the experience of others who did participate in training against the MiGs.

"Rico's" combat success continued on January 26 when, again flying F-15C 85-0114/call sign "Citgo 27," he shot down a MiG-23 with an AIM-7. Two other members of "Citgo" flight also destroyed "Floggers" with AIM-7s during that engagement. More about that fight later.

"Rico" wasn't done yet. He later went on to score a third kill (a Serbian MiG-29) on March 24, 1999, during Operation ALLIED FORCE in the Balkans, flying F-15C 86-0169/call sign "Knife 13" of the 493rd EFS.

During DESERT STORM F-15C pilots deployed from Bitburg AB also got in on the action on January 19, having been sent from Germany to Incirlik AB, in southern Turkey, very late in DESERT SHIELD. Capt Dave "Spyro" Prather and 1Lt Dave "Abby" Sveden of the 525th TFS/36th TFW (flying F-15Cs number 79-0069 and 79-0021 as call signs "Rambo 03" and "Rambo 04," respectively) each scored kills against Mirage F 1EQs with AIM-7s.

Capt Steve "Gunga" Dingee was leading the flight as "Rambo 1." From the same generation as Kelk, Graeter, and Tollini, "Gunga's" first TDY after becoming MR was to Nellis for CONSTANT PEG. At that time he was a member of the 8th TFS, which was in turn part of the Holloman-based 49th TFW. His operations officer was Don "Devil" Muller, an initial cadre CONSTANT PEG pilot and architect of the Red Eagle security program. "Gunga" was also an FWS graduate and former "Barnyard" instructor. Following his three years at Holloman, he then went to Luke AFB as an F-15 instructor in the B Course (RTU/FTU). With six years of operational and instructor experience under his belt, Dingee was posted to Bitburg AB. It was during this tour that his squadron deployed to Turkey for DESERT SHIELD.

"Gunga" concluded his career with various assignments at Nellis in the Staff and at Langley AFB again flying the F-15. His final assignment was at Nellis, and when he retired in 2003 he had 3,500 hours of flying time in the F-15.

Whilst at Bitburg "Gunga's" operations officer was Maj John "Flash" Mann, also a Red Eagle. The influence Muller and Mann had on the young officers was comprehensive and dynamic. That influence produced results in combat. "Gunga" recalled:

I had had several PEG deployments before my DESERT STORM experience. As a matter of fact, my very first MR TDY was to CONSTANT PEG. Needless to say, I was exactly the guy described in Steve Davies' book on my first ride – a wide-eyed grape. I believed that it was just as important an experience as Red Flag. CONSTANT PEG was instrumental on the eve of DESERT STORM when it came time for me to tell my young guys about what to expect and how to react. "Devil" Muller was my first Ops Officer, and "Flash" Mann was my Ops Officer during DESERT STORM. Both of these talented individuals also shaped the guys in the squadron with their vast experience flying MiGs during operations at Tonopah.

"Gunga" set up his Bitburg squadron with formed four-ship formations. Dingee was leader, Capt Larry "Von" Ludwig was his wingman, "Spyro" Prather was No 3 and "Abby" Sveden No 4. They had two engagements with Iraqi aircraft and the four-ship was credited with three victories. As previously noted, two of them were claimed on January 19, when Prather and Sveden each destroyed Mirage F 1EQ. "Abby" told me:

I did not get to fight the Tonopah MiGs. When DESERT STORM kicked off, I was a 180-hour first lieutenant wingman, having only been MR for about eight months. So, my opportunities for cool TDYs like that were limited by my brief time in the Eagle up to that point.

The night before the war kicked off, our Ops O, "Flash" Mann, got us all in a room for a chat. He gave us a "hypothetical" discussion about how someone might want to fight some of the threat aircraft in the IrAF inventory. I flew with "Devil" Muller after the war when he was at HQ USAFE and attached to our squadron. I didn't know he was a Red Eagle, like "Flash" Mann, until I saw his photo in Steve Davies' book – why would I, thanks to good operational security.

Overall, I'd give high marks to the operational training I'd received up to that point as well, with a few caveats. It was really just the normal training any F-15 squadron would be doing from month to month. As a matter of fact, our squadron was not supposed to deploy from Bitburg because the other two were slated to go to Saudi (one entire squadron, with additional pilots from the other two). We gave up most of our training sorties from October through to December to those who were to deploy (we called them the "nifty 50"). The rest of us got just enough flying to keep basic currency on the Eagle. I actually showed up for the war out of MR currency and had to get a new checkout about two weeks before the conflict started!

Our deployment to Incirlik from Bitburg was a last-minute addition to the fray (we got word in mid-December), and our clearance to actually fly from a base in Turkey was received from the Turkish government 12 hours after the deadline it had been given by the Bush administration. We didn't get the chance to deploy and then spent many months contemplating upcoming events. We were also a basic squadron. No "who's who" list of "target arms" (nickname for FWS graduates) and "experienced" players creating a dream team, while the normal drivers stayed home. We came with what we had. I flew in my first eight-ship on the opening day of DESERT STORM for the 525th TFS, and that's when we got the kills.

I will say that my own encounter with the IrAF seemed like any BVR to a visual training engagement I'd flown up to that point in my career. BVR comm/radar work, BVR AIM-7s to a visual pickup, follow up shot after bandit maneuvers and a pre-merge kill. I kind of doubt a few sorties against MiGs would have improved the outcome too much since we never mixed it up post-merge. But that's the opinion of someone who never flew a CONSTANT PEG sortie, so I don't know how valid that data point is.

The second engagement for Capt Dingee would come on February 11.

The two Mirage F 1EQ kills for the 525th TFS concluded the aerial action for the first three days of DESERT STORM. No fewer than 14 Iraqi fighters had been either shot down or run into the ground by USAF, US Navy, and US Marine Corps pilots flying F-15s, F/A-18s, and an EF-111A. Five days later on January 24, RSAF pilot Capt Saleh Al-Shamrani of No 13 Sqn, flying F-15C 80-0068 from King Abdul Aziz AB near Dhahran, in Saudi Arabia, shot down two Mirage F 1EQs with AIM-7s.

On the 26th "Rico" Rodriguez was flying as call sign "Citgo 27" when he scored another kill, as mentioned earlier. The other two members of the flight that got kills that same day were captains Rhory "Hoser" Draeger and "Kimo" Schiavi, again from the 58th TFS. The latter pilots were flying F-15Cs 85-0108 and 85-0104 as call signs "Citgo 25" and "Citgo 26," respectively. Each destroyed a MiG-23 with an AIM-7. The following website report provides details of their engagement:

This triplet of kills was a "textbook" BVR offensive sweep, with the four "Citgo" F-15Cs (the fourth was flown by Capt Bruce Till) picking up four MiG-23s and bouncing three – one of them returned to H2 air base early in the intercept, presumably after suffering some sort of mechanical problem. The targets were sorted and shot at by all four F-15s at a distance of more than 13 miles – Till's AIM-7 arrived slightly after the others, and thus he did not receive a kill credit.

Draeger, another Kadena product who also attended FWS, was killed in a car crash in Oregon in 1995.

The next day, January 27, 1991, Capt Jay "OP" Denny and his wingman Capt Ben "Coma" Powell of the 53rd TFS/36th TFW each shot down two Iraqi aircraft.

Years earlier, "OP" had taken his MR check ride in the F-15 on March 31, and the very next day, on April 1, he was at Nellis AFB for CONSTANT PEG! He was then a lowly second lieutenant in the 58th TFS. The squadron reported to the briefing auditorium in the Threat Training Facility at Nellis and was in-briefed. Pilots had been pre-briefed before leaving Eglin, but this was the real deal. Paperwork was signed in ink and each officer promised on paper never to reveal anything about the program. They were warned about bar talk at the Officers' Club and while downtown in Las Vegas. The structure was intense in comparison with Red Flag. During the latter pilots were instructed never to fly over the TTR. Now it was their assigned airspace.

Then, airborne at last, "OP" met "Paco" Geisler head-on in a visual identification pass. "OP" was flying an F-15D with a squadron mate in the rear cockpit. "Paco," who was the 4477th TES Operations Officer, was in a MiG-21. "Paco" called for the join up for the "look see" and leak check, and then the training began. "OP" had resisted the temptation to make an exclamation over the radio when he first saw the MiG. The standard building block progression then followed for the fighter pilot. After a long hard look at the MiG from both the left and right wing positions, underneath and also a glimpse looking down from above the Soviet fighter, it was time for trail formation and perch attacks. More complex and challenging training maneuvers followed that prepared this young officer for the real combat that would be his fortune in a few short years.

"Paco" made a couple of dazzling maneuvers during in-close BFM and then revealed that he had exhausted his energy (airspeed) and was now a sitting duck. It didn't initially look that way to "OP." Then, he began to understand, and the mystique of the MiG melted away.

In April 2009 "OP" and I sat and chatted over coffee at "Aunt Martha's Bed and Breakfast" in Fort Walton Beach, Florida, just outside Eglin AFB. We talked at length about those days when we learned so much. While at Eglin he had been taught how to be a wingman and then a leader. His squadron had deployed to Nellis for Red Flag (and CONSTANT PEG) and then proceeded to

Weapons and Tactics Instruction with the US Marines. Every step of the way these officers were acquiring skills that they would use for the rest of their flying careers, and especially during the combat that would follow with DESERT STORM. Every event built on the previous one, elevating the fighting abilities of the 58th TFS pilots to an incredible level. Gifted aviators joined their ranks and prepared for combat in the F-15 – "Cheese," "JB," "Sly," "Rico," "Mo," "ET," and "Logger" to name but a few by their fighter pilot "handles."

Then "Paco" Geisler was assigned to the 58th as its Operations Officer, adding to the mix his wealth of experience as an initial cadre Aggressor pilot, F-15 FWS instructor and highly experienced MiG-21 pilot. The 58th TFS was on a roll!

My discussion with "OP" covered a wide range of subjects. He remembered leaving Eglin and going to the 53rd TFS at Bitburg AB. Upon arrival there, he immediately turned around and headed back to Nellis to attend FWS. During the course he and fellow classmates, and future combat victors, "Cheese" Graeter, "Vegas" Dietz, and Rick Tollini again flew against the CONSTANT PEG MiGs. "OP" returned to Bitburg and was appointed the squadron Weapons Officer, the chief instructor, and the leader of the pack. CONSTANT PEG Operations Officer and MiG pilot John "Flash" Mann joined the 53rd TFS as its Operations Officer. If "OP" was the chief "Knight" at Bitburg, "Flash" was the "King." "OP" was also the sponsoring officer when "Flash" and his family arrived at Bitburg from the US.

Bitburg was being equipped with the more capable Multi-Stage Improvement Program (MSIP) F-15Cs at this time, and a part of "OP's" task was to ease this transition based on his Eglin experience with MSIP jets.

Bitburg generally scheduled a Friday afternoon weapons officer training session. On one notable Friday, World War II Luftwaffe ace Günther Rall, who had 275 kills to his name, came and shared his experiences with the F-15 pilots. He revealed that in World War II he and his fellow aviators were trained to a very high standard. They didn't have very many pilots left by the end of the war, but those that survived were very good. A part of that quality was attributed to the German squadron of captured American (and British) fighters that the Luftwaffe operated for training. Rall referred to the P-38 Lightnings, P-51 Mustangs, and P-47 Thunderbolts that were operated by the Germans for training, and made a veiled reference to the American squadron in Las Vegas that did the same thing. Knowing eyes cautiously glanced at each other as those American pilots "in the know" wondered who was the source for the German ace's information.

On "OP" Denny's big day, he was flying F-15C 84-0025/call sign "Opec 01" when he downed two MiG-23s with AIM-9 missiles. His wingman,

"Coma" Powell, was flying F-15C 84-0027/call sign "Opec 02" when he downed a MiG-23 and a Mirage F 1EQ with AIM-7 missiles. The following day Capt Don "Muddy" Watrous from the 32nd TFS, based at Soesterburg, in the Netherlands, claimed his unit's sole aerial victory of the conflict. Flying Bitburg jet F-15C 79-0022/call sign "Bite 04," he shot down a MiG-23 with an AIM-7. On January 29, 60th TFS pilot Capt Dave "Logger" Rose (one of seven pilots from this unit attached to the 58th TFS) used F-15C 85-0102/call sign "Chevron 17" to destroy a MiG-23 with an AIM-7.

"Logger" and "Coma," like many of the other pilots in DESERT STORM, were too young to have had a chance to fly against the Tonopah MiGs. But their training, like that of all the other F-15 pilots, was the product of a previously broken training system that was repaired in time for DESERT STORM. "Logger" also subsequently enjoyed a distinguished flying career at Nellis and elsewhere, including an assignment with the F-22 initial cadre at Edwards AFB.

On February 2, Capt Greg "Dutch" Masters from the 525th TFS, flying F-15C 79-0064/call sign "Rifle 01" destroyed an Il-76 transport aircraft with an AIM-7. Things picked up again four days later as the remnants of the IrAF tried to flee to neighboring Iran in order to escape destruction on the ground at air bases across Iraq. Capt Tom Dietz (in F-15C 79-0078/call sign "Zerex 53") and 1Lt Bob Hehemann (in F-15C 84-0019/call sign "Zerex 54") from the 53rd TFS each scored two kills, the former destroying two MiG-21s and the latter two Su-25s, all with AIM-9s.

Two helicopters were also shot down, the first of these, an Mi-8, falling to Lt Stuart Broce (pilot) and Cdr Ron McElraft (RIO) of VF-1, flying from USS *Ranger* (CV-61). Flying F-14A BuNo 162603/call sign "Wichita 103," the pair destroyed the helicopter with an AIM-9L. A few hours later Capt Robert Swain of the 706th TFS/926th TFG repeated the feat when he gunned down an MBB Bo 105 helicopter whilst flying A-10A 77-0205/call sign "Savage 01."

More victories followed on February 7, and this time they were all claimed by Eagle pilots. A single Su-7 was credited to 33rd TFW CO, Col Rick Parsons, who was flying F-15C 84-0124/call sign "Chevron 21." His wingman, Capt Tony "ET" Murphy of the 58th TFS, flying F-15C 85-0102/call sign "Chevron 22," went one better by destroying a pair of Su-22s. All three Sukhois fell to AIM-7Ms. A controversial kill claim for an Mi-24 helicopter was also made that day by Maj Randy May of the 525th TFS in F-15C 80-0003/call sign "Killer 03," his victory being claimed with a Sparrow too.

525th TFS pilots captains "Gunga" Dingee (in F-15C 79-0048/call sign "Pistol 01") and Mark "Curly" McKenzie (in F-15C 80-0012/call sign "Pistol

02") also destroyed a helicopter on February 11 when they each fired an AIM-7M at the same Mi-8. Each pilot was credited with 0.5 of a kill. Three days later captains Richard Bennett and Dan Bakke of the 355th TFS/4th TFW, flying F-15E 89-0487, dropped a GBU-10 2,000lb laser-guided bomb on a Hughes 500 helicopter whilst it was hovering just above the ground. Another Mi-8 was downed on February 14 by Capt Todd Sheehy of the 511th TFS/10th TFW, flying A-10A 81-0964/call sign "Springfield 27." Destroyed with the aircraft's GAU-8 cannon, this proved to be last gun kill credited to the USAF.

The final aerial kills of the war occurred on March 20 and 22 during the enforcement of ceasefire RoE that prevented the IrAF from flying fixed-wing aircraft following the cessation of hostilities on February 28. Helicopters were allowed to fly, however, and the IrAF also started flouting the RoE during March by sending aircraft aloft in northern Iraq. Things came to a head on the 20th when a Su-22 was destroyed by 53rd TFS pilot Capt John Doneski in F-15C 84-0014/call sign "Amoco 34," his victory being achieved with an AIM-7M. Two days later, squadron mate Capt Dietz was credited with his third victory of the war (all scored with AIM-9Ms) when he too downed a Su-22 whilst flying F-15C 84-0010/call sign "Zerex 21." Moments later 1Lt "Gigs" Hehemann also claimed his third kill when the pilot of a PC-9 that had been target spotting for the Su-22 ejected just as Hehemann (in F-15C 84-0015/call sign "Zerex 22") was about to fire a Sidewinder at his aircraft.

Eight years later in March 1999, during Operation ALLIED FORCE in the Balkans, USAF F-15C pilots were credited with destroying four Serbian MiG-29s. One of these was shot down by now Lt Col "Rico" Rodriguez (493rd EFS F-15C 86-0169/call sign "Knife 13") on March 24 for his third kill, and another was blasted from the sky that same night by my good friend Capt Mike "Dozer" Shower (493rd FS F-15C 86-0159/call sign "Edge 61"). The final two "Fulcrums" were claimed by 493rd EFS pilot Capt Jeff Hwang on March 26 whilst flying F-15C 86-0156/call sign "Dirk 21." All four MiG-29s fell victim to AIM-120 AMRAAMs, as did a fifth Serbian "Fulcrum" on May 4, claimed by F-16CJ pilot Lt Col Michael Geczy (he was flying 91-0353/call sign "Puma 11" of the 78th EFS). No American pilot has claimed an aerial victory in combat since that date.

CHAPTER 8

LIFE AFTER MiGs – THE AGGRESSORS

The MiG-21F-13 on static display outside the Aggressor squadron building at Nellis AFB is almost certainly the jet we knew as "Bort 04" when it was flown at Tonopah by the Red Eagles. Nearby, an ex IrAF Su-7 with Arabic numbers on the nose can also be found on static display outside the Threat Training Facility. This aircraft served Iraq as a fighter-bomber. There were never any Su-7s in the CONSTANT PEG inventory. SA-2 and SA-3 SAMs are on display mounted on their launchers near the Su-7. The MiG-29 on static display at Nellis is one of the airframes the US government bought from Moldova in 1997.

With the end of the CONSTANT PEG program one might logically ask "What now?" To answer that question it is necessary to briefly look back at the USAF's Aggressor program history, which began with the 64th AS flying T-38s at Nellis in October 1972. Three years after the first squadron was formed, an additional unit, the 65th AS, was also established at Nellis in October 1975. A PACAF Aggressor squadron (26th AS) then followed at Clark AB in January 1976, followed four months later by the USAFE-controlled 527th AS at RAF Alconbury, in England. Thus, by 1977 the USAF had four Aggressor squadrons spread across three major air commands, TAC, USAFE, and PACAF. The aircraft these units flew eventually changed from T-38s to F-5Es when embargoed jets that were earmarked for South Vietnam and elsewhere became available. The four F-5E squadrons provided adversaries for USAF fighter aircrews worldwide for more than a decade.

In response to the end of the Cold War all four Aggressor squadrons, like CONSTANT PEG, were shut down between 1988 and 1990. But herein lies the "lesson of the sourdough bread." Instead of totally terminating the Aggressor program, which was flying F-16s when the last squadron was shut down, a small organization called Adversary Tactics, or AT, was formed and assigned to the commander of Red Flag. Red Flag was also formally named the 414th Combat Training Squadron (CTS).

As an aside it is interesting to note that the 414th had a previous life as an F-4 unit, and in those days – from the 1960s through to the 1980s – it was officially the 414th Fighter Weapons Squadron. The original 414th occupied the building just north of the Thunderbird hangar on Tyndall Avenue at Nellis AFB. It was from this facility that the aircrews assigned to the RIVET HASTE technical order 556 were trained during the fall of 1972. These aircrews got their first taste of operational training against a MiG-17 that was flown by either Randy O'Neil, our assistant Operations Officer, or myself.

Back to the "lesson of the sourdough bread." Way back in the cowboy days, the rounding up and driving of cattle to market had many challenges, not the least of which was feeding the wranglers doing the job. Cowboy movies starring Gene Autry, Roy Rogers, and other famous actors suggested that a chuck wagon accompanied the cattle drives. The chuck wagon was stocked with plenty of beans, wheat, and sourdough starter. Cattle could be slaughtered along the way to satisfy the need for red meat. Beans weren't a problem, and neither was bread as long as the cook maintained his "starter" for making sourdough bread. On the odd chance that "cookie" used the last of the crucially important starter for a batch of bread, then there would be no more sourdough for the duration of that particular trail drive. So, the lesson is "Never cook all of the sourdough starter."

By forming the AT group and keeping the Aggressors alive at Red Flag, the USAF demonstrated understanding of this lesson. Put in other terms, it is a whole lot easier to expand an existing program than it is to start a new one from scratch. And today we are harvesting the "lesson of the sourdough bread" as Aggressor squadrons are being reformed. Initially, the Aggressors broke out of AT at Red Flag in February 2003 when the AT section of the 414th CTS became the 64th AS, flying F-16C/Ds in the adversary role from Nellis. Later, in September 2005, the 65th AS also stood up again at Nellis, but this time flying F-15C/Ds. Thus F-15s and F-16s of the 64th and 65th ASs replicate the Su-27 and later model "Flankers" and the MiG-29 "Fulcrum" in the adversary mission. GCI continues to be integrated in the squadrons as in the days of old.

The Aggressors have grown in other ways also. The adversary mission now includes surface-to-air assets. And Aggressor units train US forces by denying space and cyberspace, as any future adversary might attempt.

Since the end of the Cold War other opportunities have emerged that have facilitated the training of our fighter units. F-15 pilots from Alaska traveled to India in 2004 and participated in Exercise Cope India, during which they had the opportunity to engage Indian Air Force (IAF) pilots flying the Su-30, MiG-27, MiG-29, Mirage 2000, and a drastically updated version of the MiG-21 known locally as the Bison. F-15s returned to exercises with the IAF in 2005, 2006, and 2008, and lessons learned from these encounters have been widely discussed during classified tactics talks. Also, F-15s from the 18th Wing at Kadena traveled to Malaysia in 2006 for Exercise Cope Taufan 06, where they trained against Royal Malaysian Air Force MiG-29s, Hawk 208s, and F/A-18Ds.

American fighter units assigned to USAFE have also widely traveled to and trained with the air forces that were formerly a part of the Warsaw Pact. These air arms continue to operate aircraft either built in the Soviet Union or under license from the former USSR, further offering realistic training opportunities. Prior to selling the MiG-29s acquired from the former East Germany after "the wall" came down in 1989, the Luftwaffe brought the "Fulcrums" to Nellis AFB and the Canadian air base at Cold Lake, in Alberta. Here, they were engaged in an extensive series of training missions with US aircrews during Red Flag and Maple Flag exercises.

Three USAF pilots also undertook exchange tours with the Luftwaffe and flew the MiG-29s operationally for several years. One of those officers, Fred "Spanky" Clifton, is still working Aggressor issues and is teaching at the USAF Weapons School with me. "Spanky" recently (December 2010) flew the first airworthy civilian-owned "Fulcrum" during its initial flight tests in Quincy, Illinois. This aircraft is an ex-Soviet air force MiG-29UB sourced by owner Don Kirlin. A second USAF pilot to fly MiG-29s with the Germans was Doug "Vinnie" Russell, and in January 2011 he performed the first flight of the second privately owned MiG-29UB to be returned to the skies. "Vinnie" flew the ex-Ukrainian air force two-seater from Arlington Field, in Washington state, to nearby Paine Field in Everett, Washington.

The Aggressor mission continues to grow with PACAF forming the 18th AS at Eielson AFB, Alaska, in August 2007. Equipped with F-16C/Ds, this unit plays a major adversary role in the newly constituted Cope Thunder exercises in Alaska, its fighters being camouflaged in a variety of traditional Aggressor color schemes as well as a new arctic black and white scheme playfully nicknamed "Shamu."

Thus, times change and programs change, but the quest for training continues.

CHAPTER 9

CLOSING THOUGHTS

CONSTANT PEG could not have happened without the complete support from our military and civilian chain of command in the USAF and US Navy as well as the Departments of Defense and Energy.

To make CONSTANT PEG happen, the action officers (Peck, Frick, and Smith) generated ideas and plans, charted the course, and presented the Air Staff and TAC generals (Vandenberg, Donnelly, Currie, and Gabriel) with solutions to problems as they arose. The leadership approved generalities and concepts, allowing the action officers to run the day-to-day aspects of the project. With the authority delegated to them by the generals, the action officers made things happen. The civilians in both the Departments of Defense and Energy shared the vision and fully supported the project, enabling the contractors under their authority to build the airfield in record time.

Most importantly, the enlisted workforce restored the aircraft and equipment and gave us safe flyable MiGs. Without these, CONSTANT PEG would have been unsustainable. A US Navy Blue Angels pilot was recently featured in the August 2010 issue of *Popular Mechanics* magazine. He reflected that the demonstration team's maintenance department owned the Blue Angels' aircraft, allowing the pilots to borrow them for about 45 minutes at a time – the time it takes to fly a typical airshow routine. He went on to say that without maintenance, the Blue Angels don't fly. The same was true for the CONSTANT PEG MiGs. Without the entire enlisted MiG maintenance and logistics support team we would never have been able to fly.

CONSTANT PEG was sustained over the years by dedicated commanders and assigned men and women that were sometimes challenged instead of helped by the follow-on leadership above them. A tip of the hat also goes to the

National Intelligence community for making so many vitally important "toys" (as in airframes and parts) available to our MiG logistics team.

Looking beyond the construction of the airfield and more than 15,000 sorties directed at the training of nearly 6,000 aircrew members, the United States of America was rewarded for its investment in CONSTANT PEG with incredible combat performance, notable during DESERT STORM and the other Southwest Asian and Balkan wars of the 1990s and early 21st century.

The entire CONSTANT PEG story can be summarized by suggesting that it is important to understand the deal. Take a look at CONSTANT PEG and see what you can get when you give three determined officers a credit card and unlimited support, and then let them do the job. The project served as the ultimate building block in the process of training some of the best fighter pilots the world has ever known. The products of this training contributed to the USAF, US Navy, and US Marine Corps share of the worldwide combat success that stands in excess of 170 kills by F-15 and F-16 pilots without a single loss in return to enemy aircraft.

This project has been the most important contribution of my life to my country and its air force. I am infinitely grateful to have had the opportunity to play a role in the renaissance in fighter tactics and training. Further, to have had a key leadership position and to have stood among the men and a few women that made CONSTANT PEG happen fills me with immense pride.

To those of you that are still engaged as military men and women, learn the hard lessons and lead the way. The nation is depending on you.

POSTSCRIPT

Jerry Baker passed away.

Mike Beverlin is retired in Idaho.

Lt Gen Bobby Bond died in an aircraft accident on April 26, 1984, that was not related to CONSTANT PEG operations.

Tom Burzynski, like Mike Scott, had two tours with the Red Eagles. He was an initial cadre crew chief and served with Scott as the NCOIC of the unit. Tom retired in Las Vegas and was employed in the gaming industry. He is now deceased.

Herbert "Hawk" Carlisle is currently a lieutenant general on active duty.

Ike Crawley, Dave Hollingsworth, and Chico Noriega, among many others, retired in Las Vegas.

Maj Gen Jim Currie retired from the Air Force in 1979.

Gen Chuck Donnelly retired in Washington, D.C., and was the President of the Air Force Association during his retirement. He died of cancer in 1994.

Bob "Darth" Drabant retired from the USAF and is currently a senior civilian government executive in the test community at Nellis AFB.

CMSgt Robert O. "Bobby" Ellis retired in Las Vegas and died in February 1987.

Glenn Frick retired as a colonel and worked for many years for Lockheed Martin in Fort Worth. Glenn and Gracie bought property outside Godley, Texas, which included a grass airstrip. Glenn was a very successful aerobatic pilot in sport biplanes, and at one time was the captain of the US Aerobatic team. As a master craftsman, Glenn, assisted by Randy O'Neil, restored aircraft in one of his Godley airport hangars. Glenn died of leukemia in 2001.

George "G2" Gennin retired from the USAF in 1990 as a colonel and is currently President and CEO of SDS International, a defense services firm he founded in 1991. "G2" and his wife Laureen live in Madison, Virginia, in the foothills of the Blue Ridge Mountains, approximately 30 miles northwest of Charlottesville, where they have a ranch and raise registered Texas Longhorn cattle.

Tom Gibbs retired as a colonel and flew as an American Airlines pilot until reaching the mandatory retirement age. After several years of retirement in Colorado, Tom Gibbs passed away in 2011.

Chuck "Heater" Heatley had a distinguished naval career and retired as a US Navy captain. He lives and works in the Washington, D.C., area.

Earl "Obi Wan" Henderson retired as a lieutenant colonel after encountering a medical problem. He went on to found AVTECH Corporation, which services various contracts at Nellis AFB.

Chuck "Brows" Holden retired as a colonel and is a corporate jet pilot living in Las Vegas.

Gerry "Huffer" Huff completed his flying career working as a simulator instructor and airline pilot at the Dallas Fort Worth Airport, and then retired to Mexico.

Ron "Moscow" Iverson retired as a lieutenant general and lives in Washington, D.C.

Billy Lightfoot passed away.

MSgts Don Lyon, Steve Hovermale, and Tommy Karnes retired from the USAF and continued to work in aviation-related fields after retirement. All three were crewing F-86 Dart tow aircraft at Kadena AB when Col Peck served as the Deputy Commander for Operations and Vice Commander of the 18th TFW. Don Lyon is now retired in Idaho. "Tonopah" Tommy Karnes retired in Missouri but at last word had also moved to Idaho. Steve Hovermale is retired in Oklahoma.

Jack Manclark retired as a colonel and later transitioned into the Senior Executive Service. He is employed in the Pentagon in Washington, D.C.

Dave "Marshall" McCloud died in an aircraft accident in July 1998 while serving as a lieutenant general in the USAF in Alaska.

Tom "Squid" Morgenfeld resigned from the US Navy and then served as the Chief Test Pilot with Lockheed "Skunk Works" and flight operations. He played a key role test-flying the F-117A, F-22, and F-35. Now retired, he lives in Camarillo, California.

Don "Devil" Muller retired as a colonel, and until his death in 2010 he was an F-15C academic and simulator instructor at Tyndall AFB.

Maj Gen Richard Murray retired from the Air Force in 1985.

Joe "Jose" Oberle retired as a lieutenant colonel and had a distinguished career at Lockheed Martin in Fort Worth. He and wife Rita split their retirement time between Georgia and Florida.

Randy O'Neill retired as a colonel and worked for Lockheed Martin in Fort Worth, Texas, for many years. Randy and his wife Helen became patrons of a school in Fort Worth that cared for underprivileged children. Randy worked with Glenn Frick restoring aircraft in his spare time, and was an avid motorcycle enthusiast. After a long struggle to recover, Randy died of injuries he had sustained in a single vehicle cross-country motorcycle road trip accident in Arizona.

Gail Peck retired as a colonel and has worked as an instructor at the USAF Weapons School at Nellis AFB since 1998. Peggy Peck died of cancer in November 2002, and in 2004 Gail married Carol Rubus. He maintains his flight instructor credentials and co-owns a turbocharged RG Cessna Cardinal. He is building an all-metal two-seat experimental aircraft as a hobby.

Jim Richardson is currently among the missing.

Doug Robinson is a heavy equipment operator in Las Vegas.

Bill "Saki" Sakahara retired and continued his career in the defense industry. Bill is retired in southern California.

Mike "Scotty" Scott had a distinguished military career and returned to the Red Eagles for a second tour as the unit's final commander. He had the sad task of shutting down the program. Mike Scott retired as a colonel after serving as a television briefer and spokesman for Central Command in Southwest Asia during DESERT STORM. He is currently a captain with Southwest Airlines and lives in Las Vegas.

David "DL" Smith was promoted to lieutenant colonel and selected to lead the USAF Aerial Demonstration Team, the Thunderbirds. He died at the Cleveland Lakefront Airport in September 1981 following a bird strike on take-off while flying a non-demonstration flight in a Thunderbird T-38.

Mary Jane Smith married and moved to Pahrump, Nevada, in retirement. She is now deceased.

Dave Stringer retired as a brigadier general.

Richard "Moody" Suter retired as a colonel after completing a distinguished military career. He and Gail Suter retired to the Phoenix area. "Moody" died of cancer in January 1996 and Gail also passed away a few years later.

Maj Gen Sandy Vandenberg is retired in Tucson, Arizona.

Joseph "CT" Wang retired as a colonel and was recently engaged in advanced testing and tactics validation as a civilian analyst at Nellis AFB. He is currently retired in Las Vegas.

Phil White retired as a colonel and then flew for Southwest Airlines. He is currently retired in Florida.

The remaining fighter pilots and maintainers who served with the Red Eagles finished up their MiG tours and went on to face other challenges in life, certainly richer as a result of their CONSTANT PEG experience.

APPENDIX

RED EAGLE ALUMNI ROSTER

Best known information as of November 2011

Last Name	First Name	Service	Assigned	Position
Adametz	Karin			Computers
Adams	Billy	USAF	79-83	Admin
Addis	Steve	USAF		APG
Alford	Steve			Auto Pilot
Allen	Ray			Welder
Allen III	James P.	USAF	85-88	APG
Ames	Terry	USAF	85-88	Egress
Anderson	Doug		84-88	AGE
Anderson	Tom			Fireman
Andres	John	USAF	87-88	Admin
Arbogast	Gary	USAF		Crew Chief
Ashwood	George	USAF		ECM
Atkinson	Jim (Sam)			Hydraulics
Baca	Steve	USAF	87-88	APG
Baenan	Jeremy	USAF		
Bailey	Kevin			APG
Baker*	Jerry (Jeb)	USAF		Maintenance
Baker	Larry	USAF	84-88	Machinist
Barker	Charlie	USAF	79-85	Life Support
Barnard	Darren	USAF	87-88	Admin
Barret	Aaron			APG
Barrett	Jeff	USAF	81-84	Weapons
Bartlett	Jim			Telemetry

Bashiorka	Linda			Operations
Bayer	Bill		81-85	GCI
Bell	Jim	USAF	83-91	Crew Chief
Belt	Bob	USAF		Pilot
Bennett	Dyke	USAF	84-88	APG
Bergdarf	Ray			
Bermingham	John	USAF	85-88	Weapons Controller – GCI
Berry	Don	USAF	81-84	Machinist
Beverlin	Mike	USAF	78-83	Crew Chief
Bickford	Jerry	USAF		Avionics
Biri	Walt			APG
Birl	Levon	USAF		Admin
Black	Clyde	USAF		Paint
Black	James			APG
Black	Matt	USAF		Pilot
Bland	Dave	USAF	83-85	Pilot ("Bandit 32")
Bodenheimer	Thurman	USAF	84-88	Crew Chief
Bodner	Gary		82-88	APG
Bohman	Joe	USAF	80-84	Crew Chief MiG-17
Boma	Tom	USAF	86-88	Pilot ("Bandit 59")
Boteler	Ralph			
Boudreau	Dave	USAF		Sheet Metal
Bowers	Brad			APG
Bradshaw	Freddie	USAF	83-87	Welder
Brand	Steve	USAF	85-88	APG
Braun	Paul	USAF	84-88	APG
Breault	Robert	USAF	83-87	Machinist
Brelsford	Warren			Electrician
Brewster	Mike	USAF	83-88	Engines
Brex	Tim	USAF		Parachutes
Brick	Tom		87-88	GCI
Brown	Alvin			Admin
Brown*	Hugh	USN	79	Pilot ("Bandit 12")
Brown	Sandra		85-88	Admin
Brown	Stephen	USAF	83-86	Pilot ("Bandit 32")
Browne	Greg	USAF		Avionics
Brubaker	Guy	USN	84-86	Pilot ("Bandit 48")
Bucko	Leonard	USMC	81-84	Pilot ("Bandit 22")
Bullis	Ash	USAF		Crew Chief
Burderer	Leo		80-82	CE

Burdick	Omer		80	Contracts
Burzynski*	Tom	USAF	78-88	Crew Chief
Byrnes*	Greg	USAF		Machinist
Campbell	Jeff	USAF		Crew Chief
Caramico	Richard	USN		Engines
Carlisle	Herbert	USAF		Pilot ("Bandit 54")
Carmichael	Graling			Paint
Carr	Dave	USAF		Pilot
Carrigan	Dan			Weapons
Cartier	Roger	USAF	83-86	APG/Supervisor
Cass	Charles			APG
Castillo	Joe			Supply
Cavallo	Alan	USAF	85-88	ECS
Cazessus	Ricardo	USAF		Pilot ("Bandit 63")
Ceplecha	Chris	USAF		Pilot
Chandler	Larry			
Chandler	Richard			Supply
Chanik	Evan (Marty)	USN		Pilot ("Bandit 52")
Chitwood	Eddie	USAF	84-88	APG
Christoff	Al	USAF	81-84	Crew Chief
Chronister	Barry			Intel
Ciarlante	Mike			
Cibel*	Stan		84-88	Crash Recovery
Cieplinski	Adolph		84-88	APG
Clark	Frank		85-88	Survival Equip
Clawson	Larry	USAF		
Cleveland	Mike	USAF		Supply
Clifton	Fred	USAF		Commander (Det)
Clink	Bob			Contracts
Clough	Bob			Avionics
Clouse	Richard			GCI
Collins	Ed	USAF		ECS
Collins	Frank			
Contreras	Rich	USAF	81-85	Crew Chief
Coppick	Tim			Life Support
Corder*	Chuck	USAF		Pilot ("Bandit 15")
Coshatt	Dan	USAF	86-88	GCI
Cox	Paul	USAF		APG/COM
Craig	Gary	USAF	84-87	Pilot ("Bandit 43")
Crawley	Ike	USAF	79-85	Jet Engine Mechanic

Cruz	John			Navy Weapons
Curran	Dennis	USAF		APG
Dain	Jack	USAF		Engines
Davenport	Steve			APG
Davis	Bob	USN		Pilot ("Bandit 64")
Davis	Jack	USAF		Telecoms
Davis	Jeff			Fuels
Davis*	Terry	USAF		Supply
Day	Jim		82-86	GCI
Deatline	Mike	USAF		Crew Chief
Degraff	Dennis	USAF		Intel
Dehay	Tom			APG
Deitz	Kermit	USAF		Fireman
Devaney	John	USAF		Crew Chief
Dickson	Mike	USAF	87-88	Weapons Controller – GCI
Dill	Paul	USAF		Crew Chief
Dix	Rich	USAF		Crew Chief
Dollinger	Tom			APG
Donovan	Tim			Intel
Doty	Art			Computers
Drabant	Robert	USAF	78-79	Aero Engineer/Operations
Drake	Ted	USAF	84-87	Pilot ("Bandit 42")
Dresher	Jim	USAF	82-86	Crew Chief
Dresser	Don	USAF		APG
Drenkhahn	Vance	USAF		Pilot
Dubron	Steve	USAF		Pilot
Duncan	Jim	USAF		Paint
Dvorachek	John	USAF	86-88	APG
Ealey	Marv	USAF		Crew Chief
Eddinger	Brian			
Elder	Lawrence	USAF		Mechanical Acc.
Ellis*	Robert	USAF		NCOIC of Maintenance
Ely	Mark			
Emfinger*	Steve			GCI
Enos	Tim	USAF	79-83	APG & QA
Entrekin	John			Maintenance
Eschenbach	Doug	USAF		Crew Chief
Esquivel	Ray			Scheduling
Estes	Ken		85-88	Electrician
Ethington	Bill			Egress

Evans*	Jim	USAF		Pilot ("Bandit 67")
Falbe	Gerald			Engines
Ferrari	Bob	USAF		Crew Chief
Fields	Robert G.	USAF	82-88	APG
Fisher	Bill			APG
Fisher	Brad	USAF	81-85	Crew Chief
Fitzpatrick	Robert			GCI
Flannery	Todd	USAF		Crew Chief
Flinchbaugh	Steve	USAF	84-88	Hydraulics
Flores	Lebonicia			Supply
Ford	Earnie	USAF		Life Support
Ford	Eugene	USAF		Parachutes
Ford	Mike	USAF		Pilot
Foerster*	Hilbert	USAF		Engines
Forsythe	Laura			Operations
Fox	Ron	USAF		Operations
Frick*	Glenn	USAF		Commander (1 – order of command) ("Bandit 4")
Fuerst	Nick	USAF		Pilot ("Bandit 65")
Fuller	George	USAF	85-88	Avionics
Funke	Bryan J.	USAF	87-end	Flight Surgeon
Furgeson	Tom			
Furgeson	Virgil			Admin
Fussell	Steve			Radar
Futryk	Daniel	USAF	79-83	GCI
Gallegos	Mike	USAF		Engines
Gallegos	Robert			
Galloway	Ben	USAF	79-85	AGE
Garcia	Fred	USAF		Maintenance
Garey	Frank			Intel
Garin	Tom		83-88	Analyst
Geer	Rob	USAF	87-88	Avionics Com/Nav Specialist
Geisler	Frank K.	USAF		Pilot; DO operations ("Bandit 35")
Gennin	George	USAF	82-84	Commander (5 – order of command) ("Bandit 31")
Gibbs*	Tom	USAF	80-82	Commander (4 – order of command) ("Bandit 21")
Gibeault	Bob	USAF		Supply
Gibson	Bruce	USAF		Crew Chief

Gombarcik	Jim			
Gordon	Scott	USAF	85-88	Maintenance Officer
Green	Jim	USAF	81-84	Pilot ("Bandit 26")
Green*	Laurie	USAF	86-87	GCI Controller
Gregory	Mike			Intel
Griese	Bob	USAF		Machinist/Welder
Griffin	Willie			Admin
Gruse	Larry	USAF	80-84	Vehicle Maintenance
Haarklau	Darrah	USAF		Egress
Hadaway	George			APG
Hall	Jeremy			Egress
Hardy	Ed			
Harnden	David			Admin
Hartley	Don	USAF		APG
Harvey	Cal			APG
Hashem	George	USAF		Admin
Heatherly	Colin	USAF	84-87	Electrician
Heatley	Chuck	USN		Pilot ("Bandit 8")
Heck	Tim	USAF		Pilot
Helms	Buster	USAF		Hydraulics
Henderson	Earl	USAF	79-80	Commander (3 – order of command) ("Bandit 13")
Henesley	Robert	USN		Hydraulics
Henslee	Ken			AGE
Hernandez*	Rey	USAF		Fuels
Hicklin	Martin			Avionics
Hill	Ron	USAF		Parachutes
Hinostrosa	Louis	USAF		Fireman
Hites	Ron			Paint
Hobson	Bob	USAF	78-84	Avionics Chief
Hogue	Pat			Life Support
Hoke	Doug			APG
Holden	Chuck			TFWC
Holland	John	USAF		Crew Chief
Hollingsworth	Dave	USAF		Crew Chief
Holly	Dave			Sheet Metal
Holst	Marvin			APG
Holtsclaw	Jay			AGE
Honanie	Curt	USAF		Engines
Horan	John	USAF	79-80	GCI

Horsley*	Randy	USAF		Avionics
Hovermale	Stephen			Crew Chief
Howell	Gerry			Operations
Hubbard	Rick			APG
Huff	Gerry	USAF		Pilot ("Bandit 6")
Hughley	Art			Electrician
Hunt	Ferris			Weapons
Hunt	Jon			Radar
Huskonen*	Clyde	USAF		APG
Iverson	Ron	USAF		Operations/Pilot ("Bandit 2")
Jackson	Bobby			APG
Jeffries	Charles	USAF	80-84	Jet Engines
Johnson	Bill			Avionics
Johnson	Bob			Admin
Johnson	Jeryl			Operations
Johnson	Wayne	USAF	80-84	Crew Chief
Johnson	Wendell			1st Sgt
Jones	Larry	USAF		Operations
Jones	Mike	USAF	83-88	GCI
Judd*	Paul			Avionics
Juryn	Ron	USAF		Crew Chief
Kaiser*	Richard			NDI
Karn	Bill			
Karnes	Tommy	USAF		Crew Chief
Keiffler	Brian			ACC
Kemper	Derek	USAF		Sheet Metal
Kepler	Harry	USAF	85-88	Fuels
Keys	James	USAF		GCI
Kinney	Tim	USAF		Pilot ("Bandit 45")
Koch	Todd			
Kohout	Leonard	USAF		Admin
Kolodziej	Tom	USAF		Analysis
Komora	John	USAF	87-88	GCI Controller
Kossler	David	USAF		Pilot
Labier	Louis			APG
Lara	Gary	USAF		Admin
Larsen	Dudley A.	USAF	86-88	Pilot ("Bandit 60")
Laughter	Sel	USN	80-82	Pilot ("Bandit 18")
Lawrence	Claude			Weapons
Leckie	Ken			Flight Surgeon

LeDuc	Todd	USAF	82-85	GCI Controller
Legget	Don	USAF		Egress
Leighton	Herb	USAF		AGE
Lentz	Bryan	USAF	82-86	Crew Chief
Lewallen	Gary	USAF	77-83	Operations
Lewis	Barry			APG
Libner	John	USAF		Admin
Lider	Randy	USAF		Operations
Lightfoot*	Billy	USAF		Vehicle Maintenance
Lloyd	Lyle	USAF		Hydraulics
Long	Paul	USAF		Crew Chief
Lorenzen	John	USAF		NDI
Lossing*	Don			Paint
Lovin	Steve			Computers
Lynn	Bill			Avionics
Lyon	Don	USAF		Crew Chief
Macy	Marty	USMC		Pilot ("Bandit 49")
Magee	Bill			
Maggart	Billy	USAF	80-84	Crew Chief
Mahoney	James D.	USAF	87-88	Pilot ("Bandit 63")
Mahoney	John			AGE
Mallory	Richard			Egress
MacDonald	Jim	USAF	83-86	GCI
Manclark	Jack	USAF	86-87	Commander (7 – order of command) ("Bandit 51")
Mann	John	USAF	86-88	Pilot, Squadron DO ("Bandit 56")
Marney	Jim	USAF		Hydraulics
Martin	Linda			
Mashore	Gary	USAF		Crew Chief
Mason	Larry	USAF	82-88	Sheet Metal
Materazzi*	Maris	USAF		1st Sgt
Matheny	James	USAF	82-86	Pilot ("Bandit 27")
Mayberry	George	USAF	81-85	Life Support
Mayo	Robert	USAF	75-77	Pilot ("Bandit 1")
McArthur	Mark	USAF		Egress
McCarter	Wallace			APG
McCarty	Charles			Fireman
McCarver*	Walter	USAF		Welder
McCloud*	Dave	USAF	79-82	Pilot ("Bandit 10")

McCort	Dan	USN		Pilot ("Bandit 44")
McCoy	Brian	USAF	86-88	Pilot ("Bandit 53")
McCracken	Jeff			APG
McGuire	Tim			
McHenry	Bill	USAF		Crew Chief
McKenzie	Jim			AGE
McMurtrie	Rod	USAF	84-88	Chief, Maintenance Ops Division
Meckoll	Jim	USAF		
Meekins	Vanessa	USAF		Graphics
Melson	Doug	USAF		Pilot ("Bandit 68")
Merril	Jody		84-88	Fuels
Metzger	Bob			
Michael	Joe			APG
Miller*	Roy	USAF		APG Flight Chief
Mills	Mark	USN	82-85	Hydraulics
Mondloch	Keith			
Montgomery	Gary			APG
Mooney	Bob			Fireman
Morgenfeld	Tom	USN	76-79	Pilot ("Bandit 7")
Muller*	Don	USAF	76-79	Pilot ("Bandit 3")
Munstlerman	Lui			
Murphy	Bill			APG
Murphy	John			Supply
Murphy	Rich	USAF		POL
Musick	Jim			Training
Myers	Burt	USAF	80-83	Pilot ("Bandit 19")
Myers	Larry	USAF	81-85	Crew Chief
Nathman	John B.	USN	82-84	Pilot ("Bandit 29")
Navel	Gary	USAF		Crew Chief
Neal	J. B.	USAF	84-88	Crew Chief
Nebaker	Don			Scheduling
Nelson	John	USAF	80-85	Logistics
Newberry	Dave	USAF		Communications
Newton	Zara	USAF	86-88	Intel
Nichols*	Danny	USAF		NDI
Noriega	Chica	USAF		Crew Chief
Oberle	Joseph	USAF		Pilot/Operations ("Bandit 5")
O'Connor	Stan	USN	87-88	Pilot ("Bandit 69")
Olson	Bob			APG

O'Neil*	Dawson R. (Randy)	USAF		1972 MiG-17 Pilot
Ostus*	Russ	USAF		Crew Chief
Othold	Charlie	USAF		Crew Chief/AR
Palmer	Henry	USAF	84-88	Avionics
Palmer	Oscar			
Pappendick	Ron	USAF		Crew Chief
Parial	Renato		85-88	Egress
Pascal	Bob	USAF		Hydraulics
Payne	Ralph	USAF		Fireman, Fire Chief
Peck Jr	Gaillard R.	USAF	78-79	Commander (2 – order of command) ("Bandit 9")
Penner	Bob	USAF		Crew Chief
Peters	Joe			Admin
Peterson	Jeff	USAF	83-87	Supply
Pettaway	Tony	USAF		Avionics
Peverill	John			Engines
Phelan	Dennis	USAF	84-88	Pilot ("Bandit 47")
Phfeifer	Ken			AGE
Pinchart	Rick	USAF		Sheet Metal
Pitcher	Dan			Radar
Pittman	Greg	USAF	84-88	AGE
Pleasant	Roy	USAF		Crew Chief
Pollan	William (Bill)	USAF	86-88	Flight Surgeon
Polumbo	Rob	USAF		Pilot
Poore	Gary		84-88	Life Support
Postai*	Mark	USAF		Pilot ("Bandit 25")
Powers	Bill	USAF	83-87	Chief of Supply
Pragal	George	USAF		APG
Praytor	Jim	USAF		Egress
Press	Mike	USAF	79-81	Operations/Pilot ("Bandit 20")
Price	Jim			APG
Pridgeon	Steve	USAF		AGE
Prim	Pat	USAF		Fuels
Prins	Orville	USN	82-85	Pilot ("Bandit 30")
Pumphrey	Chris			Weapons
Puttock	Paul	USAF	85-87	CRS Superintendent
Pyle	Joe Mike			Illustrator
Rae	Gary			Radar
Ransby				
Reist	Bob			

Richardson	Jim	USAF		Crew Chief
Rieger	Bob	USAF	84-88	AGE
Ripp	Jim	USAF		
Ristow	Terry			
Roan	Jim			APG
Robb	Jim	USN	83-85	Pilot, OIC Navy/Marine Corps Ops ("Bandit 38")
Roberts	Carol			Admin
Robertson	Ronie			APG
Robinson	Doug	USAF		AGE
Robinson	Evan	USAF		Fireman
Rodriguez	Ramon			APG
Rogers	Herb	USAF		Life Support
Rogers	Shelley	USAF		Pilot ("Bandit 55")
Rose	Dave	USAF		Pilot
Rotta	Al	USAF	88	AGE
Roy	Mike	USAF	83-85	Pilot MiG-21 IP ("Bandit 36")
Royal	Dwight			APG
Russell	Doug	USAF		
Saari	Garry	USAF		Hydraulics
Sakahara	Bill	USAF	77-80	Pentagon, Air Staff CONSTANT PEG project Officer
Salazar	Dennis	USAF		APG
Salter	Wesley	USAF	83-88	Life Support
Samanich	Rich	USAF	85-88	Engines
Sanders	John	USAF	86-88	NDI
Sandoval	Emilio	USAF	87-88	Supply
Saxman	John	USAF	83-86	Pilot ("Bandit 34")
Scamp*	Larry	USAF		NDI
Schneider	Ralph	USAF		
Scott	Mike	USAF	79-83	Commander (8 – order of command) ("Bandit 14")
Shean	Keith	USN		Pilot ("Bandit 17")
Shearin	Tom			APG
Sheffield	Bob	USAF	79-82	Pilot ("Bandit 16")
Shell	Homer			Avionics
Shelley	Ron	USAF		APG
Shelton	Bob			APG
Shervanick	Larry T.	USAF	82-86	Pilot ("Bandit 28")

Shinkawa	Tom	USAF		Admin
Shumock	Dennis			Engines
Silvers	Cary	USN	86-88	Pilot ("Bandit 61")
Simione	Fred	USAF		Crew Chief
Simmons	Mick	USAF		Pilot ("Bandit 57")
Skidmore	John	USAF		Pilot ("Bandit 41")
Slusher	Jack	USAF		Avionics/Telephone Maintenance
Smith	Christine	USAF	85-87	Intel Analyst
Smith	Dave			Intel
Smith	Eugene	USAF	87-88	APG, MOC
Smith	Jim	USAF	83-87	AGE
Smith	Ricardo			Hydraulics
Snyder	Vern			Intel
Spader	Jim	USAF		Sheet Metal
Spinks	John			Intel
Springer	George			Admin
Springle	Brian			
Stage	Earl			
Stalbaum	Wayne			APG
Steed	Charles			APG/QA
Sterling	Gary	USAF		APG
Stewart	Herb	USAF	82-86	Crew Chief
Stiles	Rick	USAF		Life Support
Stoker	Ed	USAF	87-88	APG
Stringer	David	USAF	79-82	Maintenance Officer
Stucky	Paul	USAF	83-86	Pilot ("Bandit 40")
Sundell	Charles E.	USAF	86-88	Pilot ("Bandit 58")
Sztabnik*	Tom	USAF		Admin
Tabunan	Isaac			
Tarbet	Joanne			Training
Taylor	Russell (Bud)	USN	81-84	Pilot ("Bandit 23")
Tessman	Jeff			APG
Therrien	Sam	USAF	87-88	Pilot, Asst Chief Plans and Ops, TAC ("Bandit 66")
Thomas	Marlon			GCI
Thompson	Doug			Admin
Thompson	Rick	USAF	81-83	APG Flight Chief
Thompson	Ted	USAF	85-88	Pilot ("Bandit 50")
Threats	Bob			Analysis

Thurman	Jim			Maintenance
Timm	Loren E.			TFWC
Tittle	George	USAF		Chief of Maintenance
Triche	Walter (Felix)	USAF		Avionics
Trombley	Bill			
Tullus	George	USMC		Pilot ("Bandit 37")
Vance	Dick	USAF	84-88	Avionics
Vandenberg	Hoyt S.			Pentagon
Vandersyde	Dennis			APG
Vanosdol	Ken			Operations
Vargas	Johnnie			Weapons
Varwig	Ted	USAF		Pilot
Vasquez				Construction
Vinson	Jim	USAF		APG
Vogel	Ed	USAF	84-88	Paint
Wagner	Mike			Paint
Wagner	Rick	USAF	84-88	Avionics
Wakefield	Kevin			Training
Waldrop	Dennis	USAF	81-84	GCI
Walker	Don	USAF		Crew Chief
Walls	Bruce	USAF	84-86	GCI, Flight Commander
Wang	Joseph	USAF		TAC, CONSTANT PEG Project Officer
Warren	David	USAF	84-86	EMS Super/ Maint Ops Div Chief
Warren*	Eunice	CIV	80-84	Secretary
Warrens	Wade			
Watley*	Monroe	USAF		Pilot ("Bandit 24")
Weaver	Jon			APG
Webber	Richard			
Webster	Steven			Fireman
Welcher*	Bill			Egress
Westcott	George	USAF		APG
Whitaker	George			APG
White	Phil	USAF	84-86	Commander (6 – order of command) ("Bandit 46")
Whitehead	Merle	USAF		Supply
Whitney	Jay	USAF		TAC
Whitsel	Ron	USAF		Crew Chief
Whittenberg	Karl	USAF	79-82	Pilot ("Bandit 11")

Wigington	John	USAF		Instrumentation
Wilborn, Jr	Eivens H.	USAF	84-88	Avionics Instruments
Williams	Hal	USAF		Sheet Metal
Williams	Mike	USAF	84-88	APG
Wilson	Jimmy	USAF		AGE
Windhorst	Dana	USAF	86-88	Flight Surgeon
Wisnieski	Tony			APG
Witt	Mike			APG
Woodcock	Dan	USAF		APG
Woodland	Linda			Material Storage
Worland	Steve	USAF		Supply
Worthington	Robert			AGE
Wright*	Bill	USAF		Crew Chief/APG Flight Chief
Wright	John			Intel
Wright	Kevin			Operations
Wright	Neena R.	USAF	86-88	Executive officer
Wright	Pat			Paint
Wutke	Randy			AGE
Young	Dave	USAF		Electrician
Young	Phil	USAF		Plans and Scheduling
Youngblood	Warren			GCI
Zettel	Rob	USAF	83-86	Pilot ("Bandit 39")
Ziegenbein	Tom			APG
Honorable mentions				
Clements	Ron	USAF		CO of 57th FWW at Nellis start of CONSTANT PEG
Davies	Steve	CIV		Author of *Red Eagles*

* Indicates they are deceased

GLOSSARY OF ACRONYMS AND TERMS

A&E	Architecture and Engineering
A/B	Afterburner
AAA	Anti-Aircraft Artillery
AB	Air Base
ACM	Air Combat Maneuvering, meaning more than one fighter maneuvering in a coordinated fashion against one or more adversaries
ACMI	ACM Instrumentation Range
ACT	Air Combat Tactics. Advanced ACM/DACT
Admin	Administration
AF/PR	DCS Air Force Programs and Resources. Three-star organization at the Air Staff in the Pentagon (c.1978) responsible for allocation of fiscal resources
AF/PRP	Director of Programs. Two-star organization at the Air Staff in the Pentagon (c.1978) subordinate to the AF/PR
AF/RD	DCS Air Force Research and Development. Three-star organization at the Air Staff in the Pentagon (c.1978)
AF/TE	Air Force Test and Evaluation. An Air Staff function run by a civilian SES officer (currently Jack Manclark, former 4477th TES commander)
AF/XO	DCS Air Force Plans and Operations. Three-star organization at the Air Staff in the Pentagon (c.1978)
AF/XOO	Director of Operations and Readiness. Two-star organization at the Air Staff in the Pentagon (c.1978) subordinate to the AF/XO
AF/XOX	Director of Plans. Two-star organization at the Air Staff in the Pentagon (c.1978)
AF	Air Force
AFB	Air Force Base
AFFTC	Air Force Flight Test Center
AFOTEC	Air Force Operational Test and Evaluation Command
AFSC	Air Force Specialty Code and Air Force Systems Command
AGE	Aerospace Ground Equipment. Ground support equipment for aircraft, including electrical starting units, hydraulic servicing, etc.
AGM-65 Maverick	A series of air-to-ground missiles designed to destroy tanks
AGP	Airplane general (crew chief)
AIM	Air Intercept Missile

AIM-7 Sparrow	Radar-guided air-to-air missile
AIM-9 Sidewinder	Heat-seeking air-to-air missile
AIM-120 AMRAAM	Active radar guided air-to-air missile
AIMVAL/ACEVAL	Air Intercept Missile Validation/Air Combat Evaluation. Air-to-air test conducted at Nellis AFB wherein F-14 and F-15 effectiveness was tested with a variety of armament against F-5E Aggressors on ACMI
AMARG	Aircraft Maintenance and Restoration Group
AO	Action Officer
AOPA	Aircraft Owners and Pilots Association
AOR	Area of Responsibility, meaning a designated geographic area wherein combat operations are ongoing
AS	Aggressor squadron
AT	Adversary Tactics
AT	Adversary Threat
ATC	Air Traffic Control
AWACS	Airborne Warning and Control System (E-3 Sentry)
AWOL	Absent Without Leave
B Course	Initial training course in a combat aircraft. B Course follows pilot training or other flying assignment, and is followed by MR qualification in a combat squadron
B Model	Two-seat F-15
BS	Bullshit
BDM	A defense contractor that was on contract to the Air Force for Red Baron project work.
BFM	Basic Fighter Maneuvers, meaning the individual maneuvers performed by a fighter aircraft during air combat. Also relates to a phase of training wherein individual maneuvers are mastered
Bingo	Fuel state radio call directing RTB
Blackjack	Radio call sign for the Nellis Range Control
BOQ	Bachelor Officer Quarters
BuNo	Bureau number – US Navy nomenclature for an aircraft tail number
Butterfly	A pattern resembling a butterfly that is used for the initial set-up during some aerial gunnery exercises
BVR	Beyond Visual Range
BX	Base Exchange (military department store)
CAP	Combat Air Patrol, meaning an orbit or a profile flown by a formation of fighter aircraft during combat operations
CBPO	Consolidated Base Personnel Office
CC	Commander
CE	Civil engineer
CG	US Navy guided missile cruiser
CIA	Central Intelligence Agency
CJ-6	Chinese version of a Yak trainer
Class A	An accident or mishap resulting in $1,000,000 loss or more, or a fatality
Cdr	US Navy commander equivalent to Air Force lieutenant colonel

Comm	Communications
CNO	Chief of Naval Operations, which is equivalent to the USAF Chief of Staff. Four-star admiral (general officer equivalent) responsible for the naval service exclusive of the Marine Corps
Col	Colonel
Combat Dart	Aerial gunnery wherein a head-on set up culminates in a merge of the Dart tow aircraft and two fighters. A circular pattern follows as the two fighters take turns shooting at the towed dart aerial target. The Dart tow aircraft maintains an approximate 4g turn following the initial merge
CONSTANT	Call sign or nickname associated with projects under the cognizance of the AF/XOO
CONSTANT PEG	The name given to the construction of the airfield at the Tonopah Test Range, which was followed by nearly ten years of MiG operations training American fighter aircrew
CONUS	Continental US
CPR	Cardio-Pulmonary Resuscitation
CRS	Component repair squadron
CT	Continuation Training, meaning the ongoing training sequence that follows MR qualification
CV	Vice Commander or US Navy nomenclature for an aircraft carrier
CVN	Nuclear powered (CV) aircraft carrier
DACT	Dissimilar Air Combat Training or Tactics, meaning advanced ACM with increased numbers of friendly and adversary aircraft. This was initially used to describe training against a different type of aircraft at the BFM or ACM level
DAD	Dhahran (Saudi Arabia) Advisory Detachment
Dart	A towed aerial target used to train fighter pilots in aerial gunnery
DCO	Deputy Commander for Operations, which is equivalent to the current Operations Group Commander
DCS	Deputy Chief of Staff. Three-star organization at the Air Staff in the Pentagon (c.1978)
DMM	Digital Multi-Meter
DMZ	Demilitarized Zone, which in this context means the UN border between NVN and SVN
DO	Director of Operations.
DoD	Department of Defense
DoE	Department of Energy
DRMO	Defense Redistribution and Management Office (salvage yard)
DS	DESERT STORM
DSN	Military long-distance telephone service
EA	Electronic Attack
ECS	Environmental control system or electronic combat squadron
ECCM	Electronic Counter-Counter Measures
ECM	Electronic Counter Measures
ECW	Electronic combat wing
EGT	Exhaust Gas Temperature

ELF-1	Command and Control organization established at King Abdul Aziz Air Base (Dhahran) Saudi Arabia at the beginning of the Iran-Iraq War (1980). Purpose was the integration of USAF AWACS and other air defense elements into the Royal Saudi Air Force air defense posture
ELT	Emergency Locator Beacon, meaning a device both in fighter aircraft ejection seats and carried by individual aircrew members in survival equipment that emits a warbling tone on 121.5 and 243.0 GUARD frequencies. ELT can be turned on and off and is of immense value during SAR operations
EM	Energy Maneuverability
EMS	Equipment maintenance sqadron
EO	Electro-optical
EP	Electronic Protection
ESD	Element of H&N that contracted TTR Airfield
FAA	Federal Aviation Administration
FAC	Forward Air Controller: an airborne airman in a propeller-driven aircraft (versus a jet) who marks targets for attacking jet fighters. In the Vietnam War fast FACs flew jet aircraft like the F-100F and the F-4, which were used in very high threat areas. A slow FAC flew light aircraft like the O-1, O-2 or the OV-10
Fighter Weapons Review	The official publication of the FWS
"Fishbed"	NATO reporting name for the MiG-21
"Fitter"	NATO reporting name for the Su-7/17/20/22
"Flanker"	NATO reporting name for the Su-27
"Flogger"	NATO reporting name for the MiG-23
FMA	Foreign material acquisition
FOD	Foreign Object Damage
FOT&E	Follow-on Operational Test and Evaluation
"Fresco"	NATO reporting name for the MiG-17
FRG	Federal Republic of Germany
FSU	Former Soviet Union
FTD	Foreign Technology Division at WPAFB (now is NASIC)
FTR	Follow the Road
FTU	Flying Training Unit, current terminology for the RTU
"Fulcrum"	NATO reporting name for the MiG-29
Furball	A swarm of fighters engaged in a close-in dogfight
FWS	Fighter Weapons School: the nickname for the unit at Nellis (USAF) and Miramar (US Navy) that conducted the graduate school level Fighter Weapons Instructor Course (FWIC) of training. US Navy FWIC is now conducted at NAS Fallon, Nevada. USAF FWIC is now called WIC and operates under the umbrella of the USAF Weapons School at Nellis AFB
FWW	Fighter Weapons Wing (at Nellis). Is now simply the Weapons Wing
g	Force of gravity
GCA	Ground Controlled Approach, meaning ground-based radar assistance to pilots landing in bad weather
GCI	Ground Controlled Intercept, meaning a ground-based radar controlled intercept conducted against a target by a friendly fighter or interceptor aircraft

GIB	Guy-in-Back, a nickname for a WSO
GLOC	g induced loss of consciousness
GS	Nomenclature (when followed by a number) for the pay grades of Government Civil Service employees
GSA	General Support Agency
GUARD	Two unique frequencies (121.5 in the VHF band and 243.0 in the UHF band) used for emergency communications
H&N	Holmes and Narver (architectural firm for TTR Airfield)
HAVE DOUGHNUT	Exploitation of the MiG-21
HAVE DRILL	Exploitation of the MiG-17
HAVE FERRY	Exploitation of the MiG-17
HAVE PAD	Exploitation of the MiG-23
HOTAS	Hands on throttle and stick, meaning changes in fighter cockpits that placed key switches on the throttle(s) and stick to permit the pilot to keep his/her hands on these controls
HQ	Headquarters
HUD	Head Up Display
HVAC	Heating, ventilation and air conditioning
IADS	Integrated Air Defense System
IAF	Indian Air Force
IAS	Indicated airspeed
ICE-T	Mnemonic for the sequence of calculating speed in aircraft: Indicated, Calibrated, Equivalent, and True
ID	Identification
IG	Inspector General
IMI	A company formed by Gerry Huff and Bob Faye after they both left the Air Force. Bobby Ellis' employer after he retired from the Air Force
INS	Initial Navigation System
Intel	Intelligence
IOT&E	Initial Operational Test and Evaluation
IR	Infrared
IrAF	Iraqi Air Force
IV	Intravenous
JAG	Judge Advocate General
"Jay Bird"	NATO reporting name for the radar in the "Fishbed J"
JFK	John F Kennedy International Airport
Joker	Radio call made regarding fuel state indicating that it is time to disengage from an air engagement and RTB
JP4	Fuel similar to diesel that contain additives and is used in jet aircraft engines (has been replaced with JP8)
Jug	Single cylinder on an air-cooled radial aircraft engine
KIAS	Knots of IAS
KOA	Campground of America
LAX	Los Angeles International Airport
Lazy-8	Series of climbing and diving turns which resemble an S when the flightpath is projected onto the ground from above. Used for basic coordination training

LES	Leading edge slats
LINEBACKER I	Aerial campaign against NVN that commenced in 1972
LINEBACKER II	Aerial campaign against NVN that took place in December 1972 and included B-52 bombing raids to RP IV (Hanoi)
Lt	Lieutenant, meaning a rank in the US Navy equivalent to captain in the Air Force and Marine Corps
Lt Cdr	Lieutenant Commander, meaning a rank in the US Navy that is equivalent to major in the Air Force and Marine Corps
Lt Col	Lieutenant Colonel
Lt Gen	Lieutenant General (three-star).
Maj Gen	Major General (two-star)
MAX	Full power with afterburner
ME	Mission Employment, meaning the final phase of training at the FWS wherein all the building blocks are executed together in a combat like scenario
MEI	Management Effectiveness Inspection
Merge	Condition when two or more fighters pass line abreast or canopy to canopy at close range during a head-on pass
MIA	Missing in Action
MiG	Abbreviation for the Russian aircraft manufacturer Mikoyan Gurevich Design Bureau. Used as an aircraft type designation, i.e. MiG-15, MiG-17, MiG-21 etc.
MiGCAP	A CAP dedicated to finding and destroying enemy aircraft (MiG aircraft during the Vietnam War)
MIL	Military Power or full power without afterburner
MIPR	Multi-Interagency Procurement Request, a tool for transferring money between different departments of the US Government
MOC	Maintenance Operations Control
MOGAS	Motor gasoline, as in car and truck fuel
MR	Mission Ready, meaning that a pilot has completed all necessary training and is qualified for combat
MRE	Meal Ready to Eat
MSIP	Multi-stage improvement program – significantly improved the combat capabilities of the F-15
MSL	Mean Sea Level
MSM	Meritorious Service Medal
MULE	Hydraulic servicing AGE
MX	Maintenance
NAS	Naval Air Station
NASIC	National Air and Space Intelligence Center
NATO	North Atlantic Treaty Organization
NCO	Noncommissioned officers or enlisted military personnel
NCOIC	NCO in charge, usually the senior NCO in an organization
NDI	Non-Destructive Inspection
NM	Nautical Mile
NSA	National Security Agency, which is the agency in charge of code in the USA

NTS	Nevada Test Site
NVN	North Vietnam
NVOO	Nevada Operations Office (DoE)
NW	Northwest
OJT	On-the-Job Training
OPR	Officer Performance Report
Ops	Operations
OSD	Office of the SECDEF
OSI	Air Force Office of Special Investigations
PACAF	Pacific Air Forces
Pak 6	Same as RP IV
PBS	Used with a number by the VPAF to identify their pilots
Pickle	The act of pressing a bomb release button on the control column of a fighter aircraft
PO	Purchase Orders
POC	Point of Contact
POL	Petroleum, Oil, and Lubricants
POM	Program Operating Memorandum
PoW	Prisoner of War
Prop	Propeller
PSP	Pierced-Steel Planking
QA	Quality assurance
Qweep	Little unimportant (mostly) stuff that must be done in the military to survive
R-1	Doug Robinson
R-2	Evan Robinson
Racetrack	A pattern resembling a horse race track that is flown during some aerial gunnery exercises
RAF	Royal Air Force
RAG	Replacement Air Group (Wing), US Navy equivalent of RTU
RBS	Radar Bombing System, meaning a radar scoring system used to grade the accuracy of a released weapon. RBS was adapted (COMMANDO NAIL) in Vietnam to enable the ground radar site to vector the bomb-laden aircraft to a release point during poor weather conditions
Red Baron	Reports detailing all of the air-to-air engagements of the Vietnam War
Red Eagles	Nickname adopted by the personnel assigned to the CONSTANT PEG project
REECo	Reynolds Electrical and Engineering Company
Ret	Retired
RIO	Radar Intercept Officer or back seat crewmember in a US Navy F-4 or F-14
ROE	Rules of Engagement
ROLLING THUNDER	Aerial campaign against NVN prior to October 31, 1968
RP	Route Package meaning a distinct geographic area in NVN
RP I	Southernmost RP in NVN
RP IV	RP including Hanoi and Haiphong, NVN verbalized as Route Pack Six

RPM	Revolutions per Minute
RP VIA	Sub area of Route Package VI around Hanoi
RP VIB	Sub area of Route Package VI around Haiphong
RSAF	Royal Saudi Air Force
RTAB	Royal Thai Air Base (Thailand)
RTB	Return to Base
RTU	Replacement Training Unit, meaning an Air Force organization whose mission it is to train aircrews in their initial qualification in a combat aircraft
RWR	Radar Warning Receiver
SA	Situational Awareness
SAC	Strategic Air Command
SAM	Surface-to-Air Missile
SAR	Search and Rescue
S/E	Stan/Eval
SECDEF	Secretary of Defense
SG	Support Group
"Sirena"	NATO reporting name for Soviet RWR
SME	Subject-matter expert
SMS	Senior Master Sergeant
SNL	Sandia National Laboratory
SOB	Son-of-a-Bitch
SOF	Supervisor of Flying
Stan/Eval	Standardization and Evaluation
SVN	South Vietnam
TAC	Tactical Air Command, with headquarters at Langley AFB
TAC/ADO	Assistant TAC/DO (one-star)
TAC/DO	TAC Director of Operations (two-star)
TACAN	Tactical Air Navigation (ground based navigation system – generally military)
TAF	Tactical Air Force
TDY	Temporary Duty
TEF	Test and Evaluation Flight
TES	Test and Evaluation Squadron
TFS	Tactical Fighter Squadron, combat fighter unit manned with aircrew members and usually equipped with either 18 or 24 fighter aircraft
TFW	Tactical Fighter Wing, meaning an organization of USAF fighter aircraft, usually three squadrons each possessing either 18 or 24 aircraft
TFWC	Tactical Fighter Weapons Center. Located at Nellis AFB, and commanded by a two-star general
TIADS	Tonopah Integrated Air Defense System (H&N name for TTR airfield)
TISEO	Target Identification System, Electro-Optical. System included a multi-magnification telescope that was slaved to the aircraft radar. When a distant target was locked-on with radar a telescopic EO image of the target could be viewed in the cockpit, permitting beyond visual range identification

TITS	Tonopah Integrated Training Site. Very temporary initial name for the CONSTANT PEG project
TNP	Tonopah
TRW	Tactical Reconnaissance Wing
TTF	Threat Training Facility
TTR	Tonopah Test Range, meaning a land and airspace area within the Nevada Test and Training Range known also as R-4809A. Range is charted as NSN 7641014867735, with NIMA Ref No. NTTRCO1
UHF	Ultra-High Frequency
UN	United Nations
UPT	Undergraduate Pilot Training
US	United States (of America)
USAF	United States Air Force
USAFE	US Air Forces Europe
USMC	United States Marine Corps
USMTM	US Military Training Mission
USN	United States Navy
USSR	Union of Soviet Socialist Republics
VAW	US Navy air wing
VC	Viet Cong
VF	US Navy fighter squadron
VHF	Very-High Frequency
Vice Adm	Vice Admiral (3-star)
VIFF	Vectoring in forward flight (AV-8 Harrier maneuvring technique using vectored thrust)
VIN	Vehicle Identification Number
VIP	Very Important Person
VOR	Very High Frequency Omni Range (ground based navigation system – generally civilian)
VPAF	Vietnamese Peoples' Air Force, meaning the air force of NVN
VX	US Navy test squadron
WEZ	Weapons Engagement Zone
Wolf Pack	Nickname for the 8th TFW
WRM	War Readiness Materials
WSO	Weapons System Operator, or back seat crewmember in a USAF F-4
WWI	World War I
WWII	World War II
YF-110	Cover nomenclature for the MiG-21
YF-113	Cover nomenclature for the MiG-23
YF-114	Cover nomenclature for the MiG-17
YGBSM	You've Gotta Be Shitting Me
ZZ	Tail markings on Kadena-based F-15s of the 18th TFW

INDEX